Nancy Ries
12-02

Rural Reform in Post-Soviet Russia

Rural Reform in Post-Soviet Russia

Edited by
David J. O'Brien
and
Stephen K. Wegren

Woodrow Wilson Center Press
Washington, D.C.

The Johns Hopkins University Press
Baltimore and London

Editorial Offices:

Woodrow Wilson Center Press
One Woodrow Wilson Plaza
1300 Pennsylvania Avenue, N.W.
Washington, D.C. 20004
Telephone 202-691-4029
www.wilsoncenter.org

Order from:

The Johns Hopkins University Press
Hampden Station
Baltimore, Maryland 21211
Telephone 1-800-537-5487

2 4 6 8 9 7 5 3 1

Library of Congress Cataloging-in-Publication Data

Rural reform in post-Soviet Russia / edited by David J. O'Brien
and Stephen K. Wegren.
    p. cm.
Includes bibliographical references and index.
    ISBN 0-8018-6960-9 (hard : alk. paper)
    1. Land reform—Russia (Federation) 2. Rural development—
Russia (Federation) 3. Rural renewal—Russia (Federation)
4. Agriculture—Economic aspects—Russia (Federation)
I. O'Brien, David J. II. Wegren, Stephen K., 1956–
    HD1333.R9 R87 2002
    338.1'847—dc21   2001006559

ABOUT THE CENTER

The Center is the living memorial of the United States of America to the nation's twenty-eighth president, Woodrow Wilson. Congress established the Woodrow Wilson Center in 1968 as an international institute for advanced study, "symbolizing and strengthening the fruitful relationship between the world of learning and the world of public affairs." The Center opened in 1970 under its own board of trustees.

In all its activities the Woodrow Wilson Center is a nonprofit, nonpartisan organization, supported financially by annual appropriations from the Congress, and by the contributions of foundations, corporations, and individuals. Conclusions or opinions expressed in Center publications and programs are those of the authors and speakers and do not necessarily reflect the views of the Center staff, fellows, trustees, advisory groups, or any individuals or organizations that provide financial support to the Center.

Contents

Maps, Figures, and Tables

Maps

Figures

Tables

Preface

The chapters presented in this volume would not have been possible without the cooperation of a dedicated and diverse group of scholars. The individuals who contributed to this volume were willing to set aside the biases and technical language of their respective disciplines so that they might actually talk with one another. Lengthy discussions among these scholars identified ways in which their respective findings might fit into the larger picture of adaptation and change in rural Russia. As a result, the final edited versions of these chapters reflect the larger themes developed through face-to-face meetings in which the authors presented, discussed, challenged, and refined each other's interpretations of findings of empirical research on Russian rural life.

This highly productive exchange and synthesis was developed through a series of three workshops sponsored by the Kennan Institute for Advanced Russian Studies at the Woodrow Wilson Center and the College of Agriculture, Food, and Natural Resources of the University of Missouri-Columbia. The Kennan Institute has a long history of support of scholarly research on the development of civic culture and democracy in Russia. In particular, the institute's sponsorship of several workshops on social capital in Russia highlighted the need to pay greater attention to underlying social relationships, informal as well as formal, that could facilitate the development of a market economy and democratic institutions.

The College of Agriculture, Food, and Natural Resources at the University of Missouri also was a sponsor of the workshops. The College of Agriculture has a long-term involvement in research and extension outreach to support agriculture in emerging economies. Moreover, the University of Missouri's rural community–development model views the development of the social and cultural infrastructure of rural life as central to economic development in any national context. Although predating the use of the term social capital, this focus is consistent with the emphasis on understanding and developing indigenous social institutions and relationships as a precondition for more productive economic activity and a more open and democratic society.

The first workshop in Columbia, Missouri, in May 1998 was devoted to the organization of basic themes pertaining to rural development in Russia. This workshop crystallized the need for a multidisciplinary approach to rural Russia, drawing upon research from a variety of disciplines including economics, sociology, history, anthropology, geography, and political science. A second, expanded workshop was held in Washington, DC, in May 1999. Nineteen scholars, representing six disciplines, participated in this workshop. The three days of presentations and intensive exchanges among the scholars resulted in a consensus on the three major themes around which this book is organized.

In addition to the authors of the chapters that follow, there are a number of other persons and organizations without which this book would not have been possible. The University of Missouri Research Board and the University of Missouri Foundation sponsored the workshop in Columbia, Missouri. Michael Nolan, social science leader, College of Agriculture, Food, and Natural Resources, and Patricia Ramsay and Hal Jeffcoat, University of Missouri Development Office, played critical roles in gaining that support. The Kennan Institute for Advanced Russian Studies, Woodrow Wilson Center, sponsored the workshops in Washington. Funding for these workshops was provided by the Program for Research and Training on Eastern Europe and the Independent States of the former Soviet Union (Title VIII), the Woodrow Wilson Center Federal Conference Fund, and the George F. Kennan Fund.

The director of the Kennan Institute, Blair Ruble, is responsible for initiating the concept of a series of workshops on rural Russia and for seeing that a variety of human and material resources were available to the participants. Under his urging and constant facilitation, the organization of the workshops and this volume proceeded. Nancy Popson of the Kennan Institute handled the difficult organizational tasks and much of the grant writing associated with this project. Not the least of her accomplishments was to get a large number of academics to turn materials in on time and to arrive in Washington in relatively good humor. We are very grateful to her always kind but persistent efforts to keep us in line. Finally, we want to thank Sue Allmart for her patience and skill in dealing with a variety of formats, tables, maps, and figures.

Rural Reform in Post-Soviet Russia

Introduction

Adaptation and Change:
Old Problems, New Approaches

STEPHEN K. WEGREN AND DAVID J. O'BRIEN

In the early years following the collapse of the Soviet Union it was fashionable to ask whether the agricultural reforms in Russia would produce a private agricultural sector to replace the collectivist structures inherited from the Stalin era. Russia's agrarian question concerned whether private structures would supersede collectivized agriculture. During the 1990s, Western analysts were taken with privatization, which led to a rather large literature, albeit one heavily skewed toward the analysis of private farming. If the criterion for answering Russia's agrarian question is a standard based on Western European or North American agriculture, then the answer is clearly "no." The limited success of government efforts to create an economically significant class of private farmers, the inability of the executive and legislative branches of the central government to create enforceable land-tenure rules, and unfavorable macroeconomic trends lead to a negative response.

If, however, we take a broader *institutional*[1] view of Russian agriculture and rural life, our assessment of change may not be so negative. After all, agrarian reform is much broader than private farming alone. Russian agriculture and rural life may not be very close at all to the experiences of farming and rural life in the West, or for that matter even to farm households in parts of Eastern Europe, but significant changes have occurred in rural Russia since 1991. Farmland has been privatized. A land market has developed, especially in small-scale land leasing. Moreover, households have made adaptations to the collapse of the Soviet system that go beyond mere

1

survival. There is strong empirical evidence of an entrepreneurial spirit among some households in the countryside. Significant changes have occurred in the food distribution, procurement, and marketing systems. At the same time, serious problems remain in rural Russia and it is by no means clear what the ultimate form of Russian agriculture and rural life will be. Enormous problems in institutional adjustment remain. In short, the picture of what was happening in rural Russia from 1991 to 2000 is immensely complex. The first step in appreciating the nature of the changes that are taking place in rural Russia today is to understand the unique character and history of the agrarian problem in Russian society.

The Agrarian Problem in Russia

One definition of the agrarian problem concerns the relationships among people, land, and agricultural production. As technology and democratic ideas spread around the world in the nineteenth and early twentieth centuries, many nations struggled, some peacefully and some violently, with these agrarian relationships as they affected the efficiency of agriculture, the quality of life of rural people, and the sustainability of communities. From the mid-nineteenth to the mid-twentieth century, Russia experienced a series of attempts at agrarian reforms, each of which was intended to meet specific economic, political, or social needs in rural society. During the course of these reforms, Russia was transformed from a backward, rural peasant society to one that was increasingly urban and industrial, if not exactly modern. These reforms educated the Russian peasantry and mechanized agricultural production. Agrarian reforms also changed peasant-state relations, redefined class relations within the rural economy, and altered urban-rural relations.

The emancipation of the serfs and the accompanying land reform program in 1861 was intended to transfer significant portions of the land owned privately by the nobility to peasants. The Stolypin reforms in the early twentieth century did not redistribute land but sought to restructure agriculture by liberating peasants from the commune and transferring land ownership and use to individuals. Both of these reforms attempted to redress economic and social issues that arose from the land and class structure of the Russian countryside that had existed for centuries.

The main problems associated with the contemporary reform efforts, which are the subject of this book, arise from the agrarian reform program launched by the Bolsheviks. The period of Soviet rule from 1917 until

World War II created three conditions with which subsequent reform programs would have to grapple: (1) the institutionalization of two types of agricultural production organizations, large estates and very small land-holdings; (2) the elimination of private property rights; and (3) the absence of a rural bourgeoisie or middle class.

These revolutionaries wanted political control of the countryside and economic development of agriculture in order to increase the production of food for a rapidly growing urban sector. They recognized a de facto land reform from below, as peasants seized landholdings from landed estates of the nobility and even from larger peasant landowners. An important consequence of the Bolshevik agrarian reform was the destruction of the landowning class and the subdivision of estate and larger peasant lands.[2] Landholdings were small scale, but they were not individually owned.

Each household was responsible for cultivating its strips of land but the commune decided the way in which that land was used. Communal involvement in agriculture during this period included decisions regarding the distribution and redistribution of land, such as interstripping, as well as management of the agricultural calendar, including decisions about what to plant and dates of planting and harvesting. In this sense, the early Communist period returned to pre-Stolypin communal land ownership, coupled with individual household land use.

A second dimension of Bolshevik reform was the nationalization of all agricultural land. The Decree on Land of 26 October 1917 provided for the abolition of private property, the confiscation of estates with no compensation, and the prohibition of private selling, leasing, and mortgaging of land. All these prohibitions were later codified in the 1922 Land Code. Land was supposed to "belong" to all the people and to be used only by those who tilled it. Toward this end, from 1918 to 1921, local land reserves were created and administered by local land committees. Citizens who wished to engage in farming had a right to an allotment from their local reserve. This was accompanied by efforts to control grain and the food trade and supplies to meet the needs of the Red Army during the Civil War. Starting with the New Economic Policy (NEP) in 1921, state control over the food trade was relaxed, but land remained national property.

Stalin's collectivization, from 1929 to 1934, was intended to reverse the 1917–18 peasant revolution from below. During collectivization, communal holdings were reorganized into larger state (*sovkhozy*) and collective (*kolkhozy*) farms through a process of village amalgamation.[3] As larger collective farms were created and came under the political and economic control of the state, an additional goal of collectivization was to transfer resources from agriculture in order to facilitate rapid industrialization.

The attempt to destroy small-scale communal farming and to supplant it with larger collective farms created class conflict in the countryside.[4] Collectivization was resisted not only by rich peasants (*kulaky*), who actually had more incentive to join collective farms in order to protect themselves, but also by middle and poor peasants. It turned out that the distinction between kulaky—who were considered "class enemies"—and middle and poor peasants was a great deal more difficult to apply in reality than Soviet ideology had anticipated. As a result, rural dwellers of all classes suffered.

According to some Western estimates, nearly five million people were affected by efforts to eliminate alleged kulaky during collectivization.[5] Terror and coercion marked the roundup of peasants and their forcible incorporation into collective farms. Resistance by rural dwellers to collectivization led to reprisals against collective farms and their workers (*kolkhozniki*). Collective farms and their buildings were often the victims of arson and collective farmers were sometimes attacked in their fields. Another form of resistance was the mass slaughter of farm animals. In 1928, for example, there were 70.5 million head of cattle in Russia. This number fell to 38.4 million in 1933. The 26 million pigs in 1928 fell to 12.1 million in 1933, while the number of sheep and goats fell from 146.7 million to 50.2 million during the same time period.[6]

From the time of collectivization in the late 1920s, the Soviet leadership favored large, mechanized, collective farms that exercised political and social control over local village populations. Soviet agrarian policy, however, was forced to tolerate small individual land plots because of the high proportion of food produced on them. The rural "private" sector during the Soviet period was commonly referred to as "private plots." They were not, however, totally private since the land was not privately owned. A better translation of *lichnoe podsobnoe khoziaistvo* is "personal plot."

Personal plots were intended to supplement the family's diet, outside of state regulation and control over production decisions. These plots were quite small. In the post-Stalin years the overall size of a plot could not exceed one-half of a hectare, including the land on which a dwelling was built, or 0.2 hectares on irrigated land, although regional variations did exist.[7] Both urban and rural dwellers were eligible to operate a personal plot. In the rural sphere, personal plots were more prevalent among collective farmers than among state farm workers.[8]

Government policies toward the personal plot went through various phases. The first phase was one of begrudging tolerance, indicated by the

Model Collective Farm Charter of 1930 that allowed the retention of personal plots of limited size within the village. Furthermore, in 1932 chaotic channels of private food trade were replaced with a legalized system of collective farm markets where peasants could sell their produce.[9] Again in 1935, the Model Collective Farm Charter guaranteed the retention of private plots because of their importance to the national food supply.

World War II was characterized by more lenience toward personal plots. Collectivization was interrupted as farm members were allowed to leave state and collective farms, and the ability of the state to control and manage the food sector declined. During the war, the role of non-state agricultural activities expanded. Personal plots were crucial in feeding the peasantry itself during the war. Local self-reliance lowered overall demand on supplies coming from the state sector. Food from personal plots was used to provide for the massive number of people who were evacuated to the east, especially during the first two years of the war. Food grown on household plots was sold to urban residents through the collective farms' (*kolkhozny*) market.[10]

The postwar period witnessed the return of the Stalinist bias against personal plots. Stalin's last direct attack on collective farm markets came in his "will" on economic policy, published in 1952 as *Economic Problems of Socialism in the USSR*. In this short book Stalin called for the elimination of the collective farm market and the establishment of an exchange system between industry and agriculture.[11] This barter system had a devastating effect on peasants since it meant that they would have no legal outlet to sell surplus produce from their personal plots.

After Stalin's death, Khrushchev attempted to moderate state agricultural policies.[12] Early in his tenure, from 1953 to 1958, he sought to increase personal plot production by easing a number of restrictions on them. Obligatory deliveries to the state, in the form of taxes from plot production, for example, were ended. His preferential plot policy was temporary, however, and after 1958 he developed policies that strengthened state regulation of personal plots.

In an effort to improve agricultural performance, Khrushchev pursued a variety of strategies. One was to induce higher agricultural production by increasing material incentives to farms. To achieve the production increases he desired, Khrushchev announced at the September 1953 plenum that procurement prices would be increased for livestock, poultry, milk, and butter. The policy of giving farms production incentives through higher state purchase prices was pursued until the end of the Khrushchev period. In subsequent years additional purchase price increases were announced for a series of animal husbandry products.

Another strategy employed during the Khrushchev period was to expand the amount of land under cultivation with the Virgin Lands Program. The assumption here was that expanding the amount of land under cultivation could rapidly increase food production and provide protection against regional droughts in European Russia. During the latter half of the 1950s, farms assimilated more than 30 million hectares of virgin and idle land in northern Kazakhstan and parts of the Russian Republic. By 1960, the amount of arable land under cultivation increased to 220 million hectares, up from 188 million in 1953.[13] Moreover, in the hope of achieving economies of scale, Khrushchev set in motion a program of merging smaller collective farms (kolkhozy) to form larger ones. In the period from 1953 to 1962, the number of kolkhozy was reduced from 97,000 to 39,500, while the average number of households per farm rose from 208 to 440, the sown area per farm rose from 1,693 to 2,896 hectares, and the capital stock per farm increased almost twelvefold.[14] Khrushchev's policy changes, however, were largely tactical. With the exception of abolishing machine tractor stations in 1957, he did not undertake any structural reform of Soviet agriculture.[15]

Nonetheless, Khrushchev will perhaps be best remembered in rural areas for other reforms that affected the quality of life of rural citizens. These included, for the first time, allowing rural citizens to have passports and thus to have more mobility within the Soviet Union. In addition, he created a system in which agricultural workers received wages for their work on collective and state farms. The latter had the effect of increasing the monetary purchasing power of rural residents, but it also had a negative impact on the development of private plots.

Brezhnev expanded upon many of the policy initiatives begun by Khrushchev. Policies toward personal plots, for example, became even more lenient, although his "liberal" policy did not deregulate their activities. During his tenure purchase prices for the agricultural economy as a whole increased several times. Massive amounts of money were allocated to agriculture in an effort to modernize agricultural production, and rural wages increased faster than urban wages. Nonetheless, even though some limited innovations were introduced after Stalin, the basic institutional and organizational structure of the Soviet agricultural system changed very little.

The Gorbachev agrarian reform program was designed to improve and restructure but not to destroy the Soviet system of agriculture. The Soviet agricultural system did an adequate job of feeding the population of the Soviet Union, but the quality and variety of foodstuffs were low, farms were increasingly inefficient and suffered from low profitability, and agricultural subsidies consumed ever-larger proportions of state spending.[16] The Gorbachev reforms were intended to make farms more profitable and accountable for their economic activities, improve the quality and selection of their output, and decrease the level of state subsidization. He continued to believe in the viability of the state and collective farm system, and thus his goal was to adopt policies that made them work better, not to undermine their existence. He stated that,

> We reject the demand for "total decollectivization." I am convinced that those collective farms and state farms that are managing their operations skillfully, are working to improve social amenities, are providing peasants with proper living conditions and are producing large amounts of output needed by society deserve every kind of support. Naturally, they will remain an organic part of the Soviet countryside as it undergoes renewal.[17]

Gorbachev did not support individual ownership of farmland. His reform in land relations returned to the NEP era by emphasizing land leasing by individuals and families. In his view, those leasing land could become independent of larger farms by starting family peasant farms. At the June 1987 plenum when the idea of land leasing was introduced, Gorbachev stated that "the most important task today is to make people full-fledged masters of the land again."[18] He urged kolkhozy and sovkhozy to lease abandoned houses and land plots on a contract basis to urban dwellers who wanted them for productive purposes. Leasing as the primary reform policy was approved in principle in 1988. The March 1989 plenum officially codified land leasing as the party's reform package, although Gorbachev actually opted for a conservative reform when he argued that it was "scientifically and practically ungrounded" to disband kolkhozy and sovkhozy in order to hand their land over to leaseholders. The plenum approved long-term leases (up to fifty years) and permitted leases to be inherited by family members. Leases did not, however, transfer ownership of land or any leased object. The state remained the owner of all land.[19]

Another feature of Gorbachev's reforms, consistent with the Soviet agrarian tradition, was the maintenance of high levels of financial subsidies in the agricultural sector. He actually *increased* the level of capital investments into agriculture from 1986 to 1990 in absolute terms, even as the percentage of all capital investments in the Soviet economy devoted to agriculture declined somewhat.[20] By 1988, agricultural subsidies equaled nearly 12 percent of Soviet gross domestic product (GDP). In 1991, agricultural subsidies as a percentage of GDP declined to 10 percent, but total agricultural subsidies equaled 104 billion rubles.[21]

The food question was central to societal stability, in terms of dealing with both urban consumers and agrarian interests in the countryside. The regime attempted to solve both of these problems by subsidizing food prices and paying farms more for their products. The largest component of agricultural subsidies went to consumer price subsides, rising from 44 percent of all agricultural subsidies in 1988 to 77 percent of all agricultural subsidies in 1991.[22] As Gorbachev noted in his memoirs, "Any noticeable increase in retail food prices was resolutely rejected. The problem was totally divorced from economic considerations, and regarded as a purely political issue."[23]

Moreover, agricultural producers had become dependent on subsidies to pay for mechanization and modernization. Gorbachev notes that "sixty percent of expenditures on agricultural production was attributed to industrial supplies to rural areas. . . . Statements claiming that agriculture was 'unprofitable' were found to be wrong. All data pointed to the fact that much more was siphoned off from agriculture than invested in it."[24]

Thus, Gorbachev agrarian policies attempted to fudge the issues he inherited as part of the Soviet legacy. He remained committed to large enterprises (collective and state farms), while also permitting the creation of independent peasant farms based on individual or family labor. These farms could only lease land, not own it. Most important, land leasing remained inherently limited. For example, targeted leases allowed the farm director to decide which land could be leased and which crops could be grown. Individual farmers were also limited in that they were required to sell a good portion of their output back to the farm, either as rent or as payment for inputs, thus remaining dependent upon the parent farm. In addition to peasant indifference to leasing, a consequence of these limitations was that no genuine independent class of farmers developed.

As a result of the core problems that carried over from the Stalin period, the agricultural sector at the end of the Gorbachev period had become increasingly inefficient, costly, and noncompetitive. One Western economist estimated that Soviet agriculture was one-half as productive per unit of input as U.S. agriculture.[25] Restraints included the paucity of hard-paved roads and rudimentary rural infrastructure, including a shortage of food storage facilities.

The Yeltsin Reforms

Boris Yeltsin attempted institutional changes that broke sharply with the Soviet past. These included reorganization and privatization of state and collective farms, privatization of processing and agricultural enterprises, land privatization and the adoption of supportive legal institutions, the creation of an individual private farming stratum, and the development of a land market.[26] Yeltsin's reforms were intended to transform Russia's agricultural economy along market lines, create the foundations for a class of independent farmers, make food production more efficient, decrease the economic burden of food subsidies, and deregulate the food trade.

Unlike Gorbachev's efforts, agrarian policies during the Yeltsin era were not intended simply to reform the basis of Soviet agriculture, but to destroy collective agriculture as the dominant sector of food production and as the primary form of farm organization. In the place of collective farms, smaller, specialized farms using family and hired labor were expected to emerge as the backbone of Russian agriculture. Private farms were to be based on private landholdings (either leased or owned). By the beginning of 2000, more than 260,000 private farms were in existence, but this was a decrease from 284,000 in 1994.

What were the results of the Yeltsin reforms? Scholars have been divided into three schools of thought: (1) those who see beneficial transformation taking place that may lead to a more productive future; (2) those who see only destruction of the agricultural sector; and (3) those who see little real transformation in either institutions or farm behaviors. Our view is that the reality of the Yeltsin reforms is more complex than any one of the three conventional schools of thought. A central goal of this book is to present the complexity of the impact of reform efforts implemented during the 1990s. In understanding the results of agrarian reform in the 1990s, we can point to measurable "successes" and "failures."

On the success side, one of the most distinctive changes in Russian agriculture has been the privatization of farms, farm property, and agricultural land. A program of farm reorganization led to the destatization of large farms and their property. Farmland also was privatized, allowing people wishing to leave a parent farm to do so with a free land allotment in order to undertake agricultural production. Only about one in three families actually left, but farm members were free to depart from the collective farm, with land and property, and more undoubtedly would have done so in a more favorable macroeconomic environment.

Furthermore, from 1992 to 1994 a deliberate policy to promote private farms was pursued by the Russian government. A host of incentives was created to encourage people to start private farms. The most important of these incentives were free land; moving-expense grants; a five-year land-tax exemption; and, at a time when market rates of interest were 110 to

140 percent or higher, private farmers were given credits at greatly subsidized interest rates.[27] The government also mandated that 15 percent of all government investments in agriculture would be allocated to assist private farmers. The initial response during the 1992–94 period was a tremendous increase in the number of private farms, increasing from less than 50,000 on 1 January 1992 to more than 284,000 in July 1994. Since then, as incentives were either abolished or eroded by inflation, the number of private farms stagnated, although the average size of surviving farms is increasing.

According to experts in Russia, 83 percent of agricultural land is now in private hands. Legally, farm members now own collective farms and their legal successors, typically known as joint stock companies. However, while the large agricultural enterprises do not legally own, they nonetheless still *control the use of* most agricultural land. There are several reasons for their persistence. One is the unwillingness of older residents to sell their land shares because of the fear that they will be forced to leave their place of residence if they have no other way to support themselves. In addition, many households fear that they will not be able to find other providers for services that they currently obtain from the large enterprises.[28]

Nonetheless, a rudimentary land market has developed in Russia. The farm privatization process that had begun in Nizhniy Novgorod in 1993 was extended to ten other regions by 1999. This program auctioned off farmland and property, breaking up large farms into smaller economic entities with greater farm specialization. During the post-Soviet period, tens of millions of land certificates, or deeds, have been distributed to nearly every farm member and other landowners, empowering them with the right to sell, buy, bequeath, trade, lease, or give away their land share. The land market remains limited by rural demographics, macroeconomic factors, limited purchasing power of individuals, and legal restrictions. Yet, for certain types of land plots, especially those used for small-scale agricultural production, the land market is particularly robust. Land leasing—either from individuals, farms, or municipalities—is also quite popular. Thus, the land market continues to hold potential for introducing significant transformation in the agricultural sector.

At the same time, there have been many negative consequences of the Yeltsin reform efforts that arose from the inherent limitations of what privatization by itself could accomplish. At the very heart of these problems is the need to replace the whole range of institutions and organizational structures of the Soviet period with a new set of institutions that will support households and village communities that are engaged in independent farming. These include educational, health, and agribusiness support services as well as local government and voluntary associations of a civic society that support independent agricultural communities in other parts of the world.

The institutional changes that are necessary to support a sustainable Russian agriculture and rural community life need to be based on an understanding of the unique institutional and social organizational arrangements in the Soviet period. Yet, the Yeltsin administration was quite naïve about the larger institutional picture in the Russian countryside.

In contrast to the Stolypin reforms, for example, which created a large administrative organization to implement change, the Yeltsin government all but ignored administrative details. He took at best a laissez-faire attitude and at worst a deliberately hostile attitude toward the rural population's negative reactions to reform. The absence of support for broader rural development may have been due to a perceived lack of need to gain the political support of the rural population, or simply the government's inability to finance a more pro-agriculture policy, or some combination of these two factors.

The macroeconomic environment for large-scale capital intensive agriculture deteriorated significantly during the Yeltsin presidency. By 1998, prices for industrial goods had risen four times faster than purchase prices for farm products.[29] To purchase a truck or tractor, farms now have to sell 2.8 to 6 times as much produce as they did in 1991.[30] The proportion of unprofitable large farms rose from 3 percent in 1990 to 89 percent in 1998, before declining somewhat to 59 percent in 1999.[31] Farm monetary losses totaled US$2.5 billion in 1998.[32] Former Minister of Agriculture Viktor Semenov noted that federal budget allocations to agriculture declined to less than 2 percent of the total budget in 1998 compared to 19 percent in 1991.[33] Government farm support declined from US$1.75 billion in 1996 to just over US$100 million in 1999.[34]

The acquisition of tractors declined steadily from 143,700 per year in 1990 to a mere 6,416 in 1998; in the same period, truck acquisition dropped from 97,600 to 980 and grain combines from 37,800 to 717.[35] The rate of machine depreciation exceeding replacement in agriculture was 90 percent to 120 percent, or at least three times the rate in the rest of the economy.[36] Applications of mineral fertilizers declined from an average of 79.4 kilograms per hectare of arable land in 1991 to 14.6 kilograms per hectare in 1997.[37] While deliveries of fertilizers to domestic producers have plummeted, exports of mineral fertilizers have remained virtually constant. It is estimated that food producers are extracting 4.5 times as many nutrients from the soil as they apply and there are fears that soil degradation could become irreversible in some grain-growing regions.[38] Land reclamation has virtually ceased, declining from more than 4.5 million hectares annually during the late 1980s through 1991, to less than 500,000 hectares in 1997.

Since the early 1990s, average grain harvests have declined, livestock herds have shrunk to 1950 levels, and 1999 meat production was less than 60 percent of its 1992 level. The physical volume of meat output from large farms was down 68 percent, and from households, down 10 percent. As a percentage of the ruble value of total output, the share of food produced by large farms fell from 67 percent in 1992 to 34 percent in 1999. During the same time period, the share produced by households rose from 32 percent to 60 percent. The share produced by private farms rose from 1 percent to 2 percent.[39]

The conditions in the Russian macroeconomic environment that created enormous difficulties for large-scale capital-intensive producers, at the same time created opportunities for smaller-scale, labor-intensive production. As basic food production turned more to subsistence and sale of products from household plots in farmers' markets, the provision of food to large cities became increasingly dependent on foreign imports. Food imports rose from 16 percent of the nation's food needs in 1990 to 22 percent in 1993, and 29 percent in 1994. By 1997, imports accounted for an estimated 40 percent of the nation's food consumption.[40] In major cities like Moscow, St. Petersburg, and Vladivostok, imports may account for as much as 75 percent of total food consumption.[41] Of particular importance is imported meat, which has given rise to political concerns over "food security." According to one estimate, Russia imported as much as 54 percent of its meat in 1997.[42] U.S. Department of Agriculture estimates put the figure closer to 35 percent, which is still a significant increase compared to the early 1990s. With the devaluation of the ruble in August of 1998, meat imports dropped from 80,000 tons a month for the January–July 1998 period, to 50,000 tons in August, to 20,000 tons in September, to less than 10,000 tons in October. At that point, however, the trend was reversed and imports of meat climbed to over 60,000 tons in December and rose to 80,000 tons per month during the first three months of 1999.[43]

To some extent, the rural population in Russia has been shielded from some of the harsher consequences of reform by its capacity to grow its own food. Moreover, although conditions may be very difficult for rural residents, there is not as great a gap between the worse off and the better off in rural areas as there is in urban areas. Nonetheless, there has been a clear deterioration of the social service infrastructure in rural areas, including the closing of schools and clinics and recreational/cultural facilities.[44] The deterioration of social conditions is reflected in the rapid increase in the rural death rate, from 13.3 per 1,000 people in 1990 to 15.6 per 1,000 in 1998. During the same time period, the rural birth rate plummeted from 15.5 per 1,000 to 10.2 per 1,000.[45] If not for rural in-migration, largely forced migrants from the Near Abroad, the rural demographic situation would be significantly worse.

The Beginning of the Putin Presidency

At the time this introduction was written, the new Russian president, Vladimir Putin, had been in office less than one year. Although the formulation and the consequences of his policies are not yet set, it does appear that he views the agricultural sector as being more important than did his predecessor. In July 2000, Prime Minister Mikhail Kas'ianov stated that agriculture was a "special sector" of the economy and promised high state tariffs on imported foods to protect domestic producers."[46] At the end of July, a government program on agrarian policy for 2001–10 was adopted. To demonstrate this renewed interest in agriculture, the new president attended conferences on agrarian problems in August 2000 in Samara, promising federal support for agricultural production.[47]

During the late summer and early fall, there were discussions about debt relief for large farms, encompassing some debt write-off and some deferment on repayment of other debts. Discussions in the fall also raised expectations that a new land code would soon be adopted. In October 2000, President Putin's secretary of agriculture, Aleksei Gordeev, indicated that agricultural revival was a top priority of the new administration. He claimed that "today, there is not one head of an administration, [one] governor, [one] president of a republic, who is indifferent to the problems of the countryside, who is not searching for possibilities to increase support to the countryside from regional budgets and other sources."[48]

It seems likely that Putin will support higher import tariffs and more trade protectionism as well as de-emphasize the role of officially registered private farmers as the primary vehicle for reforming Russian agriculture. In turn, we may expect greater federal executive-branch acceptance of the continued existence of large agricultural enterprises. This may be seen in some combination of debt write-offs, subsidized credits, special leasing programs, or increased budget allocations.

A critical question that remains is to what extent Putin will address the larger issues of rural development, especially the development of institutions in rural villages that will support the needs of households and village community life. In particular, will the president support the notion that developing institutions at the local level is necessary in order to go beyond survival to sustainable adaptation in a market economy? These institutions include the development of real producer and processing cooperatives that will support households in the development of agricultural and nonagricultural enterprises. In addition, the ability to attract and retain talented people in rural areas requires attention to a range of social service and organizational needs of civil society that are not included in typical discussions of "agricultural issues." The empirical work in this volume addresses this full range of rural development issues.

Themes of the Book

This book employs a variety of disciplinary approaches to provide an empirical assessment of what has changed and what remains to be changed in order to create sustainable rural communities in Russia. Although attention will be given to agricultural institutions and organizations, our primary interest is larger *agrarian* issues. These include the relationship between rural interests and the changing institutional structure of Russian society; the economic and social organization of rural households; and the material well being, social infrastructure, and quality of life of rural families and villages.

The book is divided into sections that respond to four main questions: (1) To what extent has Russian agriculture adapted to a market economy? (2) What are the major obstacles blocking the transformation of Russian agriculture and its integration into a world economy? (3) What is the nature of the adaptation that Russian households and villages are making to the exigencies and opportunities they face in the post-Soviet economic, political, and social spheres? (4) How will that adaptation affect the prospects for further reforms? The central conclusions and arguments for each of these questions are briefly summarized below.

Agricultural Adaptation to a Market Economy

Russian peasant culture and social organization are not an inherent obstacle to capitalist development. Historical research shows that cooperative trust relationships in the peasant commune provided a basis for an emerging dairy cooperative movement in Siberia in the nineteenth century.

Contemporary Russian land reform is having a profound impact on the Russian village. It is changing the role of collective farms, increasing individualization of agriculture, converting the rural population from workers to shareholders, and broadening the range of options for individual choice. The rural population has lost much of the social benefits that it enjoyed during the socialist regime. Yet, it has gained ownership of land and property, additional options for independent decisions, and new prospects for mobility. Those who have begun taking advantage of these opportunities are enjoying definite benefits: They are better off, happier, and more optimistic.

Large agricultural enterprises have adapted to new conditions. They have changed the way in which they use land by shifting production mixes, curtailed expenses by reducing livestock herds, adapted to the changes in the way farms are financed, and entered into new food-marketing arrangements. Although conventional wisdom often sees rural elite orientations as antireform, farm managers have had to make substantial adaptive responses to survive in the current macroeconomic environment. Adaptations by rural elites represent a source of optimism for successful reform in the Russian countryside.

Although somewhat rudimentary, a land market has emerged in Russia. The conventional wisdom that the rural population is opposed to land reform ignores the fact that this population is now the backbone of the landowning class in Russia. In addition, land leasing has become an important vehicle for expanding household agricultural production.

New marketing opportunities have arisen in rural Russia. Regions that are more successful in adapting to change have developed vertical cooperative linkages with farms and food processors, the latter at times involving multinational firms. Food processing enterprises are generally more economically viable than farms and can establish relationships with farms that are in their interest. In addition, new types of integration are creating holding companies that can compete with imports, and thus may be one of the few practical ways that Russian producers can stay in business in an increasingly competitive market. Empirical evidence demonstrates that vertical cooperation has produced a social rejuvenation in farms by putting them into a more rigorous economic environment.

In the post-Soviet period, there has been a substantial growth of household enterprises, largely in response to new market opportunities and the decline in social services and income supports from the state. Households have developed these enterprises largely through increases in their own human and social capital. In the Soviet period, institutional development at the village level was severely retarded by its narrow position within the social organizational structure of a command economy. Essentially, the village served as a source of labor for the collective and state farms and as a source of consumption for products produced by state enterprises. These new enterprises in the contemporary period may, however, have reached their growth potential within current institutional arrangements. The challenge now is to find ways to build institutions at the village level that will support household agricultural and nonagricultural enterprises, finance social services, and support the development of civil society.

Sources and Nature of Opposition to Change

Cultural meanings and personal sentiments attached to Russian village definitions of appropriate and inappropriate social relationships can provide obstacles to the development of a monetary-based market economy. While Russian peasants are not averse to the marketplace and exchange, barter relationships and various types of indirect exchanges based on nonmaterial criteria have come into conflict with some aspects of post-Soviet reform efforts.

While rural producers are slowly adapting to the introduction of new or expanded markets at the micro level, macroagricultural development has been regressive rather than progressive. With basic economic constraints such as de-monetarization, lack of sufficient government subsidies, and massive taxes, people on the farms believe that until the government changes and adopts more pro-rural legislation farms cannot succeed. The lack of attention given to the social safety net of the village exacerbates the negative feelings many villagers have toward reforms in general.

Rural workers face several human capital disadvantages vis-à-vis urban workers. These include lower average education levels, fewer specialized (marketable) job skills, and less geographical mobility. Thus, rural workers have fewer employment and entrepreneurial opportunities and face institutionalized barriers to access of education, skills training, and social services. Rural workers are rewarded at a lower rate than urban workers for their investments.

Members of former kolkhozy are caught between the conflicting demands to farm independently in a developing market economy while maintaining a sense of community and collective. Farm directors attempt to increase output and develop profits while ensuring the social well-being of the villagers, but find little success in meeting either objective. Complaints about transportation, education, child care, and medical care are pervasive and at times outweigh those related to farm equipment and fertilizers.

Ethnic regions were more supportive of the Yeltsin regime, which is seen as a proxy for support of reforms, than were the Russian regions. This is important because ethnic regions are more likely than Russian regions to retain collective farms rather than converting them into individual peasant farms.

Substantial regional and local differences occur with respect to efforts to salvage portions of Soviet-style subsidies to large enterprises through a mechanism known as elastic budget constraints. Regional and local decisions to adopt or eschew elastic budget constraints have significant consequences for the development of incentives of large enterprises to restructure.

There is a gap between the goals of the reorganized collective farms and their realization. In some places, enterprise reorganization has led to the entrenchment of semifeudal property relations in the village, thereby generating increased opposition to further market reforms. A basic weakness is that farm reorganization focused efforts on the reform of individual enterprises to the exclusion of reform of production relations and distribution networks among a wider range of village residents.

Household and Village Adaptation to Change

In a relatively short period of time households have made significant adjustments to increase their production and sales of agricultural products. These adjustments have been largely through increases in human and social capital, the latter being the development of informal helping exchange networks. Income from household enterprises, both agricultural and nonagricultural, accounts for almost two-thirds of average household income.

The growth of household enterprises has been occurring largely through an informal economy that has some inherent constraints on growth. Rural Russians are rational economic actors who will make adaptations to improve the economic viability of their households. Relationships between peasant households and the large farms were a crucial part of the household survival strategies in the post-Soviet period, and those relationships persist in the institutional structure of Russian village life today. Further growth of household enterprises and the long-term development of private agriculture in Russia are dependent on greater local and regional support for household enterprises.

Large enterprise directors have differed widely in the strategies they have employed to deal with the challenges of farm restructuring. Individual personality differences account for the major portion of variances in managers' choices of survival strategies in the post-Soviet period.

Households' social exchange networks, which date back to Soviet times, have been increased to deal with the new demands of trying to cope with an expanding market economy, especially the increased pressure to produce on private plots and to obtain goods and services in the marketplace. The primary effects of these networks on satisfaction with life domains and life in general are *indirect* rather than direct, compensating for limitations in household human capital.

Notes

1. A discussion of institutional change in rural Russia in light of the "new institutional economics" and the "new institutionalism in sociology" is found in the concluding chapter in this volume. In this introductory essay, we focus on the historical, political, and economic background of Russian agriculture and rural social organization. The new institutional economics has been stimulated by Douglass North, *Institutions, Institutional Change and Economic Performance* (Cambridge: Cambridge University Press, 1990); and Oliver Williamson, *The Economic Institutions of Capitalism* (New York: Free Press, 1985). Representative works in the new institutionalism in sociology include Mary C. Brinton and Victor Nee, eds., *The New Institutionalism in Sociology* (New York: Russell Sage Foundation, 1998); and Mark Granovetter, "Economic Action and Social Structure—The Problem of Embeddedness," *American Journal of Sociology* 91 (1985): 481–510.

2. While collective farming was held as a long-term policy goal, in fact only about 3 to 4 percent of agricultural land in European Russia was retained for collective farming. Lazar Volin, *A Century of Russian Agriculture: From Alexander II to Khrushchev* (Cambridge, MA: Harvard University Press, 1970), 134.

3. The amalgamation process itself reached its logical end 30 years later when collective farms were amalgamated, resulting in fewer, but comparatively enormous, collective and state farms.

4. See Shelia Fitzpatrick, *Stalin's Peasants: Resistance and Survival in the Russian Village After Collectivization* (New York: Oxford University Press, 1994).

5. Robert Conquest, *The Harvest of Sorrow: Soviet Collectivization and the Terror-Famine* (New York: Oxford University Press, 1986), 125.

6. Alec Nove, *An Economic History of the USSR, 1917–1991* (Middlesex, England: Penguin Books, 1992), 186.

7. See Stephen K. Wegren, "Regional Differences in Private Plot Production and Marketing: Central Asia and the Baltics," *Journal of Soviet Nationalities* 2 (spring 1991): 118–38.

8. A. F. Kalinkin, *Lichnoe podsobnoe khoziaistvo: kollektivnoe sadovodstvo i ogorodnichestvo* (Moscow: Kolos, 1981), 11. By 1988, it was reported that nearly all collective farm families (98 percent) had a personal plot, while 79 percent of state farm families had a plot. Among urban worker and employee families, only about 25 percent had a personal plot. *Lichnoe podsobnoe khoziaistvo naseleniia v 1988 godu* (Moscow: Goskomstat, 1989), 3.

9. Naum Jasny, *The Socialized Agriculture of the USSR: Plans and Performance* (Stanford, CA: Stanford University Press, 1949), 384.

10. See William Moskoff, *The Bread of Affliction: The Food Supply in the USSR During World War II* (Cambridge: Cambridge University Press, 1990), 94.

11. See J. V. Stalin, *Economic Problems of Socialism in the USSR* (New York: International Publishers, 1952), 63–71.

12. For an overview of agricultural policy during the Khrushchev era, see Erich Strauss, *Soviet Agriculture in Perspective: A Study of Its Successes and Failures* (New York: Praeger, 1969), chapter 7; David M. Schoonover, "Soviet Agricultural Policies," in Joint Economic Committee, *The Soviet Economy in a Time of Change: A Compendium of Papers Submitted to the Joint Economic Committee, Congress of the United States*, vol. 2 (Washington, DC: Government Printing Office, 1979), 87–115.

13. See Martin McCauley, *Khrushchev and the Development of Soviet Agriculture* (London: Macmillan, 1976), chapter 4.

14. Frank A. Durgin, "Russia's Private Farm Movement: Background and Perspectives," *The Soviet and Post-Soviet Review* 21 (1994): 217.

15. See Volin, *A Century of Russian Agriculture*, chapter 14.

16. To be fair, we need to note that lower profitability occurred because of increased production costs due to rising input prices and increased labor costs, neither of which farms could control. Moreover, the bulk of subsidies to agriculture were aimed at keeping retail food prices low for urban consumers.

17. Speech at the 28th Party Congress, July 1990, in *Pravda*, 3 July 1990, 2–4.

18. *Pravda*, 26 June 1987, 1–4.

19. After the March 1989 plenum, the USSR Council of Ministers passed a resolution on leasing. "Ob ekonomicheskikh i organizatsionnykh osnovakh arendnykh otnosheniy v SSSR," *Ekonomicheskaia gazeta* no. 19 (May 1989), 7–8. That resolution was followed by the Supreme Soviet law on leases that specified terms and conditions of land leasing. See the law passed by the USSR Supreme Soviet in *Pravda*, 1 December 1989, 3–4. The law took effect in January 1990. Land leasing was also codified in the Law on Land, adopted at the end of February 1990 and published in March 1990, which provided for the leasing of land for the creation of independent peasant farms. *Izvestia*, 7 March 1990, 1–2. None of the laws cited above, however, allowed land to be sold, purchased, or mortgaged.

20. In 1990 rubles, collective farms received 156.2 billion rubles of capital investment during the 1981–85 period, but received 183.8 billion rubles in the 1986–90 period. *Narodnoe khoziaistvo SSSR v 1990 g.* (Moscow: Finansy i statistika, 1991), 435.

21. The World Bank, *Food and Agricultural Policy Reforms in the Former USSR: An Agenda for the Transition* (Washington, DC: World Bank, 1993), 218, table 8.2.

22. Ibid.

23. Mikhail Gorbachev, *Memoirs* (New York: Doubleday, 1996), 121.

24. Ibid., 120.

25. Karen McConnell Brooks, "The Technical Efficiency of Soviet Agriculture," in D. Gale Johnson and Karen McConnell Brooks, *Prospects for Soviet Agriculture in the 1980s* (Bloomington: Indiana University Press, 1983), chapter 9.

26. There are of course other aspects, such as cultural reformation, social policy, and the rural wage structure. But those are not "institutional" reforms, they are policy reforms.

27. In 1992, the interest rate was 8 percent per annum, and in 1993, 28 percent.

28. These services include assistance with cultivation and marketing of household plot production, provision of materials for household construction, and supplementary supports for social services, such as education and health care. See David O'Brien et al., *Services and Quality of Life in Rural Villages in the Former Soviet Union: Data from 1991 & 1993* (Lanham, MD: University Press of America, 1998), 115–62.

29. *Izvestia*, 25 July 1998, 1–2.

30. *Sel'skaia zhizn'*, 26 December 1996, 8–9.

31. *Rossiiskii statisticheskii ezhegodnik 1996* (Moscow: Goskomstat, 1996), 552; *Sel'skaia zhizn'*, 22 May 1997, 3, and 23 February 1999, 1.

32. Russian Ministry of Agriculture reports, available at *www.aris.ru*.

33. *Izvestia*, 25 July 1998, 1–2.

34. In January 1998, Russia redenominated the ruble, introducing new notes with three fewer zeros than pre-1998 rubles. To make the data comparable, the text refers to 1998 rubles.

35. Russian Ministry of Agriculture reports, available at *www.aris.ru*.

36. *Finansovye izvestiia*, 25 May 1995, 5.

37. *Rossiiskii statisticheskii ezhegodnik 1998* (Moscow: Goskomstat, 1998), 456.

38. Estimate of researchers at the Russian Research and Design Institute for Chemicalization of Agriculture in *Interfax Food and Agriculture Report* 6, no. 27 (1997): 12–13.

39. Calculations based on *Rossiia v tsifrakh* (Moscow: Goskomstat, 2000), 139, 198.

40. *Finansovye izvestiia*, 13 November 1997, 6.

41. Some analysts believe the foreign market share in some cities is as high as 90 percent. See "Russia Today Business Report," 7 January 1999, available at *www.russiatoday.com*, citing the Consumer Market Department at the Russian Foreign Trade Ministry.

42. *Finansovye izvestiia*, 13 November 1997, 6.

43. Recent figures on imported versus domestically produced meat can be obtained from the Russian Ministry of Agriculture website, available at *www.aris.ru/WINE/*.

44. In Soviet times there was a unified electrical power grid system. Today, a large number of the power plants have passed into private hands. "Before there were lights in every village. Today, from Kirov, Vologodsk, Voronezh and a series of other oblasts come reports that, for many weeks, the villages are without lights" (*Sel'skaia zhizn'*, 15 December 1996, 1). In 1993, an average of 250 to 300 rural stores closed in every province of Russia. In Tula oblast, for instance, the number of retail trade enterprises fell by almost a third and the number of public catering enterprises by more than a third. *Krest'ianskie vedomosti*, 23–29 January 1995, 7.

45. *Demograficheskii ezhegodnik Rossii 1999* (Moscow: Goskomstat, 1999), 52.

46. *Sel'skaia zhizn'*, 4 July 2000, 1, 2.

47. *Sel'skaia zhizn'*, 5 September 2000, 1, 2.

48. *Sel'skaia zhizn'*, 5–11 October 2000, 3.

Part One

Adaptation of Russian Agriculture
to a Market Economy

1

Entrepreneurship and the Siberian Peasant Commune in Late Imperial Russia

IGOR V. VOLGINE

Introduction

The variety of the capitalist paths may be as different as the societies that are going to take these paths. Culture, which constitutes the source of informal institutional economic practices, preconditions the specific character of capitalism in a particular country. The recent Russian rapid implementation of "formal capitalism" in law, politics, and economy has not led to the creation of the "informal" capitalist society, that is, to changes in habits, norms, and everyday practices. Informal institutions change very slowly. In the case of Russia, they are not merely the result of decades of communist rule but are deeply rooted in social consciousness and cannot be easily removed by a replacement of the formal environment. Public resentment toward present-day Russian capitalism shows that the boundary between old and new life orientations and values is still fluctuating. This includes rhetoric about "capitalist foreign abuse," resistance of workers to capitalist managers, corruption and oppression of free producers by their "egalitarian" neighbors and bureaucrats, and the emergence of the Russian Mafia.

Many theorists contend that the contemporary resentment toward capitalism in Russia is rooted in traditional cultural patterns rather than in the
Soviet legacy or the recent democratic experience. They argue that the
Russian cultural tradition fosters traits such as slackness, idleness, and lack
of initiative and hopelessness. These traits that are captured by the catch-
word *nichevo* (nothing) are alleged to contradict the basic principles of
capitalism.[1]

In short, it may appear that the rejection of capitalism is not merely a
product of ideological control under communism but the result of a deep-
seated collectivism in Russian life that can be traced to the collectivist traditions of the Russian peasantry.[2] The negative effects of this communal
mentality, it may be argued, combine with the seven decades' experience
of egalitarian Marxist ideology resulting in the strong cultural patterns that
contradict the ideas and values of capitalism.

This chapter raises the question, to what extent is the communal system
actually responsible for the emergence of anticapitalist patterns? It will
be shown that the capitalist modernization experienced by Siberian agriculture after 1861 presents a good example of a successful transformation
of the formal environment into capitalism. Siberian peasant communes
proved to be capable of economic cooperation not only with native merchants but also with foreign capitalist managers. This means that the peasant commune does possess the proper forms of economic interaction and
organization for adaptation to a capitalist environment. The results of this
study can shed light on the relationship between peasant culture and current efforts to bring foreign investment into Russian agriculture.

Methodological Grounding

Swidler's approach to culture and behavior is especially useful in understanding the role of Siberian peasant communes in the development of capitalist enterprises in the nineteenth and early twentieth centuries. She argues for the need to shift our emphasis from cultural ends to the behavioral
patterns of individuals. She observed that "people may share common as-
pirations, while remaining profoundly different in the way their culture organizes their overall pattern of behavior."[3] Values do not determine the
behavior of people but rather their distant cultural orientations. Similar
ends do not imply similar means of their acceptance. Available means determine differences in results despite similar anticipation and intention.

In this sense, culture represents a set of skills and habits rather than a set of preferences and wants. Swidler asserts that any particular individual is a kind of "architect" of his or her personal behavioral "strategies of action." Material for these strategies is supplied by culture, which is a "tool kit" of "symbols, stories and rituals, which are used in varying ways to solve different kinds of problems."[4]

According to Swidler, culture represents a "tool kit" of unit actions from which various behavioral strategies are constructed. These constructed "strategies of action" are executed through everyday practice and receive confirmation from the "ethos" (roughly, environment), which enforces repetition of successfully applied strategies. In turn, a successful behavioral strategy supports the ethos around it by repeating itself until the time when a changing environment does not correspond to this strategy any longer.

When traditional strategies of action are not justified by the ethos, individuals begin to look for ideological values to develop other "strategies of action" from "segments" of their cultural "tool kit" in order to be consistent with the new ethos. Hence, the possibility of changes in a society are greatly preconditioned by the availability of the various patterns that are provided by the cultural "tool kit." Swidler assumes that culture represents a great storage system, containing "diverse, often contradictory symbols, rituals, stories and guides to action."[5] This cultural diversity provides a variety of choices of strategies of action.

The Formation of Cultural Patterns Among Russian Peasants

Egalitarianism

The geographical factor has always been significant in Russian history. The severe northern climate, unstable crops, poor soil, and a short growing season of five and one-half to six months have demanded additional efforts in order to diminish the risk of a bad harvest. According to Wright,

> [t]he methodical German landowner, August Von Haxthausen, who visited Russia in 1843–4 and wrote a classic account of the countryside calculated that in the province of Yaroslavl he would need 7 men and 7 horses to work an area of land which, in the valley of the Main in Germany, or in France near Orleans, could be worked with 4 men and 4 horses. Moreover, these Russian estates would bring him only 2600 thalers compared to 5000 thalers that he could expect from German or French soil.[6]

The nuclear peasant family could barely secure steady economic performance on its allotment.

These circumstances led to communal practices. The most important agricultural procedures were performed collectively, under the supervision of the commune in order to diminish the risk of a poor harvest and to secure at least minimal economic efficiency (the principal of risk avoidance). The peasant commune's structure also secured the means of mobilizing available resources and was an effective mechanism for controlling deviant behavior.

Low population density, which is discussed in chapter 3 by Ioffe and Nefedova, added to the difficulties caused by unfavorable natural conditions: "[T]he basic condition in Russia . . . was that there were never enough hands to till the land."[7] All of these factors required a strict discipline among the commune's members. It resulted in a hierarchy within the community, including the family relationship. Thus, the commune represented a rigid system of authority and command wherein individual activities were tightly controlled for the common good. This system is considered to be responsible for what was later viewed as the negative effects of communal mentality, and has been traditionally considered to be the main source of Russian national character and culture.[8]

Dependence on natural conditions created a great deal of economic insecurity for peasant households. Sometimes the hardest workers were unsuccessful in securing the required minimum of return from their allotments, but in a favorable year, even the laziest peasants would receive a significant surplus. Hence, many peasants believed that it was better to fulfill the prescribed accustomed set of agricultural operations in order to receive more or less stable satisfactory returns. As to additional surplus, it was seen as depending on individual *fortune*, not on initiative.

The passive economic position of the peasant could be ascribed to his perception of economic activity as a lottery game. The dependence of the peasant's life on agricultural success resulted in a fatalistic approach to life, a feeling of helplessness before natural forces. To a certain extent it restrained the peasant's initiative in the implementation of new agricultural methods. Results were seen as depending not on personal or collective contributions but rather on supernatural will from above. The primitive feeling of omni-equality among the peasantry corresponds to this fatalistic view of life.

Egalitarianism is traditionally associated with the Russian communal practice of land repartition. It implies that all individuals should be treated on the same basis. The repartitional practice and treatment of property rights show that the feeling of equality among Russian peasants is closely connected to the feeling of justice—that is, that every family of the commune must receive its *just* proportional amount of land. Some scholars describe the peasant's egalitarianism as "a simple egalitarian passion for justice," which was preferred to the principle of economic expediency.[9]

Usually the peasant commune possessed a certain amount of cropland, pasture, and forest, and the repartition of the communal resources meant the redistribution of existing resources among communal members. "The goal of redistribution was merely to supply households with the minimum amount of land . . . that was a . . . practical and culturally conditioned adjustment to limited resources. Equalization thus became an unintended consequence of redistribution."[10]

In the long run, the redistribution practice resulted in the development of a peasant egalitarianism that turned out to be anticapitalist in nature. It was the practice of

> taking from one to give to another. One man's gain represented another's loss. . . . [The peasant's] perception of economic activity and perhaps even of social transactions in general, was a zero sum game. Any unusual accumulation of property or wealth among the peasants, even if it was acquired by special effort or ability could be treated as socially unjust by others in the community. . . . The successful peasant was resented as much as admired, often labeled a "*mir* (community) eater." Land distribution thus helped to create a strong sense of distributive justice . . . in economic terms.[11]

The communal form of property and mutual responsibility, which was fostered by the state after 1861, provided a feeling of collectivity and unity. The equalization of the economic possibilities of peasant households under conditions of limited resources was the logical continuation of the peasant's understanding of justice. Equalization in the form of repartitional practice created a strong feeling of justice "in economic terms." It came to be seen that the "fair" way of receiving the proper share of common wealth was through the redistribution procedure, that is, "taking from one to give to another." This view stressed that economic success was based on the anticipation of receiving a *fair* part of the common wealth rather than on the personal efforts of the individual. The peasant's perception of economic activity as a zero-sum game hampered the development of capitalistic households because capitalist morality contradicted peasant virtues. The cultural perception of wealth as immoral and unjust not only restrained the peasant's capitalist initiative but also condemned and rejected it. From this point of view, redistribution was viewed as the just economic alternative to unjust capitalist accumulation.

Anti-Individualism

Anti-individualistic communal traits originated in the egalitarian outlook of Russian peasants. Excessive collectivism also contributed to the peasant's rejection of self-seeking behavior. This was one of the main consequences of the communal system. Keenan observes that

> the most significant autonomous actor in peasant life was not the individual (who could not survive alone in this environment), and not even the nuclear family (which . . . was marginally viable, but still too vulnerable to disease and sudden calamity) but the village, to whose interests all others were in the end subordinated.[12]

The minimization of risk in agriculture for the sake of economic efficiency was one of the main tasks of the commune. The accomplishment of this task required rigid control over the use of natural resources and the labor force. This control also included the suppression of any kind of delinquency: "[The] community emerged as arbiter. . . . [It] maintained rigid control devices to ward off potential danger of behavior which could be harmful to the communal interests."[13] Those who deviated from the group norms of common law encountered at first ridicule, then open censure, and finally exclusion or expulsion from the commune (exile in Siberia or forced recruitment into the army). Communal justice might even culminate in death.[14]

The logic of collective life prescribed to every actor a specific role in a common game. Free improvisation was more often punished than welcomed. This is contrary to the capitalist mentality, where one could take a risk for the sake of a potentially large gain in the future. Risk as well as rational, self-oriented behavior is an unavoidable element of capitalist reality. Both not only contradict the principle of the risk minimization but also oppose peasant virtues. "Traditionally, Russians equate trade and industry (i.e., entrepreneurship, self-oriented behavior) with pure greed."[15]

According to the peasant's viewpoint, every member of the commune must show loyalty to common interests. The image of a positive peasant hero is a person who is devoted to the interests of the commune and does not look for personal reward. His devotion is so deep that he is ready to die before failing in his moral obligations to the commune. Reoccurring in peasant folklore are references to an "honorable" death, suggesting that death while conducting a deed in the name of common good is a behavioral pattern to be emulated. It also means that deviation from this type of behavior or failure to defend common interests will result in implicit or explicit expulsion from the commune. The latter means a "disgraceful" death. Even the case of a large beneficial personal contribution to the commune resulting from an individual act was seen as an immoral pursuit of money for oneself.

The Russian writer Fedor Kamanin provides an extreme example of peasant rejection of their neighbors. A resourceful peasant returns to his village after a financially successful trip to America. In order to be readmitted to the commune again, he has to show his devotion to the common interest. The procedure included the presentation of a "gift," which was a discount in some trade services and credit. To the local peasants, however, the lack of a tangible "gift," its small size, or his deviant behavior served as a reason to perceive him as an immoral, greedy, and dishonest person, which tacitly implied expulsion from the commune. The tension between this peasant and the community increased and eventually resulted in his murder by members of the commune.[16] In short, the shared feeling of equality, the common experience of shared rewards and punishments, did not encompass approval of pure personal initiative even in the solution of personal economic misfortune. Also, self-oriented behavior was a source of condemnation, even if it fulfilled common needs, due to the fact that an individual acting as an entrepreneur had received too many benefits from it. In the case just described the volume of the entrepreneur's success exceeded the limits of what was allowed. He was too successful and too rich according to the views of local peasants. This perception resulted in his neighbors' hostility and his isolation, which, in turn, provoked his murder.

In Kamanin's story, local peasants did not know how the entrepreneur achieved his success. It must be noted that in the same village there were other rich peasants and merchants who successfully operated local trade enterprises. Typically, peasants treated their "communal" entrepreneurs more tolerantly if they witnessed the origin and the process of their wealth accumulation. From the peasant's point of view, the way of making money, or the correspondence of the entrepreneur's behavior during business operations to peasant virtues, was more important than economic results. The wealthy outsider was treated more severely than his native counterpart.

It must be noted that internal gradual capitalist accumulation, within the communal framework, was relatively safer than external sources. Slow adjustments to new social, economic, and cultural phenomena by traditional peasant culture prevented social outbursts and conflicts. Capitalist accumulation that was effectively inserted from the outside, however, could collide with various obstacles, some of which were too strong to overcome.

Cultural adjustment of the traditional peasant's views to new behavioral patterns proved to be the most difficult.

> Social control was so powerful that it was impossible for peasants to exist, physically or psychologically, if they found themselves in a hostile relationship with the commune. . . . The socialization and the strong social control exercised by the commune did not allow a distinction between the individual and the group. The peasant's "I" merged with the communal "we."[17]

The overwhelming majority of peasants after emancipation refused to take their allotments as private property. They could not imagine how they could run their households independently. The low incidence of deviant behavior in the countryside also shows the power of the collective tradition and unity within the commune.

Georg Simmel asserted that a positive attitude toward changing fashions in clothing and grooming illustrated the desire of a person to be distinguished from others, and, in turn to show the level of individualism in a society. From this point of view the peasant commune demonstrated full "indifference towards fashion . . .[,] the absence of individualistic strivings to differentiate oneself, to separate oneself from the larger group."[18]

A more accurate conceptualization is that "[t]he relationship between peasant and commune may be called organic, voluntary conformity . . . political, intellectual, moral, and social, and it is made for the standardization of the peasants' needs and interests."[19] This standardization represents a kind of tacit public agreement created to provide minimal economic efficiency and it is mainly for this reason that peasants delegated their rights to the commune. With respect to other aspects of life, a peasant felt himself relatively independent insofar as his activity did not contradict the common interests. Peasant communal conformity was based on the commonality of interests and purposes, homogeneity of status, and internal unity. "Total absorption of the peasant by the commune did not occur . . . and was hardly possible. . . . [T]he commune left room for diversity and originality, even for open revolt by the individual. . . . Only in those questions that concerned the common interests of the whole commune was . . . peasant behavior strictly regulated and deviations from the norm reduced to a bare minimum."[20]

The peasantry showed little tolerance for urban life, peasants who deviated from the accepted norms, and foreigners. Every peasant was "not only the victim of oppression but very much the actor and oppressor." The communal system, through bonds of mutual responsibility, made peasants suppress their neighbors' excessive individualism for the sake of the common good.[21] The collectivist character of power in the commune

> was not an institution of representative government; it was in fact rather anti-representative. It took the burden of decisions from the individual through communal decisions . . . which were surely no more than a reflection of the great identity of interest among the members.[22]

From this point of view, the anti-individualistic rejection of the self-seeking behavior is seen as the outcome of the peasant's conformity. The peasant restricted his own initiative as well as his neighbor's for the sake of the common interest. These interests embraced only certain vital economic functions that were determined by collective land and resources property. Formally, peasants remained free to undertake any profitable business that did not affect the communal procedures, but in reality they were bound by these agricultural procedures. The commune's response to the interests of the majority was a realization of the economic instability of individual households. The commune served as an insurance institution. Even with the beginning of the commune's decline during the rapid development of capitalism, only a small number of peasants regarded the commune as a burden. "An absolute majority of the peasants . . . still supported the commune, not even conceiving of an existence outside its confines."[23]

In spite of the rising efficiency of individual labor, the amount of communal responsibilities actually increased. Under unclear judicial regulations, the commune was a more efficient defender of peasant interests than was the individual peasant.[24] The perception of shared gains and losses together with collective experience was fixed by the individual peasant during his entire life. This resulted in the psychological belief that collectivist methods were not only more efficient and dependable but also "proper" and "just." Worobec asserts that the peasants "firmly believed that collective efforts were far more effective than uncoordinated individual attempts."[25]

The peasantry felt safe behind the communal walls. These walls promoted a minimal level of efficiency and provided assistance in cases of economic misfortune and common crisis situations. The peasant's economic equality in rights and duties and equality before the state secured uniformity among commune members and their internal solidarity in external relations. However, in spite of the fact that the "concern for equality of burdens and obligations lay at the heart of the Russian repartitional commune,"[26] the commune did not attempt "to achieve complete economic equality among its members . . . but [sought] . . . to establish certain limits to differences in their economic status."[27] Governmental support of the commune after emancipation led to the continuity of some social control functions of the commune that restricted the economic freedom of the individual peasant.

The prescribed character of actions in the peasant commune and the rejection of individualistic behavior left little space for initiative, change, and development. The economic consequences are clearly visible: The lack of initiative led to the mere reproduction of traditional agricultural forms with little space for innovation. Therefore, many theorists have viewed the peasant commune as a rigid system able to provide only the prescribed traditional order of life, and thus militated against innovation.[28]

The Xenophobic Tradition

Distrust of foreigners or xenophobia is deeply rooted in Russian history. With insufficient knowledge about the outer world, Russians emphasized their own national identity. The Orthodox Church supported differences in the way of life between Russia and the West. The doctrine of the "Third Rome" asserted the religious superiority of the Russians. Russia was "Holy Russia" or "the Second Jerusalem," the only repository of true Orthodoxy, that is, true Christianity. As a result, Russian national identity still has a messianic character. To be a Russian means to be a representative of the chosen nation, which shelters the true religion and thus promotes the only way for common salvation. Hence, the relationship of Russia to other nations is ambiguous. On the one hand, there is fear of contamination by Catholic heretics and the unusual customs of foreigners. On the other hand, Russia trades with the West and profits from Western technology.

Religious rejection combined with the generalized distrust of foreigners increased peasants' suspicious attitudes toward capitalism. Because corporate capitalism came to Russia as a mature social institution and was foreign in character, the peasantry did not have an opportunity to witness its development. Thus, it was perceived as a component of the hostile foreign culture that had nothing in common with Russian tradition.

Economic nationalism and related demands for protection from the state reinforced the xenophobic tradition. The main explanation for a kind of moral innocence and lack of competitiveness that characterize Russians lies in the relatively late start of capitalism in Russia. Most Russians, except for a very small class of wealthy landlords, knew nothing about stock exchanges or financial speculation. Citizens applied to the government for protection against perceived foreign abuse.[29] Traditional Russian industries and merchants could not deal with foreign competition and demanded protection. The state responded to these demands by strong regulations and increased supervision of economic enterprises. New sectors of the economy such as the chemical and electrical industries were established and managed by foreigners with little Russian participation. These developments were perceived as simple exploitation by many Russians. This xenophobic view was found in all classes of Russian society and continued in Soviet and post-Soviet times.[30] The xenophobic rejection of capitalism and hostility toward capitalism were grounded on a low opinion of the behavior that is essential to success in the marketplace; such beliefs are also found in other societies undergoing rapid modernization. "Poverty and weakness became proofs of spiritual superiority over the adversary, whose superior technical or military power masked moral decadence."[31]

The Peasant Commune in Siberia

Although it had a clear cultural connection to European Russia, the peasant commune in Siberia evolved within a much different set of environmental constraints and opportunities. This unique historical development illustrates Swidler's argument that the same general cultural orientation may support quite different behavioral adaptations for individuals who operate within different environmental settings.[32]

The eastern region of the Russian Empire originally was conquered by the Cossacks, and then populated by exiles, criminals of all kinds, peasants who escaped from serf obligations, and religious heretics. Long distances, vast territories, weak governmental control, and rich natural resources allowed these individuals to remain semi-independent from the regulations of state and church. Thus, Siberia was historically populated mainly by socially active representatives of Russian society who possessed a higher level of individualization and initiative than did other Russians.[33]

In the second half of the nineteenth century, Siberia was more economically underdeveloped than was European Russia. Settlement of this region was slow and accelerated only after the 1880s when land shortages developed in central Russia. The absence of infrastructure prevented the government from imposing its decrees.[34]

One of the most important historic features of Asiatic Russia was the weak development of landlord ownership rights. In a legal sense, the state, the autocratic family, and the Cossack army, as well as a small number of landlords were the main landowners in Siberia. However, the overwhelming majority of the Siberian population, the peasantry, freely used state land, without proper legal basis. The government paid little attention to the peasants' seizure and use of land and forests until the end of the nineteenth century. Prior to that time, the government's primary interests in Siberia were mining precious metals and the fur trade. Revenues from these items were stable and profitable.[35] The state limited itself to the usual per-soul tax. Any attempt to impose additional taxes was difficult, given the government's weakness to impose its dictates in Siberia.

Siberian inhabitants were involved in economic activity that could be called entrepreneurial. Many people, including peasants, undertook different kinds of small businesses, such as fur hunting and trapping, gold mining, and retail trade. Sometimes these activities were economically more successful than agriculture and gave peasants additional revenue. Many visitors noted the similarities in economic activities between Russians in Siberia and individuals in Canada. Entrepreneurial initiative and individualism were features that made the Siberian people different from their countrymen in European Russia.[36]

The unique characteristics of the environment and the people who settled the region preconditioned some peculiar features of Siberian development. In spite of a similarity in status, economic conditions among the peasantry in European Russia and Siberia were different. Siberian peasants enjoyed greater freedom in their activities than did their European counterparts: They never knew serfdom and they had choices of undertaking a small business or being "pure" peasants. Most Siberian peasants did both. Weak national government control allowed the Siberians to organize their way of life almost independently, and the peasant communal system was freer from official impositions. Many of the cultural patterns of the Russian peasantry in Siberia developed with little influence from the state.

The Siberian peasant commune represented a natural form of economic cooperation for the Russian peasantry. It was "a union for the common usage of the land." The commune united both collective and individual elements. "The right of the overall power over the communal land, belonged to the commune."[37] The very idea of the commune implied the equal right of all for the "just" part of God's land, which was confirmed by individual labor. The main tasks of the commune were to regulate, promote, and coordinate the activity of its members.

The commune demonstrated a strong ability for adaptation in different environments that formally did not support it, a result of the institution's flexibility. The commune provided certain facilities that were crucial for the survival of its members. Moreover, the efficiency of Russian agriculture under the commune system, compared to European and U.S. agriculture in the nineteenth century, showed no apparent negative effects from land repartitioning.

> [G]rain yields per hectare on peasant allotment land in European Russia after the Emancipation rose almost as fast as those on private land. From 1860 to 1911 there are no reliable data that the village communal system or communal land tenure slowed down Russian rural development.[38]

The fact that the communal system was reproduced by Russian peasants who migrated to Siberia shows that this system was deeply rooted in Russian culture and that governmental impositions played a secondary role in establishing the commune in that area. Differences in the evolution of the communal systems in European Russia and Siberia mostly lie in the different functions of the commune in land regulations. Kaufman considered the Siberian type of peasant commune as the most "natural" and "clear" form of Russian peasant economic organization, which was not contaminated by governmental intrusions.[39]

However, the vast territories, rich natural resources, and high-quality arable land in Siberia undermined the main task of the Russian commune, which in the European part of the country was to maintain economic efficiency in an environment of high risk. Peasant households in the Altai region, in the southern part of Siberia, proved to be highly productive in agriculture, while peasants in northern areas often undertook fur hunting and profitable handicrafts. All of this undermined the perception of economic activity as a high-risk game of chance. Free land and rich natural resources left a place for entrepreneurial initiative. At the same time, the regulating functions of the commune, especially obligatory crop rotation, which were so common in European Russia, were absent in Siberia almost to the end of the nineteenth century. The tsarist government did not try to restrict free land usage until it was able to control peasants via police. Describing the Altai peasants, Chudnovskiy said, "Personality here dominates the *mir* . . . [P]rivate interest dominates the communal one."[40]

The relatively unimportant status of the commune in land regulation in Siberia is found in the fact that in Siberian communes land repartition did not occur until the beginning of organized settlement in the late nineteenth century. The gradual inflow of migrants from the European part of Russia, and subsequent land shortages, strengthened the government's control and laid down the foundation for the repartition practice.[41] Land repartition became more common, but it never became as common as in European Russia. Full repartitions were very rare and took place only in the western regions of Tobolsk province. The greater the perceived land shortage, the more frequent were repartition practices. However, in Siberia repartitions were performed only with insufficient allotments and meadows. Land redistribution was a response to land shortages and governmental directives. The peasantry resisted frequent repartitions and tried to sabotage government imposition of new repartitions.

Siberian peasant morality did not enforce sanctions against improper wealth accumulation. The perception of economic success as a zero-sum game was not as common among the Siberian peasants as among their European Russian counterparts. The Russian peasant morality of anticipating one's part in the common good clashed with Siberian peasant initiative and resulted in cultural conflicts. Siberian peasants despised peasants from the European part of Russia and called them *rasseiskimi* (the Russians). Siberian dwellers, the *sibiriaki,* considered themselves to be Russians, but were nevertheless distinct from and superior to European Russians.

Many foreign observers have noted differences between the peasants of European Russia and Siberia. Digby Basset described the European Russian peasant as "naive, patient, ready to receive the promised something for nothing . . . a small farmer without ambition . . . with cheap vodka."[42] Algernon Noble observed that the *sibiriak* inhabitants were more skillful and self-confident workers. He described his meeting with a Siberian colonist's family, who were in desperate straits on the eve of the coming winter—no foodstuffs, no firearms, no warm clothes, and no activity to solve these problems. Noble remarked that this was typical for people from Russia; in contrast, the sibiriaki could take care of themselves.[43]

In Siberia, the rich peasants who achieved their success within the communal framework and in small business were admired and respected. They formed a peasant "establishment," which was responsible for the decision-making process inside the commune. The British reporter Morris Price considered these independent rich peasants potential leaders of local self-government.[44]

The bonds of mutual responsibility for the commune's fiscal burden imposed by the state contradicted the peasant cult of labor. According to Rabcevich, "The role of the commune in a fiscal sense was alien to the interests of the peasantry."[45] In brief, the state's fiscal impositions restricted the formation of proper relations between poor and rich households of the commune, and governmental support of poor households led to increasing social tension within the commune. In summary, then, the original peasant commune system that was derived from European Russia, *but in the absence of government controls,* did not prevent the development of capitalist economic relations in Siberia.

The history of the Siberian butter industry provides a vivid example of flexible peasant cooperation, both with and without the help of the commune. It also illustrates how trust relations "worked" under existing conditions and to what extent communal anti-individualistic bonds limited capitalist peasant entrepreneurial activity *in practice.*

The Siberian Butter Industry

In 1894, the first dairy-product export enterprise was created by the Russian merchant Valkov. In 1896, the first peasant cooperative dairy was established in the village of Morevo. From 1888 to 1900, thirty peasant cooperative dairies operated in Siberia. Before 1900 all of these enterprises received no support from the tsarist government and relied mainly on their own resources. The lack of operating capital was a common weak point of Russian enterprises. Therefore, in the initial stage of butter-industry development, foreign investment played an important role in supplying the required capital. Foreign merchants also provided a link between the remote Siberian butter producers and foreign consumers.

Danish merchants were the first who founded highly profitable dairies in western Siberia. Denmark specialized in butter production, and increasing the output of the Siberian industry attracted the attention of Danish entrepreneurs. Despite poor transportation, good natural conditions made this business highly profitable. These conditions included a 6-percent to 7-percent fat content in the milk of the local dairy herd, compared to a 4.5-percent average in the Danish dairy herd.[46]

The newly opened dairies needed a steady supply of milk from local peasants. This initial stage of the dairy processing operations was the most difficult and dangerous. Attempts to reach agreements sometimes resulted in peasant rebellions, as peasants tried to preserve their way of life and resisted the unknown. Some communes reached agreements, but, because of the distrust of foreigners, many of them refused to supply milk to the new processing facilities.

The eventual agreements reached between foreign entrepreneurs and peasant communes reflected the customs of peasant economic practice. Through collective efforts, risk was avoided and the peasantry reconciled self-interest and solidarity, which corresponded to peasant virtues and morality. From this point of view, the commune acted as a cohesive whole, as an entrepreneur who deliberately took a risk for a potential gain in the future. The high level of trust relations within the peasant collectivity pre-conditioned the existence of dense "norms of reciprocity." According to the "folk theorem," which characterizes the mechanism of trust relations, the players were "engaged in an indefinite set of repeated games" that will punish the defector in successive rounds. The clear rules regulating differ-ent "repeated games" implied that the mechanism of punishing violators would be fast, effective, and low cost.

The norms of peasant reciprocity and the means to enforce them within the communal framework secured a high level of trust relations within the commune. Thus, the commune provided a large amount of social capital[47] in a very efficient way without governmental and judicial support. The commune prevented defections of different kinds—the defector could be punished, not only in the current round of exchanges, but also in succes-sive rounds. The folklore image of the positive peasant hero is that of an honest person, who trusts and is trusted by others. Foreign managers ob-served this feature. For example, International Harvester accepted peasant credit receipts, which did not possess any formal legal force, as the main contractual document between the company and peasants. Losses in these kinds of exchanges were very low, only 2 percent.[48]

The high level of trust relations among the Russian peasantry found its expression in the *mir* (agricultural) and the *artel* (industrial) systems of co-operation. The latter played an important role in the development of the Siberian butter industry. Communes that made agreements benefited from the cooperation, and the limits of trust were widened. Some of these com-munes even planned to participate in business. Social capital accumulates in the repetitive actions of trust relations. Thus, the amount of milk sup-pliers provided increased immensely and some peasants began to plan their own businesses. The artel model for cooperation in the industrial field was quickly adapted to the needs of the butter industry. In 1896, the first peas-ant cooperative dairy was established in Siberia and in 1899 there were 30 peasant cooperative dairies. The artel model proved to be extremely suc-cessful in terms of bringing large numbers of isolated peasant communes into new market relations.

In the next stage of industrial development, Russian entrepreneurs at-tempted to take on all aspects of establishing and running businesses. The main emphasis was on the artel, first to coordinate the efforts of existing enterprises and second to promote the creation of new enterprises. The greater level of individualization resulted in the splitting up of communes.

Some more successful peasants tried to run their own business separately. The system became more complicated. Short- and long-term credit was needed, not only for ensuring the future supply of milk but also for building butter inventories. Credit was needed for acquisition of cream separators and agricultural machinery.

Russian merchants coordinated the work of the artels and peasant entrepreneurs through the "Organization for Assistance to Butter Cooperatives." This association promoted the creation of 270 artels, encompassing fifty-two household groups of 500 persons each.[49] The organization also served as a link between foreign companies that were responsible for sales abroad, and the peasant entrepreneur artels, which remained the basic unit of the industry. The association also undertook an attempt to link Siberian butter producers directly to foreign customers through the mediation of the cooperative union. Unfortunately, World War I did not allow this task to be completed.

Nonetheless, impressive results were achieved. Prior to the beginning of World War I, Siberia supplied 16 percent of global butter production, and 61.3 percent of Russian butter production.[50] The development of the butter industry cooperatives led to a higher density of dairy herds per capita in Siberia than in the United States, Germany, or Denmark.[51] The main social and economic consequence of this development was the rapid individualization of peasant households and the undermining of the communal system. Thus, the system of peasant communes and existing cultural patterns in rural villages did not prevent the economic processes that eventually contributed to the commune's destruction as a social institution. In short, *certain features of the Siberian model of the Russian peasant communal system were very effective in the creation of new capitalist strategies of action.*

Conclusion

The realities of the democratic and market transition in Russia—legal confusion, a power vacuum, and corruption—have increased criticisms of capitalism. This has caused some scholars to search the Russian past for the cultural origins of anticapitalist sentiment. Before the Soviet period, Russian culture contained the elements for rejecting individualistic orientations. Some observers have argued that the communal system of the Russian peasantry is the source of these anticapitalist cultural patterns and norms. Moreover, anticapitalist sentiments, it might be argued, were enhanced during the Soviet era.

The example of the Siberian butter industry's development in the late nineteenth and early twentieth centuries, however, shows that *the nature of communal patterns was neutral and not anticapitalist.* The transformation of the Siberian communes and their positive involvement in market relations is a good example of how communal principles can change in a capitalist direction. The Siberian peasant commune, which differed in some ways from its counterparts in European Russia, proved to be highly flexible and adaptive to the market. It promoted a high level of interpersonal trust and flexible forms of cooperation. Communal cultural patterns were not purely anticapitalist in character. In some ways, communal regulations were strict and rigid but they did not block change. They left space for entrepreneurial initiative and innovations, secured trust relations, and helped to develop effective forms of economic cooperation. Thus, the Siberian variant of the Russian peasant communal system promoted capitalist development.

Notes

1. Miller Wright, *Who Are the Russians? A History of the Russian People* (London: Faber and Faber, 1973), 56.

2. Thomas C. Owen, *Russian Corporate Development from Peter the Great to Perestroika* (Oxford: Oxford University Press, 1995), 96.

3. Ann Swidler, "Culture in Action: Symbols and Strategies," *American Sociological Review* 51 (April 1986): 275.

4. Ibid., 273.

5. Ibid., 277.

6. Wright, *Who Are the Russians*, 62.

7. Christine Worobec, *Peasant Russia: Family and Community in the Post-Emancipational Period* (Princeton, NJ: Princeton University Press, 1991), 52.

8. Owen, *Russian Corporate Development*, 98.

9. Wright, *Who Are the Russians*, 67; T. Prudnikova, "The Influence of Equalization Ideas on the Communal Rules in Western Siberia after the Emancipation," in *Krest'ianskaia obshchina v Sibiri: XVII–nachala XX v.*, eds. L. Gorushkin and M. Gromyko (Novosibirsk: Nauka, 1977), 200.

10. Dorothy Atkinson, "Egalitarianism and the Commune," in *Land Commune and Peasant Community in Russia: Communal Forms in Imperial and Early Soviet Russia*, ed. Roger Bartlett (London: Macmillan, 1990), 8, 11.

11. Ibid., 14.

12. E. Keenan, "Moscovite Political Folkways," *Russian Review* 45 (1986): 123.

13. Worobec, *Peasant Russia*, 7.

14. Boris Mironov, "The Russian Peasant Commune after the Reforms of the 1860s," in *The World of the Russian Peasant: Post-Emancipation Culture and Society*, eds. Ben Eklof and Stephen P. Frank (Boston: Unwin Hyman, 1990), 13.

15. Owen, *Russian Corporate Development*, 98.

16. Fedor Kamanin, "*Rasshvyrka*": *pishi ty bol'she pro nashi ivanovichi* (Moscow: Sovetskiy Pisatel', 1984), 135–74.

17. Mironov, "The Russian Peasant Commune after the Reforms," 14, 19.

18. Ibid., 19.

19. Ibid.

20. Ibid., 20.

21. Worobec, *Peasant Russia*, 7.

22. Wright, *Who are the Russians*, 79.

23. Mironov, "The Russian Peasant Commune after the Reforms," 23, 31.

24. Atkinson, "Egalitarianism and the Commune," 124.

25. Worobec, *Peasant Russia*, 20.

26. Ibid.

27. Mironov, "The Russian Peasant Commune after the Reforms," 23.

28. V. P. Danilov, "The Commune before Collectivisation," in *Land Commune and Peasant Community in Russia: Communal Forms in Imperial and Early Soviet Russia*, ed. Roger Bartlett (London: Macmillan, 1990), 301.

29. Owen, *Russian Corporate Development*, 45, 151–52.

30. Ibid., 114.

31. Ibid., 115–50.

32. Swidler, "Culture in Action," 275.

33. Erwin Lessner, *Cradle of Conquerors: Siberia—The Complete Story of the Giant Land Mysterious in the Past, Menacing Today* (Garden City, NY: Doubleday, 1955); Emil Lengyel, *Siberia* (New York: Random House, 1943), 29.

34. V. Rabcevich, "The Peasant Commune in the System of Local Governing in Western Siberia," in *Krest'ianskaia obshchina v Sibiri: XVII–nachala XX v.*, eds. L. Gorushkin and M. Gromyko (Novosibirsk: Nauka, 1977).

35. Prudnikova, "Influence of Equalization Ideas," 201.

36. Lindon Bates, *The Russian Road to China* (London: Constable, 1910), 30; Emil Dillon, *Russia on the Pacific and the Siberian Railway* (London: Sampson Low, Marston & Co., 1899), 339; Henry Cooke, *Trade with Siberia: Condition and Prospects of the British Trade in Siberia* (London: Board of Trade, Commercial Intelligence Commission, 1905).

37. Prudnikova, "Influence of Equalization Ideas," 200, 232.

38. R. Bideleux, "Agricultural Advance Under the Russian Village Commune System," in *Land Commune and Peasant Community in Russia: Communal Forms in Imperial and Early Soviet Russia*, ed. Roger Bartlett (London: Macmillan, 1990), 201, 208.

39. A. A. Kaufman, "Zastyvshania istoria obshchiny: ocherk razvitia zemel'nyh poriadkov sibirskoi obshchiny," *Vestnik Evropy* no. 6 (1893).

40. S. Chudnovskiy, "The Altai Land Commune," *Severny vestnik* no. 11 (1888): 184.

41. M. Gromyko, *Trudovye tradicii russkogo krest'ianstva* (Novosibirsk: Nauka, 1975).

42. Digby Basset, *Tigers, Gold, and Witchdoctors* (London: Lane Boadley Head, 1928), 272.

43. Algernon Noble, *Siberian Days* (London: H. F. & G. Witherby, 1928), 167–71.

44. M. P. Price, *Siberia* (London: Mathuen & Co., and New York: George H. Doran Company, 1912), 8.

45. Rabcevich, "The Peasant Commune," 138.

46. Leonid Gorushkin, *Sibirskoe krest'ianstvo na rubese dvuh vekov* (Novosibirsk: Nauka, 1967), 164.

47. Robert Putnam, *Making Democracy Work* (Princeton, NJ: Princeton University Press, 1993), 165–71.

48. Fred V. Carstensen, *American Enterprise in Foreign Markets: Studies of Singer and International Harvester in Imperial Russia* (Chapel Hill: University of North Carolina Press, 1984), 156.

49. Gorushkin, *Sibirskoe krest'ianstvo*, 160.

50. Ibid., 156.

51. Ibid.

2

The Impact of Land Reform
on the Rural Population

ZVI LERMAN

Land reform in developing countries is usually implemented from considerations of equity and equality. The overall goal is to reduce poverty among
the rural population by redistributing the land concentrated in large land-
owner estates to landless peasants or peasants with very small subsistence
plots. In Brazil, for instance, 2 percent of large landowners control 98 percent of agricultural land, and the declared objective of the Brazilian land reform program is to achieve more equitable distribution of the nation's farmland. The program has not advanced much during the last two decades, but
the intentions of moving toward greater equity among the rural population
remain alive. Outside the developing world, this was basically the model observed in East Central Europe after World War I and then again immediately after World War II (between 1945 and 1950). This was also the model
implemented in Russia during the liberation of the serfs in the 1860s, then
during Stolypin's reforms between 1905 and 1914, and again immediately
after the 1917 Revolution. See chapter 7 by Macey in this book.

The fourth Russian land reform, which formally started in 1991, was essentially different. Although the rural population in the Soviet Union at
times suffered from severe mobility restrictions and the standard of living
in the village lagged behind that in towns and cities, the peasants hardly
suffered from the kind of class inequality and poverty that had characterized the pre-1917 era. Although the rural population largely lived and
worked in farm structures that had certain features in common with large

estates, the peasants could hardly be regarded as oppressed and exploited by their landlords. On the contrary, one of the main functions of the large collective and state farms in the Soviet Union was to take care of the social infrastructure and social services in the village for the benefit of all worker-members. Today, economists claim that this commitment to social obligations was one of the factors responsible for the inherent inefficiency of large Soviet farms from a pure business perspective.

The fourth Russian land reform had little to do with restoring equity and equality. Basically, it did not even focus on the individual peasant. This was a systemic sectoral reform, whose main goal was to transform the agricultural sector into a system compatible with market-oriented economic principles that were part of the overall transition to the market. These principles dictated a transition from collective agriculture to an agricultural sector based on private property and market incentives. Issues of justice, equity, and individual well-being were tackled as part of the implementation details, when decisions had to be made about the actual privatization strategy (restitution to former owners or distribution to workers) and the treatment of various beneficiaries (equal distribution to everybody or adoption of differentiating criteria). Yet, this reform has had a profound impact on the peasants in Russia and all other former Soviet republics. These changes can be grouped into the following dimensions:

- changing the role of large farm enterprises in the village,
- increasing the individualization of agriculture,
- implementing the transition from workers to shareholders, and
- increasing the range of options for individual choice.

In the following sections, I examine some of the available evidence on these dimensions of rural change and trace the adaptation of the rural population in Russia to the new conditions. The empirical data derive mainly from two large surveys of managers and employees in farm enterprises and independent private farmers conducted by the World Bank in 1992 and again in 1994 in five Russian provinces. The survey results were published in full by the World Bank.[1] Methodological details of the two surveys are presented in the appendix to this chapter. Official national statistics are also used to the extent that they are available.

The Changing Role of Large Farm Enterprises

The Soviet collective farm played a complex, multifaceted role in relation to village residents. First, it was their lifetime employer, the business that provided rural households with base income in the form of salaries that were essentially guaranteed for life. Second, it was the local government, a small-scale welfare state that, in the eyes of individuals, was completely responsible for all social services and benefits, even those that were legally the responsibility of central government (such as education and medical care). All these services were generally provided free, in line with the overall philosophy of the Soviet state. Third, it acted as a benefactor or a benevolent master by extending its support to households beyond the legally defined sphere of social services into areas that included assistance with cultivation of the household plot, as well as assistance with provision of farm inputs and sale of farm products. This assistance was part of a deep symbiosis between large-scale collective production that dominated Soviet agriculture and small-scale individual plot production that never ceased in the Soviet Union. The cost of all these business and nonbusiness activities was never a problem in an administrative command economy: As long as the farm enterprises met their production targets, their costs were automatically covered one way or another by the state.

This environment is now a thing of the past. In 1991–92, the large collective and state farms were "privatized," i.e., the land cultivated by these farms was transferred from state ownership to private ownership. However, this was not individual private ownership of the kind observed in market economies, but a joint or collective ownership of all workers and pensioners in the privatized farm enterprise. Although unusual by market-economy standards, this was regarded as the first step toward the ultimate transfer of ownership to individuals. In the process of privatization, the farm enterprises were required (or at least expected) to assume a clear business orientation and to restructure their operations so as to achieve profitability without government support through subsidies or debt write-offs.

Transition to market-based operations naturally implied elimination of central planning and production targets. This has been fully accomplished, by and large, and the farm enterprises are now free to produce what they wish and sell to whomever they wish, in direct response to market signals. In World Bank surveys, 60 percent of large farm managers indicated an increase in the degree of economic independence of their farm enterprises. Yet a market-based operation also implied freedom to shed redundant labor in the interest of increasing efficiency and the separation between business and municipal-government activities, terminating the financial responsibility for social services. These two components of the transition are far from having been satisfactorily implemented.

Table 2.1

Strategies Adopted by Managers of Large Farm Enterprises in Response to Inadequate Funds to Meet Payroll, 1992 and 1994 (percent)

Strategy	1992	1994
Borrow money	69.8	50.4
Delay wage payments	57.0	90.6
Delay other payments	64.7	—
Dismiss some workers	13.2	16.2
Keep workers, reduce wages	7.8	12.4
Shift workers to outside jobs	8.9	11.5

Surveys of farm managers in Russia indicate that they are generally committed to continuing the tradition of full employment: Their sense of duty and comradeship does not allow them to fire redundant workers. Managers prefer to borrow money to meet the payroll rather than reduce their labor force and become more productive (Table 2.1). The burden of social services also largely remains with the farm enterprises (Table 2.2), and overall only 40 percent of respondents in a 1994 World Bank survey reported that some social assets had been transferred to the village council. In many cases, it was impossible to transfer the responsibility for social services, as prescribed by law, because the newly independent local government lacked a sufficient budget and was thus unable to assume the responsibility (this answer was provided by 60 percent of survey respondents). Managers participating in the survey indicated that the cost of maintaining the social services remained at about 12 percent of total farm expenditures, as in previous years.

Table 2.2

Transfer of Social Assets to the Local Council by Large Farm Enterprises, 1992 and 1994 (percent)

Asset Type	1992	1994
Clubs	18.8	28.6
Daycare centers	18.4	29.5
Schools	17.4	26.9
Clinics	—	19.2
Shops	—	7.7
Housing	8.5	5.1
Telephones	6.2	9.4
Electric/power	6.2	7.7
Roads	4.6	5.1
Sewage/water	4.3	3.4

Freed from central planning and stripped of traditional financial support, farm enterprises remain burdened by paternalistic responsibilities, including lifetime employment and social services in the village. This in itself is sufficient to cause serious damage to profitability in the new environment, but the situation is exacerbated by the reluctance of the farm managers to undertake radical internal restructuring with the purpose of increasing efficiency and productivity. The former collective and state farms, with thousands of hectares and hundreds of workers, are much too big, given the evidence of prevailing farm sizes in market economies. The benefit of economies of scale was the main justification for the emphasis on large-scale farming in the Soviet Union, and yet empirical evidence on the whole fails to support the very existence of such economies in primary agriculture. It is well established that large farms may be much more expensive to run because agency and monitoring costs rapidly increase with size.[2] Moreover, collective or cooperative farms, whether large or small, are a rare exception in market economies. Many empirical studies provide evidence of intrinsic inefficiencies of this organizational form in agriculture and other sectors.[3] Thus, to increase their efficiency and productivity, Russian farms have to restructure from large collectives into smaller operating units based on individual incentives and individual accountability.

There has indeed been some downsizing of the large farms in recent years. The number of farm enterprises in Russia increased by about 5 percent after 1990 as some large enterprises divided into smaller entities along functional lines. Survey results indicate that average farm size in the sample declined by about 15 percent between 1990 and 1994 due to separation of smaller units and allocation of land to the individual sector (household plots and independent private farms). Farm enterprises remain very large, however, with many of them controlling between 4,000 and 8,000 hectares of land. The average number of workers naturally declined with the reduction in land resources. But, in line with the lifetime employment attitude, the reduction in the labor force was substantially less than the reduction in land: In the survey, there was a 10-percent reduction in labor compared with a 15-percent reduction in land. Farms have made some adjustments in their production profile, increasing crop production and reducing the relative importance of livestock in direct response to market price and profitability signals. Other than that, most farm enterprises continue to be managed much the same way as in the past, albeit with less administrative intervention from the state and also less financial security than in the past.

Thus, elimination of the administrative command system and central planning has not been accompanied by other farm-level changes that are essential for healthy operation in a market environment. As a result, the proportion of Russian farms reporting losses increased from 3 percent in 1990 to 60 percent in 1994–95 and then to about 80 percent in 1997–98. Farms do not have enough cash to pay salaries, and salary arrears of several months have become quite common. In World Bank surveys, 80 percent of managers reported salary delays in 1994, compared to 50 percent in 1992. Shortage of cash is forcing managers to increase even further the traditional reliance on payments in kind in lieu of wages. Finally, the financially weak farm enterprises are no longer in a position to allocate sufficient funds for social services to their workers. The percentage of farms providing the traditional range of social services and benefits dropped from about 80 percent in the 1992 survey to 60 percent in the 1994 survey (Figure 2.1). Employees report a substantial decline in access to social services in farm enterprises (Table 2.3). The reported decline covers services and benefits that the farm enterprise can no longer afford to provide, such as trans-

Figure 2.1
Provision of Social Services and Benefits, 1992 and 1994

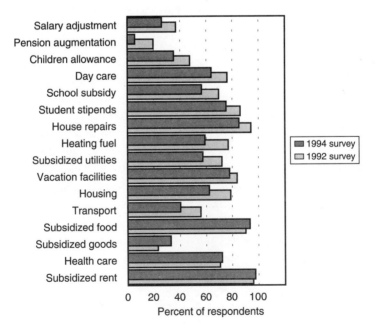

Table 2.3

Availability of Social Services and Benefits as Reported by Farm Employees, 1992 and 1994 (percent)

	1992	1994
Compensation for price increases	24.4	13.4
Pension augmentation	8.3	2.4
Child allowances	38.1	13.6
Student stipends	7.2	4.1
House maintenance and repairs	40.8	26.4
Subsidized food	63.9	62.5
Subsidized consumer goods	14.7	5.5
Medical care	82.9	51.3
Use of vacation facilities	32.3	20.5
Subsidized rent	20.8	14.4
Transport	84.6	72.0

port, house maintenance, and subsidized rent and repairs, as well as state-funded services and benefits, such as medical care and child allowances, for which the government can no longer pay. The rural population continues to have access to these services, but on a substantially reduced scale and probably at a much lower level of quality. As with many functions and operations formerly provided by or through the state, things seem to go on by inertia, while rapidly shrinking, possibly toward total oblivion in the near future.

Managers of large farm enterprises naturally feel frustrated by this course of events. In World Bank surveys, managers in 1994 were clearly more pessimistic about the expected outcomes of the ongoing process of transition and restructuring (characterized as "reorganization") than they were in 1992 (Figure 2.2). Although the central government bears some responsibility for the deteriorating situation of the farms, it is mainly the managers themselves who must face the blame because of their failure to adjust to the new reality. Managers of large farm enterprises continue to entertain the notion that in the end the government will come to their rescue, as it has always done in the past. This conception is a very strong disincentive for trying radical and possibly painful solutions on the operating level that are essential for improving the economic situation of the farm sector. See chapters 11 and 15 by Amelina and Kalugina, respectively, in this book for research on the different strategies employed by managers and regional officials to deal with pressures to restructure.

Figure 2.2
Farm Managers' Expectations of Change in Farm Situation Due to
Reorganization, 1992 and 1994

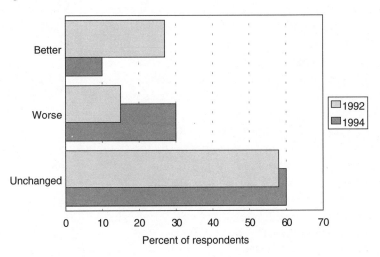

The Individualization of Agriculture

The worsening financial situation of both the farms and the state directly affects the rural population through salary and pension delays, as well as deterioration of the traditionally robust social infrastructure. The picture that is deduced by examining the performance of the former collectives is a grim one indeed. But is everything truly so dire? Is the rural population on the verge of slipping from socialist plenty into capitalist poverty? A closer examination through the eyes of individuals presents a less bleak picture.

Throughout the Soviet era, rural residents were effectively "part-time" workers in the large farm enterprises, while the remainder of their working day was spent on the household plot. The output from the household plot always contributed a significant share of the family income in rural Russia, both in the form of food products for family consumption and as a source of supplementary cash income from sales of surplus output. Household surveys routinely conducted in the past by Russian statistical organs indicate that in 1990 the average husband-and-wife couple in the village spent two and a half hours daily (and double that on weekends) working on the household plot. The products from the household plot contributed 20 to 25 percent of the total budget of rural families all throughout the 1980s and the early 1990s (this includes both the value of consumption and cash income from product sales).

One of the first achievements of land reform in Russia (and indeed throughout the former Soviet Union) was a substantial increase in the size of household plots. The total land in household plots doubled from about 3 million hectares in the 1970s and 1980s to 6 million hectares after 1992. The share of household plots in agricultural land accordingly went up from 1.5 to 3 percent. Households received additional land from the state re-distribution fund, which was created by extracting about 15 percent of the land managed by large farm enterprises with the declared purpose of pro-viding a reserve of land for new individual users.

Not all the additional land allocated to the household sector went to augment existing household plots. Part of this land was used to create new household plots for young landless families, and as a result the average household plot in Russia did not double in size. World Bank surveys indi-cate that the average household plot in five provinces increased by nearly 50 percent from 0.24 hectares in 1990 to 0.35 hectares in 1994. Despite this augmentation, household plots in Russia are still below the magic fig-ure of half a hectare. Nevertheless, the enlarged household plots have be-come a more important contributor to family income. Unfortunately, the recent household surveys conducted by Russian statistical organs no longer include information about the share of the household plot in total family income. We are thus forced to rely for comparison on World Bank farm-level surveys, which show that half of the families derive *more* than 25 per-cent of their income from the household plot. The average contribution of the household plot today thus approaches about 50 percent of family in-come (compared with 20 to 25 percent in the 1980s).

Another dramatic change in the rural scene since 1990 is the emergence of a new breed of individual agricultural producers, the so-called private farmers. Private, or peasant, farm is the accepted translation of the Russian term *krest'ianskoe (fermerskoe) khoziaistvo*, which is basically an indepen-dent family farm established outside the collectivist framework. While household plots are small subsistence-oriented farms cultivated on a part-time basis by individuals whose primary occupation is work on large farm enterprises, peasant farms are full-time operations run by individuals who are not affiliated with the large farm enterprises. Some peasant farmers in Russia are former workers in large farm enterprises who have left the col-lective with the objective of establishing an independent farm; others are newcomers to agriculture, who have applied and received land for in-dependent private farming. Peasant farms in Russia are much larger than household plots: They average 40 hectares, compared with less than 0.5 hectares for household plots. On the whole, they are commercial operations whose output is intended mainly for the market, while the small household plots sell only the surplus that remains after the family's needs for food are satisfied.

The individual farming sector in Russia consisted exclusively of household plots until the early 1990s. Today, it includes two distinct components: the enlarged household plots and the emergent peasant farms. There are about 270,000 peasant farms in Russia today. The total agricultural land of these farms exceeds the land of the 15 million household plots: Peasant farms cultivate 14 million hectares, or 6 percent of agricultural land in Russia (compared with 7 million hectares, or 3 percent of agricultural land in household plots).

As a result of land reform processes, the individual sector today controls 10 percent of agricultural land in Russia, up from 1.5 percent prior to 1990. Yet the contribution of the individual sector to agricultural production has always exceeded by a large margin its share in agricultural land. In the pre-reform period, household plots produced 25 percent of agricultural output on 1.5 percent of agricultural land, while collective and state farms with 98.5 percent of land produced only 75 percent of agricultural output. Today, the individual sector (including household plots and peasant farms) accounts for over 50 percent of agricultural output on 10 percent of the agricultural land. Perhaps paradoxically, most of this contribution continues to come from household plots: Peasant farms, controlling one and a half times more land than household plots, produce only 2 percent of agricultural output. See chapter 5 by Patsiorkovski and chapter 14 by O'Brien in this volume.

The apparently phenomenal productivity of land in household plots stemmed in the past from their specialization in livestock. Livestock could be raised with very little land, especially if grain and other animal feed were forthcoming from the land-rich collective farm. Thus, until the early 1990s livestock accounted for two-thirds of the product mix in household plots, compared to one-half nationally. After 1990, as prices began to be liberalized and livestock production turned highly unprofitable, the individual sector adjusted its product mix in response to market signals. The share of livestock in the output of household plots today is less than 40 percent, and for peasant farms it is even lower (about one-third).

Yet, despite a clear shift in emphasis to crop production, which is clearly dependent on land availability, the individual sector in Russia continues to achieve substantially higher land productivity than the collective sector.

This is one of the manifestations of the individualization of Russian agriculture. Theory and experience in market economies suggests that individual, family-based production is indeed basically more efficient than production in collectives, cooperatives, or corporations. Proving economies of scale is elusive in primary agriculture. Perhaps land reform, by strengthening the land endowment of the individual sector in Russia, began to unleash its potential.

As in the past, the superior performance of the individual sector is greatly assisted by transfers from the farm enterprise. World Bank surveys show that virtually all households (over 90 percent) have access to grain from the large enterprise, which they either receive in lieu of wages or purchase at reduced prices. For one-third of respondents, this is supplemented by access to hay and concentrated feed. In addition to animal feed, the large enterprise is an important source of many other farm inputs and services for the household plots of its employees, as well as for other village residents, such as teachers, doctors, and postal workers (see Tables 2.4 and 2.5). Virtually all farm managers (98 percent) reported that they provide a wide range of services to their employees in working their household plots. In addition to leasing farm machinery to small-holders without mechanical equipment of their own, farm enterprises also sell used farm equipment to their employees and other individual operators who may have difficulties accessing the regular commercial channels. Two-thirds of the farm

Table 2.4

Farm Inputs Supplied by Farm Enterprises to Rural Residents, 1994 (percent of 234 farm enterprises)

Input/Service	To Household Plot Farmers	To Private Farmers
Seeds, seedlings	45	48
Feed	82	14
Young animals	82	27
Organic fertilizer	38	7
Mineral fertilizer	6	3
Herbicides/pesticides	29	4
Machinery/equipment	42	36
Repairs/maintenance	31	26
Spare parts	18	18
Fuel	30	9
Veterinary medicines	62	27
Construction materials	82	15
Construction services	54	6

Table 2.5

*Services Supplied by Farm Enterprises to Rural Residents, 1994
(percent of 234 farm enterprises)*

Services	Employees	Other Villagers	Private Farmers
Farm machinery for contract work	99	86	49
Transport	99	86	42
Pasture and hay	90	72	27
Consulting	77	66	51
Credit	18	3	0
Veterinary services	93	80	53
Product marketing	67	45	12
Fuel for farm use	34	16	12
Heating fuel	47	27	7

managers indicate that their employees have priority in access to farm services and are charged preferential rates.

The availability of these farm inputs and services reinforces the intrinsic benefits of individual initiative and allows the household plots to continue achieving their high levels of productivity of land despite the shift from livestock to crops. The peasant farms, on the other hand, are definitely not achieving the same levels of land productivity as household plots. Individual incentives to succeed are there in an equal and possibly even much stronger measure. The quality of their land is about average, as World Bank surveys have not produced any evidence of large-scale discriminatory practices in allocation of land to peasant farms. But something is missing that would raise the peasant farms to the same high level of productivity as household plots. Perhaps there are difficulties with inputs, which private farmers feel more acutely in the absence of the umbilical cord to the farm enterprise. Perhaps there are difficulties with marketing and transportation services that prevent the peasant farmers from maximizing product sales. Indeed, as seen in Tables 2.4 and 2.5, substantially fewer farm enterprises provide farm inputs and services to peasant farms, and these are typically purchased by peasant farms at market prices. A new World Bank survey conducted by Maria Amelina in two provinces may reveal some details of the productivity-enhancing benefits that household plots derive from farm enterprises, which are not accessible to independent peasant farmers. See chapter 11 by Amelina in this book.

Despite the continuing higher productivity of household plots, which supports the Western belief in the superiority of individual farming, much research remains to be done before we can convincingly conclude that household plots in Russia are indeed more productive and economically more efficient than large collective structures. The sheer magnitude of the apparent productivity gap—55 percent of output on 10 percent of land in the individual sector—is too great to be accounted for by qualitative arguments of the kind presented here. This is a very important topic, especially because the contribution of household plots continues to increase: According to official statistics, household plots are approaching the 50-percent mark of agricultural output in all former Soviet republics.

New Owners, New Choices

The most publicly dramatic feature of land reform in Russia (although not in all former Soviet republics) is the abolition of exclusive state ownership of land and recognition of private land ownership. The land in household plots and in peasant farms is intended to be privately owned. The individual farmer is expected to get an official title to land, the so-called *gosudarstvennyi akt*. The actual legal status of individually cultivated land remains unclear, however. Despite efforts made through presidential decrees and government resolutions, only part of the individual land has been transferred to private ownership. World Bank surveys reveal that in both household plots and private farms about half the land is privately owned. Much of the remaining land is state-owned and is still held in the traditional Soviet tenurial forms of lifetime inheritable possession or use rights (Table 2.6). It is interesting to note that peasant farmers actively resort to land leasing as a mechanism for increasing their farm size, while in practical terms household plot farmers do not lease land. Transfer of land to pri-

Table 2.6
Land Tenure Type of Private Farms (1994) and Household Plots (1994 and 1992)

	Private Farms	Household Plots	
	1994[a]	1994[a]	1992[b]
Private ownership	50	45	30
Lifetime possession	19	17	13
Usership	7	38	56
Lease	24	0	1

[a] Percent of total plot area.
[b] Percent of total number of parcels.

vate ownership of 15 million individuals is a dynamic process, and it obviously cannot be completed in a couple of years. Survey data for household plots indicate significant progress with privatization of land between 1992 and 1994 (see Table 2.6). Yet much remains to be done, and the process is obviously continuing.

What can the new owners do with their land? They can produce what they want and sell their surplus to whomever they want. The state does not interfere in the production decisions of the individual sector, and the main operational interaction is through taxes. Other than freedom to produce and sell, however, the notion of property rights in Russia (and throughout the rest of the former Soviet Union) is quite fuzzy and in practice differs from that in the West. The first point to bear in mind is that after seventy-five years of exclusive state ownership, the very concept of privately owned land does not sit well with everybody. World Bank surveys reveal that about half the respondents who are not private farmers themselves are opposed to private ownership of land by individuals and basically prefer the old tenurial form of lifetime inheritable possession (private farmers are predominantly in favor of private land ownership). The intense political and public debate surrounding the notion of private land ownership has so far prevented the adoption of a new land code consistent with the reform principles being implemented in practice, and since 1991 land policy in Russia has been governed through presidential decrees.

The main bone of contention is the right to sell and buy land, which is of course the foundation stone of property rights in market economies. The deep divide on this issue in the Russian political establishment is a reflection of grassroots attitudes. Table 2.7, which is based on the 1994 World Bank survey, indicates that while more than half of the private farmers support buying and selling of land, 80 percent of employees and managers in farm enterprises are outright opposed to this option. See chapter 4 by Wegren and Belen'kiy for more survey findings on attitudes toward buying and selling land.

Table 2.7
Attitudes Toward Buying and Selling of Land, 1994 (percent of respondents)

	Positive	Negative	Undecided
Private farmers	52.7	36.9	10.4
Employees	14.7	79.1	6.1
Managers	15.4	79.5	5.1

Buying and selling of household plots was enshrined in the 1993 constitution, and some land transactions are occurring among rural households and by households from the state. Land transactions in land by peasant farmers are an entirely different matter. The initial land reform program in 1991–92 included a moratorium on buying and selling of land in private farms. This could be justified by the desire to prevent speculation and windfall profits by individuals who received a free grant of land from the state on the basis of a simple application. Subsequent presidential decrees and government resolutions have lifted the moratorium and allowed buying and selling of land in peasant farms, as well as household plots. In the absence of more permanent legislation, however, the legal status of such transactions remains unclear and markets for land purchases have failed to develop. Peasant farmers do resort to leasing of land, as discussed above, but actual buying and selling of land is extremely rare.

According to data recently published by Wegren and Belen'kiy, there were nearly 1 million buy-and-sell transactions in Russia between 1993 and 1996 (Table 2.8). Nearly 50 percent of these transactions were between individuals and involved land for farming purposes (all other transactions involved state-owned lands). The average size of a transaction, however, was 0.14 hectare, which implies buying land for augmentation of the household plot, as such small parcels are of no interest to private farmers who cultivate an average of 40 hectares.

But the individual sector controls only 10 percent of agricultural land in Russia. Some of the remaining 90 percent of agricultural land has been retained in state ownership, but most of it has been privatized, or more precisely "destatized," to various successors of collective farms. According to

Table 2.8
Purchases of Land by Individuals in Russia, 1993–96

	Cumulative Number of Transactions	Average per Transaction (hectares)
From the state		
All transactions	357,894	0.31
Land for private farming	1,840	21.41
From individuals and private entities		
All transactions	560,493	0.16
Land for farming uses	439,015	0.14

Source: Stephen K. Wegren and Vladimir R. Belen'kyi, "The Political Economy of the Russian Land Market," *Problems of Post-Communism*, 45 (August 1998): 56–66.

official statistics, practically all former collective and state farms in Russia
have by now reregistered in new legal forms, including various joint stock
companies, limited liability partnerships, and agricultural producer cooperatives, among others. This formal transformation from a *kolkhoz* or a *sovkhoz*
is a prerequisite for transfer of land from state ownership to the ownership
of the collective, i.e., the body of individuals constituting membership of
the new organization. World Bank surveys indicate that 90 percent of the
land controlled by large farm enterprises has been privatized and only 10
percent remains under state ownership. This first stage of the land reform
process is typically followed by the second stage, in which collective ownership is divided into individual land shares. These are not physical plots of
land but rather "paper shares," or certificates of entitlement to a certain
number of hectares in the collective farm, without specifying the exact location or boundaries of the individual entitlement. The collective property
(farm buildings, machines, and equipment) is also divided into paper shares.
In the 1994 World Bank survey, the average size of a land share was 12.5
hectares per person and the average property share was US$1,500.

Despite the fairly abstract nature of the process, the distribution of share
certificates converts the members of the collective into individual owners
or shareholders. This process is virtually completed in Russia. According to
the 1994 World Bank survey, 90 percent of farms have gone through the
process of allocating individual share certificates to their members, and 80
percent of all land resources has been distributed in the form of shares.

The prevailing legislation allows the shareowners various options for future disposition of their shares. The most extreme option is to leave the
collective with a plot of land corresponding to the share entitlement. This
option is allowed if the withdrawing individuals or families intend to establish independent peasant farms, and it is in a striking contrast to the
Soviet practice that kept the individuals in the collective and grudgingly
allowed exit without any compensation or share of jointly accumulated
assets. Surprisingly or not, the right of exit is actually exercised by the new
Russian shareowners. Some information on the number of exits from farm
enterprises according to the 1994 survey is presented in Table 2.9. Figure
2.3 shows a clear increase in the frequency of exits from large enterprises
between the 1992 and 1994 surveys. The proportion of farm enterprises
in which no employees had left during reorganization dropped from 45
percent in 1992 to 30 percent in 1994. The proportion of farm enterprises
in which more than 10 employees had left increased from 20 percent to 35
percent. In 1992 the maximum number of employees leaving a farm enterprise was 134 and there was only one farm with more than 100 exits.

Table 2.9
Exit of Employees During Reorganization of Farm Enterprises, 1994

Organization Created by Exiting Members	Managers Reporting Exits ($n = 234$)	Number of Exiting Employees	Number of Entities Established
Private farm	68.4%	3,437	1,603
Partnership or small enterprise	2.6%	1,344	8
Cooperative	0.5%	10	1
Other	0.9%	44	5

The maximum number of exiting employees in early 1994 rose to 850 in one instance and there were nine farms with more than 100 exits (4 percent of the sample). Yet half the managers believe that this increase in the frequency of exits is a passing phenomenon, and the prospects for the development of private farming in their regions will diminish in the next two to three years.

Most shareowners, however, have no intention of taking the extreme course and establishing an independent private farm outside the collective. Only 8 percent of farm-enterprise employees participating in the World Bank survey were considering the possibility of starting a private farm. The main deterrents to becoming a private farmer included insufficient capital (74 percent of respondents), difficulties with purchase of machinery and equipment (60 percent), and risk aversion (56 percent). Other factors reported by around 40 percent of respondents were reluctance to change their lifestyle and the lack of legal guarantees.

Those who do not become independent private farmers may regroup within the former collective with other members, neighbors, and friends, pooling their shares in autonomous functional subdivisions. The law provides for this possibility, enabling such a group of shareowners to take control of the corresponding amount of land and productive assets and to start operating autonomously, either as a separate legal entity or within the framework of the former collective enterprise. Although these entities are not individually run operations, they are in principle superior to the former large collectives because of their smaller size, immediate involvement of the owners, and clearer personal accountability in a relatively small team. The entities listed in Table 2.9 after private farms are examples of smaller legal bodies that separated from former large collectives. There is, unfortunately, very little information at this stage on internal regrouping that leads to creation of autonomous entities within the collective.

Figure 2.3
Exit of Employees During Reorganization, 1992 and 1994

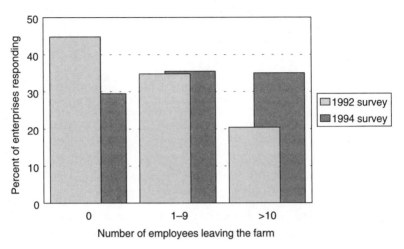

Some individuals may not be ready to exercise even this kind of freedom of organizational choice. Their preference may be toward inertia, leaving their land shares in collective management for joint cultivation. This may be the preferred solution for pensioners, who are too old to take an active part in the management of their new assets, although pensioners also may join smaller autonomous groups as passive investors. Despite the inherent inertia of this option, case studies and field observations reveal a definite change in the psychology of former collective members once they become the shareholders of their former collective. They know that they are entitled to dividends or lease payments for the shares entrusted to the new shareholding organization that succeeded their former collective. This makes them assume a much more active role on the farm, and managers indicate that they are frequently pressured by their shareholders to account for their actions and to justify their operating decisions. The evidence is still anecdotal, as the issue has not been tackled in a large-scale survey, but the phenomenon, if indeed pervasive among the new shareholders, points to a radical departure from the practice of Soviet collective management, when the members were generally disinterested and rubber-stamped the director's decisions.

The rural population in contemporary Russia faces a considerable range of new options, at least in principle. Every family has a 0.5-hectare household plot and a 10- to 15-hectare land share in their former collective. Their options fall in three broad categories: (a) maintaining the status quo, i.e., continuing to work household plots while leaving their land shares in the collective, (b) joining with a small number of other shareholders to create a new autonomous profit-motivated entity with active or passive participation, and (c) leaving the collective altogether to start an independent family farm with their land share entitlement plus the land from their household plot. These options sound very similar to those that any farmer faces in a market economy: farm independently, create a partnership, or voluntarily join a production cooperative. Current alternatives are fundamentally different from peasants' options during the Soviet era, when membership in the collective was far from voluntary and when they had practically no freedom of exit from the collective farm.

One clearly problematic area remains, however, which is basically due to the fuzziness of the concept of private ownership in Russia. The options listed above assume that the individual remains a farmer in the village. What if the individual decides to migrate to the city? In any market economy, individuals can sell property and take its cash value with them; or in a less irrevocable mode individuals can rent or lease their property and receive supplementary income, while keeping open the option of ultimately returning to the village. In Russia, a private farmer in practice cannot sell his land for lack of a proper legal foundation. Subleasing is allowed only in the short term. Farmers cannot leave their land behind while attempting to earn a living in the city, because failure to cultivate the land continuously for one or two years bears the threat of summary administrative expropriation. Thus, private farmers are essentially locked into the countryside, despite the new freedom to produce what they want and to sell it how they wish.

What about the shareowners? Can they leave and still keep their economic roots in the village? Presidential decrees and government resolutions passed since 1991 suggest that the individual can sell his or her land share to another member of the former collective, invest it in the equity capital of a corporation in return for a stream of dividends, or lease it to a legal or physical body in return for a stream of lease payments. There is, however, very little evidence of buying and selling of land shares among individuals. The land shares are either invested in the equity capital of the collective or are leased out to the collective, and no information is available on the extent to which these arrangements actually influence the mobility of the rural population.

In a certain sense, the whole question may be academic, as the rural population in Russia is notoriously immobile, with most people spending their entire life in the same village. World Bank surveys reveal that 80 percent of farm-enterprise employees have lived in a rural area since birth. Yet greater mobility will certainly be an asset as the need for labor adjustment in the

village becomes more acute. It seems that paper shares endow their owners with greater freedom of mobility than farmland. Russian legislators and policymakers need to give some thought to this difference and attempt to equalize the freedom of choice of both groups of rural residents. The apparent discrimination against private farmers may be unconstitutional, as it clashes with certain guaranteed individual freedoms, and Russia may do well to borrow a leaf from the book of the Constitutional Court in Moldova, which has consistently and repeatedly upset several laws and government resolutions that attempted to limit the practical freedoms of farmers in relation to their land.

Family Welfare

How has land reform affected the economic situation of rural families? It is practically impossible to answer this question with any certainty, as in Russia (and the rest of the former socialist countries) land reform is just one component of a complex process of transition to the market and its effects cannot be isolated from the effects of other components. I attempt to obtain a qualitative estimate of the impact of land reform on the welfare of rural families by examining two constituencies that differ radically in their role in the process of land reform, while having roughly the same exposure to other forces of transition. These two constituencies are independent private farmers, on the one hand, and shareholders of large farm enterprises, on the other.

In most cases, private farmers are former farm-enterprise employees who have decided to leave the collective and take the fate of their families into their own hands. The shareholders of the farm enterprises are basically the same human material as private farmers, but they have a different set of attitudes and priorities: They prefer the relative safety of the traditional collective framework and tend to avoid the risks and uncertainties associated with independent farming. Both groups give a fairly low evaluation of the general standard of living in their countries. Yet a comparison of their responses shows that on the whole farmers are better off and more optimistic than employees of collective enterprises.

The percentage of respondents reporting that the family budget is just sufficient for subsistence is significantly higher among farm-enterprise employees than among private farmers. At the other extreme, a much higher percentage of private farmers report that they can afford more than just bare subsistence needs, including even the purchase of durables (Figure 2.4). Private farmers offer a much more positive evaluation of the changes

Figure 2.4

Responses to Questions About What Family Budget Buys, Private
Farmers and Large-Farm Employees, 1994

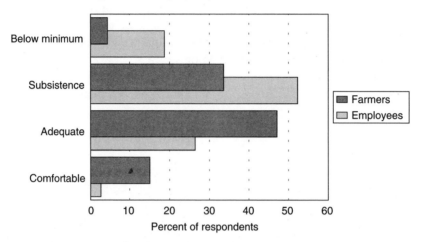

Note: "Below minimum," family income is not sufficient to buy all foodstuffs a family needs;
"subsistence," family income is sufficient to buy food and the bare necessities of life; "adequate," family can afford clothing, shoes, and so on, in addition to food; and "comfortable,"
family can also afford durable goods and experiences no material difficulties at present.

during the last few years than do farm-enterprise employees. A significantly
higher percentage of private farmers judge the situation to have improved,
while most farm-enterprise employees at best regard the situation as unchanged (Figure 2.5). Finally, private farmers face the future with much
greater optimism than employees remaining in collective farm enterprises.
The percentage of private farmers with positive expectations for the future
is much higher than the percentage of farm-enterprise employees; and conversely, the percentage of farm-enterprise employees with negative expectations for the future is much higher than the percentage of private farmers (Figure 2.6).

Private farmers are basically at the leading edge of reform. They have
made a clear decision, and there is no turning back to the safety of the collective umbrella. They are fully exposed to all the risks that producers have
to face in an environment prone to extreme economic and legal uncertainty, including the ultimate risk of not-infrequent bankruptcy. And yet
they appear to be happy and optimistic, if not in absolute terms then at
least relative to the other segment of the rural population—the individuals
who have decided to stay in the collective rather than face the risks of per-

Figure 2.5

Perceptions of Family Situation in Recent Years, Private Farmers and Large-Farm Employees, 1994

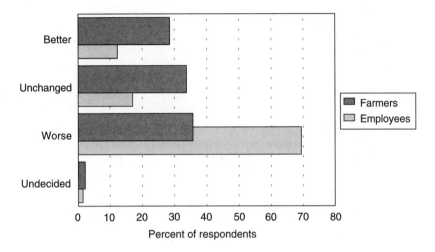

How Has the Family Situation Changed in the Last Few Years?

sonal initiative. In a certain sense, this is the most significant and most encouraging outcome of reforms: The reform efforts have not been in vain.

So, is the rural population better off or worse off as a result of land reform? Quite honestly, we do not know. But nor do we have a precise answer to this question for the urban population. The answer is not a decisive yes or no, because the picture consists of many shades of gray. It is obvious that the rural population has lost much of the comfortable benefits and the certainties enjoyed under the socialist regime. On the other hand, rural residents have gained ownership of land and property, which has definite value and under certain conditions can be converted into cash. They have gained additional freedoms of choice, additional options for independent decisions, and additional prospects of mobility, and now have the tools and opportunities for trying to shape their individual future in a more decisive way than during the Soviet era. Those who have taken this opportunity and have begun using these tools appear to be enjoying some benefits. Unfortunately, these pioneers are very few and far between. The large masses are conservative, like peasants all over the world, and their behavior is still difficult to change. But the process of change has begun, and if we are to believe the evidence provided by private farmers, further and deeper change

Figure 2.6
Perceptions of Family's Future Prospects, Private Farmers and Large-Farm Employees, 1994

How Will the Economic Situation Change in the Next Few Years?

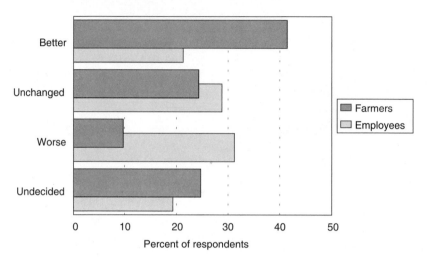

will ultimately lead to overall improvements in rural life. And this has been the basic message of land reform from the very beginning.

Appendix: Methodological Details of the Two World Bank Farm Surveys in Russia, 1992 and 1994

In addition to the overall picture of agricultural reforms that usually emerges from official Russian statistics, it is interesting and instructive to examine the process of reform on the micro level in order to understand the impact on existing farms and individuals in rural communities. Such micro-level monitoring of reforms in Russian agriculture was undertaken in two extensive field surveys conducted by the Agrarian Institute of the Russian Academy of Agricultural Sciences with the participation and support of the World Bank. The first was carried out between October 1992 and March 1993 (K. Brooks and Z. Lerman, *Land Reform and Farm Restructuring in Russia*, World Bank Discussion Paper 233 [Washington, DC: World Bank, 1994]). The second was conducted a year later, between November 1993 and April 1994 (K. Brooks, E. Krylatykh, Z. Lerman, A. Petrikov, and V. Uzun, *Agricultural Reform in Russia: A View from the Farm Level*, World Bank Discussion Paper 327 [Washington, DC: World Bank, 1996]).

Five oblasts—Pskov, Orel, Rostov, Saratov, and Novosibirsk—were included in the survey, capturing a range of agroclimatic conditions and farm specialization profiles. Four of the five provinces are located in the European part of Russia. Novosibirsk oblast is in Siberia. The general characteristics of the provinces are presented in Table 2A.1. The local research organizations in these provinces were sufficiently experienced and qualified to carry out the fieldwork.

The surveys addressed three groups of active rural agents: managers of large-scale farm enterprises (the traditional collective and state farms), which started to reorganize at the end of 1991 and still account for half of all agricultural production in Russia; members and employees of these enterprises as typical representatives of the rural population in Russia; and the emerging private farmers, who began to establish family farms outside the collectivist framework in 1991–92. Farm-enterprise managers and employ-

Table 2A.1
General Characteristics of the Five Sampled Provinces

	Saratov	Rostov	Novosibirsk	Orel	Pskov
Location	Lower Volga region, SE part of East European plain	North Caucasus region, Don basin, S of East European plain	SE of west Siberian plain, between Ob' and Irtysh Rivers	Central Russian plateau, central region	NW European Russia, border with Belarus, Latvia, Estonia
Climate	Dry continental, droughts, winds	Moderate continental, hot and dry	Extreme continental, short hot summer, drought and winds in the south	Moderate continental, warm, moderately humid	Moderate continental
Soils	50% chernozem, 30% chestnut, 11% solonetz	Chernozem, chestnut, solonetz	Podzol, serozem, chernozem	Chernozem, serozem, dernopodzol, sandy	Podzolic, marshy
Agriculture	Russia's main grain producer, livestock, large farms	Russia's main livestock producer, mechanized mixed farming	Mixed grain-livestock	Diversified crops, grain-livestock farms	Mixed dairy-beef, flax

Table 2A.2
Distribution of Respondents by Provinces in 1994 and 1992 Surveys

	1994 Survey			1992 Survey		
Province	Farm Managers	Farm Employees	Private Farmers	Farm Managers	Farm Employees	Private Farmers
Saratov	61	144	273	101	403	324
Rostov	51	110	200	35	306	293
Novosibirsk	58	110	250	43	300	142
Orel	52	113	177	70	318	125
Pskov	12	30	130	11	100	100
Total	234	507	1,030	260	1,427	984

ees were surveyed in a total of 14 districts *(raiony)* selected among the five provinces: three raiony from each of Novosibirsk, Orel, and Rostov oblasts, four raiony from Saratov oblast, and one *raion* from Pskov oblast. Survey instruments were administered to managers of most farm enterprises in the selected districts. In this way, enterprises of different organizational forms and past histories of profitability were chosen. The household sample was drawn from a subset of the selected enterprises. Farmers were surveyed in 18 districts, which included the same 14 districts selected for managers and employees, plus four additional districts in Novosibirsk oblast, where the number of raiony had to be increased to achieve a sample with the required number of private farmers. Private farmers were sampled at random from the list of all registered farmers in each district, giving preference to geographically clustered farms to save travel time for the enumerators. On the whole, the sample was constructed to include the major organizational forms of farms in the five oblasts, but it is by no means a representative sample for Russia as a whole.

By and large, the two surveys used the same questionnaires. The first survey was based on a total of 2,700 interviews, and the second on 1,800. The composition of the two samples is shown in Table 2A.2. Both surveys were conducted in the same geographical areas, but the specific respondents differed. Not all participants in the first sample could be located, and the numbers of farm units changed during ongoing reorganization. The two samples overlap, but are not identical.

Notes

1. K. Brooks and Z. Lerman, *Land Reform and Farm Restructuring in Russia*, World Bank Discussion Paper 233 (Washington, DC: World Bank, 1994); K. Brooks, E. Krylatykh, Z. Lerman, A. Petrikov, and V. Uzun, *Agricultural Reform in Russia: A View from the Farm Level*, World Bank Discussion Paper 327 (Washington, DC: World Bank, 1996).

2. T. Hanstad, *Are Smaller Farms Appropriate for Former Soviet Republics?* RDI Report on Foreign Aid and Development No. 97 (Seattle, WA: Rural Development Institute, February 1998).

3. K. Deininger, *Cooperatives and the Break-up of Large Mechanized Farms: Theoretical Perspectives and Empirical Evidence*, World Bank Discussion Paper 218 (Washington, DC: World Bank, 1993).

3

Spatial Contrasts and the Potential for Agricultural Revival

GRIGORY IOFFE AND TATYANA NEFEDOVA[1]

The embracing of market relations by Russian agriculture is by no means a straightforward process. It has numerous mediators, one of which is the Russian countryside's spatial variance—for instance, farming in Kuban' is profoundly different from that around Kostroma. Likewise, a farm in the outskirts of a large city is different from one 100 kilometers distant. Spatial variance is nothing intrinsically Russian. Indeed, it is inherent in the nature of any human–land relationship.

The imperative to adjust to variable natural conditions, coupled with the special role of the land, is the first and longest-standing component of agriculture's spatial basis. A second component is social, which is affected by transportation costs and the social differentiation of the countryside as a result of urbanization.

The concept of *economic rent* is used to assess the impact of the two aspects of spatial variance on agriculture. Economic rent is a relative measure of the advantage, or surplus productivity, that one parcel of land exhibits over another. One can distinguish between two varieties of surplus productivity: (a) that gained due to favorable natural conditions and (b) that gained due to differential accessibility to market centers (the social component). The former can be labeled Ricardo's rent and the latter von Thunen's rent, named after David Ricardo and Johann Heinrich von Thunen, respectively, who were the first scholars to conceptualize the two varieties of economic rent and pioneered their application in agriculture.[2]

In the following, we first describe the spatial pattern of Russian agriculture, introducing major variables and predictors of its productivity, and then focus on three ongoing processes with pronounced spatial dimensions that affect its adjustment to new economic conditions. We highlight the link between the existing spatial context of Russian agriculture and its potential revival.

The Spatial Context of Russian Agriculture

There is nothing extraordinary in spatial variance as such; it is the amount that matters. Russia is a country where both natural conditions and accessibility to market centers exhibit a remarkable amount of spatial variance. Contrasts within the natural environment are enormous. For example, the mean January temperature ranges from 4°C near Sochi on the Black Sea coast to minus 50°C in the Sakha republic. The mean July temperature varies from 28°C along Russia's Caspian coast, to 0° to 8°C in northern Siberia and in elevated areas. The growing season commences in February–March in the south and in late June in the north, while natural vegetation ranges from tundra to semi-desert. Only 13 percent of Russia's land area is used in sedentary farming.

Spatial contrasts within what Russians mean by the term *osvoyennost'* (its meaning embraces colonization, settlement, development of land, and habitability of space) parallel contrasts in the natural environment and even exceed them. One can speak of continuous settlement only within the triangle area of St. Petersburg, Novorossiisk, and Novosibirsk. In half the land outside this triangle permanent settlement does not exist, and within the other half, human colonization is patchy. Needless to say, the picture of the *rural* population's pressure on land is a component of the more general picture of human colonization. The centuries-old expansion of agricultural land, and of cropping area in particular, had virtually come to a halt by 1960, although the amount of cropland continued to increase somewhat in a few regions as a side effect of emerging commercial exploitation of mineral riches (in eastern Siberia) and of land reclamation projects (in the northern Caucasus and the Volga region).

One peculiar feature of human colonization and settlement in Russia is large interurban distances. Even in European Russia, cities with over 250,000 residents are twice as far apart (314 km) as Western European or U.S. cities of the same size (158 km in both cases).[3] Accessibility to vibrant urban cores matters because they are market centers consuming agricultural output and because in the modern era it is cities that have been destined to cast a web of social contacts with surrounding areas, thus integrating various local communities into a single society. It is important to point out in this regard that in today's Russia the cost of transporting produce—differentiating farm specialization and land use intensity—affects agriculture less than another differentiating factor, the quality of rural life. However, the spatial layout of this effect is similar in appearance to the von Thunen's landscape, because remote communities have been consistently worse off than peri-urban ones, that is, those located in proximity to urban areas.

Investment in the countryside's social-welfare infrastructure (roads, schools, hospitals, and community clubhouses, etc.) was assigned a low priority for so long that belated attempts to reduce the urban-rural amenities gap undertaken in the 1970s and 1980s were unsuccessful. Although rural conditions improved somewhat, the rising quality of urban life outpaced the rural; thus, the urban-rural gap remained in place. Peri-urban areas benefited from spillover effects of urban investment and from the heightened density of linear infrastructure converging on any city, just as radial spokes converge on a hub. Rural communities that could take advantage of proximity to a city became islands of relative prosperity. The possibility of commuting to urban centers, thus combining the best features of rural and urban ways of life, must be taken into account as well. Whereas in the U.S. cultural context this latter factor spurred suburbanization, in Russia it helped to prop up sundry extra-urban activities, including agriculture.

During the years and decades of rural demographic erosion, peri-urban (but rural in their status) areas fared the best. In the 1970s and 1980s—when births still outnumbered deaths in the countryside, but the rural exodus was in full swing—not only was the rural population as a whole stable and even occasionally increasing in peri-urban areas, but its agricultural component did so as well and even experienced a stronger pull to cities and towns.[4] These areas enjoyed a higher standard of living, and had a more stable and even growing agricultural labor supply. Therefore, what has been written about the negative and disruptive influence of urbanization on agriculture in the West[5] hardly fits the Russian context. In most Russian regions, particularly nonchernozem (not black-earth) zones, yields per land unit strongly resemble a classical von Thunen's landscape with output value declining the greater the distance from an urban center (Map 3.1).

In contrast, the rural periphery, located outside a two-hour (travel time) accessibility range from such centers, has experienced a prolonged social decay. In the mid-1980s, it was estimated that in such areas, agricultural output had negative elasticity with respect to land. In other words, the

Map 3.1

Gross Agricultural Output of Agricultural Land in Moscow Oblast, 1997–98, in thousands of rubles per hectare

Note: Shaded area is city of Moscow.

greater the amount of land under cultivation, the lower the productivity.[6] This phenomenon occurred regardless of the level of spatial resolution of the statistical analysis. Negative elasticity was revealed in samples of farms, rural *raiony*, and oblasts.

Thus, massive abandonment of land should hardly come as a surprise. Under the Soviet regime, this process was not accurately reported and therefore underestimated by local authorities and, in turn, by the Federal Statistical Agency. The size of landholdings was one of the central planning proxies for collective farms' supply of various inputs and equipment, such as fertilizers and tractors. Nonetheless, even in the 1980s occasional aerial photographs showed that land actually under cultivation in some rural raiony was only half of what was officially reported. The scale of land abandonment in the depopulated periphery vastly exceeded the reduction of peri-urban farmland as a result of urban sprawl. Our numerous field trips

to outlying nonchernozem raiony since the early 1970s have convinced us
that the officially recorded decline in farmland between 1970 and 1997—
15.8 million hectares, or 7 percent[7]—is a substantial understatement of
land abandonment. Farmland contraction in European Russia alone most
probably exceeds this figure by a factor of two. The official statistics of Russia's Land Committee show that in the most depopulated regions, agricultural land contracted by 20 to 46 percent between 1959 and 1989. The
biggest reduction was in the European northern region at 46 percent, and
the second largest occurred in the northwest. In Novgorod oblast, the reduction was 33 percent. In Tver oblast, in the industrial center of the
country, agricultural land contracted by 32 percent and in Yaroslavl oblast,
by 25 percent.[8]

Predictors of Spatial Differentiation

It follows from the above discussion that two variables can be used as predictors of agricultural land value across Russia. One is the fertility of the
soil and other natural factors, while the other is accessibility to urban areas.

Specific techniques for assessing the favorability of natural conditions for
agriculture have long been in use in Russia. They are based on long-term
records of yields on specially designated, regionally representative parcels
of land in the absence of irrigation and any other sophisticated cultivation
method; that is, under natural conditions of soil type, temperature, and
moisture.[9] The estimates of the so-called bioclimatic potential (Map 3.2)
thus obtained are expressed in centners/hectare (one centner = 0.1 metric
ton) yields of respective crops. The highest grain-related estimates are
those of the northern Caucasus and the western margin of the central chernozem region (approximately 30 and over 30 centners/hectare, respectively). These estimates are fairly high (20 to 25 centners/hectare) in the
central region from the province of Smolensk in the west to Bashkortostan
in the east. The European north, central Siberia, and the southern Volga
region fare the worst (see Map 3.2).

Map 3.2 shows that in European Russia the best natural conditions for
agriculture are found in the western margins of the steppe (particularly
in Krasnodar *krai* and Belgorod oblast) and forest steppe (particularly in
Voronezh and Kursk regions). In Siberia, the far-eastern Primorsky krai
and Amur oblast are best endowed. The second component of economic
rent can be approximated by urban population density (Map 3.3). The
highest density is found around Moscow and in the oblasts located east
of Moscow (Yaroslavl, Vladimir, Ivanovo, Nizhniy Novgorod, Ulyanovsk,

Map 3.2
Bioclimatic Potential of Arable Land in Russia (centners/hectare of normative grain yield)

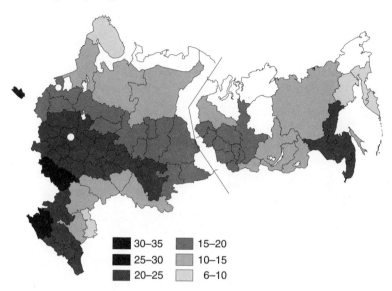

■ 30–35	■ 15–20	
■ 25–30	■ 10–15	
■ 20–25	☐ 6–10	

Source: Prirodno-sel'skokhoziaistvennoye (Moscow: Goskomstat, 1983).

Samara, and Tatarstan), and also around Kaluga, Tula, Belgorod, Chelya-binsk, Krasnodar, and northern Ossetia. Urban population density is evidently not as good a predictor of von Thunen's rent as "bioclimatic potential" (Map 3.2) is of Ricardo's rent. In this analysis however, we use urban density for want of a better proxy for accessibility at the oblast level.

When the value of normative land tax is assigned to each Russian region in 1995, its value appears to be a function of Ricardo's and von Thunen's specifications of economic rent. This is shown in the linear regression model below. The model is based on a sample of all Russian geopolitical subdivisions, with the exception of seven *okrugy* (Nenets, Khanty-Mansi, Yamalo-Nenets, Taimyr, Evenk, Chukotka, and Koryak).

$$Y = -25.171 + 73.297X + 13.943Z;\ R = 0.744;\ F = 49.048$$

In this model, Y represents the 1995 value of land tax in rubles per hectare (from 1995 on, only proportional changes were introduced; that is, in all civil divisions the land tax was augmented by a fixed number of percentage points); X, bioclimatic potential in centners/hectare; Z, 1998

Map 3.3
Urban Population Density, 1998 (inhabitants/km²)

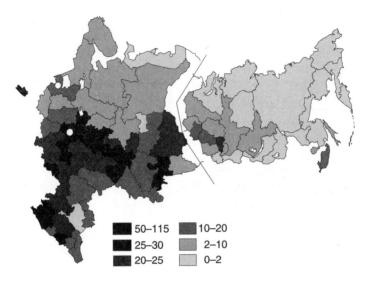

50–115	10–20
25–30	2–10
20–25	0–2

Source: Compiled based on the *Demographic Yearbook of the Russian Federation 1998* (Moscow: Goskomstat, 1999).

urban population density in people per square kilometer; *R*, multiple correlation coefficient; and *F*, Fisher value (of statistical significance).

This result means that seemingly arbitrary land tax values[10] assigned by the Ministry of Agriculture are in fact highly predictive, as they derive from the two components of agricultural rent discussed above. They should thus be treated as reasonable approximations of the variable utility of agricultural land and are proportional to its market value. Predictably, land tax values are at their highest if and when *both* economic rents are high. Krasnodar and Belgorod are cases in point.

Important questions remain concerning the comparative performance of natural and social (proximity to urban centers) components of agricultural rent. Has productivity become more dependent on one or the other of these components? Alternatively, with the passage of time, which areas have become better suited for successful farming Russian style, the most urbanized *or* the best endowed naturally? Because the deterioration of the countryside has proceeded unobstructed for decades and thus could not help but increase the attendant core-periphery gap, we hypothesized that

Table 3.1

Pearson Correlations Between Total Agricultural Output and Bioclimatic Potential and Urban Population Density, 1980, 1991, and 1997

Factor	1980 (n = 71)	1991 (n = 89)	1997 (n = 89)
Bioclimatic potential	0.46	0.37	0.35
Urban population density	0.26	0.35	0.42

Sources: Calculated based on Goskomstat's oblast-structured data on population, land area, and monetary value of total/gross agricultural output. Bioclimatic potential estimates are from *Prirodno-sel'skokhoziaistvennoye raionirovanye zemel'nogo fonda SSSR* (Moscow: Kolos 1983).

for agricultural output relative distance to an urban environment should be gaining in significance compared to natural soil fertility, which is not subject to short-term changes.

Table 3.1 tends to confirm our hypothesis. It appears that as time goes by, economic rent in agriculture becomes more dependent on its social component, whose proxy in our analysis is urban population density. In Russian conditions, therefore, urbanization has many positive effects on agriculture. While some components of agricultural output show a somewhat different spatial trend, the conclusion remains accurate overall. Grain yields, for example, become more and more dependent on natural soil fertility, which is understandable in view of a drastic reduction in fertilizer inputs in the 1990s.

Our previous research shows that grain yields have exhibited similar spatial trends in the past, for the most part during periods of economic crisis, such as during collectivization. Whereas in 1901–34, grain yields (per unit of land) in nonchernozem regions typically exceeded those in black-earth regions primarily due to differences in technology, this advantage was reversed at the time of collectivization.[11] Today the spatial pattern of grain yields shows signs of being conditioned by the natural fertility of the soil to a larger extent than was the case in the 1980s. However, rural population density is now an even stronger predictor.

In 1997, the Pearson correlation between grain yields and rural population density across 89 divisions of the Russian Federation was 0.82. (The correlation between grain yields and bioclimatic potential was 0.68.) In other words, under the current demographic conditions, production is destined to shift away from depopulated areas. It is also true that rural population density has historically been a function of soil fertility. As our previous research showed, however, the pull of urban centers is gaining in significance as a predictor of rural population density, while soil fertility is declining in importance as a predictor. On the eve of the current crisis there seemed to be parity between these two predictors of the extent to which the countryside was populated. While the current economic situation may have tipped the balance in favor of the best naturally endowed areas yet once again (after all, migrants from thoughout Russia end up in the central chernozem and northern Caucasus region more frequently than elsewhere), we think that the pull of urban centers may be experiencing only a temporary setback. Therefore, we believe that the social component of economic rent in agriculture is associated primarily with and generated by urbanization.

Prospects for Revival

In the 1990s, Russian manufacturing output declined at a higher rate than agricultural production. Nevertheless, there was a 36-percent decline in agricultural output from 1990 to 1997 (the 1998 crop failure should not be counted, because failures of such magnitude are very rare). Another sign of regress was the large share of subsidiary or household farming in total agricultural output—47 percent in 1997. Subsidiary farming refers to what rural and small-town inhabitants produce in their backyards. A typical subsidiary farm is not only worlds apart from the Western-style, private family farm envisioned by Russian reformers, but is also technologically a step backward compared with a typical collective farm.

Another sign of problems in agriculture was the drastic reduction in the number of head of cattle. Although importing meat is economically more rational for Russia than importing grain fodder and then wasting it in inefficient livestock-fattening operations (the way in which meat was produced in Russia in the 1970s and 1980s), the magnitude of the reduction in cattle herds is much greater than would be expected on the basis of inefficiency alone.

Finally, the increasing proportion of retirees in many rural regions[12] is also an unfavorable sign. Yet, the downward slide in Russian farming may have already bottomed out. Elsewhere we have expressed the view that collective forms of farming rather than private family farms are going to be the mainstay of Russian agriculture in the foreseeable future.[13] However, rather than focusing on the political economy of Russian agrarian reform, in the remainder of this chapter we discuss instead what we see as three avenues of renewal: contraction of agricultural space, demographic revival, and vertical integration of food producers.

Prospects for Russian agricultural turnaround are connected with the spatial characteristics described earlier. For example, we would expect better conditions for revival in Krasnodar and Belgorod, rated high on *both* components of economic rent than, say, in Kirov and Kostroma, which are rated low on *both* of them.

Contraction of Agricultural Space

Russia's 206 million hectares of farmland is a great asset and a heavy burden at the same time. It became more of a burden as a result of rural depopulation. Currently, only about 20 percent of Russia's socialized farms and their reorganized forms (joint stock companies) are profitable. Some experts believe that another 40 percent can achieve profitability under certain conditions. The remaining establishments, mostly outlying farms, are for the most part irremediable. When farm debts were written off again in November 1998, the survival of quite a few rural communities was ensured, but economically the write-off made as little sense as it did on previous occasions. We mentioned earlier that output elasticity with respect to land as a production factor in Russia has long been negative on any spatial level. However, because communal farming in outlying areas is a vehicle for collective survival, many economically doomed farms cannot be disbanded. Nor can they file for bankruptcy as no institution or group of people would be willing to act as a caretaker. The problem with such farms being disbanded is in fact multidimensional—economic, social, and political.

We believe that under current conditions the only realistic way to eliminate economic waste and concentrate prospective investment on economically viable farms is to resign oneself to the natural course of events. This is one instance in which public discussion of a traditional Russian question—"*Chto Delat'*?" (What to do?)—ought to be avoided. Peripheral rural communities are dying out anyway. Moreover, in contrast to the 1970s and 1980s when some efforts were being made to curb this process in its early stages, the issue has been eclipsed by a larger number of other societal problems. This may be a blessing in disguise.

For a long time the essence of economic strategies employed in the Russian countryside has been to level the playing field. From the time when the New Economic Policy (1921–27) was abandoned, the main principle of government control over agriculture has been to keep unprofitable farms afloat and to hold back progressive establishments. These policies have had a twofold effect. On the one hand, the existence of economically doomed farms was prolonged artificially, and on the other, profitable farms were deprived of the opportunity to reinvest their profits, because of the redistribution of these profits to the benefit of unprofitable farms. Although this strategy never achieved its ultimate leveling goal, it was promoted by powerful ideologues.[14]

While the ideologues are still alive and well, the federal budget is in much worse shape today than in the past and there are fewer people living in outlying areas. It is instructive to recall that plans to alter the flow of certain major rivers never materialized in the USSR because of a shortage of public funds and not because of perceived ecological damage. Likewise, cutting back on support to many outlying farms in depopulated areas— owing to a shortage of funds—and concentrating on lands that promise speedier return on investment will contribute most favorably to the viability of the farm sector in general. Contraction of agricultural space is not unlike pruning trees by cutting off dead and rotten branches. It is noteworthy that the rate of land abandonment has been relatively low not only in regions with the highest natural fertility but also in regions of relatively high population densities near urban centers.

Demographic Revival

While the Russian countryside will never be as populous as it once was, its partial demographic revival is underway and is crucial for the future of Russian farming. In fact, the direction of rural migration began to change as early as 1989. By 1992 more people moved from urban to rural areas than in the opposite direction. An almost two-centuries-old trend was reversed. The urban-to-rural migration, however, quickly diminished; by 1994, the traditional rural-to-urban migration pattern had been fully restored. Whereas "in 1993, urban areas received only 39 percent of the country's incoming migrants, and rural areas, 61 percent[,] . . . in 1996, the ratio was 81:19. Thus the countryside's share of net migration is far below its share of the total population of Russia."[15] It is also important to point out that migration to the countryside is fueled almost entirely by migrants coming from outside Russia (specifically from former Soviet republics), many of whom were urbanites in their countries of origin.

And yet one should not discount the positive influence of this process on the countryside. Analyses of rural revival in 1993–94 showed that it began in the south of European Russia and extended north.[16] It is noteworthy that the chernozem center (with the possible exception of Kursk oblast and, especially, Tambov oblast) and the piedmont provinces of the northern Caucasus had never been impacted by rural decay to the extent

Table 3.2

Snapshot of Rural Population Dynamics in Russia, 1996–97

	Number of Civil Subdivisions ($n = 86$)[a]	Rural Population/Total Population of Subdivisions (%)
Births outnumber deaths	20	12
(1) Net migration inflow to rural areas	5	2
(2) Net migration outflow from rural areas	15	10
Deaths outnumber births	66	88
(3) Net migration outflow from rural areas	22	19
(4) Net migration inflow did not offset negative natural increase in rural areas	30	41
(5) Net migration inflow offset negative natural increase in rural areas	14	28

[a] Includes oblasts, kraya, and republics.

Source: Calculated from statistics in *Demographic Yearbook of the Russian Federation, 1997* (Moscow: Goskomstat, 1998).

of the nonchernozem regions (with the exception of the Moscow and Leningrad oblasts). In terms of revival, southern oblasts have better starting conditions.

Table 3.2 shows that in 1996–97, the migration inflow into the countryside exceeded outflow (positive net migration) in 49 of Russia's civil subdivisions (see rows preceded by 1, 4, and 5). In 44 of these 49 subdivisions, deaths outnumbered births. Thus, two components of rural population dynamics—migration and natural increase—worked in opposite directions. However, in 14 such areas net migration compensated for negative natural increase, which account for 28 percent of Russia's rural population. As seen in Map 3.4, these subdivisions include Krasnodar and Stavropol kraya, and Samara, Orenburg, Leningrad, and Tiumen oblasts (south of the latter's oil producing districts), and appear to be areas of genuine rural revival. A more modest revival is unfolding in regions where incoming migration does not outweigh negative natural increase (Map 3.4 and Table 3.2). Most of these subdivisions are located in Russia's heartland (in the industrial center and central chernozem macroeconomic regions). Because most newcomers settle in the most accessible places, the current

Map 3.4
Components of Changes in Rural Population, 1996–97

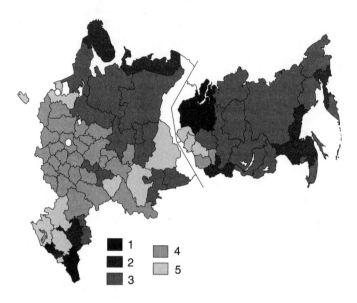

Note: Numbers 1 through 5 are defined in the first column of Table 3.2.

interplay of rural demographic processes in Russia's heartland is yet another (indirect) confirmation of the ongoing contraction of rural space. It is noteworthy that about 70 percent of Russia's rural population continues to be associated with agriculture in one way or another.[17]

The population replenishment of certain rural areas is more than just a numerical phenomenon. For years the flip side of the rural exodus has been a negative self-selection of human capital since the most industrious, independent-minded, and bright individuals left the countryside and the most passive, subservient, and alcohol-addicted remained. We are unaware of any systematic behavioral and psychosocial quality analyses (e.g., drinking habits and their implications, labor ethic, mental health, etc.) of rural communities impacted by outmigration, and thus can only fall back on personal impressions gained during numerous field trips. Just two examples follow. In 1973, while still a student at Moscow University collecting rural household statistics in the Uglich raion in Iaroslavl oblast on the basis of a rural soviet's handwritten records (so-called *pokhoziaistvennoye knigi*), one of the authors was stunned by the discovery that as many as 10 percent of all children qualified as handicapped. According to de facto social workers (*secretar' sel'soveta*), in most cases this resulted from hard drinking by at least one of their parents. Many years later, in July 1995 when both of us visited a farm in the Nekouz raion (also in Iaroslavl oblast, located in the rural periphery), our first impression was that of a few dozen cows groaning incessantly in a nearby shack. According to the farm's bookkeeper, the cows had not been milked for three consecutive days because dairy workers had received their long-delayed pay exactly three days earlier and were recovering from serious hangovers.

Although it does not befit scholars to rely on such apparently disconnected and unscientific observations, discarding them altogether is not a tenable option either. We believe that certain social environments render meaningless policy-induced transformations of any kind. Because we have made numerous observations of the above nature, we are convinced that on Russian farms the infusion of fresh blood is indispensable for a true rural revival. This infusion, however modest, is underway and there is evidence that the incoming migrants exhibit behavior and personality attributes in many ways superior to those of the lifelong locals.[18]

Vertical Cooperation of Food Producers

That Russian farming has not been transformed along the lines of market reform has several causes, including the vestigial communal experience of the Russian peasantry, the highly precarious demographic situation in the countryside, and the loss of high-quality human capital through long-term outmigration. Private farms, which are much lauded in the West, have emerged but have made little difference: 280,000 private farm units account for only about 3 percent of the country's agricultural output. Thus, socialized farms, or contemporary large-enterprise equivalents, remain just about the only framework for cooperative action of a *horizontal* type, that is, within and between grassroots communities in rural Russia. But only a few such farms are economically viable. However, forms of *vertical* cooperation—linking farms with food processors and retailers—have begun to command attention. Technically speaking, cooperative arrangements are not new in practice or in theory.

In the early twentieth century, Alexsandr Chaianov developed a theory of agricultural cooperation in which he distinguished between *vertical* and *horizontal* forms of cooperative arrangements. Horizontal cooperation involves contractual links between farms that are viewed as basic production units. Such partnerships may encompass the supply of implements and seeds, as well as selling produce. The most consistent and radical form of horizontal cooperation takes the shape of "full-scale communes where so-cialization sometimes extends to personal consumption or even to certain items of clothing."[19] It also includes co-ownership of fixed assets and land.

In contrast, vertical cooperation is an arrangement that allows peasant households to take advantage of economies of scale without undermining economic incentives by being forced into collectives. The essence of verti-cal cooperation is the establishment of harmonious economic relationships between agriculture and later stages of food production, food processing centers, and retail outlets. Chaianov did not pit horizontal and vertical co-operation against each other. He advocated forms of horizontal coopera-tion between peasant households that were far short of radical socializa-tion. In fact, both horizontal and vertical agricultural cooperation were vigorously developed in Russia from 1890 to 1914, and later from 1921 to 1927. However, it was the most radical form of horizontal cooperation that prevailed (later known as collectivization), thereby making agriculture the first stumbling block of the centrally planned economy.

In a disguised fashion, the idea of vertical cooperation staged a somewhat clumsy comeback in Russia in the late 1970s when the Soviet authorities concerned with food supplies began to dabble with the concept of APK (*agropromyshlenniy kompleks*), the Russian acronym for agrarian-industrial complex. The APK was an attempt to link farms with food processors and retailers by purely administrative means, forcing agriculture and food pro-cessing under a single government agency. This attempt failed, primarily because it was a bureaucratic solution and because it involved all large food production units regardless of their intentions or performance. At the same time it was clear that collective farming, the brainchild of the most radical proponents of horizontal cooperation, was at a crossroads. Indeed, collec-tive farming seemed to have exhausted its potential to the point that even market forces unleashed in the early 1990s could not revive it. At that time, forms of genuine vertical cooperation began to command attention.

Forms of vertical cooperation that began to emerge in the mid-1990s cannot possibly be regarded as textbook illustrations of Chaianov's theory, simply because Russia has changed so much since the 1920s. First, rural demographics and the quality of human capital in the countryside have be-come the most restrictive factors of a market-style agrarian reform. Second, the rural household can hardly be considered the basic economic unit, be-cause collective farming continues to be the backbone of Russian agricul-ture. Third, the majority of large farms are unprofitable, while food proces-sors are more successful. There is in fact an intimate relationship among all three major components of the economic environment. It is highly improbable, therefore, that vertical cooperation could proceed merely from successful farms taking over processing operations, as was the case with butter manufacturers in Siberia in the first decade of the twentieth century,[20] although such instances are not beyond the realm of possibility. See chapter 1 by Volgine in this book for a discussion of the highly successful dairy cooperatives in Siberia during that time period.

However, Chaianov did not consider the predominance of collective farming to be a barrier to the success of vertical cooperation. "Agricultural collectives," he wrote,

> . . . can in no circumstances be treated as being the opposite of . . . agricultural cooperation. They should not replace but merely supplement the system of primary cooperatives. Therefore, the question of collective farms comes down, in effect, to the question of who will be the members of the primary cooperatives: individual family farms, large farms, or collective farms. The choice would not be between *collectives* and *cooperatives*. The essence of the choice would be whether the membership of cooperatives is to be drawn from collectives or from peasant family households. And even as regards this question, the solution is by no means always or everywhere clear.[21]

Although Chaianov's and other classic Russian "organization-production" ideas have been openly discussed since 1991, the legacy of the command economy in agriculture precluded practical steps being taken in this area before 1996–97. It took an acute economic crisis, advanced polarization among farms, massive food imports, and subsequent fears of import cutoffs to introduce some modest positive changes. The dramatic reduction in food imports may have prodded many more production units to further capitalize on these changes. We believe that the sporadic attempts at vertical integration in the Russian food production system warrant scrutiny. This time, the key role is played not by the state, but by food processors—that is, production units in the latter stages of the food-production cycle.

Before 1997, up to 40 percent of the production units in Russia's food processing industry were not earning a profit. Recently, however, the share of food processing in the industrial output of large cities has grown appreciably—for example, up to 27 percent in Moscow and 19 percent in St. Petersburg. Moreover, in 1997, growth resumed in as many as 19 food-industry product categories for the first time since 1991, with the most tangible growth recorded in mineral water, beer, and potato products. The output of refined sugar, dairy products, vegetable and fruit preserves, noodles, confections, margarine, and wines all experienced growth. Only meat processors continued their downward slide.

There is growing interest by foreign and domestic investors (the latter recently overtaking the former) in Russian food processors' increasing demands for perishable produce. The Baltika brewery of St. Petersburg, controlled by a Scandinavian beverage holding company, receives high-quality barley from selected farms in Leningrad, Pskov, and Novgorod oblasts. Moscow milk-processing plants are successfully cooperating with exurban dairy farms. A potato chip factory in Kadnikov (Vologda oblast) has a contract with a formerly bankrupt potato farm, Markovskoye. There has been a great deal of publicity about the successful experiences of two meat-processing plants, Cherekizovsky in Moscow and Klinsky in the town of Klin (100 km northwest of Moscow). Both have contracts with several formerly unprofitable farms. Cherkizovsky has even acquired livestock operations of its own, buying up several cattle and pig farms. In brief, there is a large amount of evidence that farms are being economically resurrected by emerging direct links with processing operations. Examples appearing in the Russian media are located in Vologda,[22] Moscow, and Tver' oblasts.[23] Former Russian minister of agriculture Vladimir Semionov, himself a long-time farm director, has been hopeful about vertical cooperation between producers and food processors.[24]

This process seems to have received a boost after the financial debacle of August 1998. Because importers were hit hard by the drastic devaluation of the ruble, some foreign businesses shifted from selling imports to direct investments. Thus, in February 1999, the German company Ehrmann and Wydra embarked on the construction of a milk processing plant in Ramenskoe raion (Moscow oblast). It is noteworthy that the company has sold yogurt, cottage cheese, and other dairy products in Russia since 1992, and company executives insist that although they had decided on construction of a Russian plant long ago, they actually made their final decision only after 17 August 1998. In early 1999, Ehrmann and Wydra was developing plans to purchase 300,000 liters of milk from 30 local dairy farms that will be selected on a competitive basis. The company was also committed to providing the selected farms with state-of-the-art refrigerators, milking machines, and animal food components.[25]

We believe that successful vertical cooperation in the Russian food production system will likely spread to many other oblasts, particularly those that are most urbanized (see Map 3.3) and those with the most fertile land (see Map 3.2). More rigorous regional analysis of this process is a topic of our ongoing research. At this point we can only state that, by and large, the emphasis on animal husbandry on nonchernozem farms as well as their proximity to major industrial centers makes these farms more likely to establish direct links with food processors than farms in major grain-producing regions of the south. However, the latter are not going to be bypassed by vertical cooperation.

It is symptomatic in this regard that in the 1990s, the principal breadbasket regions, such as Krasnodar, Rostov, and Stavropol, suffered larger setbacks than nonchernozem regions not only in agricultural output, but also in food processing. In the past, links between farms and processors were prearranged in a top-down fashion by provincial and federal authorities. In contrast, under the new economic conditions even communist-leaning leaders of the Russian Red Belt are unable to continue this practice, which is one of the reasons behind the recent setbacks. If farming in the chernozem regions is to recover its former status as a major contributor to the domestic food supply, according to the full strength of its bioclimatic potential, vertical links will have to be reinstated on a market basis by farmers and processors themselves. This cooperation is mutually beneficial to all economic units involved. Privately owned food processors need stable supplies and nominally privatized communal farms face problems that are not solvable within the languishing system of state patronage.

Socialized farms own land, but still cannot legally sell it to a nonagricultural user. They lack stable channels for selling their produce, as well as the financial wherewithal to maintain or replace their aging equipment. With large farms now commanding only slightly over one-half of Russia's agricultural output, smallholders—households producing food in their backyards—are also gravitating to their natural partners, the registered private farms. Registered private farmers are engaging in small-scale food processing by obtaining raw produce supplies from subsistence/household farms on a contract basis.

Summary

We began by pointing to a striking amount of spatial diversity in Russian agriculture. Two variables help capture a substantial part of this diversity: natural soil fertility and accessibility to major urban centers. The latter variable has recently gained in importance. Regions with high ratings on both variables have better chances for agricultural revival.

We then considered three processes with favorable implications for Russian agriculture: contraction of agricultural space, demographic revival, and vertical cooperation arrangements. While there is no systematic and conclusive evidence at the time of this writing that all three processes are closely related with major aspects of agricultural diversity, some of the evidence presented indicates that this link may be in place. Thus, both highly fertile and heavily urbanized regions lead in the demographic revival. Conversely, the least urbanized and fertile regions lead in land abandonment, which, however, appears to be a favorable process that stems economic and financial waste. Finally, evidence of vertical cooperation between farms and food processors for the most part is underway only in the outskirts of large cities. Further insight into the spatial pattern of positive changes in Russian agriculture requires extensive research and we are currently involved in such.

The relationship between the spatial diversity of Russian agriculture and revival potential is indeed worthy of further research because all the noticeable venues of revival are place-specific and are not randomly distributed. If agriculture survives the current crisis and then becomes one of Russia's most successful economic activities, it will not happen everywhere at the same time. This process can occur more quickly in some areas than others and in some places it may not happen at all. It will definitely take place more quickly if new realities and processes are recognized and encouraged by all the economic actors involved.

Notes

1. This research was funded by the National Council for Eurasian and East European Research (grant agreement 815-7g).

2. Brian J.L. Berry, Edgar C. Conkling, and D. Michael Ray, *The Global Economy in Transition* (Upper Saddle River, NJ: Prentice Hall, 1997), 202–9.

3. Grigory Ioffe and Tatyana Nefedova, *Continuity and Change in Rural Russia* (Boulder, CO: Westview Press, 1997), 27.

4. G. V. Ioffe, *Sel'skoe khoziaistvo nechernozemia: territorial'nye problemy* (Moscow: Nauka, 1990), 90–91.

5. C. R. Bryant and T.R.R. Johnson, *Agriculture in the City's Countryside* (Toronto: University of Toronto Press, 1992), 25–26.

6. Ioffe, *Sel'skoye khoziaistvo*, 50–51.

7. *Rossiiskii statisticheskii ezhegodnik 1996* (Moscow: Goskomstat, 1997), 547; *Sel'skoe khoziaistvo v Rossii* (Moscow: Goskomstat, 1998), 181.

8. Calculated on the basis of *Zemel'nyi fond RSFSR* (Moscow: TsSU RSFSR, 1961); *Zemel'nyi fond RSFSR* (Moscow: Finansy i Statistika, 1990).

9. *Prirodno-sel'skokhoziaistvennoye raionirovaniye zemel'nogo fonda SSSR* (Moscow: Kolos, 1983).

10. Stephen K. Wegren, "The Development of Market Relations in Agricultural Land," *Post-Soviet Geography* 36, no. 8 (1995): 503.

11. G. V. Ioffe, "Osvoennost territorii i sel'skoe khoziaistvo v Evropeiskoi chasti SSSR," *Izvestiia AN SSSR, seriia geograficheskaia* no. 2 (1990): 66.

12. Stephen K. Wegren, Grigory Ioffe, and Tatyana Nefedova, "Demographic and Migratory Responses to Agrarian Reform in Russia," *Journal of Communist Studies and Transition Politics* 13 (December 1997): 54–78.

13. Ioffe and Nefedova, *Continuity and Change in Rural Russia*.

14. Perhaps the most outspoken and candid reasoning in support of keeping weak farms afloat can be found in publications by Anatoly Salutskii. See Salutskii, *V glubnke* (Moscow: Politizdat, 1988) and *Proroki i poroki: pop-nauka v zerkale realnosti* (Moscow: Molodaia Gvardiia, 1990).

15. Zhanna Zayonchkovskaya, "Recent Migration Trends in Russia," in *Population Under Duress: The Geodemography of Soviet Russia*, eds. George Demko, Grigory Ioffe, and Zhanna Zayonchkovskaya (Boulder, CO: Westview Press, 1999), 123.

16. Ioffe and Nefedova, *Continuity and Change in Rural Russia*, 186–87.

17. Ibid., 13.

18. Ibid., 279–87.

19. A. V. Chaianov, *The Theory of Peasant Co-operatives*, trans. David Wedgwood Benn with an introduction by Viktor Danilov (Columbus: Ohio State University Press, 1991), 210; originally published as A. V. Chaianov, *Osovnye idei i formy organizatsii sel'sko-khoziaistvennoi kooperatsii* (Moscow: Izd. Knigosoiuza, 1927).

20. Ibid., 8.

21. Ibid., 209.

22. *Izvestia*, 24 June 1998, 4.

23. *Expert*, no. 2, 19 January 1998, 31–33.

24. *Kommersant*, 23 December 1998, 8; *Expert*, 30 November 1998, 30–33.

25. *Izvestia*, 11 February 1999, 4.

4

Change in Land Relations: The Russian Land Market

STEPHEN K. WEGREN AND VLADIMIR R. BELEN'KIY

Russian land reform is beginning its second decade, but there is little scholarly consensus on its achievements. On the one hand, significant change in land relations is evident. There now exists in Russia private ownership of land, whereas during the Soviet period only the state could own land. During the 1990s, millions of hectares of land were transferred from state to private ownership—much of it for free, and much more land than was transferred to peasants in several Latin American nations that are considered to have had successful land reforms.[1] During the reorganization of state and collective farms, some 12 million rural dwellers received land shares, encompassing approximately 116 million hectares. More than 44 million Russians own and operate small-scale agricultural plots, encompassing about 8.4 million hectares. Private farmers possess another 13 million hectares.[2] Overall, according to two well-known Russian experts on land reform, in 1999 83 percent of agricultural land was held in private ownership, and only 17 percent as state property.[3]

On the other hand, some observers argue that little has changed in the Russian countryside. They assert that scant evidence exists of the social or economic transformation expected when reform was launched in 1990, and that large farms continue to dominate the Russian countryside. In this view, the land market has not facilitated a transfer of ownership to more efficient and productive users. A common complaint along these lines is that

88

a basic conservatism in Russia prevails, particularly in the countryside, which prevents adoption of meaningful land reform.

In summary, there is little scholarly consensus about the achievements of land reform or the obstacles to further structural change. The real issue, we argue, is not whether Russia has a land market, but what kind of market exists in that country. For a subject that is so crucial to the transformation of Russian society, the literature on the Russian land market in English is surprisingly sparse (although Russian language analyses are much more numerous). To date, published works on the Russian land market in English consist only of two oblast-specific studies, a World Bank survey that was not specific to the land market, and a study based on 1995–96 survey data.[4]

The importance of the land question can hardly be overstated. Land reform outcomes will greatly influence the nature of the Russian agricultural system and the productivity and efficiency of the rural economy, and will have a significant impact on political relations between town and countryside as well as within the countryside. The purpose of this chapter is to contribute to the literature on the Russian land market by addressing issues not covered in previous publications. We hope that by providing an analysis of the status of Russian land reform based on survey and land transaction data, a better understanding of the Russian land market will emerge. In our view, a correct understanding of the Russian land market will demonstrate that significant changes in land relations have occurred during the past decade.

Background to the Russian Land Market Surveys

In the second half of the 1990s two large surveys were conducted throughout Russia on the characteristics of the land market and motivations of buyers and sellers. The first survey by the Institute of Land Relations and Land Tenure in Moscow and the Institute of Sociology in Kaluga oblast took place in seven regions during fall 1995 and in winter 1996. Surveys were conducted in Voronezh, Volgograd, Ivanovo, Smolensk, Kaluga, and Novgorod oblasts and in Altay *krai*. The survey was designed to capture elite opinions about land reform and the land market and, important for our purposes here, attitudes of potential buyers and sellers. In the first survey a total of 5,841 respondents aged 18 and older were polled in face-to-face interviews. Survey results were based on responses from 579 agricultural experts, 2,932 actual owners or users of land, and 2,330 potential owners or users of land.[5] This survey provided important data for understanding the nature of the Russian land market.[6]

The second survey was conducted in fall 1997 and winter 1998 by the same institutes. This chapter draws mainly on evidence from the second survey. As in the first survey, respondents aged 18 and older were polled in face-to-face interviews. The second survey was carried out in eight regions. These regions included Voronezh, Volgograd, Ivanovo, Kaluga, and Novgorod oblasts, which were surveyed in the first survey, as well as Perm, Moscow, and Tula oblasts. The 1997–98 survey interviewed a total of 5,608 people, including 135 rural experts, 2,739 people wanting to obtain land, and 2,734 people who owned land or were users of land at the time of the survey and were potential sellers.[7] For convenience, we refer to the latter two groups as "buyers" and "sellers." Both the supply and demand side of the land market was captured. Buyers and sellers of land are of particular interest, and their social characteristics are shown in Table 4.1.

Respondents were grouped according to gender, age, education, and place of residence. A significant change took place between the first and second surveys for both land buyers and sellers. In both surveys, respondents were grouped not only according to the categories shown in Table 4.1, but also by the form of ownership in the enterprise where they

Table 4.1

Social Characteristics of Land Buyers and Sellers in 1995–96 and 1997–98 Surveys (percent)

	1995–96		1997–98	
Variable	Buyers	Sellers	Buyers	Sellers
Gender				
Male	44.4	47.8	41.2	36.7
Female	54.9	50.6	58.7	62.9
Age				
18–30	20.7	16.4	19.9	14.3
31–40	33.7	26.6	28.8	22.5
41–50	26.2	28.5	29.3	29.0
Education				
Incomplete secondary	3.8	6.3	6.2	14.7
General or specialized secondary	42.9	44.0	56.9	53.6
Some higher education or completion				
of higher education program	52.7	48.9	36.8	31.5
Place of residence				
Oblast center	71.6	67.4	45.5	44.6
City	17.5	16.9	40.3	39.4
Countryside	10.7	15.4	14.2	16.0

Note: Percentages for variable categories do not sum to 100 percent because experts interviewed in the same surveys were not included.

worked. There were three categories: managers in state-owned enterprises, workers in state-owned enterprises, and workers in nonstate enterprises. Respondents were further categorized depending on whether they were land buyers or land sellers. In the 1995 survey, workers in state enterprises comprised 53 percent of the sample of land buyers for urban land and 52 percent of the sample for rural land. In the 1997 survey these percentages dropped to 31.8 and 34.1, respectively. Also, among land buyers, the percentage of respondents who were workers in nonstate enterprises increased significantly, from 29 percent in 1995 for urban land and 22 percent for rural land, to 53 percent and 52 percent, respectively.

The same trend was true for land sellers, as workers in state enterprises constituted 58 percent of the sample in 1995–96 for urban land and 53 percent for rural land. These percentages declined to 35 for both urban and rural land in the 1997–98 survey. Conversely, workers in nonstate enterprises increased from 23 percent of the sample for urban land and 29 percent for rural land to nearly one-half of the sample for both types in the 1997–98 survey. Therefore, in the second survey, the proportion of state enterprise workers declined, while that of nonstate enterprises increased to about half of the respondents. This trend is important because workplace privatization has conditioned orientations toward land ownership, as shown later in this chapter.

Our analysis of the Russian land market is focused on three levels: federal, regional, and individual. At the federal level, we examine attempts to develop and reach consensus on a legal framework for land transactions (land code), and then describe general national trends in the land market. We then examine regional variations in the land market, including legal variations and regional market development. Finally, we look at individual preferences regarding land leasing and buying, attitudes toward land ownership, and the motivations of land buyers and land sellers.

Federal Level

Land reform in Russia has largely been a "revolution from above," with the state attempting to change attitudes, legal structures, and behaviors. The importance of the national government has been changing, and we will see how regional actors have become more important in a separate section below. Nonetheless, the federal level has been the arena of the most conflict, as well as the most progress. We first examine the legal environment at the federal level.

Legal Environment

The legal environment in Russia is easily misunderstood. On the one hand, Russian legislation is a good deal more conservative than that found in the Baltics, Albania, or more recently, Ukraine. Moreover, the Russian legal environment for land privatization has been muddled, leading to confusion about what is permissible and legal. On the other hand, compared to ten years ago there has been significant progress in what is allowed. Importantly, even with a lack of legal clarity, land privatization has become a significant aspect of reform and a significant number of land transactions have occurred. Peasants are generally understood as rational, conservative actors. A conservative, putatively antimarket peasant would hardly take action in an environment where consequences are not known and costs might exceed benefits. Yet, even with a less than favorable legal environment, land privatization and a land market have developed.

The legal basis for land reform has been extensively reviewed in other publications during the past several years. For our purposes, it is sufficient to note that government resolutions dating from December 1991 and presidential decrees issued in October 1993 and March 1996 form the current legal basis for land privatization and land transactions.[8] In addition, the 1993 Constitution (Article 27) permits the ownership of land, as does the 1994 Civil Code (Articles 260 and 261).

What has been missing is a federal land code that would: (1) replace the 1991 Soviet-era land code, (2) reflect new legal realities as permitted in the 1993 Constitution and 1994 Civil Code, and (3) provide detailed mechanisms for the conclusion of land transactions. The absence of a federal land code has added to the confusion over what is permissible. During the Yeltsin period, the land code was a battleground for the executive and legislative branches. The most contentious issues are related to the right of disposal of agricultural land, namely, whether large tracts of agricultural land should be allowed to be sold, and to whom and for what use.

Conservatives are opposed to selling land in large farms, arguing that agricultural land should remain in agricultural use, and they believe that only those who use the land should own it. They support a regulated land market in which only the sale of small-scale agricultural plots of land would be permitted, and agricultural land would have to remain in agricultural use. Conservatives also argue that peasants only recently obtained land, and an unregulated market would allow rich urbanites and speculators to buy up land, depriving peasants of their right to land. Liberals favor an unregulated land market in which agricultural land could be sold to anyone, and the purpose of land use is allowed to change. Owing to these differences, several versions of the land code passed in the Duma during the Yeltsin period but were never enforced.

The first Russian land code was adopted in 1922 and stayed in effect until April 1991 when a new version was approved. The 1991 version permitted the ownership of land but imposed restrictions on the purchase and sale of land. Work on a new land code commenced in 1994, as two versions were drafted, one by the Russia's Choice Party and a second by the government. These versions were simultaneously presented to the Duma for a vote in July 1994, but neither received the required number of votes to pass. In September 1994, the Duma Committee on Agrarian Questions drafted a new version after receiving more than 1,300 amendments from regional representatives. This version came up for a vote at a plenary session of the Duma in March 1995, but the Communist Party, Russia's Choice, and the Yabloko Party voted against it, all for different reasons, reflecting the incoherence of the draft.[9] Amendments were again solicited from regional representatives, but regional policies differed greatly, as some favored private ownership and others forbade it, and still others wanted significant restrictions on private ownership. The draft that came up for a vote on the floor of the Duma in June 1995 was rejected, falling 16 votes short of the 226 required for passage. Finally, the Duma adopted the fifth version, and it was sent to the regions for amendments, of which more than 840 were received. The version that resulted came up for a vote in the Duma in October 1995 but fell 35 votes short.[10]

Following the election of a new State Duma in December 1995, on 22 May 1996 a new version of the land code was passed by the State Duma, but it was rejected by the Federation Council in July 1996. This version did not envision the sale or mortgaging of land held by agricultural enterprises or private farmers. Members of the State Duma attempted to overturn the decision by the Federation Council, but were only able to muster 269 votes instead of the 300 that were required.[11] A mediation commission was established and worked for five months. One compromise that was reached allowed private farmers to sell their land after ten years. However, even after ten years, land held in private ownership by private farmers faced significant restrictions on the freedom to sell land. The commission was not able to bridge the most significant differences and, in the end, the commission could only agree to exclude altogether the clauses on land mortgaging and state regulation of land turnover, instead referring to other federal laws on these issues. A new version was considered by the Duma in December 1996, but returned to the commission without a vote.

With the changes incorporated from December 1996, a new version of the land code passed in the Duma in June 1997 by a vote of 285 to 10, and the Federation Council approved it in early July 1997. This version allowed individuals or organizations to own or lease farmland, but prohibited the purchase and sale of agricultural land. Foreigners were also forbidden to own land. In late July 1997, President Boris Yeltsin vetoed this version. Needing 300 votes to override the veto, in September 1997 the State Duma voted 304 to 52 to override.[12] Following this vote, both sides searched for an acceptable compromise, and a "roundtable" discussion was scheduled for 22 November 1997. The November meeting was postponed until 11 December 1997, and then postponed again when Yeltsin became sick, until 26 December 1997.

When the December roundtable was finally convened, not all disagreements were bridged, although some progress was reported. At the conclusion of the December 1997 roundtable meeting, the participants signed a protocol of agreement. The protocol provided for the establishment of another mediation commission, which was to work on compromise language for a new land code. The protocol set a deadline for the end of March 1998 for work to be completed and for Yeltsin to sign a new land code into law. In early February 1998, it was reported that the mediation commission had not even been formed and the work had not yet begun. Later that same month, the Federation Council upheld Yeltsin's veto of the Duma's land code.[13]

After missing the March deadline, in April 1998 Yeltsin forwarded twenty-four amendments to the Duma in an attempt to break the stalemate. The Duma Committee on Agrarian Questions considered these amendments, adopted some of them, and introduced several "corrections" of its own to the Yeltsin version. Among those changes was a restriction on the sale of agricultural land held by collective farms and their legal successors. Only land held in private ownership and land used for small-scale agricultural purposes could be sold freely, according to the committee's draft version. A few days later in April 1998, the Duma passed its version of the land code based on the committee's work, by a vote of 263 to 3. This version also passed in the Federation Council, but in June 1998 Yeltsin vetoed it, claiming that it restricted land sales too much.

A month later in July 1998, Yeltsin submitted his version with changes to the Duma, but it was twice voted down, the second time receiving 220 of the required 226 votes. Following that vote, the Duma Committee on Agrarian Questions asked the president to clarify two of the more controversial changes.[14] By early December 1998, a compromise draft was ready for consideration, but Communists asked for a delay to have time to study the changes. The compromise version that emerged finally went before the Duma for a vote on 23 December 1998. Two rounds of votes were taken, but neither vote succeeded in obtaining sufficient support; on the first vote only 217 deputies were in favor, and on the second only 178. Leading the vote against this version were the Communist Party and Yabloko, while deputies of the Agrarian faction supported the document.[15]

An impasse was reached, and a new version of the land code would have to be drafted. During 1999, however, Yeltsin's illnesses and his increasing absence from the policymaking process affected progress. Debates on a new version of the land code took place again in fall 1999, but preparations for the December 1999 State Duma elections prevented a new draft from coming up for a vote. In February 2000 after the December election, the Union of Right Forces (SPS) submitted a new draft of the land code that permitted the unregulated purchase and sale of land. In mid-March 2000, a plenary session of the Duma was supposed to consider this newest draft, but the session was postponed after the Kremlin requested continued work on the version submitted by the SPS.[16] In late June 2000, the head of the Agroindustrial Deputy faction in the Duma, N. Kharitonov, reported that the Duma would vote on a new draft of the land code by 5 July, prior to the summer adjournment.[17] However, in mid-July, it was reported that the Duma did not consider the new draft code prior to its summer vacation.[18] In July 2001, a draft supported by the Kremlin passed the second reading in the Duma and was expected to be approved in the fall of 2001. However, this draft did not address the question of rural land sales.

National Trends in the Land Market

Although Russia remains without a legal mechanism for the conduct of land transactions, Russians have embraced the land market. The government estimates that some 450,000 land transactions take place annually, and some observers maintain that an equal number of transactions go unreported to escape taxes. Market transactions consist of the buying and selling of land and land leasing. Overall, in terms of area and number of transactions, land leasing during the early years of land reform has been more prevalent than land purchases, accounting for about 98 percent of market transactions. Nonetheless, as discussed below, the purchase and sale of land are becoming more significant.

The land market consists of two types of submarkets: the municipal market and the private market. The municipal market involves purchases of

Table 4.2

Structure of Land Transactions in Russia, 1996–98

How Land Was Obtained	1996, # of Transactions		1996, % of Total	1997, # of Transactions		1997, % of Total	1998, # of Transactions		1998, % of Total
Purchase from local government (average size of land plot in hectares)	43,907	(.20)	10	20,897	(.34)	4	11,467	(.65)	3
Purchase-sale between individuals	218,759	(.15)	51	265,689	(.22)	55	234,590	(.17)	56
Gift	34,094	(.24)	8	33,581	(.18)	7	26,452	(.25)	6
Inheritance	132,171	(.97)	31	158,512	(.31)	33	144,735	(.32)	34
Mortgage	760	(3.92)	—	2,983	(1.01)	1	2,789	(1.32)	1
Total	429,691		100	481,662		100	420,033		100

Sources: Roskomzem, *Gosudarstvennyy (natsional'nyy) doklad o sostoyanii i ispol'zovanii zemel' Rossiyskoy Federatsii v 1998 godu* (Moscow: Committee on Land, 1999), 55; and authors' calculations.

land from *raion* or city land funds, and the private market refers to the sale of land between private citizens. Table 4.2 presents data from the State Committee on Land (Roskomzem) that illustrate national trends in the Russian land market.

Four interesting trends can be seen in Table 4.2. First, the data show that the private land market has surpassed the municipal land market, accounting for 51 percent, 55 percent, and 56 percent of land transactions between individuals in 1996, 1997, and 1998, respectively. Second, if we subdivide transactions into market and nonmarket transactions, it is clear that market transactions dominate the land market. The definition of a market transaction is a purchase from a local government or the purchase of land from an individual—a monetary transaction. Nonmarket transactions involve no exchange of money and include land transferred as a gift or inheritance. Based on these definitions (summing rows 1 and 2), market transactions accounted for 61 percent, 59 percent, and 59 percent of all transactions between individuals in 1996, 1997, and 1998, respectively. Third, the Russian land market has registered no fewer than 200,000 purchases or sales of land between individuals annually since 1996.[19] Among transactions between individuals, the most popular uses of purchased land were for small-scale collective gardening (*sadovodstvo*), operation of private plots, and individual housing construction. These three uses accounted for 96.5 percent, 95 percent, and 96 percent of all purchase-sale transactions between individuals in 1996, 1997, and 1998, respectively.[20] Fourth, all land transactions involve very small plots of land. The smallest average sizes of land plots are found in transactions between individuals. In 1998, for example, land transactions between individuals for the construction of individual housing averaged 0.10 hectares; for private plot operations, 0.23 hectares; and for collective gardening, 0.07 hectares.[21]

Land turnover is important, of course, for the development of a land market, which in turn decentralizes power. But often overlooked is the revenue that is generated from land taxes. Land taxes were originally established by the federal law "On Payment for Land," which went into effect on 1 January 1992. This law was subsequently amended in July 1994 by the Duma and Federation Council and these changes were approved in August 1994 by President Yeltsin.[22] This early legislation established normative prices for land as well as the level of land taxes.[23] The land tax is calculated taking into account the normative price of land, which is state regulated, and multiplied by a coefficient, which is differentiated according to tax zones. Tax zones reflect land use, urban versus rural, infrastructure, quality of land, proximity to urban centers, and a host of other factors. To account for inflation, the tax coefficient has been raised several times since 1994: by factors of 2 in 1995, 1.5 in 1996, 2 in 1997, 2 in 1999, and 1.2 in 2000.[24]

Land-tax revenue is divided between local governments and the federal government and is becoming an evermore important source of revenue. Land taxes are divided in the following manner: 50 percent goes to local governments (city, raion), 30 percent goes to the federal budget, and 20 percent is retained by the oblast government.[25] Total revenue generated by land taxes was 9 billion rubles in 1997, 11 billion rubles in 1998, and 18 billion rubles in 1999.[26] More than one-half of land-tax revenue going into the federal budget came from the following areas: city of Moscow; Moscow, Lipetsk, Samara, Rostov, Sverdlovsk, and Chelyabinsk oblasts; and Krasnodar, Stavropol, Kransoyarsk, and Primorsky kraya.[27]

Regional Level

Although Russian land reform was introduced from above and was not the result of pressures from below, unlike the case of Latin American land reform, certain trends have developed that suggest the need to turn our attention to Russia's regions, or away from the capital as the primary actor. The attempt to create a national land market is complicated by regional legal variations in land policy and, of course, by different levels of supply and demand for land, based upon natural and demographic factors.

Legal Variations

Russia's regions may be grouped into three categories based upon the type of land laws they have enacted. The first group has adopted laws that permit private land ownership and the buying and selling of land, including agricultural land. Examples of these regions include Ryazan, Rostov, Volgograd, Saratov, and Samara oblasts, as well as the Republic of Tatarstan.[28] By early 1999, more than fifty regions had adopted legislation that confirmed the right to private land ownership.

The second group of regions does not forbid private ownership by law, but it also does not allow it and relevant legislation is absent. The third group consists of regions that forbid the private ownership of land as well as its purchase or sale. Thirteen regions in Russia, mostly in the far north or Muslim-dominated regions, prohibit the ownership of land, which is contrary to the federal Constitution.[29] Cognizant of these regional disparities, on a visit to Orel oblast in April 2000, President-elect Vladimir Putin called for the passage of a land code establishing the right to own land, while the degree of freedom to pursue this right would be determined by each region individually. This option might hold the best promise if the federal-level stalemate is not resolved.

The land legislation adopted in Saratov oblast is the most well known. After lengthy discussions and the receipt of more than two thousand suggestions from companies and individuals in the oblast, of which 220 were incorporated into the draft legislation, the Duma in Saratov oblast adopted the law on land on 12 November 1997, by a vote of 26 to 3. A few days later, the governor of the oblast, D. Ayatskov, signed the law, which put it into effect. The Saratov law was unique for liberalizing the terms of land sales. This legislation reconfirmed the right of private ownership, including agricultural land, and permitted the free sale of land held as private property. According to the Saratov law, owners of land shares in collective farms and their juridical successors would be allowed to sell their shares to whomever they desired in accordance with article 250 of the 1994 Civil Code. The Saratov law allows the sale of privately held land to any other person or organization. In Saratov oblast there were 6,500 land transactions in 1997, and another 2,900 in 1998.[30] However, land market conditions in Saratov are not entirely unrestricted. For example, to purchase agricultural land, a person must be at least sixteen years old and have either an agricultural education or have worked in agriculture. Foreigners are allowed only to lease land, and cannot purchase land or obtain ownership through other means (Article 44). Only privately owned land may be sold,

Table 4.3

Results of 104 Land Auctions in Saratov Oblast as of 1 January 1999

Intended Use	Number of Land Plots Available for Auction	Number of Land Plots Purchased	Percentage of Land Plots Purchased/ Offered	Average Size of Purchased Plot (hectares)
Individual housing construction	388	149	38	.21
Small-scale gardening	64	41	64	.73
Construction of trade and nonmanufacturing facilities	408	246	60	.11
Construction of social, cultural-service buildings	56	38	68	.46
Agriculture	174	68	39	72.15
Construction of manufacturing facilities	14	2	14	1.32
Totals	1,104	544	49	9.22

Sources: Roskomzem, *Gosudarstvennyy (natsional'nyy) doklad o sostoyanii i ispol'zovanii zemel' Rossiyskoy Federatsii v 1998 godu* (Moscow: Committee on Land, 1999), 59, and authors' calculations.

not state or municipal land (Article 45). Leased land, land held in unlimited use, or land held in lifetime use with rights of inheritance cannot be sold (Article 81). Finally, agricultural land has to be used for agricultural purposes (Article 87).

Following the introduction of the land law in Saratov, a series of land auctions took place throughout the oblast. Not all land put up for auction was actually purchased. By early 1999, only about one-half of land plots offered for sale were purchased, which reflects the limited purchasing power of individuals. The Saratov land auctions were different from the auctions under the terms of the Nizhniy Novgorod farm privatization program[31] in that land was sold for money. Further, the land was not divided up prior to the auction as in Nizhniy, where land auctions only resolved competing claims to a particular plot of land. Table 4.3, which is based on data from Roskomzem, shows the most popular uses of land purchased through the Saratov oblast auction.

The most common use of purchased land in Saratov was for the construction of buildings used for retail and wholesale trade and entrepreneurial activities. The plot size involved in these purchases was very small, averaging only 100 square meters. All plot sizes involved in land purchases were very small with the exception of transactions involving agricultural land, which had the largest average size, slightly more than 72 hectares. Following the lead of Saratov, other regions held land auctions for rural land as well. One example was Moscow oblast where, in the fall of 1998, agricultural land was auctioned off, although for a fraction of the price that was received in Saratov.[32]

Regional Market Development

In addition to legal differences, the Russian land market reflects regional variations in the degree of market development. To measure that variation, the 1995–96 and 1997–98 surveys asked agricultural experts,[33] "In your oblast, at what stage of development is the land market?" The results are presented in Table 4.4.

Despite regional variations, the data clearly suggest progress in the development of a land market from the first to the second survey. Very few experts felt that a developed market already existed in their oblast. However, a higher percentage of experts responded in the second survey that a land market existed but was not developed, or that a market was beginning to form. There was also a decrease in the percentage of experts who felt that no land market existed in their oblast. Volgograd was the only region in which the majority of experts felt that a land market did not exist.[34] Regional variations in supply and demand are summarized in Table 4.5 below.

The figures in Table 4.5 show the number of persons per 1,000 inhabitants who expressed a desire to buy, sell, or lease land (either in or out). Despite progress in the land market, which was shown in Table 4.4, the figures in Table 4.5 reflect the relatively weak development of the land market in the regions where the survey was conducted. In all regions, both the gross and net number of people wanting to buy, sell, or lease land totaled less than 1 percent.

Individual Level

Legal institutions and regions aside, it is a truism, but worth repeating, that the development of the land market depends on the orientations and behaviors of individuals. Therefore, one of the most important questions affecting the outcome of land reform concerns the receptivity of the Russian population to land reform from above. During the 1990s, the notion that Russians are at best ambivalent about private ownership of land seemed to be conventional wisdom. For example, upon President Putin's suggestion

Table 4.4

Experts' Opinions on Stage of Development of Land Market by Region (percent)

Level of Development of Land Market	1995–96 Entire Sample	1997–98 Sample	1997–98 Volgograd	1997–98 Voronezh	1997–98 Ivanovo	1997–98 Kaluga	1997–98 Novgorod	1997–98 Perm	1997–98 Tula
Developed market exists	.2	.7	0	5	0	0	0	0	0
Market exists, but is not developed	14.9	19.7	31.6	25.0	5.9	9.5	5.0	45.0	15.0
Market has begun to form, but land turnover is very small	47.7	51.1	26.3	60.0	52.9	52.4	50.0	45.0	70.0
No land market exists in our region	30.4	21.9	42.1	5.0	23.5	23.8	45.0	10.0	5.0
Too hard to answer	6.8	6.6	0	5.0	17.6	14.3	0	0	10.0

Sources: 1995–96 and 1997–98 surveys, and authors' calculations.

Table 4.5

Balance of Land Supply and Demand by Regions, 1997–98 Survey

*Net Number of Persons Indicating
a Desire to Buy/Sell Land per 1,000 Inhabitants*

Oblast	Oblast Center	City	Urban Settlement	Countryside
Volgograd	−13	−55	63	164
Voronezh	−7	−11	−14	−31
Ivanovo	29	−51	−27	−14
Kaluga	−3	−11	28	−92
Moscow	—	24	54	0
Novgorod	41	−10	−42	37
Perm	13	5	27	62
Tula	14	−14	34	−60
Totals	74	−123	123	−66

*Net Number of Persons Indicating
a Desire to Lease Land (In or Out) per 1,000 Inhabitants*

Oblast	Oblast Center	City	Urban Settlement	Countryside
Volgograd	66	−27	−132	−98
Voronezh	93	5	−12	31
Ivanovo	−10	0	38	30
Kaluga	−6	−1	47	5
Moscow	—	47	0	−6
Novgorod	80	115	0	−36
Perm	70	28	16	−62
Tula	−210	296	35	0
Totals	89	463	−8	−130

Note: Negative value reflects land shortage (demand exceeded supply), while positive values reflect land surplus (more supply than demand).
Sources: 1995–96 and 1997–98 surveys, and authors' calculations.

for a referendum on land, the governor of Samara oblast stated that "at the present time, about 75–80 percent of Russians are against private land ownership because they do not understand, do not know, what private ownership of land will give."[35]

Using 1997–98 survey data, in the following we clarify individual orientations about land and the land market along three dimensions: (1) overall preferences of buying/selling versus leasing; (2) differences in attitudes toward land ownership by landowners, land sellers, and experts; and (3) diverse individual motivations for buying and selling land.

Individual Preferences: Buying/Selling versus Leasing

The first aspect to consider is the question of land leasing versus buying. For a variety of reasons, land leasing has been a primary characteristic of the Russian land market during the early years. Individuals were often interested in leasing rather than purchasing land. Rural land often was undesirable, as owners did not want to invest in the land; buyers found it difficult to obtain financing for large purchases; and prospective owners did not want to risk losing the land through confiscation.[36]

Therefore, an important finding of the 1997–98 survey is that the buying and selling of land is by far the most preferred type of transaction among experts. This orientation was true across all eight regions. Buying and selling were at least twice as popular as leasing, and the fact that all regions registered similar responses suggests that buying and selling of land will continue to increase in importance in the future, providing an important impetus to the land market. Experts' responses about the type of land transaction they themselves were prepared to become involved are shown in Table 4.6.

Across all eight regions, the buying and selling of land is more popular than leasing. Interestingly, to be a lessee was more popular than to be a lessor, perhaps because of complications in calculating land taxes or collecting rents. We should mention, however, that our conclusion about preferences for buying/selling land over leasing remains somewhat of an open question and other evidence contradicts that which is presented here. A survey of privatized farms that had adopted the Nizhniy Novgorod model of farm privatization by the Agrarian Institute in Moscow found that land shareholders overwhelmingly preferred to lease their land shares. In a survey of privatized farms in five regions where farms had privatized, on average 85 percent of land shares were leased out.[37] Only 0.1 percent of land shares were sold to enterprises or privatized companies, and 0.2 percent were sold between individuals.[38] A previous pilot survey (first wave, 1993–94) of pri-

Table 4.6

Experts' Preferences for Type of Land Transaction by Region, 1997–98 Survey (percent)

Preference	Volgograd	Voronezh	Ivanovo	Kaluga	Moscow	Novgorod	Perm	Tula
Sell land	63.4	82.3	88.9	77.1	90.7	82.8	84.7	79.3
Buy land	70.1	69.0	86.3	72.5	87.1	77.5	86.4	71.2
Lease land out	36.6	17.7	11.1	22.9	9.3	17.2	15.3	20.7
Lease land in	29.9	31.0	13.7	27.5	12.9	22.5	13.6	28.8

Sources: 1997–98 survey, and authors' calculations.

vatized farms in Rostov oblast by the same institute found that income from leasing accounted for 35 percent of farm workers' income, making it the single largest component of income, and thus more than wage payments from the farm or private plot income. In addition, 24 percent of pensioners' income came from the leasing of land shares, third in importance after pension payments and income from private plot production.[39]

Individuals' Attitudes Toward Land Ownership

A crucial issue is whether the policies advocated by the federal center have resonance among individuals. In particular, one of the most contentious policy questions has been over the private ownership of land. The attitudes of rural Russians are especially important, since they have been perceived as less supportive of market reform, more wary of privatization, and suspicious of a land market. A World Bank survey conducted in five regions in 1994 found that 80 percent of farm managers

> expressed a negative opinion of the option to allow buying and selling of land in Russia. . . . Managers' opinions regarding land markets are roughly consistent with those of employees surveyed, although employees are slightly more supportive of land markets. . . . On the whole, it appears that many people in rural Russia do not consider marketability as a necessary attribute of private ownership of land.[40]

The Russian Center for Public Opinion Research, which publishes the journal *Monitorig obshchestvennogo mneniya: ekonomicheskiye i sotsial'nyye peremeny*, has consistently reported since 1994 that rural Russians favor stopping market reforms more than do urban residents. According to these reports, rural residents perceive their families' living conditions to be inferior compared to urban areas, and are generally less optimistic about the future. Clearly, the wording of a survey question is of crucial importance, and thus questions about perceptions toward "market reforms" often connote inflation, declines in standard of living, decreased consumption, and other assorted negative consequences in the mind of the respondent. More specific questions about land, however, paint a different picture. Survey data on the desirability of private ownership of land are presented in Table 4.7.

Table 4.7, based on 1997–98 data, shows a high degree of support for private ownership of land among three groups of respondents. Elite responses were more conservative than those of buyers and sellers, although the differences were not statistically significant. According to the survey, 90

Table 4.7

Attitudes Toward Private Ownership of Land of Sellers, Buyers, and Experts, 1997–98 Survey

Survey Item/Responses	Sellers		Buyers		Experts	
	%	(*n*)	%	(*n*)	%	(*n*)
Should private ownership of land be permitted?						
Yes, without any limitations	27.8	(761)	30.7	(841)	12.8	(16)
Yes, but with some limitations	53.7	(1,469)	54.9	(1,503)	71.2	(107)
No, there should not be ownership of land	10.1	(277)	7.1	(195)	13.5	(11)
Too hard to answer	8.1	(221)	6.8	(187)	2.2	(2)
No answer	0.2	(6)	0.5	(13)	0.4	(1)

Sources: 1997–98 survey, and authors' calculations.

percent of land sellers, 93 percent of buyers, and 86.5 percent of experts responded that there should be a land market. For all three groups of respondents, the most preferred form of private land ownership is ownership with some restrictions. Available data also allow us to subdivide attitudes toward the land market, depending on whether the land in question is rural or urban. Elite attitudes on land market types are shown in Table 4.8.

Table 4.8 shows that there is support for a land market. Eighty-one percent of the experts supported some type of rural land market. There was very little support, however, for an unregulated rural land market, and the overwhelming preference (76 percent of respondents) was for a rural land market with restrictions. Less than one in five (17.5 percent) answered that a rural land market was not needed at all.

There was a high level of support for an urban land market as well; 82.5 percent supported some type of land market in these areas. Support was much higher for an unregulated urban land market, supported by 19 percent of respondents, than there was for an unregulated rural land market. A lower percentage of respondents, 63.5 percent, said that there should be a restricted urban land market. There were also fewer respondents who felt no urban land market was needed, just 12 percent. Elite preferences reflect the entrenched belief that land should belong to those who work it, and that agricultural land should remain in agricultural use. Elite responses also suggest that it will be much easier to liberalize the urban than the rural land market, a process that is already underway.[41]

Survey data allow us to view support for private ownership of land for both buyers and sellers according to the form of ownership of the enter-

Table 4.8

Experts' Opinions on Type of Land Market Needed by Region, 1997–98 Survey (percent)

Land Market Type Preferences	Volgograd	Voronezh	Ivanovo	Kaluga	Novgorod	Perm	Tula	Entire Sample
Agricultural								
No restrictions	10.5	0	11.8	0	0	10.0	5.0	5.1
Some restrictions	73.7	80.0	47.1	81.0	80.0	85.0	80.0	75.9
No land market	15.8	20.0	41.2	14.3	20.0	5.0	10.0	17.5
Can't answer	0	0	0	4.7	0	0	5.0	1.5
Nonagricultural								
No restrictions	26.3	40.0	0	9.5	25.0	20.0	10.0	19.0
Some restrictions	52.6	45.0	82.4	71.4	60.0	75.0	60.0	63.5
No land market	21.1	15.0	11.8	4.8	15.0	0	20.0	12.4
Can't answer	0	0	5.8	14.3	0	5.0	10.0	5.1

Sources: 1997–98 survey, and authors' calculations.

Table 4.9

Attitudes of Land Buyers Toward Land Ownership, 1997–98 Survey (percent)

	Management in State Enterprise	Workers in State Enterprise	Workers in Nonstate Enterprise
Should private ownership of land be permitted?			
Yes, without any limitations	26.3	25.0	33.7
Yes, but with some limitations	58.7	56.0	55.3
No, there should not be ownership of land	7.7	10.7	5.5
Too hard to answer	6.9	7.5	5.2
No answer	.4	.7	.2

Sources: 1997–98 surveys, and authors' calculations.

prise where the respondent worked. These responses are shown in Tables 4.9 and 4.10.

Tables 4.9 and 4.10 indicate that land sellers were slightly more liberal—defined as favoring land ownership without limitations more than land ownership with some limitations—than land buyers. The tables also indicate that workers in state enterprises (both buyers and sellers) were somewhat more conservative than managers and workers in nonstate enterprises, using the same definition. It is interesting to note that except for workers in state enterprises who own land, managers and workers who were landowners favored private ownership of land *less* than did land buyers. The basic conclusion from these tables is that there is a high level of support for private land ownership from buyers and sellers across enterprise type, although both groups prefer land ownership with some restrictions.

Individual Motivations: Why Buyers Buy and Why Sellers Sell

We have seen there is a high degree of support for land privatization, that several hundred land transactions occur in Russia annually, and that most of these transactions involve very small plots of land. Why are individuals motivated to obtain land? What is their intended use of this land? Why do sellers sell their land? The answers to these questions are important for they define the nature of the Russian land market.

Previous survey data suggested that land ownership was not seen as economically advantageous and risky as an investment. In the 1995–96 survey

Table 4.10

Attitudes of Land Sellers Toward Land Ownership, 1997–98 Survey (percent)

	Management in State Enterprise	Workers in State Enterprise	Workers in Nonstate Enterprise
Should private ownership of land be permitted?			
Yes, without any limitations	33.1	26.0	32.9
Yes, but with some limitations	47.3	59.1	50.5
No, there should not be ownership of land	15.0	7.5	9.5
Too hard to answer	4.6	7.2	6.9
No answer	0	.2	.3

Sources: 1997–98 survey, and authors' calculations.

by the Institute of Sociology in Kaluga, respondents were asked, "Where is it advantageous to invest money?" One-third of buyers but only 12 percent of sellers answered "to buy land." The most advantageous sphere was the resale of goods, followed by the resale of homes and apartments. In the 1997–98 survey, respondents were asked which sphere of economic activity was "most advantageous." Regarding land, the situation had worsened, with only 13 percent of experts, 10 percent of buyers, and 8 percent of sellers answering "to trade land."[42] Thus, attitudes toward land ownership as an investment in land deteriorated in the time between the two surveys. What do these responses mean for the Russian land market?

It is important to bear in mind that the speculative side of the land market has always been quite small, as the 1995–96 survey clearly showed. In that survey, land buyers were grouped into four subcategories:

- Operators, who obtained land for the conduct of small-scale agriculture, such as collective vegetable and fruit gardens. Operators comprised 60 percent of the responses.
- *Dachniki,* who were largely urban residents looking for a place for rest and relaxation for family members. Dachniki comprised 20 percent of the responses.
- Owners, who were motivated to obtain land in order to pass it to their heirs or to protect themselves from inflation. Owners comprised 17 percent to 18 percent of the responses.
- Speculators, who obtained land for the sole purpose of resale. Speculators comprised 2.5 percent of the responses.[43]

Thus, the Russian land market has not been defined by land speculation or by land as a tradable commodity. Instead, land users drive the land mar-

Table 4.11

Reasons for Obtaining Land, 1995–96 and 1997–98 Surveys (percent)

Intended Use of Land	1995–96 Entire Survey	1997–98 Entire Survey	1997–98 Buyers	1997–98 Lessees
Agricultural production for consumption	58.9	68.4	72.6	54.2
Family relaxation	40.8	28.5	34.7	7.1
Construction of country home, cottage	28.5	19.6	23.3	7.0
Production of agricultural products for sale	19.5	12.4	8.7	25.2
Provide services	—	7.7	5.7	14.6
Production of nonagricultural goods for sale	—	2.5	2.0	4.2
Construction business	—	2.2	2.0	2.6
Resale of land	—	2.2	2.6	0.6
Leasing of land	—	1.1	1.0	1.1

Note: Percentages do not sum to 100 because some respondents indicated multiple reasons.
Sources: 1995–96 and 1997–98 surveys, and authors' calculations.

ket. Consequently, the important questions are: Why do buyers buy land? What are the intended uses? Survey data are useful for illustrating the primary motivations for obtaining land. The full list of motivations for acquiring land is shown in Table 4.11.

Considering first the 1995–96 and 1997–98 survey results as a whole, for both land buyers and lessees, the most common motivation for obtaining land was for the production of agricultural products intended for consumption. This motivation became stronger between the two surveys, rising from 59 percent to over 68 percent of responses. The second strongest motivation for obtaining land was for family relaxation, although overall the percentage declined in the latter survey from 41 percent to 28.5 percent. The third strongest motivation was for the construction of a country home or cottage, and the fourth most popular motivation was for commercial agriculture.

Interesting differences in motivations emerge when we distinguish between land buyers and land lessees in the 1997–98 survey. Nearly three-quarters of land buyers obtain land to produce agricultural goods for consumption, but only a little over one-half (54 percent) of land lessees do. Nearly 35 percent of land buyers wanted to buy land for family relaxation, but only 7 percent of land lessees. Conversely, the second strongest motivation for land lessees was for commercial agriculture, indicated by 25 percent of respondents, while only 9 percent of land buyers obtained land for

Table 4.12

Reasons for Selling Land, 1995–96 and 1997–98 Surveys (percent)

	1995–96	1997–98
Need for money	48.0	62.7
Land requires large capital investments	18.8	14.5
No time to tend to plot	16.7	15.5
High transportation costs to reach plot	14.4	17.6
Cheaper to buy than to grow food	—	13.0

Note: Percentages do not add to 100 because some respondents indicate multiple reasons.
Sources: 1995–96 and 1997–98 surveys, and authors' calculations.

this purpose. Thus, both land buyers and lessees obtain land to raise food for their families, but beyond that motivation, land buyers wanted to obtain land for family relaxation while land lessees wanted to conduct agricultural operations for resale. Lessees are also twice as likely to use land to provide services as land buyers. Thus, land buyers and lessees have a different ordering of motivations and differing strengths of motivations. Lessees look at land as a means to make money, adopting a more temporary approach to land use, while land buyers have a more permanent stake in their land plot.

Turning to the supply side, the survey data in Table 4.12 indicate why sellers sell their land. It appears that the primary motivation is monetary.

In both surveys the overwhelming motivation for the sale of a land plot was the need for money, indicated by 48 percent in the 1995–96 survey and 63 percent in the 1997–98 survey. Other reasons were grouped together but trailed far behind the need for money. Respondents indicated that the sale of a land plot raised money needed for an expensive personal expenditure such as an apartment, car, or furniture, accounting for 39 percent of responses. Secondary reasons were to repay a debt (22 percent of responses), or for bank investments (20 percent). Interestingly, proceeds from land sales were seldom used for everyday expenses such as food or clothing, cited by only 7.5 percent of the respondents. The data therefore suggest a basic inclination to hold onto land plots unless a special need arises.

Conclusion and Prospects

In contrast to the Soviet period, private ownership of land exists and large numbers of land transactions are occurring annually in Russia. In a previous article, Wegren argued that Russia had land transactions, but not really a land market.[44] In general, we agree with that assessment, but upon deeper reflection it seems that Russia has begun to develop a land market as well, thus representing real and significant change from the Soviet period. We would argue that "market" conditions exist for the following reasons:

- The state does not regulate the price at which land may be bought or sold; rather, supply, demand, and other market based features influence the price of land.
- Individuals have benefited from the changes in land laws. People have become empowered to buy land or not, expand land plots to whatever size they wish, lease, bequeath, or even give away their land. It is their choice.
- While the purpose of the land market is to transfer land to more productive and efficient users, it is premature to conclude that even with small plots being traded this process is not occurring. Data do not exist to answer this question at present, but it would be unwise to conclude that such is not the case. Future research may be able to shed further light on this issue.

In this chapter, three levels of analysis were used to further our understanding of the Russian land market. At the federal level, we saw that a stalemate over the land code is now in its seventh year. Despite optimism that a new land code version, along the lines introduced by the SPS early in 2000, will ultimately be approved, the best hope for the development of the Russian land market may lie with Putin's suggestion to allow regions to decide the question of land sales. The upside of that strategy would be the adoption of a land code that would then permit the passage of other land-related legislation that has been languishing. The consequence of that strategy would be increased economic discrepancies in investments and attraction of foreign capital among regions. Such regional differences may be the spark that laggard regional governments need to adopt more progressive legislation. From a political standpoint, it is important to note that there is significant popular support for a regulated agricultural land market. If separate laws, independent of the land code, were adopted that regulated the agricultural land market, it would represent congruence between elite and mass attitudes, and thus present real opportunities to build rural support. Elite versus mass attitudes about the rural market during the Yeltsin period were conflictual.

Regarding the national land market, several trends that recently emerged are likely to continue:

- The municipal market will continue to decline and the number of transactions in the private market will increase.

- Market transactions will be more popular than nonmarket transactions.
- The size of land plots involved in land transactions will continue to be very small.
- Revenue from land taxes will become an increasingly significant source of revenue for government.

Regional variations in legal provisions are unlikely to be removed and in fact may endure for quite some time if Putin pursues a "states' rights" policy to the land question. With or without regional legal variations, there are differences in the development of regional land markets, and these too are unlikely to be abated owing to vast differences in economic and political climates, as well as to differences in land quality, resource base, and level of development.

At the individual level, the preference to purchase land is likely to increase if the legal environment can be clarified, either through regional legislation or a national land code. Support for private ownership of land is also likely to continue to increase. Too many Russian families already own land shares or possess land deeds for the clock to be turned back. However, it is unlikely that an unregulated land market will become the primary preference in the near future. If a referendum on land is held, the outcome is likely to support a regulated market, and in that respect liberals have misread popular attitudes and are likely to be disappointed if they expect popular support for their position.

Moreover, the size of land plots involved in land transactions are likely to remain very small, and in that respect it is hard to imagine the land market leading to social or economic transformation in the short term. Even if a new land code is adopted that allows relatively unregulated sales of land, we should not expect that land investors are anxiously waiting for a legal breakthrough to jump in and start buying up large tracts of land for resale. As seen in the surveys, land ownership simply for resale is not considered economically advantageous, and land speculators are not likely to become a significant segment of the overall land market, although certainly their impact will be emphasized in the national media. The land market has been, is, and is likely to remain, a market of land users.

The biggest question, and the biggest unknown, is what effect an economic rebound will have on individual motivations to buy or sell land. It is hard to predict what behaviors will emerge under different economic conditions, but the survey data considered herein were very instructive in illustrating motivations behind land transactions and the way Russians view uses of land. It has been commonly assumed that as the Russian economy rebounds and personal incomes increase the land market will benefit, but our survey data suggest that assumption may be wrong. If personal incomes rise, one would expect greater purchasing power on the part of buyers for larger land plots or to increase the number of land transactions in general. Demand for land might in fact increase. But along with increased incomes, the primary motivation to obtain land—to grow food for the family—would decrease. It would be easier, and more affordable, to purchase food than to grow it. Thus, it is not clear what impact higher incomes would have on demand.

On the supply side, there are also more questions than answers about the effects of rising incomes. First, land sales involve very small plots of land, and sale prices are relatively low. As seen in the survey data, the three most popular types of land sales were for small-scale collective gardening, operation of private plots, and individual housing construction. The mean size of the land plot involved in these transactions was 100 square meters for individual housing construction, 230 square meters for private plot operations, and seven square meters for collective gardening.[45] Of course, regional land prices vary, sometimes considerably, especially around the largest cities, but average land price data for transactions between individuals in 1998 illustrate the small sums of money that are generated from land sales. In 1998, using mean land plot size per transaction and mean land price (a weighted mean including both urban and rural land prices), the sale of a land plot for individual housing construction would generate 1,650 rubles, 115 rubles from the sale of a private plot, and 47.6 rubles from the sale of a collective garden plot.[46] If personal incomes rise, then the relative monetary benefit from land sales will decrease, which in turn may lead individuals to retain their land plots. Moreover, if personal incomes increase, individuals might be able to pay for expensive purchases without the sale of land, which would reduce the amount of land available for purchase. Thus, increased personal incomes may have the unintended effect of reducing the supply of land for sale.

Notes

1. For a summary of the legislation and the process by which land was received free, see *Krest'yanskaya rossiya*, 29 November–5 December 1999, 2.

2. *Krest'yanskiye vedomosti*, 8–14 March 1999, 2.

3. A. Petrikov and V. Uzun, "Zemel'nyye otnosheniya: problemy i resheniya," *APK: ekonomika, upravleniye* 6 (June 1999): 9.

4. In order: Stephen K. Wegren, "The Development of Market Relations in Agricultural Land: The Case of Kostroma Oblast," *Post-Soviet Geography* 36 (October 1995): 496–512;

Stephen K. Wegren, "Land Reform and the Land Market in Russia: Operation, Constraints, and Prospects," *Europe-Asia Studies* 49 (1997): 959–87; Karen Brooks and Zvi Lerman, *Agricultural Reform in Russia: A View from the Farm Level*, World Bank Discussion Paper 327 (Washington, DC: World Bank, 1996); and Stephen K. Wegren and Vladimir R. Belen'kiy, "The Political Economy of the Russian Land Market," *Problems of Post-Communism* 45 (July–August 1998): 56–66.

5. Institute of Land Relations and Land Tenure and Institute of Sociology (Kaluga oblast), *Formirovaniye rynka zemli v Rossii: regional'nyye aspekty* (Kaluga: Institute of Sociology, 1997).

6. V. Belen'kiy, "Menyaya sotsialisticheskiy zemel'nyy uklad," *Voprosy ekonomiki* 11 (November 1997): 46–59; and Wegren and Belen'kiy, "Political Economy of the Russian Land Market."

7. The number of respondents by region for both surveys is available from the authors.

8. Zvi Lerman and Karen Brooks, "Russia's Legal Framework for Land Reform and Farm Restructuring," *Problems of Post-Communism* 43 (November–December 1996): 48–58.

9. The Communist Party objected to the right of private ownership, while Russia's Choice objected to restrictions on the sale and purchase of land.

10. V. Plotnikov, "Zemel'nyi kodeks—osnova zemel'nogo prava," *APK: ekonomika, upravleniye* 5 (May 2000): 9.

11. *Krest'yanskaya rossiya*, 15–21 July 1996, 1.

12. *Krest'yanskiye vedomosti*, 29 September–5 October 1997, 2.

13. *Sel'skaya zhizn'*, 21 February 1998, 1.

14. Plotnikov, "Zemel'nyi kodeks," 17–18.

15. *Sel'skaya zhizn'*, 24 December 1998, 1.

16. *Sel'skaya zhizn'*, 16–22 March 2000, 1.

17. *Sel'skaya zhizn'*, 22–28 June 2000, 2.

18. *Sel'skaya zhizn'*, 11 July 2000, 1.

19. In "Political Economy of the Russian Land Market" (60–61), Wegren and Belen'kiy presented data on land purchases during the 1993–95 period.

20. Roskomzem (State Committee of the Russian Federation on Land), *Gosudarstvennyy (natsional'nyy) doklad o sostoyanii i ispol'zovanii zemel' Rossiyskoy Federatsii v 1998 godu* (Moscow: Committee on Land, 1999), 60.

21. Ibid.

22. For an analysis of the 1992 law and its revisions of 1994, see I. Vyskrebentsev, "Plata za zemliu," *APK: ekonomika, upravleniye* 8 (August 1995): 38–49.

23. A "normative price" was defined as the price below which land could not be sold. If the market price was higher it would be sold for the market price. If the market price was lower the selling price would revert to the state-defined normative price. For more detail, see Wegren, "Land Reform and the Land Market in Russia."

24. *Krest'yanskaya rossiya*, 31 January 6–February 2000, 5. For the interested reader, this source also specifies tax rates per square meter according to type of land and intended use.

25. In addition, land transaction fees were important until the Civil Code entered into force. Prior to the Civil Code, transaction fees for notarial services could equal up to 3 percent of the value of the transaction (on a sliding scale depending on the value of the transaction). This fee and the notarization of the transaction were a legal requirement for the transaction to be considered valid. Following the introduction of the Civil Code in late 1994, the transaction fee no longer was obligatory and now depends on the willingness of the participants in the transaction.

26. *Krest'yanskiye vedomosti*, 7–13 February 2000, 3.

27. Roskomzem, *Gosudarstvennyy*, 62.

28. S. I. Gerasin, "Pravovaya baza reformirovaniya zemel'nykh otnosheniiy v sel'skom khozyaystve (obzor regional'nykh zakonodatel'nykh aktov)," *Gosudarstvo i pravo* 12 (December 1998): 70–71.

29. E. Ivankina and I. Rtishchev, "Osobennosti zemel'nogo zakonodatel'stva v Rossiiskikh regionakh," *Voprosy ekonomiki* 7 (July 2000): 77, 82.

30. V. Prokopchuk, "Zakon Saratovskoy oblasti 'O Zemle,' " *APK: ekonomika, upravleniye* 12 (December 1999): 12.

31. A detailed description of the Nizhniy Novgorod farm privatization program is found in Stephen K. Wegren, *Agriculture and the State in Soviet and Post-Soviet Russia* (Pittsburgh, PA: University of Pittsburgh Press, 1998), 94–106.

32. *Sel'skaya zhizn'*, 3 November 1998, 1.

33. "Agricultural experts" include farm managers, agricultural officials in regional governments, and academics who focus on agriculture.

34. The likely reason is that in 1997 a legal basis was absent. In mid-2000, the regional administration had expressed its support for private ownership of land and was drafting a regional law on land. Ivankina and Rtishchev, "Osobennosti zemel'nogo," 82.

35. *Krest'yanskaya rossiya*, 6–12 March 2000, 2.

36. Under present law, agricultural land that is left idle, damaged ecologically, or not used properly is subject to confiscation.

37. The oblasts included Nizhniy Novgorod, Orel, Rostov, Kirov, and Volgograd.

38. V. Ia. Uzun, ed., *Sotsial'no-ekonomicheskiy analiz rezul'tatov reorganizatsii sel'skokhoziaistvennykh predpriiatii* (Moscow: Entsiklopediia rossiiskikh dereven', 1999), 32–33.

39. V. Ia. Uzun, ed., *Sotsial'no-ekonomicheskie posledstviia privatizatsii zemli i reorganizatsii sel'skokhoziaistvennykh predpriyatii (1994–1996 gg.)* (Moscow: Entsiklopediia rossiyskiy dereven', 1997), 84.

40. Brooks and Lerman, *Agricultural Reform in Russia*, 34.

41. An "experimental" sale of urban land was announced in Zelenograd (Moscow oblast) in late 1999, to be carried out in 2000. See *Krest'yanskiye vedomosti*, 11–17 October 1999, 3.

42. The respondents were also asked to identify the least risky economic activity. Trading of goods was the first choice of land buyers, sellers, and experts, followed by trading of homes, apartments, and banking activities. Trading land was seen as risky by each of the three groups, and the only response considered more risky than trading land was the production of industrial goods.

43. Wegren and Belen'kiy, "Political Economy of the Russian Land Market," 62.

44. Wegren, "Development of Market Relations in Agricultural Land."

45. Roskomzem, *Gosudarstvennyy*, 60.

46. Ibid., 61.

5

Rural Household Behavior, 1991–2001

VALERI V. PATSIORKOVSKI

Since the collapse of the Soviet Union, most Western observers have agreed that major structural changes must be made in the organization of Russian agriculture if it is going to compete in a global economy. The question remains, how can such a restructuring occur within the constraints of the historical and contemporary Russian economic, political, and social situations?

In order to truly transform rural institutions to support a market-based agriculture, it will be necessary to develop the core social organizational unit in the Russian countryside, the *krest'ianskoe khoziaistvo* or peasant household. The peasant household is more than just an agricultural production system. Its human and social capital have the potential to play a central role in the development of the social and cultural infrastructure that is necessary to build the civil society that will support both a market farm economy and a democratic society. At the end of 1998, peasant households produced 57 percent of total Russian agricultural output. In 1992, the proportion of agricultural output accounted for by households was only 32 percent, but it has increased every year from 1991 to 2000. During the same time period, the share of agricultural output contributed by the large enterprises, the former *kolkhozy* (collective farms) and *sovkhozy* (state farms), declined from 67 to 41 percent.[1]

In 1999, the Moskovski Obshestveni Nauchnii Fond (Moscow Public Science Foundation) funded a survey that examined the adaptation of households following the financial collapse in Russia in fall 1998. This sur-

116

vey was the fourth wave of a panel survey of households in three rural villages. The three previous waves, from 1995 through 1997 were funded by the National Science Foundation. (See chapter 14 by O'Brien and chapter 16 by Dershem for more details on the 1995–97 panel studies.) A comparison of the 1995–97 data with the 1999 data shows five statistical associations between the economic collapse and the economic behavior of rural Russian households:

- Increasing agricultural production (from 8,236 weighted kg in 1997 to 8,765 weighted kg in 1997) and sales (3,630 weighted kg in 1997 to 4,463 weighted kg in 1999). (A weighted kilogram is a standardized measure for the purpose of statistical comparison across product type.)
- Increasing amount of rented land, from an average of 0.12 hectares per household in 1997 to 0.40 hectares per household in 1999.
- A nearly threefold increase in the overall mean adjusted income, when including both monetized and nonmonetized sources (from 512.1 rubles per month in 1997 to an average of 1,524.7 rubles per month in 1999).
- Increasing household differentiation of income (coefficient of differentiation went from 5.6 in 1997 to 10.2 in 1999).
- Using only monetized income, an increase in poverty from 69.8 percent of households in 1997 to 82.9 percent of households in 1999. However, when both monetized and nonmonetized income sources are included, the percentage of households living in poverty actually decreased, from 28.9 percent in 1997 to 17.1 percent in 1999.

The growing importance of peasant households in agricultural production means that we cannot ignore this basic social organizational structure of Russian life. At the same time, however, it will be impossible to modernize peasant household production and bring at least a portion of these households into mainstream, global sustainable agrieconomic systems unless there are fundamental changes in the institutional structure of Russian rural villages. This will require major changes in relationships among households, large enterprises, and local governments.

Overlooked in the midst of the attention given to land reform and the creation of a new farmer class are small but crucial changes that are occurring in the krest'ianskie khoziaistva. Because there has been virtually no systematic empirical analysis of how peasant households are adapting to the new market economy, these changes are barely known in Moscow, let alone in the West. The development of peasant household production offers hope for the overall development of Russian agriculture because it rests on a solid base of human and social capital.[2]

As noted in chapter 3 by Ioffe and Nefedova, in some regions, especially in the north and far east, there has been a persistent loss of population in rural areas. In other regions, especially in the south and the Volga River region, however, rural populations have been sufficiently strong to support an ample labor supply for agriculture. In total, my colleagues and I have identified five distinctive trends in different rural areas of Russia in the last ten years.[3]

Moreover, even when demographic trends point to future population declines, as in trends toward lower birth rates, there remains sufficient labor in rural households today to increase human capital and, in turn, to increase household production and sales. Rather than importing human and social capital from urban areas, a simpler and more efficient way to develop Russian agriculture is to use existing strengths in the countryside that are found at the household level. In our panel study in three Russian villages from 1995 to 1999, for example, we observed an increase in household labor in spite of the fact that birth rates in the study villages actually declined during this period.[4]

Social capital, which refers mainly to informal and formal helping networks, as well as attachment to the local community, is associated not directly with demographic structure and trends but rather with institutional development in rural areas and in the country as a whole during the post-Soviet period. Chapters 14 and 16 by O'Brien and Dershem, respectively, present empirical data on the development of social capital in Russian villages in recent years.

In order to understand the changing role of the peasant household in Russian agriculture it is necessary to illustrate the structure of institutions in rural Russia during the Soviet period and during the contemporary transition to a market economy. The next two sections of this chapter discuss these institutional changes.

Institutional Structure in the Soviet Period from 1929 to 1990

The relationships between the various institutional elements in the Russian village during the Soviet period are shown in Figure 5.1. This period began with forced collectivization in 1929 and continued until the breakup of the Soviet Union in 1991.

Figure 5.1
Institutional Structure of Rural Life in Soviet Russia

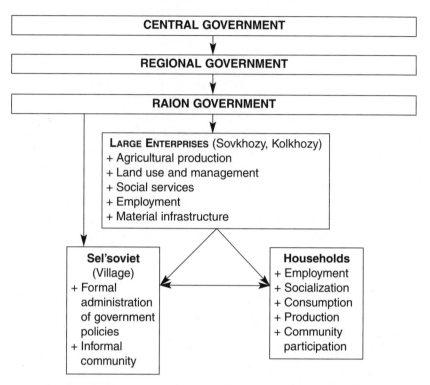

The core institution in the Soviet agricultural system was the large collective and state enterprises, the kolkhozy or sovkhozy. These large enterprises were designed as agricultural factories that received production quotas (*obiazatel'naia postavka*) from government officials. Being outside of a market economy, the managers of these large enterprises were primarily concerned with staying in the good graces of officials at higher levels. Questions concerning where grain or meat was to be processed and sold were handled administratively at higher levels, beginning in Moscow, and then transmitted by decree to the regions, provinces and, eventually, to the large enterprises themselves.

Moreover, the large enterprises also were entrusted with a very diffuse set of responsibilities, including provision of consumer goods through village shops, social services such as health and education, material infrastructure such as roads and utilities, land management, and employment of all able-bodied residents in rural villages. Because of technological advances, Soviet agriculture became more capital intensive over time and thus became less dependent on local village labor. By the end of the Soviet period there was a substantial surplus of labor attached to the kolkhozy and sovkhozy.

In the Soviet system, the local village and the households within it, were expected to do the bidding of the large enterprises. Local villages had two main functions. The formal function provided by the village council, the *sel'soviet*, was to keep records of the demographic structure of the households in the villages, such as births, deaths, and marriages, household plots, and housing. In effect, this served the needs of the large enterprise by keeping track of the condition of its labor force. The informal social function of the village was to provide individuals and households with an opportunity for informal community interaction. In most instances, the village predated Soviet collectivization and provided individuals and families with a psychological and spiritual connection with their ancestors and history.

Households were expected to serve the following five basic functions in the Soviet system:

- Provide labor for the kolkhoz or sovkhoz.
- Socialize children and maintain informal constraints on adults to support the goals of the large enterprise and thereby support the goals of the Soviet state.
- Be consumers within the Soviet command economic system. Their preferences often were not treated with a great deal of respect, especially in comparison to their more politically powerful urban-industrial counterparts.
- Maintain the village community. This was encouraged by the large enterprises because it was necessary to sustain the communal basis of their labor force. The nature of that participation, however, was severely restricted by Soviet fears about competition from nongovernmental associations.
- Keep small plots of land around their house, normally not more than one-third of a hectare, on which they were able to grow food and raise animals for their personal consumption. This provided a positive incentive for households to remain in the countryside, as well as providing a safety valve for the state when production quotas were not met.

There were, however, constant struggles between households and the government on the priority of these functions. The government viewed the households primarily as sources of labor for the kolkhozy and sovkhozy.

Even during the beginning of the Gorbachev period, the official government policy identified household production and income derived from that production as "nonlabor income" (*netrudovye dokhody*). Alternatively, households placed greater emphasis on socialization, consumption, and occasional sales. These different priorities created considerable tension between rural households and the government during the entire Soviet period.

Institutional Structure and Household Survival Strategies in the Post-Soviet Period (1991–99)

Reports on attempts to restructure Russian agriculture, from both Russian and Western sources, usually give the impression that there has not been very much real change since the collapse of the Soviet Union. Since 1990, the executive branch of the Russian federal government (starting under President Boris Yeltsin) has issued a series of decrees that outline a program for selling land to private entities. The legislative branch, the Duma, led by the Communist Party, however, has balked at these decrees and has refused to pass land reform legislation that would be signed by the executive branch. This struggle has resulted in a stalemate that has left people at the local level in a state of uncertainty regarding ownership of land.

Discussions of land reform have centered on breaking up the large enterprises, the kolkhozy and sovkhozy. These efforts, however, have not been very successful. The large enterprises continue to exist, although they have been officially reorganized, usually into a "joint stock company of the closed type" (*tovarishchestvo s ogranichennoi otvetstvennostiu,* or TOO). The TOOs only permit membership and share ownership from collective farm members, and individual members do not have any real input into decision making, which is left to the collective farm chairman. In short, the TOOs are really not that different from the kolkhozy they were supposed to replace.

Despite the aforementioned, there have been some important incremental changes in the institutional relationships in agriculture and rural life in the post-Soviet period, which are summarized in Figure 5.2.

Even though the large enterprises continue to exist, their relationships to the Russian government, villages, and households have changed. Government subsidies to the large enterprises have declined continuously since the breakup of the Soviet Union. As a result, a large proportion, 82 percent in 1997,[5] of the enterprises simply has gone bankrupt. Those that remain must compete in the marketplace. In 1994, the government decreed

Figure 5.2
Institutional Structure of Rural Life in Contemporary Russia

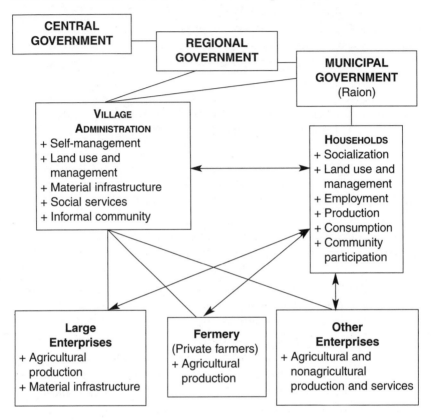

that the large enterprises stop providing social services, although many continue to do so. This has meant that the large enterprises have divested themselves of responsibility for nonagricultural activities, such as support for social services, to the local village council (formerly sel'soviet) or, increasingly, to the private sector.

As shown in Figure 5.1, the large enterprise was the dominant social organizational structure in rural villages during the Soviet period. All other social organizations, including the family and local government, were subordinate to the large enterprise. Moreover, the large enterprise coordinated all relationships between the other organizations in the village.

At present, as shown in Figure 5.2, the local village council mediates between all rural social organizations and the central and provincial governments. The traditional large enterprises currently are one of several enterprises in rural areas. Local government, which is more representative of local village interests than the old sel'soviet, is now the official link between the national and regional governments and the village. Because the federal government has been in an almost constant fiscal crisis since 1991, it has not been able to provide much support for local services and thus, rural villages have experienced an overall decline in social service support. Yet, the informal relationships between individuals and households in the village community continue to exist, although the strength of these relationships has diminished.

One of the new types of enterprises in rural areas is the new private farmers (*fermery*). Fermery are registered as individuals, not as households. The numbers and political influence of this group, however, have remained small. From 1993 to 1994, the number of persons registered as fermery increased from 182,800 to 270,000, but the size of this group increased only slightly in 1995 (279,200) and in 1996 (280,100) and actually decreased in 1998 (274,000). The total amount of land held by officially registered fermery increased from 7.8 million hectares in 1993 to 12.2 million hectares in 1997 (about 6 percent of the arable land in Russia).

The average amount of land farmed by fermery has changed only slightly, from 43 hectares in 1993 to 44 hectares in 1997.[6] Approximately two-thirds of the newly registered fermery in 1991 were urban dwellers who typically had very little direct experience with agriculture. Because of their relatively small impact on total agricultural production, the fermery remain politically weak, which prevents them from exerting a significant influence on national or oblast agricultural policies.

The inability to induce families to become private farmers is based in part on the failure of the federal government to resolve the land tenure problem. Ordinary rural Russians, who are rational economic actors, have very reasonable fears that if they buy land they may end up losing it, paying some type of penalty for it at a later point in time, or both. There are, however, four other obstacles faced by private farmers. First, the general economic uncertainty in Russia reinforces a natural caution that peasant households have with regard to risk.

Second, there is a lack of suitable infrastructure for small-scale processing plants and lack of support for small business services. Third, high tax rates create further disincentives to officially register as fermery. Finally, families that become disconnected from the large enterprises no longer can receive valuable benefits, such as discounted meals in the TOO cafeteria or help in getting supplies and inputs for agricultural operations. As a result, most peasant households operate in an informal economy in which their income is shielded from the official tax collection agencies.

The functions of the household in rural areas have changed from the Soviet period, as shown in Figure 5.2. Compared with the earlier period, households now are expected to serve six basic functions, listed below. Five of these functions are similar in some respects to what occurred in the Soviet period, shown in Figure 5.1. In these areas, households are doing some of what they did in the Soviet period, but new economic and social conditions in the post-Soviet period have altered the way in which these functions are realized. The sixth function, however, is totally new.

- Household members are no longer required to work for the large enterprises. Nonetheless, a substantial number of households continue to provide labor for these enterprises, in spite of the fact that they frequently do not receive regular salaries and benefits.
- Households continue to socialize children. But they have lost support from both the national government and the large enterprises. Each family with children needs to find extra money to pay for various educational expenses (e.g., school lunches, textbooks, clothes, and college or institute fees).
- Households continue to be consumers, but they have become significant agricultural producers in recent years. As noted earlier, peasant households produced 57 percent of total Russian agricultural output in 1998.
- Households continue to be involved in and maintain the village community. Now, however, households have more economic and social relationships with neighbors and local government while their relationships with the large farms have become more difficult and complicated.
- Households have kept their small plots of land, but they are beginning to rent additional parcels of land. Local government provides rental land for households.
- Recent laws on privatization have made households the legal owners of land that was formerly owned by kolkhozy and sovkhozy. At this time, the vast majority of households do not have title or personal use of that land. Nevertheless, all large enterprises must rent their land from rural households. This situation is creating very strong tensions between households and large enterprises.

As noted earlier, most adult workers continue to work for the large enterprises. However, as shown on Table 5.1 there has been a significant increase in the numbers of workers who are employed by other types of agricultural and nonagricultural enterprises. From 1995 to 1999 large enterprises lost approximately 25 percent of their workers. The large enterprises employed over 77 percent of the workforce in the three study villages of the Russian-American village project in 1995, but by 1999 they employed approximately 55 percent of that labor force. During the 1995–99 period, the large enterprises in the study villages went through various new reorganization schemes, which varied from one village to another. The large enterprise in Bolshoe Sviattsovo in Tver' oblast remained a traditional kolkhoz, while the kolkhozy in Latonovo in Rostov oblast and in Vengerovka in Belgorod oblast were reorganized in 1992 into TOOs. In 1998, the TOO in Vengerovka was reorganized again into a *sel'skokhoziiastvenyi proizvodstenyi kooperativ* (SPK).

Most important, the largest proportion of workers who left the large enterprises are now self-employed in either agricultural or nonagricultural small-scale informal enterprises. Table 5.1 shows that in 1999 17.3 percent of rural adults in the three study villages identified themselves as self-employed; 90 percent of them are women. Extrapolating these trends onto the total Russian rural adult population would indicate that from 2.5 million to 3 million rural adults have created a new working environment outside of the large enterprises. Moreover, the percentage of adults who are employed in different types of small businesses (fermery, other agribusi-

Table 5.1

Types of Enterprises Employing Working-Age Adults in Three Russian Villages, 1995–99 (percentage of workforce employed)

Type of Enterprise	1995 (n = 513)	1996 (n = 513)	1997 (n = 504)	1999 (n = 486)
Large enterprise	77.4	73.1	70.3	54.9
Kolkhoz	16.6	19.1	15.7	10.5
TOO	60.8	54.0	54.6	18.7
SPK	—	—	—	25.7
Public services	16.7	20.1	21.4	16.9
Fermer (officially)	2.6	2.1	3.2	4.7
Other agribusiness	1.1	0.8	0.6	1.9
Other business	2.2	3.9	3.9	4.3
Household enterprise (self-employed)	—	—	—	17.3
Total	100.0	100.0	100.0	100.0

Source: Data from the Russian-American Village Project, 1995 to 1999.

ness, and other business) went from 5.9 percent to 10.9 percent from 1995 to 1999.

Although peasant households have not received much legal protection, land, or credit from the federal government, they have made substantial changes during the past few years. While households continue to be a source of labor for the large enterprises, and an important social organizational unit for socialization, consumption, and community participation, critical changes have occurred in their agricultural production. The weakening of restrictions on the ability of households to sell products in the marketplace has provided a powerful stimulus for the development of household agricultural production.

The crisis in the Russian economy, including the agricultural sector, caused hyperinflation during the first few years of the post-Soviet period. This meant that many Russians lost their entire life savings and at times had to go without many of the necessities of life. In spite of enormous difficulties at the macro-economic level, however, Russian households have made remarkable adjustments in their own *micro-economies*. It is at this level where some of the most creative adaptations to the market economy have occurred.

Nowhere has the adaptation of households been more remarkable than in the Russian countryside. Despite the failure of the central government to resolve the problem of land ownership and the absence of any real restructuring of the large collective farms, the average amount of agricultural products sold by peasant households, krest'ianskie khoziaistva, has increased markedly since the end of the Soviet period. From 1996 to 1998, for example, the proportion of the total amount of meat produced in Russian agriculture accounted for by these small households increased from 51.6 percent to 56.6 percent. The proportion of milk products, including milk, butter, sour cream, and cottage cheese, produced by these households increased from 45.4 percent to 48.2 percent during the same time period.[7] This was accomplished by making major adjustments in household practices, often adding value-added processing to meat and dairy commodities they had produced. Many households have developed complex marketing strategies with members of their extended families and other households to sell products in hotels and restaurants in urban centers, as well as in urban farmers' markets.

Although official figures showed declines in rural household income, because of the lack of wage payments from the reorganized collective farms, many households have been able to purchase new durable goods during the past few years. From 1995 to 1999, the percentage of households in our three study villages that owned automobiles increased from 16.4 percent to 28.4 percent, which is an increase of almost 58 percent in a five-year period. The percentage of households with telephones went from 14.7 percent to 21.1 percent during the same period. These data indicate that ordinary Russians have made substantial adjustments to the new economy.

The success of individual rural households in adapting to the market economy has varied considerably, although the gap between the well-off and the not-so-well-off has not been nearly as large as in large metropolitan areas such as Moscow and St. Petersburg. Although some individuals have made substantial economic gains in the post-Soviet period, one is not likely to see "New Russian" tycoons driving fancy automobiles in rural Russian villages. Moreover, rural family and neighbor support networks do mitigate some of the harsher consequences of the market economy for those who are dependent. In this respect, the more vulnerable portion of the rural population would seem to have a significant advantage over its urban counterparts. A visitor to the Russian village does not encounter the beggars or homeless people who have become commonplace in large cities.

At the same time, however, households vary considerably in their capacity to take advantage of an economic niche in the new economy. Those households with the largest amount of labor, as indicated by the number of working-age adults, produce almost four times more agricultural commodities than their neighbors with the smallest amount of household labor. Households with larger amounts of social capital, as indicated by having more persons in their helping networks and being more involved in the social life of their villages, have additional advantages over their neighbors. In turn, households with more human and social capital are able to increase their advantages by gaining access to various types of physical capital. Because agricultural sales account for roughly one-third to one-half of household income, these advantaged households have significantly higher purchasing power than do other households. See chapter 14 by O'Brien for more details on this matter.

The different degrees of success of Russian rural households in making adjustments in their micro-economies can be viewed in two ways. One view is that this is merely a temporary adjustment until more substantial macro-level changes are made to truly reform the Russian economy. From this perspective, although the creative adaptability of Russian households is admirable, their "making do" with present circumstances will not produce fundamental change.

A second view, and the one proposed here, is that although macro-economic adjustments are crucial for reform of the Russian economy and

Russian society, the micro-level adjustments of households are more than temporarily "making do" with a transitional situation. Rather, these micro-level adjustments are based on a fundamental reorganization of peasant household production and sales, and of rural institutions, that will provide the foundation for the future development of the agrarian sector in Russia. In turn, these adjustments mean that in order to understand and assist in the process of reforming Russian agriculture it will be necessary to understand the role of human, social, and physical capital within the peasant household.

The basic social organizational unit of Russia agriculture in the pre-Soviet period was the krest'ianskoe khoziaistvo. Peasant households produced agricultural commodities using their own labor, largely manual labor, and developed informal production, processing, and marketing networks with their kin and neighbors. The Soviet period changed this entirely, by forcing peasant households to become suppliers of labor for the state-sanctioned large agricultural enterprises, the kolkhozy and sovkhozy. The Soviets did permit peasant households to produce commodities for consumption and for sale on small household plots (usually one-third of a hectare or less). Nevertheless, the state monopolization of processing facilities and markets, and, at times outright repressive measures, created disincentives for households to improve their human or social capital.

In the post-Soviet period, state monopolization of markets has weakened. Outright prohibitions against marketplace activities have virtually ended, and even though the tax structure would be considered unduly burdensome by Western standards, peasant households have found ways to get around these constraints and develop an informal economy. These changes, coupled with the inability of the large enterprises to provide wages in cash, have produced strong incentives for peasant household members to see themselves as members of household economic enterprises rather than as workers.

The persistence of the large enterprises, the kolkhozy and their reorganized forms, the TOOs, and the apparent inability of the Russian central government to produce effective land-reform legislation may obscure these profound changes in Russian agrarian life. Moreover, these household enterprises are quite small by Western standards. Nevertheless, their recent growth represents, in a nascent form, a social organizational structure that, in our view, eventually will produce much larger farms that can become the basis for a sustainable Russian agriculture.

This view of the peasant household as a viable agricultural production unit does not mean, of course, that all rural households contribute in significant ways to the Russian agricultural economy today, or that all current producers will be contributors to that economy in the future. Extrapolations from our findings suggest that at least 50 percent, or roughly 7 million, of the 14 million rural households in Russia today make some type of contribution to agricultural sales. A conservative estimate, based on our findings, would be that roughly half, or 3.5 million, of these households, would be able to expand their production capacity sufficiently to continue to be viable farm households as the Russian agricultural economy evolves.[8]

One of the key research tasks now is to identify specifically how the different levels of capital (human, social, and physical) in the peasant household are transformed into varying degrees of success in adapting to a newly emerging agrarian system in Russia. The completion of this task will have two benefits for public policy formation, both for Russians and for international organizations that have an interest in the development of the Russian agrarian sector. The first of these is to better understand how to improve the efficiency of Russian agriculture by stimulating the growth of household capital. The second benefit will be to identify ways in which selective intervention by government, nongovernmental organizations, and other interested parties might assist those households with limited human or social capital that are having difficulty creating household enterprises.

Future Institutional Structure and Rural Life in the Post-Transition Period

The relationships among the various institutional elements in the Russian village that need to occur in the post-transition period in order to create viable rural communities are shown in Figure 5.3. When Figures 5.2 and 5.3 are compared to each other there are large differences between the contemporary institutional structure of Russian villages and what is necessary to produce more viable communities in the future. None of these changes are in any way inevitable and there are strong forces resisting these changes. Nevertheless, there are certain changes, listed below, that would create an environment that is more conducive to the development of a more sustainable Russian rural village life and agricultural system.

(1) *Devolution of power from the central and regional governments to the local level.* During the 1991–2000 period, there was a substantial devolution of power from the federal to the regional governments. This process has created a great deal of tension between these power bases, and has transformed all aspects of Russian society.

Figure 5.3
Future Institutional Structure of Rural Life in Russia

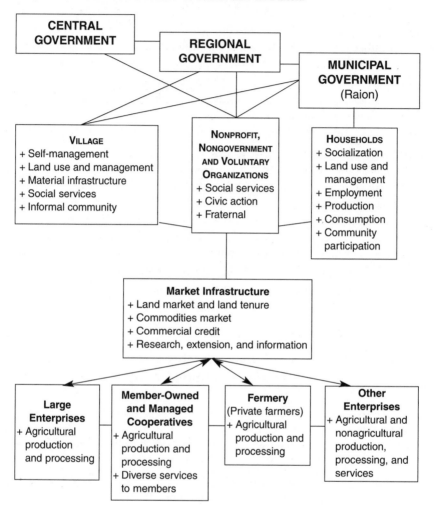

However, while power has devolved from the federal government to the regional governments, the latter have been very reluctant to give power to local-level governments at the *raion* and village levels. On many occasions during the past ten years, regional governments have attempted to create their own highly centralized system, much like the Soviet system of earlier times. See, for example, the discussion of regional "elastic budget constraints" in chapter 11 by Amelina.

Many regional governments refuse to recognize the municipal level as part of the power structure. Some regional administrations, such as those in the Komi Republic, Karelia Republic, and the Udmurt Republic, have actually violated federal law and have made local government merely a branch of regional administration. In its concern with strengthening the position of the federal government, the Putin administration in 2000–2001 has made an effort to improve linkages between the federal, regional, and local levels of government (*vertical' vlasti*). This policy shift, however, has in some ways weakened the position of local governments and strengthened the regional governments who wish to control them. On the other hand, the new law recently passed by the Duma regulating arable land usage and transactions may improve the status of local government because it legitimizes local government as one of the main actors dealing with the transfer and operation of different types of land.[9]

In order to improve the position of local government in relation to the regional and federal governments it will be necessary to develop a strong legal system for property rights, including land, which are ultimately local issues. The formal institutionalization of property rights, in turn, may facilitate the decentralization of power, thus improving the influence of local interests, through municipal government and village administration, on decisions affecting everyday life. If such a process occurs, it will be a key element in creating a true participatory democracy in rural Russia.

(2) *Creating institutional and organizational support for different types of agricultural producers.* During the past decade, the forms of agricultural production in Russia have become increasingly differentiated. There are three main types of producers—large enterprises, private farmers, and households. Many experts in Russia view the large enterprises, including new cooperatives, as the main producers and see them as continuing in that role in the future. When asked what they believed to be the most likely form of agricultural production in Russia in the future, 48 percent of the experts in a recent survey said production cooperatives and 30 percent named large commercial companies. Only 12 percent saw family farms as the dominant type of production unit in the future.[10]

However, as noted earlier, households and private farmers produce over 60 percent of all agricultural output in Russia today. The gap between the experts' perceptions of production structures and the actual contributions of different types of enterprises to agricultural output is a major source of difficulty in gaining support for institutional changes in rural Russia. The simple fact is that much of the thinking about institutional changes necessary to support private agriculture has been directed at supporting large enterprises and large commercial operations. In the survey of experts referred to above, there was recognition that subsidiary household plots have played an important role in contemporary Russia (this was noted by 26 percent of the respondents).[11] Much less attention, however, has been given to developing institutional and social organizational support for smaller-scale producers, largely because many Russian experts see them as merely a temporary contributor to national production.

In order to encourage a qualitative development of household agriculture beyond subsistence and its limited temporary role in maintaining a food supply in Russia during economic transition, it will be necessary to develop a complete local market infrastructure. This includes, as noted earlier, securing property rights and further development of the land market. The latter is discussed in chapter 4 by Wegren and Belen'kiy. This change would further the development of local-level commodities markets and commercial credit for smaller producers, and new organizations to transmit agricultural research and marketing information to local producers.

Although skeptics may argue that rural Russia is too far removed from modernization or that rural residents are too conservative and will resist change, there are numerous examples of changes in local institutions that have produced substantial gains in productivity. These include the land market in Saratov oblast, the rural credit unions in Volgograd oblast, the credit program for building household infrastructure in Belgorod oblast and the Chuvash Republic, and the commodites market in Stavropol *krai*.

The Russian Rural Net (*www.fadr.msu.ru*) and the Agroresources Net (*www.aris.ru*) on the Internet are growing very rapidly. Globalization and the information society reduce some of the advantages that urban areas have had over rural areas in industrial society. The new information technology has the potential not only to improve agriculture but to improve the general quality of life in rural areas and to connect rural citizens with the entire world. This technology will make it possible for more people to leave big cities and live comfortably in rural areas.

When people move from large cities to rural areas in the future, they will not have the urgent need to access land, a large water supply, or a workplace at the plant or office. Their basic need is access to electronic communication and a computer. In this new period, households will play a much larger role in the social organization of economic life. Like small corporate units, these households will combine human and social capital with the global economy and the information society. This transformation will have a very important influence on the agricultural sector, market infrastructure, and rural community life.

(3) *Development of civil society institutions: local government and the non-profit sector.* Even if power is devolved from the federal and regional governments to the local level, there remains the problem of creating organizations and institutions at the local level to deal with everyday problems of community development. Our research has shown that the transfer of responsibility for social services from the federal to the local levels has had a much more negative impact on rural than on urban areas.[12] A key problem here is the lack of nongovernmental, not-for-profit, and voluntary organizations. These organizations, which provide the backbone of civil society in developed countries, can play a crucial role in encouraging local citizens to become involved in finding ways to improve living conditions and economic opportunities for 14 million peasant households.[13]

The changes described above will require substantial adjustments in the relationships among the key institutional elements in Russian rural villages: households, large enterprises, and local government. A main concern here is to develop *at the local level* a consensus on community goals and to find good management for the large agricultural enterprises. Both of these issues have a very important impact on sustainable agriculture. There are many examples today in rural Russia where through community consensus and good management, large agricultural enterprises and households have developed a high level of cooperation that has resulted in marked improvement in production output and the quality of rural life. See chapter 15 by Kalugina in this book for a discussion of different strategies employed by large enterprise managers and how these have affected community consensus.

Even with economic growth and improved quality of life for many households, there remain serious social problems in rural Russia that are increased by income differentiation. Here again, nongovernmental organizations and civic action must take a more active role in dealing with problems of poverty and marginalization.

Notes

1. *Rossiia v tsifrakh 1999* (Moscow: Goskomstat, 1999), 203.

2. David J. O'Brien, Larry Dershem, and Valeri V. Patsiorkovski, "The Transition to a Market Economy in Rural Russia: Assertions and Findings," *Eastern European Countryside* 3 (1997): 75–90; David J. O'Brien, Valeri V. Patsiorkovski, and Larry D. Dershem, "Rural Responses to Land Reform in Russia: An Analysis of Household Land Use in Belgorod, Rostov and Tver' Oblasts from 1991 to 1996," in *Land Reform in the Former Soviet Union and Eastern Europe*, ed. Stephen K. Wegren (New York: Routledge, 1998), 35–61; David J. O'Brien, Valeri V. Patsiorkovski, Larry D. Dershem, and Oksana Lylova, "Peasant Household Production and Symptoms of Stress in Post-Soviet Russian Villages," *Rural Sociology* 61, no. 4

(1996): 674–98; David J. O'Brien et al., *Services & Quality of Life in Rural Villages in the Former Soviet Union* (Lanham, MD: University Press of America, 1998); David J. O'Brien, Valeri V. Patsiorkovski, and Larry D. Dershem, *Household Capital and the Agrarian Problem in Russia* (Aldershot, UK: Ashgate, 2000).

3. Valeri Patsiorkovski, David J. O'Brien, and Larry D. Dershem, "Population and House-hold Structure in Rural Russia," in O'Brien, Patsiorkovski, and Dershem, *Household Capital and the Agrarian Problem in Russia*, 56.

4. O'Brien, Patsiorkovski, and Dershem, "Household Structure and Labor," in O'Brien, Patsiorkovski, and Dershem, *Household Capital and the Agrarian Problem in Russia*, 88.

5. V. A. Semenov, "Ob itogakh raboty v pervom polugodee 1998," *Sel'skaia zhizn'*, 23 June 1998.

6. *Rossiia v tsifrakh 1997* (Moscow: Goskomstat, 1997), 298.

7. *Rossiia v tsifrakh 1999* (Moscow: Goskomstat, 1999), 204.

8. Patsiorkovski et al., "Population and Household Structure," 49.

9. Postanovleniye Gosudarstvennoi Dumy N 1079-III G D, 25 January 2001. For more details, see *www.akdi.ru/gd/proekt/GD01.HTM*.

10. Eugenia Serova, "Public Opinion Concerning Russia's Agrarian Reforms," in *Russian Views of the Transition of the Rural Sector*, ed. Alexander Norsworthy (Washington, DC: World Bank, 2000), 80.

11. Ibid.

12. O'Brien et al., *Services & Quality of Life*.

13. N. M. Rimashevskaia, ed., *Rossiia-98: Sotsial'no-demograficheskaiia situatsia* (Moscow: Institute for the Socio-Economic Studies of Population, Russian Academy of Sciences, 1999), 269.

Part Two

Sources and Nature of
Opposition to Change

6

The Cultural Dimension: Social Organization and the Metaphysics of Exchange

MARGARET L. PAXSON

Anthropology chooses, as its methodological bias, to take long, hard looks at single places. Like any bias, this brings certain features into focus, even as it blurs and distorts others. The strength of the anthropological method lies, of course, in the patience with which it allows the chaotic whirl that is culture to settle into some semblance of deeper order. At its best, anthropology watches and listens carefully—allowing human agents to be complex and multidimensional. Then and only then does it map the mechanisms of social relations.

This chapter derives from a year-long fieldwork project in a village in Russia's northern region.[1] As a contribution to this volume on adaptation and change in rural Russia, the text that follows has two main goals. The first is ethnographic: I offer a broad sketch of the social organization of one Russian village, with a special emphasis on the ways that the most intimate categories of belonging are formed and maintained. In other words, I present, in broad strokes, who it is that Russian villagers tend to act with and tend to trust (and, conversely, whom they tend to avoid and whom they tend to fail to trust). In looking at how rural Russians might react to changes in their social and economic worlds (brought on by attempts at reform, for example), this is an important overall matter.

The second goal of this chapter is more specific: identification and analysis of certain exchange mechanisms in the context of the village's dominant categories of belonging. Exchange, of course, can be monetary or nonmonetary and certainly involves more than simple acts of buying and selling. In the Russian village, it is an act embedded in an entire nexus of social interaction. Consequently, exchange can be laden with the emotions that on the one hand, bind people together, and on the other, cause tension and fear. What, it can be asked, does this imply for the course of agrarian reform?

This chapter is based on data gathered during a year-long stay in the northern Russian village of Solov'ovo[2] from October 1994 to December 1995 (with subsequent research done in the summers of 1996 and 1999, and the winter of 2000). Located on the shores of a small lake and along the edge of a red pine and birch forest, Solov'ovo is a typical small village of Vologodskaya oblast. Fieldwork there included all of the basic methods of ethnographic research: active participation in local cultural and social activities; formal and informal interviews on life histories, on noteworthy historical events, on the subjects of "modernity" and "tradition," and on certain religious themes; and the gathering of data from folklore and oral histories. A wide range of data was collected, particularly concerning the basic structures of social, economic, and political life.

The subsequent discussion offers evidence gleaned over the course of a year. It includes anecdotes and stories, aimed in part at giving the village a measure of breath and life to the reader. I begin with a brief description of the village of Solov'ovo.

Introduction to Solov'ovo

When I landed in Solov'ovo for the first time, it was a bright, quiet day in midsummer. A crowded bus had left me off along with a small group of students from the university. The village was nearly empty of noise and people. We found a grassy spot on a hill near the crossroads where the village begins and sat for what felt like hours, waiting for something to happen. Later, it was exactly in that spot that people threw dirt over their shoulders as part of the funeral ritual of Marfa's eight-year-old granddaughter. And I would turn at that crossroads countless times when walking to the village of Vershina, or off into the forest, or over into the potato fields, or down to the store, or leading the family cow to pasture. Tanned and towheaded children would race over that path with their one shared bicycle, zooming along and whooping with joy. But in those first hours of what would be my life in Solov'ovo, that spot was simply a quiet, summer-sunlit place where I waited to see what might be in store for me.

The first movement came in the form of slowly walking figures, returning from distant fields in small groups, carrying roughly hewn scythes and rakes and bundles of hay, and dressed in white shirts and hats and scarves. I blinked at this unexpected aesthetic. A woman who worked in the club-house, who was vaguely expecting a group of students, was also coming in from the fields. I noticed her right away. She was dark-skinned, small, beautiful, and had an air of calm about her. After some negotiation, she agreed to find us places to sleep that night.

If I had carried with romantic dreams of what a Russian village would be like, the romance was about the change. It was about to grow quieter. It was about to gain no small measure of dignity.

In the village of Solov'ovo, there are 36 houses (including a clubhouse, post office, and a more-or-less abandoned medical station). During the cold winter months, the village is mostly inhabited by people in their fifties and older. This is a typical sight in the Russian countryside—it has been spoken of for generations—the slow death of the village. The official population of Solov'ovo is around 30 people, but in the spring, summer, and fall months the village fills up with friends and relatives of the permanent residents, who come to help with farm work and harvesting or to simply relax and enjoy the clean air, the nearby cool lake, and the gifts of an ample forest. In July, Solov'ovo bustles with children and young people, friends, and visitors.

The collectivization of Solov'ovo took place in 1933. Villages were slow to collectivize in this region, and only with the urging of the local communists did people join. The *kolkhoz* went through several forms and sizes in Solov'ovo—from the size of three villages per kolkhoz brigade (work team), and four brigades to a kolkhoz, to its present form where the entire *sel'soviet* (administrative center) of Gulyaevo has only one brigade, that of Agrofirma Belozerska. The kolkhoz still exists in the region of Gulyaevo, but employs fewer and fewer people. The last three workers from Solov'ovo left the kolkhoz by 1996: One young man found another job and moved to a larger village, a second was fired for drinking, and a third was killed in the winter of 1996 when a tree fell on him in the forest.

Over the years, the kolkhoz in Solov'ovo became mainly involved in dairy production, as well as forestry, linen production, and animal husbandry. Corn was introduced to the region in the 1960s, but it was quickly understood that corn was not a suitable crop for the area. Today, kolkhoz lands still surround the village of Solov'ovo—and negotiations for the use of these lands for grazing, firewood, hunting, and gathering are still an issue, as they have been in rural Russia over the centuries.[3] Currently, the kolkhoz lands are not used to grow grain. Every year, villagers encroach on them more boldly for the abovementioned purposes.

As privatization was introduced in the early 1990s, the local kolkhoz went through some dramatic changes. Most profoundly, hundreds of dairy cattle were slaughtered in the nearby village of Yurino and production shifted from dairy to logging. Agrofirma Belozerska is now struggling to keep itself afloat and grappling with questions of the attractions of local forests to investors.

The fact that the kolkhoz has changed so dramatically over the years, from an employer of nearly everyone to an employer of only very few, has encouraged an overall demographic shift in the area toward an older population. Although there are young families and children, particularly in the sel'soviet of Gulyaevo, there are few such families. Work prospects are less than optimistic and opportunities to move to bigger villages or to nearby towns are often welcomed.

In Solov'ovo and the surrounding villages, I saw very little evidence of the development of private farming. Villagers do sell excess produce and meat (as they have for years), but at a very small scale. This may be due to the notoriously poor soils of the Russian north, which makes it very difficult—even under the best conditions—for farming to be profitable. It is clear that farming persists in a form that is almost entirely at a subsistence level.

Social Organization in Solov'ovo

In certain important ways, social organization has changed radically in the Russian village in the past 150 years. The emancipation of the serfs in 1861, the peasant reforms (Liberal and Bolshevik) of the early twentieth century, and the adoption of the kolkhoz in the 1930s all served to transform certain key features of social organization. On the other hand, it appears that there has been a degree of continuity in the basic makeup of social life and production. Except for the very elderly few, the villagers in Solov'ovo make their living through agricultural labor. For this labor, they rely on premechanized technology. Like the peasants of pre-Revolutionary Russia, they face the precariousness of the weather with a certain foreboding. Like those pre-Revolutionary peasants, they work on family plots and distribute the fruits of their labor outward to those who have shared in the labor. They live in a world of exchange that is largely nonmonetarized. The rhythms of their days and years are bound in large part to the movements of the natural world. Their relationships to unseen worlds and forces—ones that can intercede in times of trouble—have also been marked by continuity to the past. Mass collectivization and industrialization at the national level did not fundamentally change these basic features of agrarian life. It is not surprising, therefore, that certain elements of social organization have preserved earlier forms as well.

For centuries, the village has been a social hybrid in Russia, operating with a degree of self-definition and self-sufficiency, on the one hand, and economic and political controls at local and national levels, on the other. Such back and forth between an organization suited to small-scale agricultural production and one suited to serfdom and the exigencies of a powerful, centralized state, has made for particularly complex social forms. Echoing this point, in 1932, Geroid Robinson, the eminent social historian of rural Russia, wrote:

> The student interested in the realities of peasant life is hounded by a desire to assign each common interest and each collective function to the group which actually shared that interest and exercised that function; but to do this would require an interminable study, such as had never yet been made, of the actual practice of the peasants, as more or less modified and aborted by the agrarian laws, the interpretations of the Senate, the rulings of the local courts, and the actions of the local bureaucracy.[4]

If the question was so complex in 1932, it is not less so today. Indeed, the convoluted quality of social organization has been intensified in post-Soviet Russia. In the village, social organization is today marked by chaos and confusion, as the kolkhoz dies a slow death and social groups form and re-form. The question of land ownership, so crucial to any analysis of social groups in agrarian societies, has been blurred by the efforts at post-Soviet privatization. The kolkhoz is a truncated institution, which still exists, but is hobbled with the weight of its unviability in a new Russia. The kolkhoz that once employed most villagers in Solov'ovo now employs only a handful of men from the neighboring sel'soviet of Gulyaevo. Land, the crucial element in agricultural production and a primary obsession of any agriculturalist, is still a question in rural Russia, as it has been for hundreds of years. Privatization has been slow and incomplete. A social analysis of the village today is a social analysis in and of transition. In the three summers I spent in Solov'ovo, I watched as farmers inched their way into kolkhoz lands to harvest hay. They quietly elbowed each other into and out of strips of land. Next year, there could be a kolkhoz crackdown. Or an unofficial committee could form locally to solve the problem of land distribution in a more organized way. Or the Communist Party could return to power and re-nationalize agricultural production entirely. At this time, it cannot be said by anyone with any assurance which way things will go, even if intelligent guesses can be made.

The eye for physical geography seeks shifting patterns in physical landscapes—the places where hills rise and fall, where water drains and flows, and where there are trees or grasses or wildlife. The eye for social geography seeks clusters of people engaged in some shared activity, including working together, or living or sleeping together; distributing resources; passing knowledge to each other and to the next generation; and evoking transcendent worlds. The shapes of the social clusters that form and reform make for their own landscape of sorts. In this chapter, I identify some of these clusters. I begin with a brief description of residential, marriage, lineage, work, and ritual groups. Next, I look at the categories of collectivity in the village and offer a basic portrait of their dynamics. This includes a description of certain specific social categories in both human and otherworldly spheres, as well as larger imagined communities that extend beyond the borders of the village and into the national realm. I then briefly outline the dynamics of exchange in a rural setting and some of its underlying principles. Finally, I summarize how this analysis sheds light on questions of agrarian reform.

Solov'ovo's Social Groups and Categories

Three terms that are crucial to the analysis of social organization in rural Russia must be introduced before going further. The first is the term svoi, translated most directly as "one's own." Being svoi can mean being a member of one's immediate or extended family, a co-villager, a dear friend, or a compatriot. The term svoi is a marker for belongingness of a wide range of types. *Chuzhoi*, the second term, is the opposite of svoi. Related to the same word that means "wonder" or "miracle" (*chudo*) and other words that denote dangerous beings (such as *chudovishche*, monster), chuzhoi refers to being a stranger—one who is a foreigner or outsider. Chuzhoi can be a person from another family or village or region or country.

Rodnoi, the third term, is related to svoi in its evocative range. The definition of rodnoi is first "own," and then "native, home, intimate, familiar." The root of rodnoi is the very productive term *rod,* or family line, which ranges in meaning to cover "family, kin, clan, birth, origin, stock, generation, genus, sort, kind." There is a relationship between the sense of being rodnoi, and that of coming from the same *rodina,* or motherland, or being from the same *narod,* or people. But the term is far from being simply one of affiliation; it has a profound set of emotions associated with it. A person who is rodnoi can feel as close as one's flesh and blood and there is perhaps no dearer term for a beloved than *moi rodnoi.*

The senses of svoi, chuzhoi, and rodnoi permeate this chapter, and understanding the social and symbolic power of their various configurations is important to my thesis. The first social group that I focus on is the residential group that clusters within the peasant household, or *dvor.*

Residence in the *Dvor*

Traditionally, village households (*dvory*)[5] were inhabited by extended families, where a patriarchal family head (*khoziain*), his wife (*khoziaika*), his children (*deti*), and as time went by, his sons' wives and their children all lived together under one roof. When these extended families became too large and unwieldy through the natural process of reproduction, the residential group would split. At that time, a son would establish a new home for himself and his wife and children, usually in the same village. I heard such scenes described in the memories of Solov'ovo's villagers, where one man told how his grandfather had cut a loaf of bread in two, "*Raz, popolam!* With one stroke, in half!" symbolizing the breaking of that household and the redistribution of its wealth and property.[6]

In the lifetime of the current villagers of Solov'ovo, marriage customs included a preference for, if not an absolute practice of, intervillage exogamy and patrilocality. Young men would tend to take wives from a village that was not an immediate neighbor, but rather several kilometers distant. In Solov'ovo, the "best" villages to get wives from were ones like Filipovskaya and Yorgovsk, both more than 10 kilometers distant. Although there were occasionally marriages between co-villagers, such unions were considered less than ideal. There were two reasons given for this. First, it was "uncomfortable" for a young man to live in the same village with his in-laws, and second, it was suggested that a village is "like a family," and marrying co-villagers was therefore somewhat akin to incest.[7]

The preference for patrilocality as a residence pattern has become secondary to broader migrations out of rural Russia. In any case, the village regularly fills up with extended family members. Every summer, relatives come from great and small distances to help with farm labor. In return for their assistance, household resources are freely shared and crops are later distributed outward to them. Solov'ovo's population was roughly 30 people during the winters that I lived there. In summer 1995, my khoziaika, Sof'ya, and I counted 180 people who spent more than a couple of weeks there. Sons and daughters come along with their own children, as well as the sisters, brothers, aunts, uncles, nieces, and nephews of the khoziain and khoziaika. The household is fluid in these summer months, and though it is filled with mostly extended family members (of both the male and female lines), friends can come and stay as well. Anyone who resides under the roof for a period of more than a few days becomes a de facto member of the residential group.

Once under one roof, living together in a home carries with it an absolute requirement of participating in household labor and sharing resources. Guests always come with goods to share (bread, tea, cheese, salami, sweets, cans of meat or fish, etc.) and ready to work. *Khoziaistvo*, or the total of all tasks required to maintain a household, is also shared by all members of the residential group. As a female member of the household, it was implicit that I would help with cooking, cleaning, general care of sheep and cows, fire tending, water hauling, cow herding, sheep shearing, wood preparation, wood transportation, hay transportation, hay harvesting, potato planting, and potato reaping. Women are also expected to tend animals (milking, cleaning, and helping with calving and shearing), prepare food, and carry out most of the gardening and work involving manure. Men plow, cut down trees, heat the *pechka* (large Russian stove), hunt, make repairs of tools and other items in the house and yard, care for horses, and build homes and bathhouses. Both men and women gather mushrooms, berries, and healing herbs in the fields and forests. On the lake or the banks of streams, men, women, boys, and sometimes girls, fish. Family members alternate in pasturing the cows and sheep, bringing a book or some music to pass the time of day.

Fulfilling these tasks is not only a pragmatic issue, but also a moral one. The khoziain and khoziaika bear the brunt of the moral responsibility to keep khoziaistvo running smoothly. When obligations are not fulfilled, it is they who must answer to the dead ancestors, who can show their displeasure in a variety of ways. In light of this heightened responsibility, the khoziain and khoziaika have more power than other householders when decision making is necessary. Such decision making includes both the small, daily decisions of how to maximize the available labor force to do all the many tasks at hand (given constantly varying weather conditions), and larger decisions such as those concerning slaughtering animals, going on trips, or making large purchases. It is popularly understood that the khoziain has the last word in any decision, but in my village experience that was not always the case. Matters of importance are discussed at length until some decision is arrived at. Consultation is a crucial part of agricultural production of the kind practiced in the Russian north, and input from several sources is welcomed. Mikhail Alekseevich, the khoziain of the household where I lived, had more say than others, but no absolute say. Under circumstances where domestic violence is not practiced, there is plenty of room for female voices and power in the village. In fact, all householders—even friends who are staying for short periods—are allowed a certain weight to their opinions, even as they are expected to share in labor. This is a significant point: The household has a leader or leaders, but it also has many more-or-less equal voices. Decisions are made through group discussion and negotiation. Being a householder means landing in a social domain in which resources, work, and decision making are shared. It is as unseemly to not share in resources and in work as it is unseemly to raise one's voice far above other householders.

There is one important residue of patrilocal patterns of residence: Most of the women villagers in Solov'ovo come from someplace else, and spoke to me many times of the difficult passage from their home village to a village of strangers. For them, if not for many of their daughters, patrilocality sometimes was a harsh reality.

Arriving in her new home, a young bride is at the bottom rung of power in the residential group. She is given tasks of particular difficulty, to such a degree that it is sometimes not clear whether she is marrying a man or his residential group, joining it merely to become a new laborer.[8] Even though patrilocality is not practiced today as commonly as it was in the recent past, conflict between mothers-in-law and new brides is quite common. In all my time in the village, I only once heard a woman make spontaneously warm comments about her mother-in-law. The feeling is mutual. Mothers-in-law typically see their daughters-in-law as lazy, citing examples where their sons are required to do women's work.[9] Often, they intercede on the side of their sons when difficulties arise between a son and his wife. Correspondingly, the son typically offers no protection to his bride against the judgment or wrath of his mother, and the bride's time in her new home can be a lonely one, indeed. If that weren't bad enough, ethnographic texts suggest that in the past, brides were often subject to sexual advances by their fathers-in-law.

Good parents will investigate the family into which their children will marry. As Anna Grigorievna S—explains, it is important to know not only the character of the young person, but also that of his or her "tribe."[10]

> Before, it was such that they wouldn't let rich young men marry a poor girl. The bride needed to be rich. They avoided taking a far-away girl because you need to know all of her relatives. Her grandmothers, great-grandmothers, great-grandfathers, from which tribe/race/family the girl comes. If she was beautiful or ugly [you need to know from which tribe]. If it's a good one, the girl will be good. . . . They considered if they were busy, hard-working, if the family was a working one, not lazy.

The bride, in other words, does not simply marry a man, but does in fact, join with his residential group where she is beholden to its requirements of work, sharing, and decision making. Arriving *chuzhaia*, she slowly comes to be considered *svoia*. If she is lucky, a feeling of warmth develops. Bearing children improves her situation, and failing to do so right away will elicit questions from the community. The children take the father's last name, and receive his patronymic. They are linked in this way to his family line.

The Family Line or Rod

The family line, or rod, is a concept of great importance in rural Russian life. Defined as the "generational line emanating from one ancestor,"[11] the rod provides a model for group belonging that goes beyond the world of the living and into the realm of the dead ancestors. As well as the term rodnoi (adj., blood kin) introduced above, the root word rod produces terms such as rodina (motherland), *priroda* (nature), *rodit'* (to give birth), *roditel'* (parent), *rodstvenniki* (relatives), and *narod* (people). A household contains part of a rod; a marriage continues the line of the rod.

The term rod carries with it a sense of deep and ancient belonging. The ancestors included in the rod are invoked for help both as individuals, and collectively in yearly rituals intended to bring fertility to the land. They also provide guardianship of individual households and have powers of intercession in the human world. These are figures of great importance in rural Russia.

In the living material world, the lines of descent are both patrilineal and matrilineal. Where it is clear that the practice of patrilocality is widespread in Russian villages, peasant social organization has features of both patri-linearity and matrilinearity. There are, in fact, arguments to the effect that ancient Russian belief systems, including the "religion of the rod," were part of broader matrifocal tendencies, in which females and the female line held crucial administrative powers in social and religious life.[12] In this ar-gument, patrilinearity and patrifocality came about only after the church and state made considerable efforts to wrest religious power from the hands of women.[13]

Whether or not women were the focus of pre-Christian[14] religious life, there were elements of both patrilineal and matrilineal descent in pre-Revolutionary village culture. Inherited from the father's line is one's last name and one's patronymic. Houses, garden plots,[15] and family property (such as livestock) were also generally passed through the male line.[16] Agri-cultural land was a complex matter; it cannot be said that land passed through the male line of a given family in pre-Revolutionary Russia. In So-viet Russia, land was not legally "owned," but private plots were granted to the families of kolkhoz and *sovkhoz* workers, which, for all intents and purposes, were passed on to children via the father's line. In addition, in a practical if not legal sense, houses, family gardens, and most property con-tinued to be passed on patrilinearly during the Soviet period. Today, the legalities of land ownership are in chaos because of the process of privati-zation and the residues of the Soviet kolkhoz system. Other forms of prop-erty do not appear to pass exclusively through male lines. There is one point that can be fairly generalized: Property clusters around a household. Given the patrilocal tendencies of this century, in the lifetimes of most of Solov'ovo's residents most property fell into the hands of male heirs, even when this practice was not legally dictated. It could be supposed that with the decline of patrilocality, inheritance of property through the male line will continue to wane as well.

Matrilineal descent is not so tied to material property but is linked to other crucial features of social life. Through the maternal line, religious icons are passed. Icons are endowed with broad-reaching powers that are linked not only to Orthodox rites, but to pre-Christian religious practices as well. They are the bearers of otherworldly powers, and are generally un-derstood to be women's property. Furthermore, the systems of healing, both through foods and waters, on the one hand, and incantations, on the other, are generally the domain of women, and knowledge of them tends to be passed through women. Knowledge of Christian and pagan rituals tends to be passed through the maternal line, as well.[17]

Neither patrilineal nor matrilineal descent practices are strictly followed. There are male healers and female homeowners. The problem can be slightly turned around for better understanding. It is clear that the family line, or rod, is of tremendous importance in the conceptual world of rural Russia. Most, but not all, scholars of peasant Russia would agree that the rod is linked most profoundly to the male line of descent. It seems to me that the question of the relative powers of the male or female lines is secondary to the overall sense of belonging to the line of a given residential group. It appears that *when one lives in a given residential group, one's primary invocations are to the ancestors of that household and, beyond, those of the local village (or, more specifically, rodina)*. The line is actualized in the domain of the household, as is the sharing of resources and the sharing of decision making. The most important feature of any given rod is its locality, its rootedness. The affairs of property and knowledge are important, but are subordinate to the powers of this deep and local line. The term rodina, which means both motherland and Mother Russia, resonates with belonging to an earth-bound territory.

Extended Family Members (*Rodstvenniki*)

In terms of social groups in village Russia, it is worth making a distinction between more-or-less permanent members of a household and the extended family. The extended family members, or rodstvenniki, include family members from both the maternal and paternal side (and their spouses). Not all rodstvenniki are permanent members of a residential group. In terms of village social life, rodstvenniki become particularly important in the summer months, when even rather distant kin come to the village, stay for a while (becoming temporary householders), share in the major summer jobs, and leave. Important here is the fact that their work in the village allows them to receive the fruits of the harvest and sometimes even parts of slaughtered animals. They receive goods, in other words, not as members of a household, but as members of a work group. Strictly speaking, this is not understood to be payment. It is simply fitting that kin members help with these large tasks, and fitting that goods are received in exchange for the farm labor. Interestingly, it is not necessarily the workers themselves who will be given a portion of the harvest. If a niece or nephew is sent from a nearby town to help with summer farm work, potatoes (for example) will be later sent to their parents as well as to them. The niece and nephew appear to represent their branch of the family. The extended family as a whole helps and the extended family as a whole receives.

Part of this phenomenon is due to the fact that not every brother and sister of a given household will live in that household upon the death of the parents. They do, however, seem to feel that it is, in part, their own domain.

Certain tasks are more likely to require the assistance of extended family members. Specifically, help is given with the potato planting in the early spring, *senokos* or hay harvest in the summer, potato harvest in the early fall, and wood preparation in the late fall. At these times, relatives will come from distant towns and cities and converge on the village for weeks. At that time they become temporary householders, and share in all the tasks outlined above. Their participation in the arduous tasks mentioned here gives them certain implicit rights to portions of the harvest.

Social organization in the village appears to cluster around the linked notions of the household, family line, and extended family. There are other groups that are not tied to this household/family cluster. In Soviet Russia, the kolkhoz was a work group that was not family based, but based on a collective (brigade) that spanned one village or even a few villages. *Kolkhozniki* worked together on state-owned land and for this labor were paid in money and sometimes, in lean years, in goods.

The matter of collective khoziaistvo, its origins, and its viability as a part of social organization is a complex one. In the village, there are certain social groups that reach past the boundaries of the dvor and the extended family. In the next section, I outline the important ones. The problem of defining "collectivity" in rural Russia is one that has occupied the attention of generations of scholars.

Obshchina: That Which Is Common

Collective and "Collective":
Including the Other in the Social Sphere of the Self

Part of the reason for the complexity of this issue is the very fact that the village "commune" was so meaningful to Russian intellectuals. The history of the study of social organization in the Russian village has been marked by a certain attachment to an idealized form of community that the Russian village is said to possess. This attachment, often for ideological reasons, has succeeded in raising the pitch of rhetoric surrounding the issue, even as it has often failed to enlighten scientific analysis. Among Russians who attempted to scientifically question the natural communal quality of the village, and shift attention to the residential group (most notably, in the work of Chaianov), martyrs were made. The "village" is an opaque symbol that is marked by a particularly broad and powerful resonance. It has been a matter of great consequence to many thinkers that the Russian village does or does not house the idealized collective. Granting that the problem of collectivity is a crucial one in rural Russia, social scientists must endeavor to not confer an a priori primacy to any one manifestation of it.

It is therefore important to separate three sides of the concept of collectivity. First, a "collective" could be considered, simply, any social group. Social groups can, of course, be analyzed by looking at shared activity and the distribution of property. I have already discussed this with regard to the residential group, rod, and rodstvenniki. The social group of interest when historians speak of "communes" in rural Russia is any suprafamilial one that is linked to the territory of a village or sometimes a parish community. Even given the great importance of the family-centered dvor and the family-generated rod, there are such social groups in the village. The analysis of suprafamilial groups has been attempted by historians and social scientists who deal with the social history of rural Russia. In the next section I describe what such social groups look like today.

The second side to the concept of "collectivity" is its contextualization in academic and political discourse. Aptly called by one author an "intellectual shibboleth,"[18] the question of the place of collectivity in the broader context of the defining discourses in Russian history is a major one. Given the interest in the subject of radical nationalism and the revolutionary movements of nineteenth-century Europe and Russia, it could well be argued that the very debate over the meaning of Russian collectivity has generated some of the more gruesome paths of Russian revolutionary history.

Finally, there is the symbolic sense of suprafamilial collectivity that the villagers themselves express, mostly through narrative. More than the names for things and the detailed study of social groups, this side of the concept marks the way that symbolic configurations are housed in memory, regardless of (or complementary to) the specifics of social group formation.

A Brief History of the Problem

It has been suggested that the Russian collective grew, historically, from an ancient collectivity that was, indeed, family based. Richard Pipes writes:

> The basic unit of the ancient Slavs was a tribal community, estimated to have consisted of some fifty or sixty people, all related by blood and

working as a team. In time, the communities based on blood relationship dissolved, giving way to a type of communal organization based on joint ownership of arable land and meadow, called in Russian *mir* or *obshchina*.[19]

The specific communal nature of the mir and obshchina is explained below.[20] In any case, it well may be that the feeling of communal belongingness and the need for shared resources and cooperation evolved from the family group in ancient Russia. But why form such suprafamilial groups? North American farming, though not exclusively so, is (like so many other things in North America) conceived as an individual enterprise. Pipes convincingly argues that the type of communal-based agriculture known in rural Russia is a direct result of the poor soil and short growing seasons of northern Russia. He writes:

> The geography of Russia discourages individual farming. A general rule seems to exist which holds that northern climates are conducive to collective farm work. There are many reasons why this should be so, but in the ultimate analysis all of them have to do with the brevity of the agricultural season. . . . The unalterable fact is that all the field work in Russia must be completed in four to six months (instead of the eight to nine months available to the [W]estern farmer) calling for work being performed with great intensity, and induces the pooling of resources, human as well as animal and material. An individual Russian peasant, farming with his wife and minor children and horse or two simply cannot manage under the climatic conditions prevailing in the forest zone. He needs help from his married children and neighbors.[21]

Because of the necessity to quickly finish work in harsh conditions, a system of village-wide interdependence appeared in rural Russia, where groups formed that reached beyond the residential group and the extended family. Villagers learned to rely on each other for the tasks that the short growing season presented them with. James Billington, in his landmark work, *The Icon and the Axe*, makes the same general point, but underlines the importance of communal action in the peculiar political history of Russia. See also chapter 1 by Volgine in this book.

> The [historical] weakening of central authority and the presence of new enemies—both natural and human—forced a deepening of family and communal bonds within the widely scattered communities of the Russian north. . . . Later attempts to find in the "Russian soul" an innate striving toward communality (*sobornost'*) and "family hap-

piness" may often represent little more than romantic flights from present realities. But the practical necessity for communal action is hard to deny for the early period; and already in the fourteenth century the word "communal" (*sobornaia*) apparently began to be substituted for the word "catholic" (*kafolicheskaia*) in the Slavic version of the Nicene Creed.[22]

There is, historically speaking, another reason for the evolution of the Russian brand of collectivity: Any "natural" proclivity for mutual aid due to poor geography and political need was reinforced by the specific relationship between the Russian state, feudal lords, and local serfs.

> Cooperation between peasant families living in isolated villages under severe climatic conditions is a natural phenomenon. But the Russian peasant communes grew out of the feudal system rather than as a form of voluntary mutual assistance. The *pomeshchiki* found it more convenient to deal with a village commune via an elected or appointed chairman than with individual families.[23]

If communal action arose for reasons of poor land and a short growing season, it was reinforced through the legal relationship that developed historically among feudal landlords, the state, and agricultural laborers. The peasant obshchina, as it happened, provided a bridge between these very different sorts of Russians. A special legal relationship was formed. In the introduction to *Soviet Peasants, Or, The Peasant's Art of Starving*, by journalist and social anthropologist Lev Timofeev, this side of the obshchina's role—with its range of powers—is explained with precision.

> [T]he *obshchina* was a social institution which arose with the state's active support and functioned as a fiscal entity whose members were collectively responsible for the taxes levied against the *obshchina* as a whole. The *obshchina* had considerable powers: it divided tax payments among its members, made sure peasants did not flee from the landowners. . . . [I]t was responsible for furnishing army recruits and could also punish its lazy or criminal members, who could be exiled to Siberia without trial, exclusively upon the *obshchina's* decision. In addition, the *obshchina* assigned to each family a land plot roughly based on the number of family members and periodically redistributed land to account for the differences in the fertility of soil. All decisions were made democratically at public assemblies.[24]

The obshchina was, then, responsible for the mediation between the village community and the outside worlds of the state and the landlord. In order to appease the state through taxes, and the landlord through rent, and so on, the obshchina placed certain controls over the community. Land was redistributed according to family size[25] once a generation or so. This served to lend a community-based "fairness" to plot size; pragmatically, it gave large families the amount of land they needed to generate surplus for taxes. The obshchina also controlled the movement of villagers, often limiting migration from villages in order to maximize local production. Furthermore, legal disputes were solved by the obshchina without reference to outside courts. In short, order was kept at a local level by the obshchina. The centralized state and the landlord, though benefiting greatly from the labor of the peasant-serfs, could treat the village community as a surplus-producing black box.

This legal, political, and social isolation gave rise to an interesting range of views of the peasantry. City dwellers and rulers filled the symbol of the peasant and his obshchina with a plethora of imaginary qualities—some cheerily romantic, others soberly religious, and still others inspired by the fear and loathing of a distant other. While intellectuals were seeking the "unspoiled wisdom of the noble savage,"[26] rulers imposed burdensome taxes and local elites exploited their labor and all its products. Peasants and their obshchiny were useful in that way. Historically, the obshchina became increasingly fixed and opaque, both in the conceptions of rulers and in that of the peasantry itself.

In terms of social organization, the obshchina was a fascinating institution. Given the fact that the suprafamilial obshchina was charged with the redistribution of land, the concept of land ownership in the village resonated with both a sense of transience, in relation to the rod, and permanence, in relation to the village. The village layout echoes this: Houses are clustered together, and outside of the residential part of the village, individual plots are clustered together. When people work on their land, they work in close proximity—they can holler and joke with each other. If most labor was (and is) family based, the powers of decision making over the land as a whole were obshchina based.

Kolkhoz and Obshchina

After collectivization, the obshchina waned in importance. The kolkhoz created a new suprafamilial group, one that pulled labor out of family-based groups and into local work brigades, run by brigadiers and not village elders. In the lifetime of most of the Solov'ovo villagers, the kolkhoz was the official farming unit. Eventually, private plots were given to peasants (always vastly more productive than kolkhoz lands), which could only be worked in "free time." The obligations to the kolkhoz were the first priority and this often meant that "one's own" work had to be put aside for the end of the day and the end of the season.

The kolkhoz could be as small as a village or as large as an entire region. The larger kolkhozy were made up of several brigades and were controlled centrally. The will of the party was inserted in this system, as peasant-workers were beholden to the (often wildly unrealistic) production quotas.[27]

In terms of leadership, the kolkhoz had a *predsedatel'* (chairperson) and the brigade (a kolkhoz work group) had a brigadier. The brigadier was in charge of the day-to-day running of the kolkhoz, and could be well liked or resented. Whereas the obshchina was regulated by a group of elders, the kolkhoz had a different tone of leadership. The brigadier was a leader with powers as an individual who reported to extra-village officials. Villagers were now answerable not to their local council of elders, but to the socialist state.

Historians have written about the fundamental difference between the obshchina collectivity and that of the kolkhoz: Where the obshchina organization granted the family controls over production, the kolkhoz had little place for familial autonomy. Pipes writes:

> One occasionally hears analogies drawn between the pre-Revolutionary communes and the collective farms (*kolkhozy*) introduced in 1928–32 by the communist regime. The analogy has little to recommend it, except for a negative factor common to both institutions, i.e. the absence of private ownership in land. The differences are quite basic. The *mir* was not a collective; households carried out farming in it privately. Even more significantly, the peasant living in the *mir* owned the product of his labor, whereas in the *kolkhoz* it belongs to the state which compensates the farmer for his work.[28]

Given that the obshchina-based organization had only a cursory resemblance to the kolkhoz, peasants of this century consistently failed to feel that the kolkhoz was "theirs." Sheila Fitzpatrick writes in her recent monograph, *Stalin's Peasants*:

> The collective principle that was formally embodied in the *kolkhoz* structure seemed to have no resonance at all with Russia's peasants, despite the legacy of communalism. Peasants never admitted that they were in any sense co-owners of *kolkhoz* land and property. They made

a point of describing themselves as a mere workforce, toiling in the *kolkhoz* fields for somebody else's benefit.[29]

Even if the kolkhoz failed to be adopted by villagers as their own, it does not necessarily follow that a sense of suprafamilial collectivity never existed. In fact, the concept of collectivity is rich and nuanced in rural Russia today; the names for things are not always what one would expect, but their properties remain predictable.

Conceptualizing the *Kollektiv*

The institutions of the obshchina and the kolkhoz are one thing, and the way that collectivity is housed in the imagination is another. Like any dominant symbolic representation in a given cultural context, there are many terms (with correspondent resonantial fields) that revolve around the basic sense of "collectivity" in the Russian village. A few have already appeared. Billington refers to *sobornost'*, a concept from Russian Orthodoxy, which—as it is used in theological discourse—tends to underline the special holiness of the Russian people. *Mir* has been used, a word with separate senses of "the entire world," and "peace."[30] The word obshchina comes from the very productive root *obshch-*, one that is used to form words for all kinds of social intercourse (*obshchenie*/intercourse, relations; *obshchat'sia*/to associate with; *obshchestvo*/society; *obshchii*/common; etc.) Obshchina connotes a variety of basic human interactions, but it also still refers specifically to the pre-Revolutionary institution. The most common term in Solov'ovo for a suprafamilial group is *kollektiv*. Foreign in origin, the term likely came into popular use after collectivization and the kolkhoz (*kollektivnoe khoziaistvo*, or collective farming).

If these terms each have their own resonance, they are used with a certain amount of looseness in Solov'ovo. Whether or not historians tell us that the obshchina and the kolkhoz had little in common as institutions, they are, in certain contexts, discursively interchangeable, as when Sof'ya explained to me the meaning of obshchina:

> In every village there was a kolkhoz. That's an obshchina. About 40 houses. Sometimes villages.

Not every villager would so freely trade the term obshchina for kolkhoz. On the other hand, a certain set of qualities could be said to animate the notion of the collective—whether called obshchina, kollektiv, or even sometimes kolkhoz. Five of these qualities are delineated below.

1. The collective is linked to happiness and ideal social life.

In interviews and discussions with villagers, it was implied, countless times, that the collective was a crucial feature of an idealized social world. The following is a very typical comment:

> In the collective, in the kolkhoz, we lived. . . . They send you off to the kolkhoz—they sent you off, we had 80 people as our workforce. We went [off to work] singing. Oi. Went to work with songs. And there, everything was peaceful, well.

Time and again, happiness was associated with the act of working together (and, more broadly, associating with each other) in a suprafamilial group.

2. The collective implies interdependence.

In notions of the collective, there is a morality of group mindedness. It is good, in other words, to depend on one another:

> Sof'ya was complaining about how neighbors are constantly gossiping about each other and criticizing each other. I teased and pointed out that she does the same thing. She and Mikhail Alekseevich laughed. Mikhail Alekseevich says: "We used to be an obshchina." I ask, "What's an obshchina?" Mikhail Alekseevich answers: "Everyone lived together and helped each other and lent things to each other. That stopped after the *pereselenie* [resettlement]."

In this part of the notion of the "collective," interdependence is seen as a positive quality. Such interdependence involves a certain morality attached to the will of the group taking precedence over the will of the individual.

3. Decisions are made on a collective basis.

The fact of collective decision making at the level of the residential group was discussed previously. The suprafamilial collective is also charged with decision making. Some of this collective decision making is in evidence today, even if production mostly happens at the level of the family (residential group and extended family). Noticing that separate families began large farm tasks (such as the potato planting) at nearly the exact same time, I asked how people chose the time to start their work.

Q: Why choose to plant when you do?

Everyone else was planting and if everyone is planting, you don't want to do it alone. It's the same with the harvest; you don't want to do it alone. If everyone starts, you cannot endure waiting [*ne vyter-pish'*]. We work collectively [*kollektivno*]. We do things together.

Q: So even if the group chooses a bad time to begin, it's still worth it to work while everyone else is working?

Yes.

The sense that it is better to act in concert is alive in the village, even if the obshchina is not. What is more, older, respected villagers have more weight as decision makers than do younger villagers. Trust in elders, though not institutionalized as before, appears to permeate decision-making procedures.

4. The collective is linked to a given territory.

A collective is a local group. Though it is not always linked to a village, it resonates with a sense of local place. Below, Konstantin Andreevich links it to a parish, where the operative part of his definition of an obshchina is its rootedness in place.

Q: Is the obshchina the same thing as kollektiv?

Well, sort of a kollektiv, where people are attached to one place. To my temple. Where people relate to one another through one church, mostly. Linked to that.

The sense of rootedness and place associated with a kollektiv is analogous to the importance of place with regards to the rod. Because a given kollektiv is associated with a given territory, rearrangement of communities causes a certain cognitive (and organizational) dissonance. The pereselenie of the 1970s (when smaller villages were forcibly merged into larger ones) was met with great disapproval by all involved. After the pereselenie, the sense of community, because it is linked to place, was fractured (as when Mikhail Alekseevich commented above that the obshchina "stopped after the pereselenie").

5. The collective, when formed, grants otherworldly powers.

This, again, is a theme of tremendous importance in the village. The act of forming a community of any kind is a magical act. The formation of a suprafamilial collective is one example of such a magical act. Below, I note in my journal how the gathering of the obshchina can change the weather.

> There has been a terrible dry spell. I asked if there had ever been any way to influence the weather. Mikhail Alekseevich and Sof'ya told how they had heard that the people of the village would get together and pray for rain. And if there wasn't a priest? People would still gather. As Sof'ya put it, "the obshchina would get together and pray." Mikhail Alekseevich later added that after those prayers, the rain would begin even before people could reach their homes. This was due, he guessed, to the collective energy of the prayers.

The weather is only the beginning of the otherworldly effects of forming a group. Group formation of this kind gives rise to land fertility and sexual fertility and in certain cases, healing. It is a subject of primary importance in the text that follows.

These features of the obshchina and its conceptual corollaries are the most basic symbolic characteristics of social circles. In the next section, I describe social groups in the village beyond the residential group. I begin with looking at the territory of the village and see what, if any, social groups arise.

The Village Bounds

If the village was once linked directly to an obshchina—where the two overlapped neatly as social circles—it is no longer. Land is not redistributed by a council of elders, nor are collective decisions made regarding the migration of villagers. Taxes are neither levied nor paid by a group. The village also fails to delimit a kolkhoz; even brigades are much larger than a village territory. Does a village exist at all in a social sense?

Certainly, a village is an important conceptual category. One's *dom rodnoi* (native home) is found in a village, and deep attachments are made to the place of one's birth. When speaking of their native villages (*rodiny*), villagers' voices would lilt with nostalgia. The village is the place where one's people (*svoi*) live, where one uses the familiar second person (ty) with everyone, and the region where one's dead are buried.

Aside from the conceptual level and the obvious fact of living in tight clusters of houses, an eye for "that which is common" within the village would notice shared property and communal work efforts. Shared properties include horses that were granted by the kolkhoz during the first privatization efforts. Other post-kolkhoz inheritances are distributed as well in Solov'ovo, both legally and illegally. The bricks from a decrepit kolkhoz building are being appropriated load by load. Fields used for hay harvesting are also divvied up, if chaotically, and no council oversees these decisions as villagers inch their way into unused kolkhoz lands. Pasturelands, the lake, and forest lands are all shared, if not strictly between members of a given village (and, in the case of fishing and logging, permits must be obtained and fees paid).

There is also shared work in the village. In Solov'ovo, there was one clear case where the village delimited a work group: At the time of the potato planting, all villagers help each other, in addition to the help given to them by their extended families. This is explained by the need to use the communally owned horses with maximum efficiency. In addition, there are tasks that are shared among villagers. Most often these involve families taking turns at given tasks. For example, the Belovs will pasture one week and the Petrovs will pasture the next week. Pasturing is one such shared task, as is care of the horses (where families each give a portion of their hay and each are charged with a rotating turn feeding the animals and cleaning the barn).

The ethnographer Marina Gromyko (as summarized by Jovan Howe) delineates three types of "collective aid" in the traditions of rural Russia:

> Type One was aid performed for each household in turn. . . . Type Two aid was extended by the commune at the decision of its assembled household heads to one of its member households, which by no fault of its own had fallen on especially hard times. . . . Type Three was organized by one household in the commune on their own behalf, using communal labor.[31]

Modern habits of mutual aid are more or less in keeping with traditional habits, in the sense that the community members aided one another as *household units*. The household was, and continues to be, the most important unit of agricultural labor in rural Russia.

Politically, there is a less impressive range of shared activities that are delimited at the village level. During the Soviet period, the party gave villages a means of parlaying their needs and grievances to the state through locally elected deputies. Today, there is an administrative leader elected for a nine-village region. When troubles arise, she must be contacted and results are often slow. In addition, villages choose a *starosta* (from the traditional term for elder, though without the connotation of age today). In theory, this starosta should speak for the village when there are problems (such as flooded roads or downed power lines), but in Solov'ovo, the person chosen for this position simply refused to do the work. No one has arisen in his stead.

On the other hand, even if there is only a very limited political body in the village, it has already been suggested that decision making with regards to planting is often done collectively. Collective decision making appears to be a habit, even without institutions (such as the obshchina or the kolkhoz) to support it. Villagers discuss the rains, the soil, the frost, and simply decide. Working together, as they say, is better.

The village per se also appears, periodically, as a unit of religious ritual. In funeral rites, a procession—comprised of the casket, a cross, and rows of family members and mourners—is led to the edge of the village. There, villagers do not pass the threshold of the village, but turn facing the village and throw a lump of dirt over their shoulder. In addition, the person charged with carrying excess materials from building the coffin is charged with burning them at the village threshold. Though less frequent today, village pasturelands have been delimited in early May with a ritual *obkhod* (circumnambulation), designed to protect cows within that territory from beasts and otherworldly forces.

The village is in flux today. Its legal, political, economic, and social categories are in a state of transition. Nevertheless, a certain amount of continuity can be found in the broad conceptual strokes of social organization outlined above. If the village, the obshchina, and the *prikhod* (parish) are only cursorily linked to institutions, the sense of forming communities at various levels appears to be fixed in villagers' memory, according to certain regular patterns.

Regular patterns also emerge in the village's economic life. Habits of exchange are broadly revealing, and deserve discussion.

Basic Economic Structure in the Village: On "All Things Being Equal"

Inflation has caused tremendous hardship in the post-Soviet years. Prices have skyrocketed and, in cities, there is a serious question of whether people will survive these terrible times. Given normal weather conditions, the village is the safest place in the country for economic survival, for the simple fact that villagers are able to—even if they are not thrilled by this fact—live mostly outside of the market economy. One way or another, through agricultural labor and hunting and gathering, villagers meet their basic economic needs without much money. Those young enough to work still receive salaries, and those unable to work receive pensions. The amounts are nearly trivial (while I lived in Solov'ovo, salaries and pensions ranged from US$20 to US$50 a month), and it is very difficult to accumulate any capital these days to buy the things that an open market has provided. Goods such as a lawn mower would be appreciated, if there were money for such things. Or a motor for a boat. A VCR, perhaps. Or a car, of course. Solov'ovo residents have few such luxuries.

It is worth writing a short list of the things that villagers have without money.[32] In their gardens, they produce potatoes, cabbage, carrots, tomatoes, cucumbers, onions, garlic, beets, lettuce, sorrel, squash, peas, beans, berries, apples, herbs, flowers with healing properties, and so on. Most have built the roof over their heads and the bathhouse where they clean and heal themselves. They keep bees for honey. They produce their own alcohol. People in good health keep cows, sheep, sometimes goats and sometimes pigs, chickens, and roosters. Milking cows are a particularly important part of khoziaistvo: They provide milk, cheese (*tvorog*), sour cream, butter, and yogurt (*prostokvasha*). Solov'ovo is located on a lake (which, by the bucketful, provides all the water villagers drink and bathe with), and in that lake are abundant fish, including bream, ruff, perch, and the highly prized pike. In the forest there is game, including wild boar, elk, wild birds, as well as perhaps a dozen types of berries and twice as many edible mushrooms.[33] The forest provides wood, and sheep, wool. The open fields grow grasses spotted with clover, which is cut and fed to animals. The world of the peasant is a generous and sometimes bountiful one. It offers almost all of what one needs, if one is careful and hard working, and the whims of the weather and other "dark forces" do not lash out against the community.

The list of what must be purchased or otherwise obtained is shorter, but not insignificant. The farms and forests do not provide sugar. Nor are grains such as wheat (or the staple *kasha*) produced any longer. *Kombikorm*, a popular animal feed, must be purchased. Gas and electricity must be paid for (though most heating is done with wood, which it costs a small amount to cut down), as must certain hunting permits and taxes. Clothing must be purchased, even if village women still spin wool in the traditional way. Radios, televisions, and cars are the kinds of things that villagers want that only money can buy. Villagers now buy city-made furniture, as well, although they make and repair many of their own tools.

Most of what must be purchased is not essential to survival. This lack of dependency on the market is not only a clear advantage in these troubled times but tends, once again, to reinforce the self-sufficiency of the village, echoing back to the time of the obshchina.

In between that which one labors directly for and that which must be purchased, there is a large gap made up of all the things that individual households need and that they cannot or will not pay for. Old women living alone need someone to light their stoves for them. Some men are stronger and better at plowing than others, or are particularly good at slaughtering animals. Others have lots of time to fish. Some know the arts of healing, either through foods or sorcery. Some women keep cows and have milk, and others have none. There are times when a bathhouse needs repairs and other villagers can offer theirs to use. Knowledge of gardening or the places where the best berries and mushrooms grow is guarded like any other form of capital. In cases like these, the villagers engage in exchange.

Exchange comes in several forms; some are formal, if not always monetarized. Goods and services can be offered in exchange for goods and services. For example, milk can be exchanged for specialty vegetables; a nephew who catches fish for his elderly aunt will be given food and shelter; in return for making healing potions, one villager receives produce, fish, or goods such as tea, chocolate, or beer; and for plowing or slaughtering a cow, a villager can receive meat or vodka. Vodka is used more or less as currency; villagers pay for all kinds of services (from grave digging to woodcutting) with vodka. Money for these purposes comes from pensions, which range in size depending on the work that a person did during her life: Culture workers receive the least, kolkhozniki get more, and kolkhozniki who were war veterans of some kind receive the most. Money also comes from selling goods and handicrafts, usually in Belozersk or other villages. One very hard-working woman in Vershina has two milking cows; she gets on a bus once or twice a week to sell her milk and cheese in Belozersk, mostly through word of mouth. She rides the bus for free as a retiree, and in this way can make a little extra money for herself and her children. She is the only one in the three-village range of Solov'ovo, Vershina, and Maksimovo who manages to do this, because of the huge demands that it puts on one's time. Some young men work in construction on the side, and sometimes cut wood for pay.

Money is useful, of course, but can be an especially uncomfortable form of capital, particularly in certain contexts. The reasons for this appear to be two: First, the symbolism of "money" inherited a great deal of negative resonance during the Soviet period. Within the ideology of socialism, the lust for money (and endeavors to generate it, disdainfully called *spekulatsia* or speculation, even today) was seen as one fundamental sin of the capitalist enemy. Dollars, the most stable form of world currency available to Russians today, inherited the mother lode of negative associations. Owning dollars made one a criminal in Soviet times, and dollars still bear this sort of underworld association.

The second reason for the negative charge attached to money is a deeper one and has to do with certain fundamental principles of exchange. Money is used in exchange where debts are precisely calculated, and promptly erased. Money is comfortable where debt and the social connections it implies are uncomfortable. Within the context of the village, there are intricate webs of social connection: Villagers are, deeply, *svoimi* (one's own) to each other. Money (with its exacting ability to quantify debt and erase social connection) becomes problematic in the village for reasons that will be clearer below. The principle can be briefly noted as follows: Money is appropriate to use in exchange if there is great social distance between the traders; the closer the relationship, the more uncomfortable and socially inappropriate the use of money becomes. Exchange of goods and services is something that is done with categories of svoi ("one's own" people). Money is more appropriate to dealings with *chuzhie* (outsiders). Along with chuzhie, it carries associations of strangeness and danger.

In light of this principle, there is reluctance in the village to formalize economic exchanges with money. When villagers occasionally sell each other milk or potatoes, they name prices only with difficulty. On the other hand, it is—in terms of one's reputation and status in the village—absolutely essential to reimburse people for their services. In the following example cited in a journal entry, a neighbor, Zh—, comes to the house of Sof'ya and Mikhail Alekseevich to slaughter a lamb.

S: What will you take? Money, alcohol, or meat?

Zh—: I don't need anything.

Zh— says that he needs nothing, but it is clear to all involved that they must pay him somehow for his service. Sof'ya explains that she finally decided on a bottle of vodka and a kilogram of meat. Later I ask about Zh—'s statement that he needed nothing for his work, in light of his finally accepting meat and vodka.

Q: So, when a person says "I need nothing" (*nichevo ne nado*), it's not true? Is it true when *you* say it to people who come for potions?

MA: Yes, all I need is the cost of the bottle.

Q: How much is that?

MA: Around 500 rubles.

S: And the bottle cap.

MA: And the bottle cap, around 250 rubles. [Pause.] But it is not for me to ask.

Villagers certainly keep close track of exchanges. An outsider to the village first sees countless examples of generosity. One villager has an abundance of fresh onions or berries and brings them by when she comes to a neighbor for a visit. The host offers her tea and perhaps a shot of vodka or two. The next week, tvorog (homemade cheese) may be sent over. When produce is sold, it is sold at rock-bottom prices (there even appears to be a certain pride in selling for the lowest possible price). When giving each other milk, the milk literally overflows the jars into which it is poured. Tea is nearly always offered any guest who walks in the door. A guest coming with a gift will be sent home with one worth twice the value. To the outsider, such giving appears to be an outpouring of goods and services.

Offerings are not always accepted. There are certain implications to accepting or rejecting the hospitality of the various kinds offered. If I am invited for tea, acceptance means establishing (or reinforcing) a social link of some kind, which is often a good thing. On the other hand, some invitations are only formalities and it is inappropriate to accept them. One family constantly invited my hosts to tea, but the invitations were always refused. Months of asking finally granted me an answer. The invitation was "*radi prilichiia,* for the sake of politeness," and must be refused because of a comment some time ago by the husband of that family that "the Belovs come for tea all the time." The implication that the Belovs had taken advantage of hospitality, leaving them in a position of debt, caused them to maintain social distance from this second family. In head-to-head social confrontations, "winning" requires that one gives more. This could be called "one-downsmanship": spreading out one's surplus wins status in the community. That is, the "circle" of exchange groups appears to include an aspect of verticality. In short, vertical extremes (of wealth) are avoided in the village economic system in favor of relative social "evenness." Status is won by being an agent of redistribution (and not of individual accumulation).

As time goes on, it becomes clear to the outsider that accounts are indeed carefully kept in the village, even without formalizing them through money: Giving a basketful of green onions does not imply a basket of potatoes in return, but it does create a debt which must be "paid" eventually. The debt is not one that is meant to be quantified and then erased, but one that will, in the future, continue to encourage interdependence on a local level. The green onions of today become labor on a potato field next year, which becomes help in extinguishing a bathhouse fire in the next. The interdependence of villagers is fed and reinforced by such a system. As Marcel Mauss generalizes in his classic work, *The Gift*,

> If one gives things and returns them, it is because one is giving and returning "respects"—we will say "courtesies". Yet it is also because by giving one is giving oneself, and if one gives oneself, it is because one "owes" oneself—one's person and one's goods—to others.[34]

Exchange, most generally, is one of the mechanisms for summoning the "other" into the realm of the self. In rural Russia, the outpourings of one villager to the next are part of the procedure for making the subject a transindividual one. Becoming svoi, in large and small ways, is at the foundation of social organization in the Russian village.[35]

There is a final general point with regards to exchange in the village. The unspoken rule that one should return more than what one has received is the hallmark of a broader system of exchange that, more deeply, tends to encourage economic homogeneity in the village community. The axioms of this system could be summarized as follows: *It is good to be generous with one's possessions; in terms of one's social status, it is crucial to meet generosity with equal or greater generosity.* In other words, a redistribution of wealth that gives rise to a rough equality among households is reified in an explicit morality of generosity. Anthropologist Jovan Howe writes about the logic behind the practices of redistribution in the pre-Revolutionary village:

> The peasant through working on his own plot of land can seldom rise above the level of productivity required merely to secure the welfare of his family, hence, his own reproduction, and any attempt to improve his lot, can be so disruptive of the intricate network of reciprocity through which risks to the reproduction of allied families are apportioned. . . . For this reason, it is assumed, usually correctly, that the individual can get ahead in a peasant community only at the expense of others, so that even "good luck" is suspect and a windfall may be given away to avoid envy. The peasant calculates his costs and benefits, but in a different currency from the small commodity producer.[36]

It must not be assumed that peasants never wish to own beautiful things or receive more salary than their neighbors. The point is that such inequality of means can become a social liability. When generosity doesn't work to keep things more or less equal, there are other mechanisms that encourage homogeneity. Tattling on each other for infractions of permit laws has been practiced (and resented) for decades. The envy that arises from inequality is not, however, a mere social unpleasantness; it is a particularly generative part of the workings of unseen worlds and unpredictable forces. Envy awakens unseen forces (such as *sglas*, the evil eye) that can cause all types of ruination. Social unevenness, in other words, sets the dark forces in motion, which can and will topple the haughty.

This symbolic configuration is common to agrarian societies—especially ones where there are terribly harsh conditions and a terribly capricious growing season. Sticking together serves you well, and the opposite is fundamentally dangerous. This is the point of the classic work of George Foster, "Peasant Society and the Image of Limited Good."[37] Citing Foster's work, Jovan Howe writes on the nineteenth-century peasant's fear of accumulation of "the better things in life":

> An individual, who seeks to acquire things and, generally, "better himself," attributes of "consumerism," traditionally was not simply "bad," but positively dangerous, motivated himself by *zavist'*, "envy" and likely to incite envy in others. Alternatively, he might be a sorcerer (witch) or insane (bewitched), and was dealt with accordingly.[38]

This dynamic is very much alive in the Russian village today. It does not *determine* social relations but it does, indeed, mark certain unseen dynamics within them.

Leadership from Within: *Khoziain* and *Khoziaika* (*Svoi*)

The term khoziain is defined[39] as "owner, proprietor; master, boss; landlord; host." It means so much more than any one of those terms. The household head is the khoziain, and the term is also used for anyone in charge of a given group of people, or a given territory. When the term is brought to its ideal culmination, the khoziain is not only the leader; he is the figurehead and emblem of the group over which he has dominion. He has moral leadership, and duties of heavy-handed fatherly discipline. No less important, he is a channel for otherworldly powers, ones that can protect and heal the entire community over which he has dominion. The usage of the term khoziain falls into three subcategories:

1. The khoziain of a household. He has special powers of decision making. Also known as *batyushka* or *bat'ka*, a household is seen to be his,

and that of his father before him. Ideally, he is in charge, along with the khoziaika, of the workings of the household. Both successes and failures are on his shoulders.

2. The khoziain of a larger group, such as a factory or a town or, at its ultimate limit, a nation. Like the khoziain of a household, the khoziain over any domain is the emblem of leadership there. Like the tsars before him, Stalin was considered the "khoziain" of the Soviet Union. Such *khoziainy* are ideally strong leaders. They rule with a heavy hand, and bring about social order.

3. Supernatural *khozyaeva* (plural of *khozianin*) of natural domains, such as the forest (*khoziain lesavoi,* or *leshii*), house (*khoziain domovoi*), barn (*khoziain khleva*), or bathhouse (*khoziain banii*). These beings are in charge of their realms and must be supplicated and appeased periodically. The domovoi must be invoked before moving into a new house, and the khoziain lesavoi should be asked permission before entering the forest. When such precautions are not taken, these khozyaeva (like the others, when they are not properly deferred to) can lash out against those in their domain. They can be visible or invisible and their forms change.

The term khoziaika, the female counterpart to khoziain, has less overall symbolic impact. A khoziaika is also in charge of a given domain, usually a household but sometimes a forest or field or barn, but she usually does not carry the extra weight of national leadership in her symbolic range. The symbolism of womanhood has a great deal of power, but the female khoziaika does not carry the ferociousness of her male counterpart.

The emblem of leadership from within a svoi-formation is the focus of a great deal of emotional and symbolic attention in rural Russia. Such figures are not resented for their power. On the contrary, the khoziain in its many forms appears as a positive role (even if a given khoziain, such as Stalin, is hated or feared in given instances). For example, the role of the *barin* or feudal landlord is generally a positive one in the stories of villagers. Serfdom was abolished in Russia in 1867, but the sense that a powerful khoziain-like figure held dominion over a portion of land continued into this century and is alive in the narratives of several villagers. Relationships to a given landlord appear to have varied depending on the people involved. Solov'ovo remembers the Polish family that had been landowners in the region: Relations with the former barin were good enough (he would hire people for wage labor and the work was well appreciated), but his wife was disliked for her nitpicking about use of the forest lands. She was murdered after the revolution by a "*durak*" (idiot) who wanted her samovar. Other *bariny* in the region were decidedly well liked: One was known to give honey to the children in the villages, and another was appreciated for his hard work. As one woman told the story:

> We had at home a barin (*bara*). This one, he lived, he lived. My father, he said that they were very good [people], the ones where I was from, in Krotovskoe. He said that they were very good people. So if you have no bread, he would absolutely give you a loan, as much as you needed. And never offended people and he himself worked. Well. Worked himself. That was the barin. There was our rich one (*bogach*). They say he didn't even wear pants. During the senokos. [Wore] white underpants. He said, "I never wear pants. I always go in underpants." He would leave at 6 or 7 for senokos. Went himself. There. That was the kind of barin he was.
>
> Q: So it's not how they describe?
>
> No! No, they all lie! So, now there's a barin. The brigadier. He, for example, goes in a car. He has stuff. This barin had . . . a son, there were daughters. They all worked. When they arrived, they were dekulakized. . . . What rich ones? . . . In the family were six children. And they killed his son. What kinds of rich ones were these? Would lead them to the senokos. The little ones would bang and bang [at the work]. And he himself would dig with a wooden stick (*lapatoi*).

It appears that the role of the barin is a respected one, even if a given barin is not respected. Though nearly absent in narratives from the village of Solov'ovo, history tells many tales of peasant uprisings against landlords.[40] In the above narrative, the barin was respected for his hard work that mirrored that of the villagers. The stories about how he would work in his underwear underline this feature, i.e., that he was "one of us." The brigadier, for his haughtiness and lavish displays of wealth, was not. This is because the brigadier falls into another category of hierarchy, one that is not appreciated in the village setting. On the contrary, this form of social inequality (and the social agents who reinforce it) fundamentally ruptures a sense of well-being in the village.

Hierarchy from Without: Chuzhie Leaders

There does not appear to be an important presence of class within the Russian village of this or earlier centuries. There is no "we-the-*bedniaki* (poor peasants)" who essentially oppose "we-the-*kulaky* (rich peasants)." It is relevant to point out that collectivization, and the corresponding movement of dekulakization, were remembered nearly universally as unjust, even by people who were otherwise very sympathetic to communist ideals. Time and again, when speaking of the deportation of the kulaky (those deemed rich peasants), villagers would say, "What kulaky? They were simply hard workers!" This is not to say that there was never any resentment against these richer families. The greater injustice appears to be understood as the one perpetuated against the village as a whole, that is, against the village svoi.[41] Given the organization of the obshchina, for centuries the village had been inwardly organized and directed, even while answering to outward demands for production and taxes.

Although the khozyaeva who are the figureheads of given svoi-formations are conceptually "comfortable," there is a layer of power-holders (mostly administrators from outside the village) who are not. According to historians, the attitude of peasants toward the tsar was a warm one; he was a fatherly khoziain figure—a protector and bearer of otherworldly powers. The *boiary* (members of the administrative class below the tsar) were, by contrast, widely feared and hated.[42] In the same way that contemporary peasants say that it was not Stalin who devastated the Soviet Union with persecutions, but those under Stalin, it was the boiary who were blamed for inhumane practices of the tsarist state. The khoziain-figure is understood to intercede on behalf of the narod (the people) to his administrators: In pre-Revolutionary times, those administrators were the boiary (and more local ones such as *zemskie nachal'niki*, or land bosses), and in this century they became the *kommunisty*. A three-tiered organization is evident, filled by the roles of the khoziain figure, the administrators, and the narod. The narod and the khoziain figure are svoi to one another and have a synergistic relation one to the other. The administrators are chuzhie, and can be hated and feared as outsiders.

When the centrally organized party was introduced into the village, not only was the chuzhoi administrative layer of power still a part of peasant life, it became an intimate one as villagers themselves became party members. In the post-Revolutionary village, there were local party members, *deputaty* (representatives in the local Soviet), kolkhoz brigadiers, *agitatory* (party agitators), *stukachi* (party spies), *predsedatel' kolkhoza* (president of the kolkhoz), and so on. These sorts of administrators and nachal'niki (bosses) did not come with a comfortable range of power. This was a hierarchy that was defined not by the internal workings of village social organization (khoziainy and starosti of the obshchina), but by external, centrally controlled authorities. With the extension of those authorities into the village, chuzhie landed in the circle of svoi.

Indeed, if there was little remembered resentment against the supposed kulaky for their relative wealth (they were still part of a village-level svoi formation), there was a great deal of resentment against the party representatives who sometimes betrayed co-villagers, and against town officials whose duties were dictated by the centrally organized party. Many narratives reflect this resentment. There are very concrete reasons for this: Many people lost family members to the purges. One story vividly reflects the feeling for outsider/party leaders. Here Fyodor Sergeevich S— and his wife Antonina Mikhailovna tell how a "regional boss" was left to die.

> In our region, we had a boss. He crashed into the river. Into the Sheksna River. And they saw him lying by his car and could have saved him. No one went up to him.
>
> Q: Why?
>
> On the one hand, they were afraid. And on the other hand, here— you see he's lying there. Let him die. The devil—you go to him to save him, and he can find that person guilty for something. Something might happen. No one went up to him.
>
> Q: So everyone decided to let him die?
>
> Let him be in his car and die in his car. He perished. He was the head of the police. That's who he was. He sentenced many innocent people. For that, he crashed in his car, went into the canal or something. And he was alone. And so no one went to help him. He was in his car, driving by himself. And let him lie. No one wanted to save him.
>
> AM: Maybe no one dared. They walk up and he blames them. As if you had done something with him.

This very powerful story reflects not only hatred toward a specific man, though this is certainly clear. The head of the police was part of a stratum of leadership that is made of chuzhie. This sort of leadership is associated with fear and distrust where part of the fear comes about simply because they are within the category of chuzhie, who bear associations of unpredictable, sometimes miraculous dangers.

Gathering the Other into the Realm of the Self

Certainly, there is much emphasis on the needs of the group in rural Russia, just as the needs of an individual are de-emphasized. When entering a residential group, one's resources and one's tasks are defined by that group. Happiness is linked to group harmony. Semantically, it is awkward to speak of an "individual" who has an essential personality there. *Lichnost'* (from *lik*, face) is the closest term (and is also used to mean "a celebrity"), and is used rarely in the village. One's *kharakter* (character) can be spoken of, but this character does not seem to be the object of obsessive attention. A person can be described as soft or hard, nice or genuine, intelligent or silly, kind or cruel, but interestingly, a person "with a character" (*s kharaktorom*) is understood to be, most generally, a difficult or socially awkward person. Character, in other words, comes negatively marked.

Perhaps the most difficult symbolic barrier to an elaborate concept of an individual self is the fact that the individual will—in the sense that a given person can force her way into the universe and change the course of fate—is very weakly elaborated. The Russian "will," or *volia*, is a very important concept, one that points to the deep vibrancy that emanates out of a person and into the world. But the universal humming of volia does not imply that it is easy to take control of life and mold it into the forms we choose. More specifically, when faced with outside forces of various kinds (from the weather to the regional administration), villagers will rarely attempt to take on these forces. When regional buses aren't running for weeks on end, for example, villagers are very reluctant to call and ask why. When children drown every year in lakes and rivers, there is a sense that this is fate (*sud'ba*) and not something that can be changed by teaching children to swim.

There are most probably several reasons for this relatively weakly defined individual self. For one thing, the special fashioning of the sort of highly willed self that is found in the West cannot be separated from its history of industrial capitalism. Russia did not share this long-term development and, it could well be argued, never inherited the sort of self that tightly merges will and personality. On the contrary, this chapter has dealt with the sorts of monadic, locally defined groups that Russian history gave rise to, where the self was subsumed under the rubric of the democratic larger order. Of course, another reason for the de-emphasis of the individual will may be that Russians have taken note of the consequences of going against the larger wills of outside forces, and by laying low, as it were, they are acting for their own protection.

On the other hand, the self, as attached to an individual person, certainly exists in rural Russia. Aside from the connection between self and individual "personality," there are the deeper currents of how the self is symbolically bounded. In Solov'ovo, I found evidence of differing modes of the self that were idealized in both positive and negative ways: One form was considered open, expansive, and "soulful" (and in excess, is marked by

physical and moral slovenliness), and the second, controlled and disci-
plined (and in excess marked by soullessness).[43] The openness of the self
can come about in many ways (drinking decidedly helps the "soul" to
raskroitsia, open itself up) and is linked to the explicit morality of generosity and hospitality.[44] On the other hand, self-discipline and control
(*sdirzhennost'*) are linked in their own way to the proper leadership of a
family or other svoi formation.

As an individual, one's actions have consequences back onto the self, and
further onto the broader social sphere. Interestingly, these consequences
often fall on the family line and even the future rod, particularly with
regard to misdeeds. In village stories, destroying a church, for example,
can curse the long line of an individual's descendants. An individual, as a
sociocultural unit, also comes into existence when a person becomes the
object of group-driven shame.

Given these preliminary remarks on the Russian "self" and on certain social implications to rural Russian pronominal usage, I now conclude with
a few generalizations on what is really the overarching theme of this chapter: creating and configuring a svoi formation.

Svoi versus Chuzhoi

The most abstract, and probably the most important, concept in social organization is the notion of being svoi (one's own) versus being chuzhoi
(someone else's, alien, strange, foreign). Svoi is not necessarily linked to
any given kinship relationship, but certain relations imply it. If the reference were the village locale, then svoi would refer to householders and visiting kin and perhaps friends. In the context of the region, svoi refers to
those from the *derevnya* (village) or *prikhod*. The context can broaden several times and svoi can refer to Russians or Soviets, even. Furthermore, a
sense of svoi, it is clear, can accumulate. For instance, after an absence
of several months, when I returned to the village I was deeply moved to
be greeted with "*ty sovsem stala svoei* (you became fully our own)." A sense
of being one's own, of gathering and being gathered into a larger social
sphere, is accompanied by feelings of warmth. It is a good thing, in this
symbolic configuration, to live among one's own.

Creating a svoi formation implies the production of bounded social
groups. This activity can be done at various "levels." For example, in the
household, the production of svoi brings about work groups. The produc-

tion of svoi around the table when drinking together can serve to (for example) change the weather or create a bond of friendship that will have implications of loyalty and sacrifice. Svoi formation has a crucial symbolic function as well as its social function. In the act of svoi formation, something is fashioned that is more than the sum of its parts. Such groups can battle the unpredictable dark forces in the world at large, and channel otherworldly powers. The svoi formed in the forest with invocations to grandfather forest can protect one from the dark forces that cause one to get lost. The svoi formed with ancestors at the graveyard during the festival of Troitsa channel in powers of fertility and healing. There is a sense of svoi that surrounds being a peasant as opposed to a city dweller, or of being a Russian as opposed to any other nationality. The svoi of the rodina sends people to near-holy battle.

Svoi and the Land

Land has more than a little to do with a sense of *svoi*. As Sof'ya told me, referring to the era of pereselenie, when outsiders were forced to move to Solov'ovo:

> We didn't abuse anyone. Everyone was here. There was enough space for everyone. But anyway, somehow. . . . If people would start to fight over some petty thing, they would start saying, "why did the leshii bring you here?" There were discontents. Because those [in the village] were svoi. Svoi among svoi, that is, villagers among villagers. They live friendlier together. Those who originated from Solov'ovo lived much more as friends. There were no fights. There was enough of everything for everyone.

Perhaps the deepest form of being svoi is being rodnoi. People who are *rodnye* to each other have one of two connections: They are tied to the same family line, or to the land on which they live. These two notions are so symbolically close that the resonance from one nearly merges with the other. Rodina, the land of the rod, is kin, and rodina is the ground itself. The idea of rodina can nearly smell of local soils; when it is Mother Russia (the soil is still there), it is a vast expanse that one loves. Land has an intimate relationship to the concept of being svoi. Being rodnoi is a special form of being svoi, with an emphasis on the fact that that soil and kin are shared.

Summary

Russian peasants, like members of any society, form social groups in the performance of collective action. They create categories that distinguish between those who are included and those who are not. Three broad points on Russian social organization can be gathered from the preceding analysis. First, where it is clear that group identification and group action are crucial in rural Russia, these groups are many. There is no single Russian collective (with essential qualities) that is linked to one Russian village. This is borne out in historical studies. Second, these groups are mostly flexible: They form and re-form and include both the world of living actors and beings from other planes. Finally, there is a great deal of power to the act of forming and maintaining these groups. Some of this power is seen to have an otherworldly quality to it, which explains some of the far-reaching emotional appeal associated with local notions of the "collective." It is clear from the above analysis of village social organization that there are certain basic features of social life in rural Russia that have "survived" the sociopolitical tumult of the twentieth century. The focus on the family as an organizational unit, the economic, political, and symbolic features of local "collectives" and certain treatments of social verticality persist to this day, in spite of organized attempts to undermine their persistence.

But what does this say, most generally, about prospects of reform in rural Russia? There seem to be two main issues that arise from what has been presented.

The first involves the question of how rural communities interact with nonrural communities. In the preceding analysis, I sketched some of the dynamics of inclusion and exclusion in categories of belonging at the local level. I noted that exchange takes place constantly within the village, and often between the village and outside the village, but that money exchanges are not a particularly comfortable form of exchange among people who are svoi to one another (where being/becoming svoi relates to family ties, proximity, working and exchanging together, and even simply living on the soil of one's ancestors). Crudely put, the closer the relationship, the less comfortable exchange involving money becomes. At the same time, the closer the relationship, the more the people involved enjoy the intricate web of interdependence sometimes known as "trust." So, you bring vegetables and tea to your friends, you give more than you get, you help your family with one thing and they help you with another, and the mechanism churns on and on.

Comfortable versus uncomfortable exchange can be considered something of a conundrum when looking at rural reform, and particularly the notion that peasants must turn more actively toward the market, but it does not have to be considered an ultimate barrier to monetarization. It would be a great mistake to consider a dynamic such as this one as culturally deterministic. Plenty of money exchanges occur in the village (from the arrival of Gypsies with truckfuls of woolen underwear and scarves, to trips to the doctor 40 kilometers away, to buying grain or precut wood or cigarettes or vodka). The only question becomes how these factors could, particularly in times of economic shortage, keep the villagers exchanging through the comfort of what is known as "barter."

The second point is also not meant to be deterministic, but does need to be taken seriously. In rural Russia, as in many other peasant societies, there is a dynamic of social interaction that includes gaining status from gestures of generosity, and risking various forms of social and metaphysical danger by private acts of accumulation.[45] This does not mean that villagers will never buy anything for themselves and will never lord what they have over each other. But it does mean that there is an unspoken, powerful mechanism for eliminating the extremes of wealth, which can result in both social censure and retribution from unseen forces. This is part of an overall dynamic that strives to maintain a certain measure of group cohesion. While not, in principle, preventing the development of rural capitalism, this dynamic can, in a quiet way, discourage its more extreme forms.

Notes

1. My dissertation is based on this research: Margaret Paxson, "Configuring the Past in Rural Russia: An Essay on the Symbolic Topography of Social Memory" (Ph.D. diss., Université de Montréal, 1999). This research was supported by the International Research and Exchanges Board, the Social Science Research Council, the Kennan Institute for Advanced Russian Studies, the Faculté des Etudes Supérieures de l'Université de Montréal, the Département d'anthropologie de l'Université de Montréal, and the Phi Delta Epsilon Memorial Scholarship, McGill University.

2. This, like all the other names of people and places in this article (except for larger towns and cities), is a pseudonym.

3. See Geroid Robinson, *Rural Russia Under the Old Regime* (1932; reprint, Berkeley: University of California Press, 1969); Richard Pipes, *Russia Under the Old Regime* (London: Weidenfeld and Nicholson, 1974); and Zhores Medvedev, *Soviet Agriculture* (New York: W. W. Norton and Company, 1987).

4. Robinson, *Rural Russia Under the Old Regime*, 70.

5. See Jeffrey Burds, *Peasant Dreams and Market Politics* (Pittsburgh, PA: University of Pittsburgh Press, 1998), 17–18, for a description of the nineteenth-century dvor.

6. For a description of this rite, see Olga Semyonova Tian-Shanskaia's *Village Life in Late Tsarist Russia*, ed. and trans. David L. Ransel (1906?; reprint, Bloomington: Indiana University Press, 1993), 127–29.

7. Because of the patrilocal practices through which large households would split again and again over time, villages tend to be made up of a few family names (in Solov'ovo, the old and important names are Stepanov, Sokolov, Belov, Valov, and Zhitov) and many of the children who "*begali vmeste*" (ran together) were cousins of one kind or another. In Russian, cousins are usually called "brothers and sisters." Villages are thus populated with many, many brothers and sisters of different kinds, which perhaps reinforces the idea that the village is "like a family."

8. This was evidenced in the comment of one man who told me of his decision to marry. One day his mother said to him, "*Zhenis'. Nado pomochnitsu.* Get married. I need a helper."

9. I cannot count the daughters-in-law who, according to their mothers-in-law, would "sleep while my son does the cooking and cleaning." Never having witnessed that actual event, or anything like that actual event, I would have to treat such comments contextually.

10. The word used here was *plemenia*.

11. From P. Yu. Chernykh, *Istoriko-etimologicheskii slovar' sovremennogo russkogo iazyka* (Moscow: Russkyi Iazyk, 1994). My translation.

12. See Joanna Hubbs, *Mother Russia* (Bloomington: Indiana University Press, 1988), 81.

13. Ibid., 91.

14. In *Mother Russia*, Hubbs argues that the "religion of the rod" was separate from the religion in which ancient Slavic gods (such as Perun and his pantheon) were worshipped. She claims that these gods were the chosen ones of the princes of Kiev before the conversion to Christianity. They shared with the God of Christianity their patriarchal quality.

15. See Watters, "The Peasant and the Village Commune," in *The Peasant in Nineteenth Century Russia*, ed. Wayne Vuchinich (Stanford, CA: Stanford University Press, 1968), 143.

16. Part of this depends on the type of property. As Tian-Shanskaia wrote in her 1906 ethnography, men were understood to own "house, grain, horses, sheep and agricultural implements" (*Village Life in Late Tsarist Russia*, 124). Women pay for and "own" household items. From handicrafts and extra labor, men and women possessed their own money, and Tian-Shanskaia writes that "theft between the spouses is not uncommon" (p. 126). In comments such as these, the division between the sexes appears to be a substantial one. There is another way to look at this problem: Husbands and wives are made from two separate family lines that come together in one household unit. The division of family lines may be at least as important as gender divisions. The wife is one of "one's own," living under the same roof with her in-laws, but she maintains her own interests.

17. This topic is treated in detail in Paxson, "Configuring the Past in Rural Russia," chapter 8.

18. Watters, "The Peasant and the Village Commune," 133.

19. Pipes, *Russia Under the Old Regime*, 17.

20. In *Russia Under the Old Regime*, Pipes, like many authors, uses "mir" (which means, in this case, "world") and "obshchina" (from the root *obshch-*, meaning "shared" or "common") interchangeably to refer to ancient collectives. Acknowledging that there is a debate surrounding this issue, I will do the same. I never heard mir mentioned in the village of Solov'ovo, but the obshchina was mentioned in this sense several times. If there is a distinction between these institutions in their historical manifestations, such a distinction has not survived in the present cognitive landscape.

21. Pipes, *Russia Under the Old Regime*, 16.

22. James Billington, *The Icon and the Axe* (New York: Vintage Books, 1970), 19.

23. Medvedev, *Soviet Agriculture*, 7.

24. Pisato and Zaslavsky cited in Lev Timofeev, *Soviet Peasants, Or, The Peasants' Art of Starving* (St. Louis, MO: Telos Press, 1985), 6–7.

25. Only males were counted, generally, in this redistribution. Called *edaki* (eaters), the males would, it was assumed, contribute the most to agricultural production. Land was therefore distributed with reference to laborers and not to actual family size. One of the reforms of the Soviet distributional system was to count women as well as edaki—and apportion private plots accordingly.

26. Billington, *The Icon and the Axe*, 324.

27. For an in-depth discussion of the mechanical problems of agricultural production under the kolkhoz system, see Medvedev's *Soviet Agriculture*.

28. Pipes, *Russia Under the Old Regime*.

29. Sheila Fitzpatrick, *Stalin's Peasants: Resistance and Survival in the Russian Village After Collectivization* (Oxford: Oxford University Press, 1994), 14.

30. The two words were spelled differently until the Revolution. The important sense here is that of the "entire world."

31. In Jovan E. Howe, *The Peasant Mode of Production* (Tampere: University of Finland, 1991), 46.

32. It is worthwhile particularly because this list contrasts so sharply with the list of foods that urbanites lack during times of trouble.

33. Berries, and especially mushrooms, are commodities that can be sold for very high prices outside of the village. Villagers mostly choose to not sell their mushrooms or berries, considering them essentials of their own diet.

34. Marcel Mauss, *The Gift: The Form and Reason for Exchange in Archaic Societies* (1950; reprint, New York: W. W. Norton, 1990), 46.

35. It also happens to be one of the crucial means for summoning powers from otherworldly planes.

36. Howe, *The Peasant Mode of Production*, 17.

37. In *American Anthropologist* 2 (1965): 293–315.

38. Howe, *The Peasant Mode of Production*, 18.

39. Marcus Wheeler, *Oxford Russian-English Dictionary* (Oxford: Clarendon Press, 1992).

40. Vologda oblast falls into the category of provinces in which there was the least amount of peasant revolt. This is likely due to the fact that in this region, a relatively small proportion of peasants were serfs (16 percent to 35 percent). In Martin Gilbert's *The Dent Atlas of Russian History*, 2d ed. (London: J.M. Dent, 1993), 57–58. For an overview of the character of peasant revolts in the past century, see Eric R. Wolf, *Peasant Wars of the Twentieth Century* (New York: Harper Torchbooks, 1969).

41. One great betrayal of the era was that it was often villagers themselves—ones who had become active in the party—who chose the families to be dekulakized.

42. See Michael Cherniavsky, *Tsar and People: Studies in Russian Myths* (New York: Random House, 1969) for a characterization of this dynamic of love for the tsar and hatred/distrust for the court.

43. These generalizations are not derived from an exegesis on the subject; this is not a natural topic of discussion. Rather, they derive from symbolic gestures gleaned from long-term fieldwork.

44. The subject of the symbolic configuration of the *dusha* (soul) is an extremely rich one that has been treated with depth and subtlety in Dale Pesmen, *Russia and Soul: An Exploration* (Ithaca, NY: Cornell University Press, 2000).

45. This subject is treated in depth in Paxson, "Configuring the Past in Rural Russia," chapter 7.

7

Contemporary Agrarian Reforms in a Russian Historical Context

DAVID A.J. MACEY

It has been observed that reform was endemic to Soviet-style political systems. Indeed, every one of the so-called communist states on the Eurasian continent has, since its establishment, been in a perpetual search for that felicitous combination of policies that would enable them to "catch up and overtake" the capitalist world. While comparative communist studies developed a respectable pedigree during the Cold War years, over the last decade or so, within the newly developing genre of post-communism transition studies, it has become especially popular to compare Russia's choice of transition strategy to a market economy and the apparent failures of this latest round of reforms to the very different but also apparently much more successful path adopted by China since the late 1970s. The differences are especially noticeable in the realm of agriculture, where the changes that led to the de-collectivization and individualization of Chinese agriculture (based on long-term leases) have not only proved extremely successful but have helped fuel the rapid growth of China's light industrial, consumer goods, and service sectors as well.

In contrast, the de-Stalinization, "de-collectivization," and "privatization" of Russian agriculture during the Yeltsin years have resulted in the virtual collapse of Russian agriculture. Currently, the entire Russian economy is in a state of free fall, with both total industrial as well as agricultural output having fallen some 50 percent since the collapse of the Soviet

Union.[1] Further, as a result of the financial crisis in fall 1998, the ruble has lost some 80 percent of its value, and by all accounts the economy has been turned into a "virtual economy" conducted almost entirely on the basis of barter, *blat* (influence), and *sviazy* (connections).[2] In sum, a series of reforms—designed to radically transform and reinvigorate the lethargic Soviet-era state and collective farms, paralleling similar reforms in the industrial and service sectors—while producing major shifts in the juridical forms of ownership and management, have not produced the apparently desired economic impact. However, the reforms have certainly resulted in a huge reduction in government expenditures on agriculture, both direct and indirect—certainly an implicit if not explicit goal of reform.[3]

Further comparison between Russia and China, of course, makes it quite clear that the path followed by China was not, in fact, open to Russia because the proportions of the population involved in rural (agricultural) and urban (industrial) occupations were exactly reversed, thus making it impossible for agricultural reform to make the same kind of contribution to overall economic growth in Russia as in China. At the same time, the correlation of political forces was markedly different: In Russia the penetration of government and party was far deeper, and hence they and the population were far more invested in the existing system than was the case in China. Further, not only had China established its "communist" system some 30 years later than Russia but, in the course of the Cultural Revolution, had essentially replaced its original cadres prior to the onset of reform with a new and younger generation. Thus, the power elite in China contrasted sharply with Russia's gerontocracy. As a result, whereas change in China, in fact, developed from below among the peasantry themselves, and quickly won the support of the new managers and *apparat* (party functionaries) and, ultimately, the party's leadership, in Russia reform came from above and met with widespread opposition, among both the managers and the apparat as well as the population at large. Russia's "transition" is, indeed, unique and without precedent among other societies exiting from communism.[4]

Given the above background, I compare the past decade in the history of Russian agrarian policy and agricultural development with previous eras of great political and economic change in Russia's own recent past, rather than with the very different case of China, or the equally different cases of the former Soviet bloc countries of East Central Europe. While there are also obvious differences of context involved in such a comparison, I believe that focusing on both similarities and differences with Russia's own history of reform will enable us to reach a better understanding of what we are currently witnessing and what direction the recent changes may eventually take. In the analysis that follows, I utilize an important distinction between "land" reform and "agrarian" reform: Land reform involves a transfer of ownership from one social class to another, generally in a revolutionary context, and has traditionally been associated with agrarian policies of extensification; and agrarian reform involves a variety of more moderate changes in the management and/or structure of landholding and land use, usually with the essentially reformist goal of agricultural intensification, without significant changes in underlying ownership patterns.[5] At the same time, and to the extent that there are clear disparities between them, I distinguish three key phases of the reform process: the enactment of policy at the center; local implementation; and social, economic, and political outcomes.

Major Political and Economic Transformations in Russia's Recent Past

There have been five major eras of political and economic transformation in Russia's recent past: the emancipation of the serfs in 1861, the Stolypin reforms in 1906, the agrarian revolution of 1917–18, the New Economic Policy in 1921, and the collectivization of agriculture in 1929.[6] Each of these eras shared some key features. Above all, they were all introduced by the state from above for predominantly political reasons, though at the heart of each period of change lay a concern with agrarian policy. However, in all but one case, the agrarian revolution of 1917–18, the respective governments were also pursuing a common set of longer-term economic goals as well: to increase agricultural productivity as a means for stimulating Russia's industrial modernization. Yet, these reforms in agriculture were also quite different from one another—so much so that one might consider any comparison with the present to be without any heuristic value. First, therefore, I highlight some of the similarities and differences among government policies during these quite distinctive periods of change, and then I analyze how these comparisons can help throw light on the current and future situation.

The Emancipation of the Serfs

A moderate land reform undertaken in nonrevolutionary circumstances with some of the same goals as agrarian reform, the emancipation focused on transforming the peasantry's juridical status, administrative structure, and fiscal relationship to the state, while transferring approximately half of the agricultural land in European Russia to the peasantry's direct control. The long-term motivation for change was that of increasing economic productivity and the intensification of peasant agriculture. This goal, however, was ultimately subordinated to the immediate political goals of both enacting a policy that would preserve the peasants' presumed support for the tsarist regime while maintaining social, economic, political, and fiscal stability. At the same time, this reform imposed by the state from above in the midst of a military defeat and leadership succession, while compulsory for the peasantry, was made voluntary for the landowning nobility. As a consequence, the process of implementation, which was managed by the state but conducted by elected officials drawn largely from the local landowning nobility, dragged out until the 1880s when the process was finally made compulsory, following another political crisis and the assassination of the tsar-emancipator himself. Nonetheless, about 90 percent of peasants had been "emancipated," and, hence, the reform could on a number of levels—political, administrative, and fiscal—be considered a success.[7]

By the turn of the century, however, both liberal and conservative observers, within educated society as well as the government, had concluded that emancipation had been an economic failure and that a "second emancipation" would be necessary to achieve the increases in productivity and output still needed to fuel Russia's industrialization—much as the emancipators had originally planned. This time, however, the peasants were believed to need an emancipation from the traditional system of communal landownership and, even more important, the communal system of land use that had developed under serfdom and had subsequently been legally enforced by the emancipation process to guarantee social and fiscal continuity and stability. For while each peasant household was individually responsible for its own strips, agricultural practices—including the assignment of those strips, crop choices, and the calendar—were all collectively managed by the commune.[8]

The Stolypin Agrarian Reforms

This "second" emancipation, as it was called at the time,[9] was a classic agrarian reform in that it deliberately rejected a revolutionary redistribution of land in favor of the more moderate and reformist path of restructuring existing forms of landownership and use. Today, these reforms are often characterized as a "privatization," hence creating an immediate analogy with recent government policies that sought to create a stratum of individual private farmers. Such, however, is a misnomer. It would be more accurate to describe Stolypin's reforms as an attempt to liberate the peasant household from the collective power of the commune and thereby individualize rights of usufruct. In this more limited respect, however, and unlike the case of the emancipation, direct comparisons with the present are valid. There were other similarities as well. For Stolypin not only sought to break up the traditional and collectivist structure of agricultural management, represented by the peasant commune, he also adopted juridical measures to facilitate the formation of individual peasant family farms by the newly enfranchised members of the commune. In addition, steps were taken to enable peasants to purchase land from a state land fund, again with the goal of forming individual family farms. In both cases, however, ownership rights were restricted so as to prevent fragmentation but especially excessive accumulation, branded "speculation." Further, the right to alienate former communally owned land was restricted such that only sales to other peasants were permissible. And, of major importance, and also analogous to the present, the Stolypin reforms were almost entirely voluntary in nature. However, unlike today, separators and individualizers were privileged by the law and granted a near absolute right to separate so long as certain procedures were observed. Similarly, as is also the case today with the collective farms, communes that had the support of a majority of their members were legally entitled to preserve their existing structure. So, too, a variety of intermediary forms and partial improvements were tolerated and even encouraged, based on the assumption that either they would subsequently lead to further changes in the direction of more individualistic forms of agriculture or at least have some potential for increasing peasant agricultural productivity in the short term.[10]

While these similarities are important and instructive, there are also four significant differences. First of all, there was a difference of context, for the Stolypin reforms were introduced within a developing market economy that already possessed much of the institutional infrastructure necessary for further development, even if the peasant economy was still a primarily subsistence or consumption-oriented (*polu-natural'noe*) economy and far from being fully monetized.[11] Second, the government actively participated in the process of implementation, both by establishing locally elected supervisory bodies with joint executive, legislative, and judicial powers, and by dispatching large numbers of newly trained officials, both administrative and technical (surveyors), into every province and county of European Russia to argue the case for reform and to provide peasants with the necessary expertise and assistance to realize the reforms' relatively complex juridical and technical components. At the same time, given that these reforms were not simply imposed from above, extensive collective bargaining procedures were also established to reconcile conflicting interests within the commune. Meanwhile, reinforcing its commitment to an actively interventionist policy, the government's macroeconomic policies were similarly pro-agricultural and resulted in the provision of new forms of agricultural credit as well as the creation of the juridical bases for collateral; a huge expansion of agronomical aid and general extension services that were initially targeted for the newly formed individual farmers but soon became available also to peasants remaining within communes, so long as they led to improvements in land-use; a rapid development of credit and other forms of agricultural cooperatives; and a variety of tax and other privileges. Finally, it must be noted, the government's entire policy was predicated on the goal of keeping as many peasants as possible on the land and preventing either the formation of a landless rural proletariat or a too rapid expansion of the urban proletariat, on the assumption that such would help preserve social, economic, and political stability.

Yet, for all of the reforms' positive elements, their political origins, in the midst of a revolutionary challenge to the government, resulted in the immediate political goal of deflating the widespread demands from both the peasantry and the revolutionary intelligentsia for what amounted to a second "land reform"—or the compulsory expropriation of all remaining private noble and state land for redistribution to the peasantry, and hence overshadowing and distorting the reforms' long-term economic goals, albeit only for the initial two or three years. By 1909, the economic goals inherent in the reforms had resurfaced and remained paramount throughout the subsequent implementation process.[12] At the same time, the necessity of winning back peasant support to the government continued to be a recurrent theme in these as well as other reforms—especially local electoral reforms that sought to favor the new Stolypin peasants[13]—proposed by the government during the years preceding World War I.

Finally, like the emancipation, though unlike the present, it would be fair to say that, even within the relatively short time span of about ten years, the Stolypin reforms were achieving a degree of success. This success can be measured in terms of the number of individual farms formed during this period, which accounted for approximately 10 percent of all peasant households—not including those on the drawing boards when World War I broke out—and in absolute terms, totaled about five times the number of individual farms existing today. Another measure of success could be that of agricultural output, which also grew during these years at about 4 percent per annum.[14] And even if most of the latter growth was a result of favorable climatic conditions, the fact that output did not plummet is itself a positive indicator. Further, and again in contrast to the recent past, it is important to remember that while agriculture was, indeed, collectively managed under the commune prior to the Stolypin reforms, each household was individually responsible for its own strips. In the end, as I have argued elsewhere, the government also seemed to have been winning the political battle for the peasants' hearts and minds, as measured by the retreat of revolutionary demands for radical land reform during these years.[15] Ultimately, however, the circumstances of war, in conjunction with a social and political revolution, led to the abandonment of Stolypin's gradualistic, evolutionary, and economistic policies of agrarian reform and a revival of demands for the eminently political policy of land reform.

The Agrarian Revolution of 1917–18

Despite the return to a policy of radical "land" reform, the revolutionary change of direction should not be seen, as has been traditional, as a judgment of failure on the Stolypin reforms. Rather, the new policy was first launched and largely implemented by the peasants themselves from below, in response to new and virtually unlimited opportunities to realize their centuries-old dream of expropriating the nobles' lands that were created by the near total breakdown of political authority both before and immediately after the abdication of Tsar Nicholas II and his brother Mikhail. The Bolsheviks' subsequent decision to embrace the peasants' initiative was no more than a politically expedient and temporary recognition of a fait accompli in the countryside.[16]

In fact, policy developed in several stages. First were the spontaneous peasant seizures of nobles' lands, which began in the spring of 1917 and continued through the summer of 1918. These were subsequently "approved" by the Bolsheviks' famous "Decree on Land" of 26 October 1917, abolishing all forms of private landownership. However, as is well known, the Bolsheviks' plans for Russia's economy would ultimately come into conflict with peasant desires for local autonomy and require a new attempt to launch an "agrarian" reform or further restructuring. For while the wartime breakdown of distribution mechanisms (the market), the de facto abolition of private trade during the first six months of the new regime, and the immediate needs of survival all dictated a resurgence of the commune and return to agricultural practices characteristic of pre-emancipation Russia, these practices were in sharp contradiction to the Bolsheviks' long-term program of economic development and modernization.

Thus, in a first step toward resolving this contradiction, on 19 February 1918, the anniversary of the emancipation of the serfs in 1861, the Bolsheviks adopted a new decree, "On the Socialization of Land," which nationalized all land and placed it under state control. This decree had several goals: to impose as egalitarian a distribution of land as possible among the different peasant classes under the supervision of locally elected institutions of revolutionary self-government (soviets), encourage collective forms of production, and help lay the groundwork for a future program of both agricultural and industrial development. However, the government was unable to implement any of these policies directly. Nonetheless, a remarkably successful and highly egalitarian redistribution of land did take place, but under the control of the peasant commune rather than the local soviet. The leveling that occurred was, thus, exclusively local in nature, rather than regional or national as the government had intended.

Overall, the Bolshevik policy of supporting these spontaneous changes should, indeed, be seen as a pro-peasant, if not pro-agricultural development. However, as the winter of 1917–18 came to an end, the peasants' unavoidably subsistence orientation soon led them into near irreconcilable conflict with the Bolsheviks' need for grain to feed their urban supporters, and then, following the outbreak of civil war in the summer of 1918, the newly formed Red Army. Thus did the government declare what amounted to open warfare on the peasantry as it began systematically sending out groups of proletarians to requisition grain. Then, by a decree of 11 June 1918, so-called committees of poor peasants were formed to assist in this task. The conflicts these measures generated, culminating in the peasant uprisings that began to snowball toward the end of 1920 and the beginning of 1921 following the regime's victory in the civil war, led to the regime's acknowledgment of the complete failure of its previous policies, dubbed War Communism, and the introduction of its New Economic Policy.[17]

The New Economic Policy (NEP)

The NEP was neither a land nor an agrarian reform, for it changed neither property rights nor the structure of landholdings or land use. Nor did the regime abandon its overarching goal of establishing collective forms of agriculture. Yet, the NEP had a major impact on the macroeconomic environment and produced immediate and significant economic results, above all returning both agricultural and industrial output to pre-war levels. In this respect the NEP would subsequently serve as one possible model of reform throughout the post-Stalin years and down to the present.[18]

The essence of the NEP reforms, as they concerned the peasantry, was the abandonment of grain requisitions, a shift to a "tax in kind," and the legitimization or reestablishment of a semi-market economy in agricultural and consumer goods that enabled peasants to market their surplus and purchase consumer goods and agricultural inputs.[19] In inspiration, this was an essentially political move. Moreover, the NEP was seen more as a retreat than a model for the future (except, perhaps, for Lenin, as he reflected on Russia's future development following his stroke),[20] and thus also launched a series of economic debates. Wide-ranging in content, with both industrial and agrarian variants, the ultimate goal of these debates was to identify the keys to economic growth, industrialization, and modernization, and a socialist exit from the apparent restoration of capitalism.[21]

Simultaneously, many of the agrarian reformers, surveyors, and agronomists who had received their training during the era of the Stolypin reforms reappeared on the rural scene responding both to the debates as well as to a revival of peasant demands for assistance to improve their agriculture. Under the auspices of the Stolypin-era professionals, a new and voluntary process of agrarian reform was thus launched as they began to help peasants once again to separate from the commune and establish more individualized forms of peasant agriculture and to introduce other forms of improvements. These years also saw a huge growth in the formation of consumer and marketing cooperatives, which were seen in part as the path to higher levels of socialist organization.[22] However, while these efforts had the support of the agricultural ministry, other initiatives were simultaneously being conducted under government auspices that sought to foster genuinely communal or collectivist forms of agricultural production.[23]

All of these developments were advancing slowly during the twenties, in conjunction with a significant growth in agricultural output. Left in place, the NEP might perhaps have produced results similar to the current Chinese reforms. However, by 1926, industrial production had already more or less reached its limit, based on existing capital stock, at which point the terms of exchange turned against the village. Thus appeared the famous "scissors crisis," which resulted in peasants refusing to market their surpluses in the face of shortages of consumer and capital goods and correspondingly high prices. The peasants' "grain strike," as it was called, eventually resulted in the government resorting once again to the forced requisitioning of grain.[24]

It has been argued that one way out of this situation might have been to readjust agrarian prices to bring them into line with the prices of industrial goods.[25] However, the state's ideological and ultimately political inability to reconcile itself to the market and the use of market levers to achieve its economic goals brought the NEP experiment to a sudden end in 1929 when Stalin launched his singular conception of returning to the economic model of War Communism and imposed a state-dominated system of agricultural management on the Russian countryside, while also eliminating all forms of agricultural trade.[26]

Collectivization

This new and highly coercive policy, imposed from above, was a complete departure from previous models of agrarian or land reform, though technically it could be considered an agrarian reform in that it sought to restructure the entire system of agricultural production and land use. At the same time, the term "reform" seems particularly inappropriate given the revolutionary methods and goals that it pursued. Moreover, in contrast to the pro-peasant, pro-agriculture motivation of previous reforms, collectivization can only be regarded as an antipeasant, anti-agricultural policy that had the explicitly political goal of imposing total state control over the peasantry as a class. From the perspective of economic theory and political ideology, this policy was both rationalized and legitimized as a development strategy designed to extract every available surplus, and even more besides, from the agrarian sector in order to fuel a rapid expansion of the heavy industrial sector. Such "primitive socialist accumulation" would thus serve as the basis for Russia's modernization and the construction of socialism.[27]

Not surprisingly, this policy of total and rapid mass collectivization inspired widespread peasant opposition that within a few short months forced the government, first to adopt a more gradual pace, and eventually to reauthorize a system of private or "collective-farm" markets for the sale of produce grown on small-scale private peasant plots.[28] However, despite the huge costs—which included the widespread slaughter of livestock, the forced deportation of several million supposed *kulaky* or opponents of collectivization, as well as famine and the starvation of millions—collectivization has been judged successful on a number of levels. It was successful first of all on the political level. From the regime's perspective, it was also successful economically in both the short and long terms. In the short term, collectivization was successful because it provided uninterrupted supplies for a rapidly expanding urban and industrial Russia and for the military, even during World War II. In the long term, it was judged successful because during the 1950s through the 1970s agricultural output grew steadily within the basic framework established by Stalin.[29] At the same time, these "successes" were bought at the expense of huge declines in rural living standards during the 1930s and after.

However, the attempt to transfer wealth from agriculture to industry did not succeed. For, as several scholars have demonstrated, during the 1930s there was a net inflow of capital to agriculture, though this was largely hidden to regime and peasants alike by the atmosphere of violence that surrounded the entire collectivization process.[30] On the other hand, collectivization did result in a huge transfer of labor out of agriculture, and to that extent agriculture did make a major contribution to Russia's modernization, not to mention victory in World War II.[31]

Despite the notable economic successes of collectivized agriculture, especially in the post-Stalin era, bought literally by returning to a genuinely pro-peasant, pro-agricultural policy that led to massive investments in agriculture and in rural social capital, by the 1970s, marginal rates of return on these investments were becoming increasingly costly and, hence, unacceptable. Meanwhile, the positive social policies that increasingly guaranteed Russia's agricultural workers a minimum and quite reasonable standard of living seemed to many to be undermining both incentive and innovation—thus setting the groundwork for the reforms of the *perestroika* and post-Soviet eras.

The post–World War II period until the collapse of the Soviet Union was the heyday of the state and collective farm system. Even though the peasant standard of living grew substantially as a result of deliberately pro-peasant policies initiated by the regime, this era was also one of repeated efforts to improve agricultural productivity and output through a never-ending series of administrative reforms. These reforms included Khrushchev's Virgin Lands scheme, increasing mechanization and "chemicalization," as well as numerous efforts to improve incentives based on NEP models, the most famous of which was associated with Ivan Khudenko.[32] However, increasingly the costs outweighed the benefits, and the regime never seemed to be satisfied.[33] The perestroika years under Gorbachev were but a continuation of this reformist impulse, though with a more explicit effort to harness the perceived benefits of the NEP model. These efforts were, however, no more successful in breaking the logjam, while expenditures on agriculture continued to grow. Part of the problem was the regime's inability or unwillingness to recognize the radically different macroeconomic environments that existed in the 1980s compared to the 1920s, which, by comparison, could be described as a fully market economy.[34]

De-Stalinization/De-Nationalization/Privatization

The Yeltsin reforms that followed the collapse of the Soviet Union contained six major components. First was a politically motivated de-Stalinization that sought to destroy the existing system of state and collective farms. Frequently referred to as privatization, in fact this policy had several components, none of which was strictly speaking a "privatization," any more than the Chinese reforms of the late 1970s and the 1980s were a privatization. The potentially most significant component of the new policy, in fact, involved a "de-nationalization" of collective and state farms and either their reorganization as joint stock companies, limited liability partnerships, or genuine collectives, or the reaffirmation of their existing status as collective or state farms. A second component involved permitting, if not exactly encouraging, the leasing of agricultural land and the establishment of individual family farms. Third was the privatization, though not de-monopolization, of supply and marketing organizations. Fourth was the sponsorship of the Nizhniy Novgorod/International Finance Corporation/British Know How Fund strategy of breaking collective farms into functionally specialized units. Fifth was the almost complete termination of government assistance or subsidies to agriculture. The final innovation involved a huge expansion of private-plot agriculture.[35]

On the surface, it would seem that this complex of agrarian reforms certainly had real potential for transforming Russian agriculture and, beyond simply introducing competitive and market principles, perhaps even, finally, for rationalizing Russian agriculture. However, as we have seen, the results, as measured by either output or of peasants' standard of living, have been overwhelmingly negative.[36] In part, these results have been due to the unfavorable price scissors that developed immediately after the lifting of price controls in January 1992, when prices for inputs of urban origin soared while prices for agricultural output dived. In part, too, however, the net costs of agricultural production remained too high—and, most important, higher than in the world market. As a result, a newly liberated import market was flooded with foreign agricultural produce driving down demand for the higher-priced Russian produce, further exacerbating the problem.[37] There is also a third factor, which becomes clear when we compare the contemporary "reforms" with those in Russia's past—namely, the overwhelmingly antirural impact of the current government's policies.

The antipeasant, anti-agricultural orientation of the current regime invites immediate comparison, of course, with Stalin's collectivization. And indeed, many commentators have observed a number of similarities between Stalin's utopian leap of faith—which sought in effect to jump directly from feudalism, over capitalism, straight into socialism—with Yeltsin's adoption of "shock therapy," which involved a similar developmental leap of faith into market capitalism from a feudalistic type of socialism. Indeed, the shock therapists' argument that you can't jump over an abyss in two leaps applies equally to Stalin's agricultural policies of the late 1920s and the 1930s.[38] One might also compare elements of the current reforms with the emancipation, in that the abolition of collectivization has also been characterized as a second emancipation from serfdom, in this case of serfdom to the state by means of the system of state and collective farms.[39] On the other hand, the current reforms have little in common with the agrarian revolution of 1917–18, though they could have had if the government had decided to launch a new redistribution of land on radically egalitarian principles as the means to break up the inefficient *sovkhozy* and *kolkhozy*. Of course, such a measure would have smacked of Bolshevism—which was a sin clearly equivalent to Stalinism in Yeltsin's eyes. On the other hand, it might also have had more economic success than the current policies.

Beyond these comparisons, however, there is little similarity in content between the current policies and these three precursors. That leaves either the NEP or the Stolypin reforms as a potential comparison. And, indeed, the NEP did at first inspire Gorbachev's later plans for agrarian reform and, in part, helped prepare the groundwork for the later Yeltsin reforms.[40] However, the reformers seem to have falsely assumed that the mere withdrawal of the government from the direct management of agriculture would stimulate a massive transformation and that the peasantry would take care of everything else by themselves. At the same time, the successes of the NEP, like those of present-day China, seem unlikely to have been repeatable in Russia, if only because of the reduced role of agriculture in the Russian economy. That leaves the Stolypin reforms. I might be suspected of a certain bias in my choice, since most of my research has been focused on the Stolypin reforms. However, I hope to show how a comparison between the implementation processes of the two reforms in conjunction with a look at the historiographical debate over the evaluation of the Stolypin reforms can help us better understand the situation of Russian agriculture today, rather than to demonstrate the applicability of the Stolypin model to the present situation as a model of "correct policy."[41]

A Comparison Between the Stolypin Reforms and the Current Situation

I have already pointed out the essential similarities and differences between the Stolypin reforms and the current situation. The salient points for justifying a comparison here, however, are less the socioeconomic context within which the reforms took place than the short- and long-term goals of the respective reform programs and the methods adopted for their realization. In both cases, the government sought an essentially voluntary transition from a system of collective management to one of individual management. Furthermore, both adopted juridical measures that would legalize the breakup of existing collective forms and the establishment of a variety of other organizational forms, including outright individualization. Further, both governments eschewed the immediate adoption of private property, preferring a variety of transitional forms.[42]

Beyond this similarity of goals, however, there is the complete dissimilarity of results. Part of the explanation for this may lie in the radically different demographic environments within which the two reforms played out in the countryside, without even taking into account that Russia's rural population in the 1990s can hardly be characterized as a peasantry, in the sense of having long experience in conducting all agricultural tasks.[43] Russia's collective farmers had long ago been transformed into workers who specialized in one or at best a small number of the tasks necessary to raise livestock or produce a satisfactory harvest. But, a further comparison between the actively pro-peasant, pro-agriculture policy of the Stolypin years with the actively antirural policies of the Yeltsin government leads one to reconceptualize the current situation in terms not of agrarian reform but of its absence. Let me explain.

I would argue that, in comparison to the tsarist government in its final decade, the Yeltsin government, while expressing similar goals, effectively had no real agrarian policy of reform, because there was no reform administration. Moreover, the Yeltsin government did very little to implement those goals, and, hence, there was also no genuine reform process.[44] In contrast, the Stolypin government created a new and dedicated administrative structure as well as trained and mobilized a huge cadre of executive official and technical specialists, including surveyors and agronomists, to assist the peasantry in implementing reform; established complex inspection systems; expanded the system of administrative justice to permit appeals, while accommodating a huge growth of legal cases within the existing judicial system; and poured ever-growing sums of money into the expansion of credit and agronomic aid, rural education, and other rural social services such as various forms of insurance, credit and consumer cooperatives, and so on.[45] Indeed, as the Stolypin reforms, like the emancipation before them, make absolutely clear, when a government undertakes rural reforms that appear to many rural inhabitants to go against their immediate interests, the key to success ultimately lies with a comprehensive system of implementation that can persuade the subjects of reform—both

intellectually and through practical government activity (a real "propa-
ganda of the deed"), as well as by the practical results—that the government is, in fact, acting not only in its own interests but also in their long-
term interests.[46]

Finally, if we turn to outcomes or projected outcomes, by 2000 the
Yeltsin reforms had run about the same length of time as the Stolypin
reforms—some eight years or so—which only further emphasizes the failed
possibilities of the former compared to the relative successes of the latter.
Here, however, we face a historiographical debate, an understanding of
which is essential to the assessment of both sets of reforms. The traditional
interpretation of the Stolypin reforms, both Soviet and Western, has almost
universally considered them to have been a failure, both politically and economically.[47] For a number of years, I have challenged this viewpoint by
pointing out the fundamental weaknesses in the arguments of the so-called
pessimists as well as pointing to different categories of evidence that suggest an alternative conclusion.[48]

However, the essence of my positive arguments was not—as with earlier
pro-Stolypin liberals or monarchists—based on the demonstrable growth
in agricultural output during the Stolypin years. For the sources of this
growth cannot be clearly identified, though the likelihood that such newly
enacted reforms could have had so significant an economic impact in so
short a time is a priori impossible. Hence, with Soviet scholars, I am willing to ascribe these increases to fortuitous climatic conditions—though I
would add that these favorable conditions undoubtedly redounded in favor
of the reforms' success. Nor is my argument based on the actual numbers
of separators, which was a modest 10 percent—though five times larger in
absolute terms than today's 275,000 individual farmers.[49] Nor even do I
rely upon the significantly greater percentage (some 25 percent) of peasants who had claimed title to their strips of land within the commune
though had neither consolidated nor physically separated them from the
commune. I do not consider this figure of importance, because the procedure for claiming title, while of some value in facilitating loans, was in certain respects counterproductive and was, in any event, ultimately abandoned by the government in favor of complete land reorganization.[50]
Rather, my argument is based on my efforts to quantify the nature of the
peasants' changing relationship to a government that they clearly opposed
in 1905–6 but had increasingly come to trust by 1914–16 as evidenced by
the fact that, over the course of this ten-year period, about 50 percent
of all peasant households had petitioned the government for some form of

assistance to form an individual holding or merely rationalize holdings within the commune.[51]

Beyond this kind of argument, I have focused on the reform process itself, studying the actual process of implementation, the ways in which the government relied on voluntary initiative, and especially the way peasants contributed to determining the reforms' direction and outcomes. Particularly important are how quickly the government was convinced that, without the peasants' active and voluntary involvement and support, reform would be a dead letter and the way this conviction came to be embodied in the central government's instructions to its local officials. To be sure, at the level of the peasant commune, during this decade there was, in effect, a competition under way in the countryside between those peasants who thought that the commune continued best to serve their interests and those who thought that consolidating their strips into an integral family farm served their interests better. However, it seems to me that, given the rapidity of the changes under way and the number of peasant households involved—all within the context of a gradually expanding market economy—the latter were most likely to predominate.[52] Clearly, the tsarist government's approach to agrarian reform was a far cry from that of the current Russian Federation—with predictable results.

The ultimate test of the Stolypin reforms was, of course, political. Specifically, most authors have argued that if the peasants did not abandon their traditional dream of a *chernyi peredel'*, the Stolypin policies should be viewed as failures. However, rather than viewing the resurgence of the commune in the circumstances of 1917–18 as proof that the dream persisted and hence the Stolypin reforms failed, I would argue that such millennial dreams should be expected to persist during the peasants' gradual transfer to a system of individual family farms and a market economy for quite a long time. The persistence of such dreams was also in evidence in past centuries when peasant dreams of freedom were overshadowed by the experience of serfdom, similar to the way in which in our own experience, real life tends to overlay our ideals and dreams. Of greater concern in trying to evaluate the reforms' outcome would thus be whether the peasants' pragmatic adaptations to the market economy received positive reinforcement from the day-to-day experience of life in a market system. For if that were the case, it would seem that peasant dreams of seizing the nobility's land would indeed be gradually displaced by the complex tasks of maneuvering within an expanding market and money economy. And this, indeed, seems to have been the case during the years prior to World War I.[53]

The question before us, then, is whether the most recent changes in the agrarian sphere that have taken place in Russia are sufficient. Will the adaptations that have taken place—as agriculture has been forced to live within a gradually marketizing, if not exactly monetizing, economy, one that is, moreover, often perceived in negative rather than positive terms, especially in rural Russia—ultimately produce the desired transformation of Russian agriculture into a more efficient and productive enterprise? Or will these adaptations simply reinforce the subsistence agriculture that has once again spread across the Russian land, just as it did during a previous time of troubles, following the Revolution of 1917? My answer would be that, under present conditions, a positive and productive transformation is extremely unlikely or at best far distant. Again, the analogies with the past seem obvious. Today's collective farmers have been at least as reluctant to abandon their dreams, in this case a nostalgia for the golden era of socialism, as prerevolutionary peasants were to abandon their dreams of "black repartition." Such is, moreover, a quite rational response in the circumstances. On the other hand, were individual farmers to have received or had they been able to anticipate positive reinforcement from an evolving market environment, they too might have gradually adapted as well. As it is, however, farmers have been forced to adapt to a hostile environment by returning to subsistence forms of agriculture, based largely on manual labor by elderly women on private plots, simply in order to survive. Thus, it would seem that until the government adopts a macroeconomic policy favorable to agriculture, a positive outcome will be impossible. In a free market economy, when the terms of trade between country and city are as negative as they currently are, the future can only bring further decline, especially when foreign agricultural products can be imported more cheaply than they can be produced at home. To be sure, the August 1998 financial crash has had a positive impact in this respect, by increasing the cost of imported foods and, hence, increasing demand for Russian produce. The crash has not been sufficient, however, to change the general picture, at least thus far.[54]

All of the above raises a number of questions concerning the nature and goals of the Yeltsin government's policy. In particular, was this policy either completely misguided or was it simply a product of necessity, reflecting the state's virtual bankruptcy? Alternatively, one might hypothesize that the government decided to completely abandon agriculture. Such a decision may have been dictated by a surviving Marxist-style bias against the peasant and the countryside or by the assumption that, compared to the past, agriculture will necessarily play a far smaller and even negligible role in Russia's further economic as well as political development, and that the regime will therefore be less and less dependent on rural support for its survival. Another explanation for the hypothesized abandonment of agriculture may be, as some have suggested, that the government adopted the Leninist strategy of "the worse the better" on the assumption that a new, private agriculture will ultimately and spontaneously arise, phoenix-like, from the ashes of the old collective agriculture and that the country can survive in the interim on imported food.[55]

Conclusion

In conclusion, I would argue that there are a number of important similarities and differences between the current reforms and the earlier Stolypin reforms. Both sets of reforms can be seen as attempting to break up the existing collective forms of agricultural management and replace them with more individualistic forms. However, for the current reforms to have the same potential for success as the Stolypin reforms, the government will have to adopt a policy that explicitly favors, supports, and actively implements these reforms and manifests its support for the rural population in practical terms. Only in this way can the government expect to win the rural population's support for its agricultural goals, whatever they may ultimately be. The alternative seems to be a further decline of Russian agricultural output and the population's increasing resort to subsistence agriculture. The government might indeed do well to reflect on the circumstances that led to the NEP and the imperatives that forced Lenin to shift his government's policy from an anti-rural orientation to a pro-rural one.

As we look both into the past and ahead, and based on my own study of the Stolypin reforms, what factors might we look for as harbingers of a more positive outcome? The key factors must be the state's macroeconomic policy, especially price and taxation policies; for without changes in these areas that will redound positively on agriculture, little else matters. However, should government policy, the terms of exchange between town and country, and the provision of tax and credit preferences change for the better, then we would look for all of the phenomena listed below, and more, in order to assess the impact of such changes. Further, there are two dimensions of change that need to be kept in mind: government-initiated changes and spontaneous changes from below. The obvious areas of interest for observers to watch follow:

- A revival of growth in the number of family farms
- Continuing progress in the breakup of collective farms

- Adoption of a national law on the private ownership of agricultural land
- Increasing land mobilization
- Expansion and increased availability of rural credit
- Remonetization of the rural economy
- Development of agronomic aid and other extension services and cooperatives
- Changes in crop structure favoring more intensive and market-oriented crops
- Growth in output and especially markets for crops and animal products
- Decline in food imports
- Demographic changes indicating a rejuvenation of the countryside and the emergence of a rural bourgeoisie

Today, of course, rural Russia plays a smaller political role than it did in the past. Nonetheless, the economic stakes remain very similar: Can Russia afford to allow its agriculture to continue to decline and the rural (and even portions of the urban) population to revert to subsistence agriculture while the state simultaneously seeks to enter the modern industrial, high-tech world? Such developments seem to be as potentially subversive of the current government's declared goals as the "second economy" and *blat* were of the Soviet system before it.

Notes

1. See Minxin Pei, *From Reform to Revolution: The Demise of Communism in China and the Soviet Union* (Cambridge, MA: Harvard University Press, 1994), chapters 3 and 4.

2. Clifford Gaddy and Barry Ickes, "Russia's Virtual Economy," *Foreign Affairs* 77 (September/October 1998): 53–67; Marshall I. Goldman, "The Cashless Society," *Current History* 97 (October 1998): 319–24. In 1999, in the aftermath of the August 1998 fiscal crisis, there was extremely modest growth in industrial output, though more as a result of the devaluation of the ruble than any deliberate reform policy. See Neela Banerjee, "Signs of Stability Are Identified in Russia's Economy," *New York Times*, 14 April 1999, C5; Banerjee, "Russia's Embryos of Enterprise," *New York Times*, 20 July 1999, C1; Thane Gustafson and Eugene K. Lawson, "The Good News from Russia," *New York Times*, 28 September 1999, A25; Alexander Mikhailiants, "Breathing Room," *Harriman Review* 11, no. 4 (June 1999): 46–47; and for a contrary view, Anders Aslund, "Think Again: Russia," *Foreign Policy* 125 (July–August 2001): 20–25.

3. The most recent overviews of agricultural reform in Russia are Grigory Ioffe and Tatyana Nefedova, *Continuity and Change in Rural Russia: A Geographical Perspective* (Boulder, CO: Westview Press, 1997), especially chapters 6 and 7; and Stephen K. Wegren, *Agriculture and the State in Soviet and Post-Soviet Russia* (Pittsburgh, PA: University of Pittsburgh Press, 1998).

4. For recent comparative studies, see Mark Selden, "Post-Collective Agrarian Alternatives in Russia and China," in *China After Socialism: In the Footsteps of Eastern Europe or East Asia?* eds. Barrett L. McCormick and Jonathan Unger (Armonk, NY: M. E. Sharpe, 1996), 7–28; Ivan Szelényi, ed., *Privatizing the Land: Rural Political Economy in Post-Communist Societies* (New York: Routledge, 1998), especially chapters 5 and 6; Center for Cooperation with Economies in Transition, *Agro-Food Sector Policy in OECD Countries and the Russian Federation* (Paris: Organization for Economic Cooperation and Development, 1996); Johan F.M. Swinnen, ed., *Political Economy of Agrarian Reform in Central and Eastern Europe* (Brookfield, VT: Ashgate, 1997); and Stephen K. Wegren, ed., *Land Reform in the Former Soviet Union and Eastern Europe* (New York: Routledge, 1998). On China, see also Jonathan Unger and Jean Xiong, "Life in the Chinese Hinterlands Under the Rural Economic Reforms," *Bulletin of Concerned Asian Scholars* 22 (April–June 1990), 4–17; and Yunxiang Yan, "The Impact of Rural Reform on Economic and Social Stratification in a Chinese Village," *Australian Journal of Chinese Affairs* 27 (January 1992): 1–23.

5. E. H. Tuma, *Twenty-Six Centuries of Agrarian Reform: A Comparative Analysis* (Berkeley: University of California Press, 1965), 8–14; D. Warriner, *Land Reform in Principle and Practice* (Oxford: Clarendon Press, 1969), xiii–xx; Russell King, *Land Reform: A World Survey* (Boulder, CO: Westview Press, 1977), 3–25.

6. Recent comparative works on the new subject of reform in Russian history include Robert O. Crummey, ed., *Reform in Russia and the U.S.S.R: Past and Prospects* (Urbana: University of Illinois Press, 1989); W. E. Mosse, *Perestroika Under the Tsars* (London: I. B. Tauris, 1992); Theodore Taranovski, ed., *Reform in Modern Russian History: Progress or Cycle?* (Washington, DC: Woodrow Wilson Center Press; New York: Cambridge University Press, 1995); B. V. Anan'ich, *Vlast' i reformy* (St. Petersburg: Dmitrii Bulanin, 1996); and A. N. Sakharov, ed., *Reformy i reformatory v istorii Rossii: sbornik statei* (Moscow: Institut Rossiiskoi istorii, RAN, 1996).

7. The classic recent study is Daniel Field, *The End of Serfdom: Nobility and Bureaucracy in Russia, 1855–1861* (Cambridge, MA: Harvard University Press, 1976). On the aftermath, see David A.J. Macey, *Government and Peasant in Russia, 1861–1906: The Prehistory of the Stolypin Reforms* (DeKalb: Northern Illinois University Press, 1987), chapter 1. For a comparative study of emancipation, see Jerome Blum, *The End of the Old Order in Rural Europe* (Princeton, NJ: Princeton University Press, 1978).

8. Macey, *Government and Peasant*, passim.

9. V. I. Ger'e, *Vtoroe raskreposhchenie, 19 fevralia 1861–14 iiunia 1910* (Moscow: N.p., 1911); Dorothy Atkinson, *The End of the Russian Land Commune, 1905–1930* (Stanford, CA: Stanford University Press, 1983), 41.

10. For the ideas behind the Stolypin reforms and an interpretation of the government's goals in adopting them, see Macey, *Government and Peasant*.

11. See David A.J. Macey, "Agricultural Development and Agrarian Reform in Pre-Revolutionary Russia (1861–1917): Old Debates, Unresolved Questions, and New Paradigms" (paper presented at conference on "Social Capital in Rural Russia," Rural Russia Workshop Series, University of Missouri, Columbia, MO, 11–13 May 1998); and I. N. Slepnev, "Novye rynochnye realii i ikh prelomlenie v mentalitete poreformennogo krest'ianstva," and N. G. Rogalina, "Reformatorstvo XX veka i krest'ianskii mentalitet," in *Mentalitet i agrarnoe razvitie Rossii (XIX–XX vv.)*, eds. V. P. Danilov and L. V. Milov (Moscow: ROSSPEN, 1996), 209–14, 215–27. But see Adrian Jones, *Late-Imperial Russia—An Interpretation: Three Visions, Two Cultures, One Peasantry* (Bern: Peter Lang, 1997), chapter 9.

12. On the implementation process and changing government perspectives, see David A.J. Macey, "Government Actions and Peasant Reactions During the Stolypin Reforms," in *New Perspectives in Modern Russian History*, ed. R. B. McKean (London: Macmillan, 1992), 133–73. Alternate interpretations are held by George Yaney, *The Urge to Mobilize: Agrarian Reform in Russia, 1861–1930* (Urbana: University of Illinois Press, 1982); Jones, *Late-*

Imperial Russia, chapter 10, especially 369–86; Judith Pallot, *Land Reform in Russia, 1906–1917: Peasant Responses to Stolypin's Project of Rural Transformation* (Oxford: Clarendon Press, 1999); and A. P. Korelin, "The Social Problem in Russia, 1906–1914: Stolypin's Agrarian Reform," in *Reform in Modern Russian History*, ed. Taranovski, 139–62.

13. On the reform of the *zemstva*, see Robert Philippot, *Société civile et état bureaucratique dans la Russie tsariste: Les zemstvosi* (Paris: Institut d'études slaves, 1991), 142–44; and Francis W. Wcislo, *Reforming Rural Russia: State, Local Society, and National Politics, 1855–1914* (Princeton, NJ: Princeton University Press, 1990), 210–27.

14. This was double the average for the previous half century. See S. G. Wheatcroft, "Agriculture," in *From Tsarism to the New Economic Policy: Continuity and Change in the Economy of the USSR*, ed. R. W. Davies (Ithaca, NY: Cornell University Press, 1991), 82–83; and cf. Paul R. Gregory, *Before Command: An Economic History of Russia from Emancipation to the First Five-Year Plan* (Princeton, NJ: Princeton University Press, 1994), 29–31, 43–45.

15. David A.J. Macey, " 'A Wager on History': The Stolypin Agrarian Reforms as Process," in *Transforming Peasants: Society, State and the Peasantry, 1861–1930: Proceedings of the Fifth World Congress on Slavic and East European Studies, Warsaw, August 1995*, ed. Judith Pallot (London: Macmillan, 1998), 149–73; and cf. B. N. Mironov, *Sotsial'naia istoriia Rossii perioda imperii (XVIII–nachalo XX v.)*, vol. 1 (St. Petersburg: Dmitrii Bulanin, 1999), 479–84.

16. P. N. Pershin, *Agrarnaia revoliutsiia v Rossii*, 2 vols. (Moscow: Nauka, 1966); Graeme J. Gill, *Peasants and Government in the Russian Revolution* (London: Macmillan, 1979); John J.H. Keep, *The Russian Revolution: A Study in Mass Mobilization* (New York: W. W. Norton, 1976), 153–239, 385–463; Atkinson, *End of the Russian Land Commune*, 117–230; *Istoriia krest'ianstva SSSR*, vol. 1, *Krest'ianstvo v pervoe desiatiletie Sovetskoi vlasti, 1917–1927* (Moscow: Nauka, 1986), 5–218; Lars Lih, *Bread and Authority in Russia, 1914–1921* (Berkeley: University of California Press, 1990).

17. E. H. Carr, *The Bolshevik Revolution, 1917–1923*, vol. 2 (1952; reprint, Baltimore, MD: Penguin Books, 1966), 35–61, 151–76; Orlando Figes, "The Russian Peasant Community in the Agrarian Revolution, 1917–1918," in *Land Commune and Peasant Community: Communal Forms in Imperial and Early and Soviet Society*, ed. Roger Bartlett (New York: St. Martin's Press, 1990), 237–53; John Channon, "The Peasantry in the Revolutions of 1917," in *Revolution in Russia: Reassessments of 1917*, eds. Edith R. Frankel, Jonathan Frankel, and Baruch Knei-Paz (New York: Cambridge University Press, 1992); Alessandro Stanziani, "The First World War and the Disintegration of Economic Spaces in Russia," in *Transforming Peasants*, ed. Pallot, 174–93.

18. On the NEP model, see Mikhail Gorbachev, *Perestroika: New Thinking for Our Country and the World* (New York: Harper & Row, 1987), 25–26; Herbert J. Ellison, "Perestroika and the New Economic Policy (1921–1928): The Uses of History," in *The Transformation of Socialism: Perestroika and Reform in the Soviet Union and China*, ed. Mel Gurtov (Boulder, CO: Westview Press, 1990), 21–35; Mark von Hagen, "The NEP, *Perestroika*, and the Problem of Alternatives," in *Socialism, Perestroika, and the Dilemmas of Soviet Economic Reform*, ed. John E. Tedstrom (Boulder, CO: Westview Press, 1990), 40–64; Alexander Dallin, "The Uses and Abuses of Russian History," in *Soviet Society and Culture: Essays in Honor of Vera Dunham*, eds. Terry L. Thompson and Richard Sheldon (Boulder, CO: Westview Press, 1988), 181–94; R. W. Davies, "Soviet Economic Reform in Historical Perspective," in *Perestroika: The Historical Perspective*, eds. Catherine Merridale and Chris Ward (New York: Edward Arnold, 1991), 117–37; Davies, *Soviet History in the Gorbachev Revolution* (Bloomington: Indiana University Press, 1989), 27–46; Richard B. Day, "The Blackmail of the Single Alternative: Bukharin, Trotsky and Perestroika," *Studies in Soviet Thought* 40 (1990): 159–88; Lars T. Lih, "NEP: An Alternative for Soviet Socialism" (Princeton, NJ: Princeton University), photocopy; D. Kh. Ibragimova, *NEP i perestroika: massovoe soznanie sel'skogo naseleniia v usloviiakh perekhoda k rynku* (Moscow: Pamiatniki istoricheskoi mysli, 1997); David A.J. Macey, "Stolypin Is Risen! The Ideology of Agrarian Reform in Contemporary

Russia," in *The "Farmer Threat": The Political Economy of Agrarian Reform in Post-Soviet Russia*, ed. Donald Van Atta (Boulder, CO: Westview Press, 1993), 97–120.

19. On the NEP, see Carr, *The Bolshevik Revolution*, 2:280–96; V. P. Danilov, *Rural Russia Under the New Regime* (Bloomington: Indiana University Press, 1988); *Istoriia krest'ianstva SSSR*, 1:220–343; Helmut Altrichter, "Insoluble Conflicts: Village Life Between Revolution and Collectivization," in *Russia in the Era of NEP: Explorations in Soviet Society and Culture*, eds. Sheila Fitzpatrick, Alexander Rabinowitch, and Richard Stites (Bloomington: Indiana University Press, 1991), 192–209.

20. See Moshe Lewin, *Lenin's Last Struggle* (New York: Pantheon Books, 1968).

21. Alexander Erlich, *The Soviet Industrialization Debate, 1924–1928* (Cambridge, MA: Harvard University Press, 1960); Susan Solomon, *The Soviet Agrarian Debate: A Controversy in Social Science, 1923–1929* (Boulder, CO: Westview Press, 1977); Markus Wehner, "The Soft Line on Agriculture: The Case of *Narkomzem* and Its Specialists, 1921–27," in *Transforming Peasants*, ed. Pallot, 210–37.

22. George L. Yaney, "Agricultural Administration in Russia from the Stolypin Land Reform to Forced Collectivization: An Interpretative Study," in *The Soviet Rural Community*, ed. James R. Millar (Urbana: University of Illinois Press, 1971), 3–35; Yaney, *Urge to Mobilize*, 510–57.

23. Robert G. Wesson, *Soviet Communes* (New Brunswick, NJ: Rutgers University Press, 1963); E. H. Carr and R. W. Davies, *Foundations of a Planned Economy, 1926–1929*, vol. 1 (1969; reprint, Harmondsworth, Middlesex, England: Penguin Books, 1974), 112–253.

24. Carr and Davies, *Foundations of a Planned Economy*, vol. 1, 3–111, 254–89; R. W. Davies, *The Socialist Offensive: The Collectivization of Soviet Agriculture, 1929–1930*, vol. 1, *The Industrialization of Soviet Russia* (Cambridge, MA: Harvard University Press, 1980), 39–108; Moshe Lewin, *Russian Peasants and Soviet Power: A Study of Collectivization* (Evanston, IL: Northwestern University Press, 1968); James Hughes, *Stalin, Siberia, and the Crisis of the New Economic Policy* (Cambridge: Cambridge University Press, 1991).

25. James R. Millar, *The Soviet Economic Experiment* (Urbana: University of Illinois Press, 1990), 26–89; Jerzy Karcz, "Thoughts on the Grain Problem," *Soviet Studies* 18 (April 1967): 399–435; Karcz, "Back on the Grain Front," *Soviet Studies* 21, no. 2 (October 1970): 262–94.

26. See the discussion by Sheila Fitzpatrick, "The Civil War as a Formative Experience," in *Bolshevik Culture: Experiment and Order in the Russian Revolution*, eds. Abbott Gleason, Peter Kenez, and Richard Stites (1985; reprint, Bloomington: Indiana University Press, 1989), 57–76; Moshe Lewin, "The Civil War: Dynamics and Legacy," in *Party, State, and Society in the Civil War: Explorations in Social History*, eds. Diane P. Koenker, William G. Rosenberg, and Ronald Grigor Suny (Bloomington: Indiana University Press, 1989), 399–423.

27. See n. 25. On collectivization, see Davies, *Industrialization of Soviet Russia*, passim; *Istoriia krest'ianstva SSSR*, vol. 2, *Sovetskoe krest'ianstvo v period sotsialisticheskoi rekonstruktsii narodnogo khoziaistva: konetz 1927–1937* (Moscow: Nauka, 1986), especially 136–276.

28. Sheila Fitzpatrick, *Stalin's Peasants: Resistance and Survival in the Russian Village After Collectivization* (New York: Oxford University Press, 1994); Lynne Viola, *Peasant Rebels Under Stalin: Collectivization and the Culture of Peasant Resistance* (New York: Oxford University Press, 1996).

29. Millar, *Soviet Economic Experiment*, 90–110; cf. S. G. Wheatcroft and R. W. Davies, "Agriculture," in *The Economic Transformation of the Soviet Union, 1913–1945*, eds. R. W. Davies, Mark Harrison, and S. G. Wheatcroft (Cambridge: Cambridge University Press, 1994), 106–30. See also Lazar Volin, *A Century of Russian Agriculture: From Alexander II to Khrushchev* (Cambridge, MA: Harvard University Press, 1970), 235–574.

30. See n. 25.

31. Moshe Lewin, *The Gorbachev Phenomenon: A Historical Interpretation* (Berkeley: University of California Press, 1988), 13–56.

32. See Alexander Yanov, *The Drama of the Soviet 1960s: A Lost Reform* (Berkeley: Institute of International Studies, University of California, 1984).

33. On the post-Stalin era, there have been few monographic studies but a number of valuable collections: Erich Straus, *Soviet Agriculture in Perspective: A Study of Its Successes and Failures* (New York: Praeger Publishers, 1969); Millar, ed., *Soviet Rural Community*, D. Gale Johnson and Karen McConnell Brooks, *Prospects for Soviet Agriculture in the 1980s* (Bloomington: Indiana University Press, 1983); R. C. Stewart, ed., *The Soviet Rural Economy* (Totowa, NJ: Rowman and Allanheld, 1984); Stefan Hedlund, *Crisis in Soviet Agriculture* (New York: St. Martin's Press, 1984); Zhores A. Medvedev, *Soviet Agriculture* (New York: W. W. Norton, 1987); Josef C. Brada and Karl-Eugen Wädekin, eds., *Socialist Agriculture in Transition: Organizational Response to Failing Performance* (Boulder, CO: Westview Press, 1988).

34. William Moskoff, ed., *Perestroika in the Countryside: Agricultural Reform in the Gorbachev Era* (Armonk, NY: M. E. Sharpe, 1990); Stephen K. Wegren, "Private Agriculture in the Soviet Union Under Gorbachev," *Soviet Union/Union Sovietique* 16 (1989): 105–44; Stephen K. Wegren, "From Stalin to Gorbachev: The Role of the Soviet Communist Party in the Implementation of Agricultural Policy," *Studies in Comparative Communism* 23 (summer 1990): 177–90; Stephen K. Wegren, "Dilemmas of Agrarian Reform in the Soviet Union," *Soviet Studies* 44 (1992): 3–36; Donald Van Atta, "Back to the Future in the Soviet Countryside," *Problems of Communism* (January–April 1991): 155–64; Michael P. Claudon and Tamar L. Gutner, eds., *Putting Food on What Was the Soviet Table* (New York: New York University Press, 1992); David A.J. Macey, "Is Agrarian Privatization the Right Path? A Discussion of Historical Models," *The Soviet and Post-Soviet Review* 21 (1994): 165–68.

35. The only monograph to deal with this subject is Wegren, *Agriculture and the State*; see also Wegren, "The Conduct and Impact of Land Reform in Russia," in *Land Reform in the Former Soviet Union and Eastern Europe*, ed. Wegren, 3–34.

36. Jim Butterfield, Mikhail Kuznetsov, and Sergei Sazonov, "Peasant Farming in Russia," *Journal of Peasant Studies* 23 (July 1996): 79–105; Stephen K. Wegren and Frank A. Durgin, "The Political Economy of Private Farming in Russia," *Comparative Economic Studies* 32 (fall–winter 1997): 1–24; *Koordinatsionnyi tsentr izbiratel'nogo ob'edinneniia "Agrarnaia partiia Rossii": kratkie itogi Rossiiskikh agrarnykh "reform" v 1991–1994 godakh* (Moscow: n.p., 1995).

37. For general overviews, see Karen Brooks and Zvi Lerman, *Land Reform and Land Restructuring in Russia*, World Bank Discussion Paper # 233 (Washington, DC: World Bank, 1994); Karen Brooks et al., *Agricultural Reform in Russia: A View from the Farm Level*, World Bank Discussion Paper #327 (Washington, DC: World Bank, 1996); John Channon, *Agrarian Reform in Russia, 1992–5*, Post-Soviet Business Forum, 3d Series (London: Royal Institute of International Affairs, 1995); "Status of Agricultural Reforms in the NIS/B Countryside in 1997," in U.S. Department of Agriculture, Economic Research Service, *International Agriculture and Trade Reports: Newly Independent States and the Baltics*, Situation and Outlook Series, WRS-91-1 (May 1997), 4–9; Ioffe and Nefedova, *Continuity and Change*; Stephen K. Wegren, "State Withdrawal and the Impact of Marketization on Rural Russia," *Policy Studies Journal* 28, no. 1 (2000): 46–48.

38. See Macey, "Stolypin Is Risen," 97–120; David A.J. Macey, "Reforming Agriculture in Russia: The 'Cursed Question' from Stolypin to Yeltsin," in *Russia and Eastern Europe After Communism: The Search for New Political, Economic, and Security Systems*, eds. Michael Kraus and Ronald D. Liebowitz (Boulder, CO: Westview Press, 1996), 103–22. Donald Van Atta had previously noted a similarity between Gorbachev and Stalin's methods in his article, " 'Full-Scale, like Collectivization, but without Collectivization's Excesses': The Campaign to Introduce the Family and Lease Contract in Soviet Agriculture," in *Perestroika in the Countryside*, ed. Moskoff, 81–106. Cf. S. A. Nikol'skii, "Kollektivatsiia i dekollektivatsiia: sravnitel'nyi analiz protsessov, posledstvii, perspekti," in *Krest'ianovedenie: teoriia, istoriia,*

sovremennost', ezhegodnik, 1997, eds. V. P. Danilov and T. Shanin (Moscow: n.p., 1997), 223–40.

39. Donald Van Atta, "Yeltsin Decree Finally Ends 'Second Serfdom' in Russia," *RFE/RL Research Report* 2 (19 November 1993): 33–39.

40. See n. 18. See also Nikolai Shmelev, "It's Déjà Vu All Over Again: Russia's Economic Reforms in the 1920s and 1990s," in *Russia and Eastern Europe After Communism*, eds. Kraus and Liebowitz, 91–102.

41. In contrast to my articles "Gorbachev and Stolypin," "Stolypin Is Risen!" and "Is Agrarian Privatization the Right Path?"

42. See Macey, *Government and Peasant*, passim, especially 243; Stephen K. Wegren, "Rural Reform and Political Culture in Russia," *Europe-Asia Studies* 46 (1994): 215–41; Wegren, "Yeltsin's Decree on Land Relations: Implications for Agrarian Reform," *Post-Soviet Geography* 35 (1994): 166–83.

43. Stephen K. Wegren, "Rural Migration and Agrarian Reform in Russia: A Research Note," *Europe-Asia Studies* 47, no. 5 (1995): 877–88; Stephen K. Wegren, Grigory Ioffe, and Tatyana Nefedova, "Demographic and Migratory Responses to Agrarian Reform in Russia," *Journal of Communist Studies and Transition Politics* 13 (December 1997): 54–78; Susan Bridger, *Women in the Soviet Countryside* (Cambridge: Cambridge University Press, 1987); Bridger, "Rural Women and the Impact of Economic Change," in *Post-Soviet Women: From the Baltic to Central Asia*, ed. Mary Buckley (Cambridge: Cambridge University Press, 1997), 38–55; Norton D. Dodge and Murray Feshbach, "The Role of Women in Soviet Agriculture," in *Russian Peasant Women*, eds. Beatrice Farnsworth and Lynne Viola (New York: Oxford University Press, 1992), 236–63.

44. See, for example, Z. S. Beliaeva and O. A. Samonchik, eds., *Agrarnaia reforma v Rossiiskoi Federatsii: pravovye problemy i resheniia* (Moscow: Institut gosudarstva i prava, RAN, 1998), especially 91–119; and I. A. Ikonitskaia, *Zemel'noe pravo Rossiiskoi Federatsii: teoriia i tendentsii razvitiia* (Moscow: Institut gosudarstva i prava, RAN, 1999), especially 75–126.

45. Macey, *Government and Peasant*, 224–38; Macey, "Government Actions and Peasant Reactions"; Macey, "Agricultural Reform and Political Change: The Case of Stolypin," in *Reform in Modern Russian History*, ed. Taranovski, 180–89; and Macey, " 'A Wager on History.' "

46. Macey, *Government and Peasant*, xi–xiv, 239–48; Macey, "Agricultural Reform and Political Change," 163–89; Macey, "Government Actions and Peasant Reactions"; Macey, " 'A Wager on History.' "

47. D. Atkinson, "The Statistics on the Russian Land Commune, 1905–1917," *Slavic Review* 32 (December 1973): 773–87; S. M. Dubrovskii, *Stolypinskaia zemel'naia reforma: iz istorii sel'skogo khoziaistva i krest'ianstva Rossii v nachale XX veka* (Moscow: Nauka, 1963); Jones, *Late-Imperial Russia*; V. S. Diakin, ed., *Krizis samoderzhaviia v Rossii, 1885–1917* (Leningrad: Nauka, 1984); G. A. Gerasimenko, *Bor'ba krest'ian protiv stolypinskoi agrarnoi politiki* (Saratov: n.p., 1985); Gerasimenko, "The Stolypin Agrarian Reforms in Saratov," in *Politics and Society in Provincial Russia: Saratov, 1590–1917*, eds. R. A. Wade and S. J. Seregny (Columbus: Ohio State University Press, 1990), 233–54; P. N. Zyrianov, *Krest'ianskaia obshchina evropeiskoi Rossii 1907–1914 gg.* (Moscow: Nauka, 1992); Pallot, *Land Reform in Russia*.

48. Macey, "Agricultural Reform and Political Change"; Macey, "Government Actions and Peasant Reactions"; and Macey, " 'A Wager on History.' "

49. For the Stolypin reforms, see S. M. Sidel'nikov, ed., *Agrarnaia reforma Stolypina (Uchebnoe posobie)* (Moscow: izd. Moskovskogo universiteta, 1973), 145–51, 170–78.

50. See Petr A. Stolypin's comment on the secondary significance of claiming title as cited in K. A. Krivoshein, *A. V. Krivoshein (1857–1921 gg.): ego znachenie v istorii Rossii nachala XX veka* (Paris: n.p., 1973), 86; as cited in Diakin, *Krizis samoderzhaviia*, 352; and my articles cited in n. 48.

51. Macey, " 'A Wager on History,' " 161–67; cf. Mironov, *Sotsial'naia istoriia Rossii*, 1:479–84.

52. Macey, "Government Actions and Peasant Reactions," 157–64.

53. Mironov, *Sotsial'naia istoriia Rossii*, 1:479–84; Stanziani, "First World War"; Jeffrey Burds, *Peasant Dreams and Market Politics: Labor Migration and the Russian Village, 1861–1905* (Pittsburgh, PA: University of Pittsburgh Press, 1998), 143–85; Jeffrey Brooks, *When Russia Learned to Read: Literacy and Popular Literature, 1861–1917* (Princeton, NJ: Princeton University Press, 1985), passim, especially chapters 5, 8, epilogue; A. V. Gordon, *Krest'ianstvo i rynok* (Moscow: 1995).

54. See n. 2.

55. Such assumptions have been reliably reported to me as being bruited about within Russia's younger generation of economists and politicians, including advisers to the government.

8

Human Capital and Income Inequality

DENNIS J. DONAHUE

The collapse of the Soviet Union and the end of communism were expected by many to lead to rapid growth and greater economic well-being for Russian citizens. Other nations looked forward to the opening of new markets, while Russians eagerly awaited the coming of an age of abundance, or at least the end of ration lines. This promise of abundance reawakened the Russian dream of a "radiant future,"[1] only this time it was to be accomplished through the devices of the free market. At the point of transition, the Russian labor force was known to be highly skilled, and possessed a high average level of education. Most scholars predicted that workers would experience a short period of austerity, followed by rapid increases in economic well-being as they adjusted to an open labor market.

The persisting economic privation for many Russians is underscored by disparities between the lives of most workers and the relatively few, yet highly visible success stories. The fact that the popular media highlights those successes that do not appear to be directly linked to motivation, effort, or ability only helps to intensify the bitterness of perceived inequality. The inevitable comparisons are a constant reminder that the rules workers were told would bring them prosperity appear to have been broken.

Researchers interested in economic inequality were forced to remain covert during the Soviet period, so there is a limited history of research on the subject. The little research available suggests, however, that most income inequity and other types of social stratification were quite low.[2]

This chapter examines trends in human capital formation as well as how workers utilize previous human capital investments in the Russian Federation following the adoption of free market policies. I focus on the disparity in human capital and economic opportunity between urban and rural workers. Rural workers face substantially greater obstacles because they have been burdened by past inequities in human capital formation, and they continue to receive disproportionately low levels of economic and social assistance.[3]

Claims that rural workers are better situated to endure hardship because they have ready access to food and other resources[4] overlook the fact that rural Russians now must also learn to compete in a global market. During times of economic hardship it may well be true that access to food provides rural residents with a short-term coping mechanism. But rural residents have also come to expect access to the conveniences of the modern world. Furthermore, lower educational levels and the continuing neglect of the economic infrastructure will lead to long-term disadvantages for rural workers, particularly as the Russian economy becomes increasingly integrated in the world system. This chapter explores the differentials in human capital attainment between rural and urban workers and examines how individuals with varying levels of skills, education, and other valued characteristics navigate the transition to a competitive labor market.

Human Capital in Theory versus Human Capital in Russia

Fligstein defines human capital simply as "skills that the labor market rewards."[5] Given that the Russian workforce is both highly skilled and very well educated, this simple definition suggests that the problem lies within the labor market itself. This is true to a large extent, but Western theories of human capital do not fully explain the current Russian context.

Since the publication in 1964 of Becker's *Human Capital*[6] it has been clear that investments in the education, skills, and health of individuals provide substantial returns to both the individual and society. Schooling is the leading type of investment in human capital and it is also the focus of most studies on the subject.

Broadly defined, schooling is any knowledge and training from organizations not directly involved in the production of goods.[7] Every industrialized nation has some type of public education program for children and young adults that is funded by society as a whole. The function of these institutions is to bring the populace up to the recognized norm of general knowledge. At this point, individuals do one of three things. The first option is to enter the workforce immediately, usually in very low positions and with little opportunity for upward mobility. Another option is to seek further job-specific (vocational) training and skills in an institutional, non-classroom setting. Individuals taking this route expect to enter the workforce relatively early, but hope to begin at a higher level due to their increased investments. The third option is to continue to increase personal knowledge in specialized areas through secondary and post-secondary institutions. The educational structure in Russia is similar to the standard for most industrialized nations, but with a few important differences.

Russian children begin school at the age of seven and the typical primary education lasts eight years. Some students then attend a PTU (*prof-tekh uchilishche*) or FZU (*fabrichno-zavodskoye uchenichestvo*), which are low-level vocational training schools, while the majority of primary school graduates go on for a two-year secondary education. In the two decades prior to the breakup of the Soviet Union, state agencies made major investments in education and vocational training.[8] The goal of universal education was reasonably successful. By the time of the 1989 census, the vast majority of employed persons had completed the equivalent of an eighth-grade education.[9] Literacy rates jumped from less than 30 percent at the turn of the century to nearly 99 percent by 1959.[10]

Educational levels increased rapidly in rural regions, but still lagged far behind those of urban areas. Because the central government strove to coordinate training with expected increases in industrial production, workers often had little choice in the direction their education would take. Education beyond the secondary level became more common but, particularly in rural areas, tended to be of a vocational or technical nature. The result was a highly skilled and well-educated workforce with workers who had little experience making personal decisions on how to compete in the labor market. In addition, workers faced a global disadvantage because Russia's industrial technology was further behind global industrial standards than experts had predicted and workers were likely to be overeducated or miseducated for the jobs that were available. The number of college graduates grew during the late Soviet period, but not at a pace to keep up with other industrialized economies.[11]

Historically, the knowledge and skills attained during childhood and early adulthood have been useful throughout a lifetime. However, as the pace of technological change has increased, workers find that they must continually update their skills in order to remain competitive in the labor market.[12] This leads to a rapid depreciation in the value of earlier investments, putting workers at greater risk of becoming obsolete with the passage of time, and thereby changing the nature of the employer/employee relationship. In other words, education loses its value with age, and only with high levels of relevant experience can individual workers remain competitive.

During labor shortages, employers find it more efficient to assist present employees with job training that is directly applicable to the operation of the specific enterprise. More often, especially when there is a surplus of labor, workers must finance their continuing education either privately or with the assistance of state social services.

Russians considering their educational choices face two liabilities. First, the ability to choose the type and direction of self-education is relatively new, so they have limited experience to guide their choices. Second, the presumed goal of education (in human capital theory at least) is to maximize future returns, but this requires knowledge of how a competitive labor market operates and the ability to predict future demands for educational attainment, neither of which is available to most rural Russians.

After education, experience in the labor market is the most useful indicator of a worker's human capital. Becker discusses two types of experience, general and specific, as closely related yet distinct components of an individual's total human capital.[13] General experience is common to a variety of occupations, is easily obtained, and has little marketable value (such as ditch digging and sweeping). Specific experience is defined as specialized, often on-the-job training that increases productivity in a narrower range of occupations and job types (such as in-depth knowledge of company policies, or the establishment of trust and rapport with clientele). Work performed for one employer does not necessarily increase the value of skills to other employers. This type of experience is rewarded at a higher rate because the employer invests resources in training the employee and wants to retain the investment. Mark Rosenzweig suggests that experience is more valuable to rural (agricultural) workers because practical knowledge is learned through application rather than formal education.[14] The value of experience diminishes in all sectors of the labor market with the introduction of new technology, because old skills and training are made obsolete.

The Soviet-era policy of zero unemployment created workers with high levels of general experience in four ways.[15] First, the centrally planned economy required methods of production to be standardized, resulting in a lower skill level required for most work, and a large number of identically trained workers. Second, the Soviets focused on quantity of output over quality.[16] The combination of massive production targets and an ideology

Table 8.1

Unemployment Rates for Men and Women, 1992–98 (percent)

	Men	Women
1992	5.1	5.1
1993	6.0	5.9
1994	8.3	8.1
1995	9.8	9.5
1996[a]	10.1	9.6
1997	12.3	11.8
1998	13.7	13.3

[a] The Federal Employment Survey is normally conducted in October every year. In 1996 the survey was conducted in March.
Source: Current Statistical Survey Quarterly 29, no. 2 (Moscow: Goskomstat, 1999).

promoting zero unemployment created many machine-tending and assembly-line jobs, with only a few workers gaining high levels of specific experience.

Third, due to the increasingly rapid advance of technology, experience characterized as specific only a few years ago loses its value as the specific production process becomes obsolete.[17] The fourth factor, also related to the goal of zero unemployment, is worker redundancy. Overemployment is a continuing problem, especially among government and factory workers, and the layoff of tens of millions predicted to occur in 1991 has yet to occur.[18] Some analysts maintain that the endurance of the Soviet-era over-hiring policy has led to a crisis in work values, where workers' primary, and often only, goal is to minimize the expenditure of effort at work.[19] As shown in Table 8.1, unemployment has remained surprisingly low, particularly during the early years of the economic transition.

Geographic and occupational mobility are measures of human capital that directly influence a worker's ability to adapt to the transition economy. In almost every society, single young men and women have a geographic mobility advantage because they have fewer obligations and lower relocation costs. Russia has experienced massive internal migration of young workers from the countryside to Moscow, St. Petersburg, and other large cities. These migrants often become immigrants as they leave the country altogether in search of better employment opportunities.

Occupational mobility, the ability to move successfully from one occupation to another, is a human capital measure that has increased in value during the economic transition. The manufacturing sector, which was thought to be the most stable sector in Russia's economy, has shrunk by 45 percent.[20] Workers who are able to move into the service sector from either manufacturing or agricultural industries have two distinct advantages. First, most high-paying, service sector jobs require a population density and an established economic infrastructure that exist only in cities. Second, in general rural residents lack the education and skills necessary for a successful career move.

Demographic characteristics such as gender, age, and health are controls in most models of human capital. In Russia, women earn significantly lower incomes than men. Moreover, the gender gap has increased during the post-Soviet period.[21] This is not surprising because the position of women in the Russian labor force was already precarious, despite the communists' claim that male and female workers had equal rights.[22] Any economic upheaval will tend to disproportionately harm the disadvantaged worker population first, because other workers will be protected by unions, political power, and their cost of replacement. There is other evidence, however, that women play a more valuable role in the labor market and in overall household well-being than previous research suggests, but that they do not necessarily benefit from their increasing importance to the household.[23]

Finally, age must be controlled for in models of human capital because it is so highly correlated with other variables of interest, particularly education and experience. Very young workers tend to have relatively high levels of education compared to older workers, but they have little or no experience relevant to an enterprise. Older workers may have much lower educational levels, but will often be able to compensate for this through more years of experience, both in general work environments and in work experience specifically valuable to their current employer.

Specific Functions and Dysfunctions of Human Capital in Rural Russia

Significant inequalities in favor of urban residents persist in access to education and in existing levels of educational attainment. The literature suggests that education in all arenas is losing its value in Russia.[24] The Soviet educational system was designed to meet the needs of a socialist economy, so education is less likely to impart the type of knowledge that is rewarded in a capitalist economy. Workers in both rural and urban settings still realize an income benefit for higher education, but it is lower than would be expected in a capitalist economy, and lower still in rural than in urban areas. When the labor market in Russia stabilizes, we are likely to see that specific educational credentials (e.g., business degrees, computer science, law, etc.) will receive the higher rewards predicted by human capital theory. If this is the case, however, rural workers will still be less likely than urban workers to have received a valuable education.

In his study of human capital in rural India, Rosenzweig found that rural workers developed valuable human capital through practical experience rather than through education.[25] Similarly, Russian workers, both rural and urban, are more likely to "learn by doing" than through formal education. Because of this, we should expect that both rural and urban labor markets would place a lower value on education and a greater value on experience and tenure (job stability). This decline in returns to education is greater for rural workers because there are fewer opportunities for educated workers and because educational infrastructures are slower to change in rural areas. Many people in rural areas simply do not have access to higher education, which helps to explain some of the huge disparities in overall educational levels.[26] Rural workers are less likely to receive the kind of advanced, technical education that is easily transported to new work environments.

Rural workers, in general, face numerous geographic and institutional disadvantages. Low population density and geographic remoteness make job placement and social service provision highly inefficient.[27] Urban residents have easier access to employment opportunities and social services. Urban residents also have higher levels of geographic and occupational mobility due to functional and sociocultural closeness to Russia's economic center. Workers living near one of the major economic centers, such as Moscow or St. Petersburg, not only have more jobs open to them, but they also find it easier and cheaper to move to find a better job than do rural workers.

Measuring Human Capital in Russia

There is a wealth of data available for the study of human capital in contemporary Russia. Goskomstat publishes yearly and quarterly reports on levels of education, employment, and earnings, as well as a number of other demographic characteristics of the population. These publications compile data from the vital statistics registration system and a yearly survey of the working-age population.[28]

The empirical analysis in this chapter uses data from rounds V (1994) and VII (1996) of the Russian Longitudinal Monitoring Survey (RLMS).[29] The RLMS contains nationally representative, detailed information on households, families, individuals, and communities, providing a rare opportunity to study a broad range of the demographic and human capital variables of concern in this study. From a sample population of 4,718 households, round V had a response rate of 84 percent of households and 97 percent of individuals within those households. Additional respondents were lost to attrition from round V to VII, but the representativeness of the sample was not seriously damaged.[30] This level of cooperation is very respectable for this type of in-depth research, especially given the circumstances in Russia at the time. American survey experts have concluded that the methods and sampling frame used by the RLMS staff were as rigorous as those employed in most surveys in the United States.[31]

The subsample employed in this analysis includes all individuals between the ages of 17 and 60, which does not coincide with Russian or United Nations definitions of the working-age population. However, the subsample includes all but a few statistically outlying workers in the RLMS sample and serves as a pragmatic compromise, especially given the changing demographics of the Russian workforce. The samples contain 6,631 and 6,175 respondents, for rounds V and VII, respectively. Approximately 54 percent of each sample were female. These samples were split again into rural and urban subgroups. Table 8.2 shows the descriptive characteristics of the sample, with full and subgroup characteristics displayed by year of interview.

The variables in the analysis include total income, hours worked, age, years of labor market experience, years at current job, education (by highest grade level and by specific levels of academic achievement), percentage rural, health care availability (access to emergency medical service), functional distance to an economic center (cost of travel to Moscow), sociocultural distance to the center (timeliness of national newspaper delivery), and the availability of state employment services.

While all of the variables in Table 8.2 have theoretical importance, some were dropped from the regression analyses for statistical reasons, such as lack of explanatory power or statistical "cleanliness." The availability of state employment services, for example, has an uncontested effect on a worker's ability to utilize and enhance his or her human capital. However, 100 percent of the respondents who coded "urban" also had access to employment services, and thus the variable has little statistical value.

The dependent variable in the regression models is total income, measured in rubles and converted into natural log units.[32] Total income is the sum of all income received from primary work, secondary work, entrepre-

Table 8.2

RLMS Sample Descriptives

	1994 (Round V)			1996 (Round VII)		
	Full	Urban	Rural	Full	Urban	Rural
n =	6,631	4,982	1,649	6,176	4,726	1,450
Mean total income (per month, in rubles)	217,757	242,015	143,454	511,781	582,329	283,581
Mean hours worked (per month)	104.8	105.7	102.0	103.0	103.2	102.2
Mean age	37.7	37.6	38.0	37.8	37.7	38.0
Experience (years in labor market)	20.4	20.2	21.0	20.4	20.2	20.9
Tenure (years at current job)	5.7	5.8	5.5	4.6	4.9	3.8
Education						
Highest grade level	9.3	9.4	9.0	9.4	9.5	9.2
PTU/FZU/FZO, no secondary	9.4%	8.9%	10.8%	8.1%	7.9%	8.8%
PTU and secondary	16.4%	16.5%	16.1%	16.1%	16.2%	15.7%
Tech/med school	26.3%	28.3%	20.3%	24.5%	26.8%	17.0%
Institute/university	18.9%	21.8%	10.2%	17.2%	19.7%	8.9%
None of the above	29.0%	24.5%	42.6%	34.1%	29.4%	49.6%
% rural	24.9%	N/A	N/A	23.5%	N/A	N/A
Access to emergency clinic	84.1%	100.0%	38.5%	80.7%	97.2%	28.5%
Cost of travel to Moscow (in rubles)	188,322	190,168	183,078	769,541	763,016	790,649
Receive Moscow newspaper same day	33.7%	37.3%	22.8%	53.5%	62.3%	26.6%
Employment service available	78.1%	100.0%	15.8%	77.5%	100.0%	7.6%

neurial activity, pensions, and other sources, including the value of goods received in lieu of wages. Despite the breadth of this measure, total income is likely to remain underestimated, particularly in regard to the value of goods that are both produced and consumed within the household, which others have shown to be a major source of household income.[33] The measure of total income comes closest to encompassing all possible economic benefits of human capital. While income earned from the primary occupation is used in typical analyses of human capital, primary occupations in Russia capture only a part of the total economic activities engaged in by individuals. Total income is significantly lower for rural residents than for urban residents in both rounds V and VII.

General experience is measured as the total number of years spent in the labor market, with little variation between groups or over time. Specific experience is measured as the number of years at the current job (tenure).

The sharp drop in years at current job between round V and round VII, particularly for rural respondents, reflects the continuing economic turmoil accompanying the transition, and the privatization effect of workers moving from state to private enterprises.

The process of codifying and quantifying academic achievement variables in Russia is problematic because of the convoluted infrastructure of the Soviet education system, and by rapidly changing demographic characteristics over the past 40 years. In general, the rates of educational attainment in the RLMS sample (as with most other demographic variables) are comparable to the national statistics published by Goskomstat. Education was first measured on a continuous scale in terms of highest grade level achieved. As expected, rural respondents have slightly lower rates, but both urban and rural subsamples show small increases over time. Again, this is most likely due to changes in the structure of the sample, because 59- and 60-year-olds are retired out and 15- and 16-year-olds are brought in. Reported levels of educational attainment, that is, receiving a diploma for a specific academic threshold, have dropped substantially. The literature suggests that due to the shortage of suitable jobs Russians have held education to be less valuable in recent years. The short period of time between measures, however, may mean that much of the decline is due to the migration of those with the highest academic credentials, and lower individual-question cooperation rates.

A larger number of respondents had taken courses outside of school in the second survey than in the first (84 percent in round VII compared to 77 percent in round V). This suggests that workers are actively investing in educational human capital, but they are not relying on the traditional education system to do so. These results provide further evidence that the Russian educational system is failing to meet the demands of the market economy. Courses taken outside of school can mean anything from tractor repair to how to use the Internet. Some of these courses might lead to higher earnings, but because of the imprecise nature of the question, it is not included in the regression models.

The remaining variables are proxy measures for the availability of social services and functional proximity to valuable resources. Access to an emergency clinic indicates the likelihood that a worker will be able to receive prompt medical attention, with the assumption that easy access should be correlated with higher levels of health. This variable was omitted from the regression models because there was no variance among urban respondents.

The cost of travel to Moscow is a proxy measure for functional mobility. Lower expenses are correlated with the likelihood that a worker will migrate in search of economic opportunities. This is a dummy variable coded "1" if it would cost more than the average for the respondent to travel to Moscow, and "0" otherwise. This variable is not identical to a measurement of physical distance between two points; rather, it attempts to gauge the difficulties due to the unequal development of infrastructure in the Russian countryside. Workers might find it more difficult to migrate from Krasnoyarsk in Siberia to Moscow, than from Vladivostok to Moscow, for example, even though the former is only half the distance of the latter. The law of supply and demand tells us that workers who are less likely to migrate will be paid less because the supply of labor in their area will be higher.

Sociocultural distance from Moscow is measured through the availability of the national newspaper. Respondents who do not receive the paper on the same day it is published face a human capital disadvantage. They do not receive timely information from the government center, and are more likely to miss information on new laws, regulations, and opportunities. Respondents receiving the paper on the same day were coded "1," with all others coded "0."

Statistical Evidence of Rural Disadvantages

Table 8.3 shows the results of four separate regression models for each round of the survey. Each model uses the full sample and includes a variable for urban or rural residence, along with several other dependent variables. The education variable is measured continuously in the first column (by grade level) and then by educational achievement thresholds in the second column. Because experience is calculated as a function of age and grade level, it is included only in the absence of those variables. The third and fourth models for each round are identical to the first two, with the inclusion of new proxy variables for geographic mobility (cost of travel to Moscow) and sociocultural capital (timeliness of newspaper delivery). The strongest predictor of total income in all models is gender. Males earn substantially higher incomes, even after controlling for education, experience, and all the other human capital variables. The effect of gender is even greater than the effect of urban residence. Urban males earn significantly more than their rural counterparts.

The models using educational achievement levels have the greatest descriptive power. The models using highest grade level completed are not able to pick up the nuances peculiar to Russia's educational system, because grade level says nothing about the value of specialized, vocational

Table 8.3

OLS Regression Models, Human Capital Variables on Total Income, 1994 and 1996 (natural log)

Independent Variables	1994 (Round V)				1996 (Round VII)			
	Grade Level Simple	Educational Attainment Simple	Grade Level Full Model	Educational Attainment Full Model	Grade Level Simple	Educational Attainment Simple	Grade Level Full Model	Educational Attainment Full Model
Intercept	-0.43	1.66***	-0.06	1.77***	-1.95	0.11	-1.56	0.13
Gender: male	3.57**	2.44***	3.36*	2.44***	1.86	2.87***	1.46	2.79***
Urban	1.25***	1.03***	0.94***	0.76**	1.46***	2.42***	2.46***	2.21***
Tenure	0.13***	0.12***	0.13***	0.12***	0.17***	0.15***	0.17***	0.15***
Experience		0.17***		0.17***		0.11***		0.12***
Age	0.17***		0.17***		0.13***		0.13***	
Grade level	-0.03		-0.06		0.05		0.02	
PTU/FZU		0.65*		0.61*		0.68		0.76*
PTU/Sec		1.14***		1.07***		1.06***		1.05**
Tec/Med		1.14***		1.18***		1.87***		1.88***
Ins/Uni		1.69***		1.62***		2.32***		2.27***
Travel to Moscow expensive			-0.82***	-0.76***			-0.92***	-0.75***
Paper same day			0.90***	0.79***			0.47***	0.40*
Interactions								
Male* tenure	-0.05**	-0.04*	-0.06**	-0.04*	-0.07*	-0.05	-0.06*	-0.04
Male* experience		-0.10***		-0.10***		-0.06***		-0.06***
Male* age	-0.09***		-0.09***		-0.05**		-0.05**	
n size	6,618	6,631	6,263	6,276	6,159	6,176	5,786	5,801
F value for model	92.79***	85.56***	78.44***	73.84***	66.36***	66.55***	53.80***	54.95***

* = $p < .05$; ** = $p < .01$; *** = $p < .001$

schools in relation to a general secondary education. By contrast, the models that include specific educational attainment levels show that education has a statistically and substantively significant effect on income. The pattern is clearly monotonic, with higher educational attainments at each subsequent level showing higher overall incomes.

Residing in an urban area has a strong positive effect on income in every model, and the urban advantage is significantly higher in Round VII. Number of years with the present employer (tenure) has a small positive effect for each year of service. Age and experience have a positive yearly effect, but the effect is curvilinear, diminishing over time.

The full models confirm the hypotheses regarding functional mobility and sociocultural distance from the nation's center. When travel is more expensive, workers have less mobility and suffer an income penalty. The increased magnitude of the penalty over time suggests that the expense of moving has gone up in relation to available resources. There may also be some selectivity bias, insofar as those respondents who were most likely to be mobile have already left. Timely access to news and information (measured by same-day receipt of the Moscow newspaper) has a moderate, statistically significant effect.

Table 8.4 compares the full educational threshold model for the total sample with the separate urban and rural samples. Each regression equation shows how experience, tenure, educational threshold, travel cost, and news availability affect total income. The value of labor market experience drops significantly between 1994 and 1996, with rural respondents experiencing the greatest decrease. Experience is measured continually, so between 1994 and 1996 rural workers with several years of experience suffer huge declines in the value of their human capital when compared to urban residents with the same characteristics. The value of tenure (job stability) remains steady, although all groups experienced a decline in the average number of years spent with the current employer (see Table 8.2).

The value of specific academic credentials decreased in relative terms for both urban and rural residents between 1994 and 1996. While the coefficients for highly educated urban workers are slightly higher in absolute value, they do not compensate for inflation and, thus, translate into lower *real* returns to human capital investment. One surprise is that the achievement of specific educational thresholds is of greater value to rural respondents in 1994, even though it does not make up completely for the lower incomes they experience in relation to urban workers. That education has some value in 1994 is not too surprising, given that it is a scarce commodity in the Russian countryside.

Table 8.4

OLS Regression Models, Human Capital Variables on Total Income with Separate Models for Total, Urban, and Rural Samples, 1994 and 1996 (natural log)

	1994 (Round V)			1996 (Round VII)		
Independent Variables	Income Total Sample	Income Urban Sample	Income Rural Sample	Income Total Sample	Income Urban Sample	Income Rural Sample
Intercept	6.15***	7.56***	5.26***	4.30***	6.75***	4.25***
Experience	0.06***	0.06***	0.08***	0.05***	0.05***	0.04**
Tenure	0.05***	0.06***	0.02	0.06***	0.06***	0.06*
PTU/FZU	0.26	-0.15	1.11*	0.37	0.46	-0.13
PTU/Sec	0.67***	0.54**	0.86*	0.64**	0.52*	0.66
Tec/Med	0.85***	0.65***	1.34***	1.31***	1.34***	0.98*
Ins/Uni	0.90***	0.64***	1.92***	1.87***	1.90***	1.69**
Urban	1.08***	N/A	N/A	2.28***	N/A	N/A
Travel to Moscow expensive	-0.50***	-0.29	-0.49	-1.26***	-0.92***	-1.83***
Paper same day	0.62***	0.29	1.68***	0.73***	0.21	2.65***
n size	6,275	4,702	1,572	5,800	4,382	1,417
F value for model	47.62***	28.24***	18.14***	65.77***	28.77***	19.39***

* = $p < .05$; ** = $p < .01$; *** = $p < .001$

Tchernina found that rural workers were somewhat protected from the shock of transition by their ability to rely on natural resources and self-produced goods.[34] The reversal of the value of education in 1996 (rural workers in 1996 received a smaller benefit from education than did urban workers in that year), suggests that the shock was delayed and did not affect rural workers until sometime after 1994. It should be noted that although urban residents have consistently higher returns on their investments in human capital, most of the t-tests of the differences in the coefficients between the urban and rural models are not significant.

The negative impact of geographical mobility costs remains significant in these models. The effect on rural respondents is just about double that of urban respondents in both rounds of the survey. This is to be expected, given that it took the average rural worker 38 days to earn the equivalent of a trip to Moscow in 1994, while it took an urban resident only 23 days. In 1996, it took even longer—83 days for a rural worker and 39 days for an urban worker. These values (calculated by dividing the cost of travel by average monthly income) show that rural workers need to make a much larger investment (in terms of proportion of total income) if they wish to become geographically mobile.

Receiving the Moscow paper on the same day it is published had a small positive effect for urban respondents in 1994 but none in 1996. Rural newspaper readers, however, benefit substantially over rural nonreaders.

Prospects for Rural Workers

Rural workers in Russia face several disadvantages in their efforts to navigate the economic transition and the newly competitive labor market. The first disadvantage is their lower level of human capital. Rural workers have lower average education levels, fewer specialized (marketable) job skills, and are significantly less mobile, both geographically and occupationally, than their urban counterparts. Unfortunately, any investments in human capital will likely have to come from within Russia, because foreign governments and companies find it difficult to justify spending money on another nation's workers. Furthermore, the assistance Russia does receive inevitably comes with strings attached, insisting on further financial reform and investments in the service sector, which does very little to help rural workers.

A second disadvantage is that institutional barriers in access to education, skills training, and social services may be exacerbated by an unwillingness to accept new ideas and technologies.[35] Russians in general, and rural Russians in particular, are already falling behind in the use of new technology, and this disparity will increase exponentially if the cultural and bureaucratic impediments to innovation are not eliminated.

The third disadvantage is that the rural workforce typically works in industries that are highly affected by price and demand fluctuations. The rate of de-collectivization of Russian farms is closely correlated with the individual farmer's assessment of the risk involved in starting a private enterprise.[36] That many farm workers are hesitant to leave the collective is not surprising, given their lower average education levels and their minimal experience with competition in the global market. However, rural Russians in general show surprising savvy and skill in negotiating the economic transition.[37]

Finally, rural workers have fewer employment options and entrepreneurial opportunities than do urban workers. The spatial distribution of persons and resources makes many business opportunities too inefficient to be feasible. The highest-paying service sector jobs require the presence of a dense, centrally located population base that is not available in rural regions.[38]

Urban and rural workers differ greatly, both in their current levels of human capital and in their capacity to gain more. The ability of workers to navigate the economic transition can be predicted by their education level, labor market experience, mobility, and access to social services. Individuals residing in urban regions held advantages in every measure of human capital during the Soviet period and it appears that these differentials have been increasing in the post-Soviet period. The perception that education is becoming less valuable, however, is misplaced. Very high levels of education continue to be a strong predictor of economic success. Unless major investments are made in the educational infrastructure of rural regions, rural workers will have no chance to catch up.

Notes

1. Michael Burawoy and Janos Lukacs, *The Radiant Past* (Chicago: University of Chicago Press, 1992). See especially chapter 5, "Painting Socialism," for an explication of the place of ideology in Soviet workers' lives.

2. See Valentina S. Sycheva, "Measuring the Poverty Level: A History of the Issue," *Russian Social Science Review* 40 (1999): 19–33; and Theodore P. Gerber and Michael Hout, "Educational Stratification in Russia During the Soviet Period," *American Journal of Sociology* 101 (1995): 611–60.

3. Gerber and Hout, "Educational Stratification"; Michael Paul Sacks, "Ethnic and Gender Division in the Work Force of Russia," *Post-Soviet Geography* 36 (1995): 1–12.

4. Natalia Tchernina, "Unemployment and the Emergence of Poverty during Economic Reform in Russia," *International Labor Review* 133 (1996): 597–611. The intent of this article is not to suggest that the problems faced by rural Russians are inconsequential. But, the article serves an example of a disturbing tendency in much of the recent literature, which is to imply that rural residents suffer less than urban residents, because they are accustomed to living off the land.

5. Neil Fligstein, "The Economic Sociology of the Transitions from Socialism," *American Journal of Sociology* 101 (1996): 1074–81.

6. Gary Becker, *Human Capital: A Theoretical and Empirical Analysis* (Cambridge: Cambridge University Press, 1964).

7. Ibid., 29.

8. Loren Graham, "Adapting to New Technologies," in *Soviet Social Problems*, eds. Anthony Jones, Walter D. Conner, and David E. Powell (Boulder, CO: Westview Press, 1991), 296–318.

9. For an overview of educational stratification in Russia, and an analysis of consequences on Russia today, see Theodore P. Gerber, "Educational Transitions in Post-War Russia: Effects of Demographics, Social Origins, and Politics" (paper presented at annual meetings of the Population Association of America, New York, March 1999).

10. Sources for aggregate statistics are *Demograficheskii ezhegodnik Rossii 1998* (Moscow: Goskomstat, 1999); *Rossiiski statisticheskii ezhegodnik* (Moscow: Goskomstat, 1999); *Current Statistical Survey Quarterly*, no. 29 (Moscow: Goskomstat, 1999).

11. Walter D. Conner, "Labor Politics in Postcommunist Russia: A Preliminary Assessment," in *The Accidental Proletariat: Workers, Politics and Crisis in Gorbachev's Russia*, ed. Walter Connor (Princeton, NJ: Princeton University Press, 1991), 329–53. For an analysis of the situation immediately prior to the breakup of the Soviet Union, see also Walter D. Conner, "The Soviet Working Class: Change and Its Political Impact," in *Understanding Soviet Society*, eds. Michael Sacks and Jerry Pankhurst (Boston: Unwin Hyman 1988), 31–51.

12. Andrei Balaban, "Technology Commercialization in Post-Soviet Russia" (paper presented at IREX/UT-CREES Symposium, "Science, Technology, and the Public in Russia," Center for Russian, East-European & Eurasian Studies, University of Texas at Austin, 12 February 1999).

13. Becker, *Human Capital*, 18.

14. Mark Rosenzweig, "Population Growth and Human Capital Investments: Theory and Evidence," part 2, *Journal of Political Economy* 98, no. 5 (October 1990): S38–S70.

15. David Lane, "Full Employment and Labor Utilization in the USSR," in *Understanding Soviet Society*, eds. Sacks and Pankhurst, 221–38.

16. Graham, "Adapting to New Technologies," 304.

17. Burawoy and Lukacs, *The Radiant Past*, 122.

18. Alexander T. Samorodov, "Transition, Poverty and Inequality in Russia," *International Labor Review* 131 (1992): 335–53.

19. Vladimir S. Magun, "Work Values in Russian Society," *Russian Social Science Review* 39 (1998): 20–38.

20. V. Medvedev, "Problems of Russia's Economic Security," *Russian Social Science Review* 39 (1998): 4–14.

21. Sacks, "Ethnic and Gender Division,"; Theodore P. Gerber and Michael Hout, "More Shock than Therapy: Market Transition, Employment, and Income in Russia, 1991–1995," *American Journal of Sociology* 104 (1998): 1–50.

22. Zillah Eisenstein has written extensively on women's rights and their struggle for equality around the world, including those inequalities that existed prior to, and continue after, the breakup of the Soviet Union. For her most recent remarks on global gender inequalities, see Zillah Eisenstein, "Women's Publics and the Search for New Democracies," *Feminist Review* 57 (1997), 140–67.

23. Sandra L. Hofferth and John Iceland, "Social Capital in Rural and Urban Communities," *Rural Sociology* 63 (1998): 574–98; Cynthia Buckley, "Obligations and Expectations: Renegotiating Pensions in the Russian Federation," *Continuity and Change* 13 (1998): 317–38.

24. Gerber and Hout, "Educational Stratification"; Alexander T. Samorodov, "Transition, Poverty and Inequality in Russia," *International Labor Review* 131, no. 3 (1992): 335–53.

25. Rosenzweig, "Population Growth and Human Capital Investments."

26. Gerber, "Educational Transitions"; Hofferth and Iceland, "Social Capital in Rural and Urban Communities."

27. Leann M. Tigges and Deborah M. Tootle, "Labor Supply, Labor Demand, and Men's Underemployment in Rural and Urban Labor Markets," *Rural Sociology* 55 (1990): 328–56.

28. Sources for aggregate statistics are *Demograficheskii ezhegodnik Rossii 1998*; *Rossiiski statisticheskii ezhegodnik*, and *Current Statistical Survey Quarterly* 29.

29. Detailed information on the RLMS can be found at the Web site for the University of North Carolina at Chapel Hill, Population Research Center, at *www.cpc.unc.edu*. Data used from the RLMS comes from the income, work, and community sections of rounds V and VII. All data, including many sections that are not mentioned here, except for the community-level sections, are available to the public at no charge.

30. Steven G. Heeringa provides an analysis of the sampling strategies and an evaluation of the methodology used in the RLMS, as well as additional support for the validity of many of the measures used in this analysis. Heeringa, "Russia Longitudinal Monitoring Survey (RLMS): Sample Attrition, Replenishment, and Weighting in Rounds V-VIII," in *Special Report on the RLMS* (Ann Arbor: Institute for Social Research, University of Michigan, 1997).

31. Ibid.

32. The log conversion is commonly used in regression analysis of income because income distributions are rarely linear. The log transformation creates a more normal distribution, making linear regression more productive. The natural log also corrects for a positive skew in the income distribution by increasing the influence of low values and decreasing the influence of very high values.

33. Richard Rose and Ian McAllister, "Is Money the Measure of Welfare in Russia?" *Review of Income and Wealth* 42 (1996): 75–90; Tchernina, "Unemployment and the Emergence of Poverty."

34. Tchernina, "Unemployment and the Emergence of Poverty."

35. Graham, "Adapting to New Technologies," 315; and Balaban, "Technology Commercialization in Post-Soviet Russia."

36. Erik Mathijs and Johan F.M. Swinnen, "The Economics of Agricultural Decollectivization in East Central Europe and the Former Soviet Union," *Economic Development and Cultural Change* 47, no. 1 (1998): 1–26.

37. An analysis of how rural Chinese peasants under a socialist system try to compete in the global market is found in Victor Nee, "The Theory of Market Transition from Redistribution to Markets in State Socialism," *American Sociological Review* 54 (1989): 663–81. See also Victor Nee and Rebecca Matthews, "Market Transition and Societal Transformation in Reforming State Socialism," *Annual Review of Sociology* 22 (1996): 401–35.

38. Tigges and Tootle, "Labor Supply, Labor Demand."

9

Communal Coherence and Barriers to Reform

LIESL L. GAMBOLD MILLER

Introduction[1]

Russian peasants are not inherently risk averse and resistant to change. They, like many rural dwellers, make decisions based on weighing the outputs (labor and resources) and risks against potential gains.[2] Given the current situation with agricultural reforms, rural Russians have made the most rational, adaptive choice: to maintain the collective organization of their labor, economy, and social structure. This decision may not be easily understood in the context of standard, cost-benefit economic agricultural theory, but it is congruent with their circumstances and needs. What is exhibited is a *communal coherence*, a natural tendency toward holding the community together, marked by a logical consistency. Galina Radionova, a Russian sociologist working for the agricultural reform organization Fond Zerno, contends that "maintaining collective work would be best due to the deeply engrained sense of community responsibility." Rural villagers have not emerged as great advocates of independent private farms, not because they do not support reorganization, but because they are mindful of the bigger picture.

Most villagers were initially supportive of agricultural restructuring, but have now grown disillusioned and unenthusiastic about "independent farming" and the "market economy." The promised benefits of agricultural reforms have yet to be realized. Instead, reforms have nearly stripped them of the few, but reliable, benefits they enjoyed as members of the collective. Given the current state of farming, and of their lives in general, most villagers believe that there are too many barriers for them to experience significant success in independent farming. Due to these barriers, the peasants continue struggling to maintain the *communal coherence* that has marked their existence for decades. The fact that they cling to the *kolkhoz* is being misinterpreted as a sign that they are averse to risk and change. I argue that this behavior signals a deeper understanding of their cultural and economic needs. Considering the historical, social, and financial situations in play, it is clear that the barriers to reform far outweigh the paltry potential gains. These barriers can be divided into two main areas, fiscal and sociodemographic.

Research Background and Methods

The collapse of the Soviet Union in 1991 signaled a prodigious opportunity for social scientists. At that time, contemporary ethnographic information available on rural Russia was nearly nonexistent.[3] Communist policies had kept Western ethnographers closely guarded in Soviet cities and allowed few of them access to the Siberian region.[4] Accounts of Russian peasant culture were based in the folklore collected by Soviet ethnographers who had traveled to villages gathering handicrafts, local histories, songs, and mythic tales. The traditional anthropological participant-observation method was absent due to their general requirements of freedom of access, independently guided inquiries, an assumed integrity in the interviewing process, and the probability that matters of politics, economics, social structure, religion, and communication would be explored.

When Western social scientists began working in post-Soviet Russia, the field of agricultural studies necessitated rural research. With Russian agricultural reforms under way in early 1993, consultants were being sent to the countryside to facilitate the restructuring of collective and state farms.[5] The resultant material on post-Soviet agricultural restructuring was surprisingly devoid of data collected directly from the villagers who were being most affected by the changes. Some researchers noted that understanding the cultural elements of village life was critical for understanding the present and future course of reforms.[6] Still, most ground-level inquiries into village life did not delve beyond the farm director's impressions or hastily gathered surveys. In 1995, roughly three years after the first round of reforms, the British Know How Fund (BKHF) made its first attempt to assess the mood of people living in rural villages.[7] That period of fieldwork lasted ten days.

This chapter is based on one year of fieldwork in Nizhegorodskaia oblast from May 1997 to May 1998. In a village called Moshkin, I assessed the cultural and economic impact of agricultural reforms. Through anthropological fieldwork and survey data collection I became a regular, though atypical, fixture in the village. The farm director, who was sympathetic to my research goals, facilitated my entry into the village. Initially, my time was spent with her and the other administrators in the small farm offices in the center of the village. Soon, however, I wandered the village freely, spending time with the villagers at work in the fields, in the garage, eating at the canteen, at village meetings, and in their homes. My freedom of access and the trust gained over the months of my stay gave me a unique position from which to learn about the village situation at the ground level.

Farm Reorganization in Nizhegorodskaia Oblast

Nizhegorodskaia oblast is large by central Russian standards, and longer from north to south (430 km) than from east to west (360 km). In general, agriculture is more productive in the southern part than in the north, both for climatic and agronomic reasons. In the southern half, soil quality is generally good, with some qualifying as the extremely productive black-earth (chernozem) soil of southern Russia. In principle, large-scale grain production can be expected to be profitable here. In the north of the oblast, the summer season is estimated to be two weeks shorter than in the south. Much of the northern area is forested and is better suited for cattle raising or smallholder agriculture.

According to Russian agricultural experts in Nizhniy Novgorod, the regional differences in land quality have had a paradoxical consequence in this period of reform. Farmers further north are said to be more enterprising and capable of adapting to market methods. This is because while under central planning they always had to find ways to supplement their meager agricultural incomes. During that time period, the oblast's southern farmers were able to make a satisfactory living by sticking to administrative orders. Hence, farmers in the north are more entrepreneurial and accustomed to relying on their individual efforts to fulfill subsistence requirements. Some are even said to be leaving agriculture altogether to develop small businesses or to become part-time farmers.

Development of Reforms

The failed coup d'etat in August 1991 and the collapse of the Soviet Union in December 1991 gave way to a multi-party system and a market economy. By the end of 1992, Nizhegorodskaia oblast had become a leader in economic reforms in Russia. The first privatization in the country took place here in April 1992 with the International Finance Corporation (IFC) providing assistance in the privatization of retail and wholesale trade enterprises.

The oblast continued to play a leading role in the privatization process, pioneering the reform of truck transport and the use of privatization vouchers. Led by the 34-year-old, reform-minded governor, Boris Nemstov, the reforms were based on two main principles, as explained by the IFC:

- Freedom of choice for individuals: Privatization was a process designed to return control to individuals and must itself be driven by individuals.
- Fairness: In order to give equal access to all individuals, the process had to be transparent and radically different from the old way of "behind-the-scenes" decision making.

Therefore, the privatization procedures developed in Nizhegorodskaia oblast employed a public auction method as the allocation mechanism for privatized resources. Despite enterprise managers' mixed responses to the auction method—since along with the opportunity to control or even own assets went a risk that the assets would go to some other individual or group—auctions were held without significant problems. The initial speed of the reforms, along with their notable success in improving the food supply, gave the process further momentum.[8]

The pilot farm reorganization program was requested by Nemstov for several reasons. First, it would bring private ownership to the full chain of food production and distribution, thus guaranteeing the further development of the Russian agricultural, processing, and food marketing system. Second, it could help to resolve the seemingly permanent problem of low productivity and resultant poverty in the countryside. Finally, there was the challenge that many considered Russia's collectivized agriculture incapable of reform, irreversibly ruined by inadequate labor, discipline problems, alcoholism, poor demographics, and general hopelessness.

Thus, Nizhegorodskaia oblast became the pioneer of farm reorganization in Russia. Before the program started in 1993, many farm units were formally privatized, converting from collective (*kolkhoz*) or state (*sovkhoz*) ownership to limited liability partnerships or joint stock companies. However, little had changed in practice.

Moshkinskoe

My research took place on the Moshkinskoe farm, located 87 kilometers north of the capital, Nizhniy Novgorod. It had been part of a kolkhoz that was organized in 1930 during Stalin's first five-year plan and the sweep of forced collectivization. In March 1994, this collective underwent a highly publicized land auction with Prime Minister Viktor Chernomyrdin in attendance along with administrative representatives from over 30 regions in Russia. At this third pilot farm auction, most of the 3,109 hectares of the collective were distributed to three newly reorganized farms: Mir, Kolos, and Moshkinskoe.

Moshkinskoe is located in the village of Moshkin. At the reform auction, the farm was reorganized under the direction of Ekaterina Nikolaevna Makaricheva, former accountant, economist, and subchairman of the kolkhoz. Ekaterina had worked on the farm for 16 years before assuming the role of director for the newly formed farm.[9] Moshkinskoe received 1,477 hectares of land, the largest of the three newly formed farms. As of March 1999, there were 80 paid workers, down from 92 one year earlier.[10] The population of Moshkin as of 1 January 1998 was 426. Moshkin is located seven kilometers from the village of Kovrigino and falls under the Kovrigino *okrug*, which includes the three limited liability partnerships, Mir, Kolos, and Moshkinskoe.

Barriers to Reform

"The collective farm is the school of communism for the peasants."[11]

Very few Moshkin residents were firmly opposed to agricultural restructuring. The majority simply did not know what to make of the changes that swept through their quiet village over the previous five years. Those who spoke out against reforms claimed that the communist ideals were correct: Land was not for individuals to own and extract profits from, because it belonged to the people collectively and should be worked and enjoyed collectively. To these individuals, the potential for the economic success of

Russian agriculture mattered little. Vladimir, a 38-year-old tractor driver, explained, "We can't worry about ourselves alone. No one can succeed that way, except maybe the director, but I don't think so. Maybe in the city, but we are peasants. We want to live with basic food and drink as we always have. It should be simple!"

In collectivized rural Russia, an individual worked in the collective organization under the belief of benefiting the state and the community. Since farming support and organization were state controlled and success was measured collectively, not individually, independent inspiration and innovation were limited to personal household gardens.[12] Personal gains were measured in basketsful, not rubles. Peasants had neither the means, nor the incentive, to amass wealth. State controls and substantial informal social canons maintained rural egalitarianism.[13] Despite this culture of scarcity, however, peasants were able to provide themselves and their families with basic necessities and the occasional luxury item such as a radio, a television set, or new furniture.

The financial impact of reorganization on most collective farms has been steady and substantial economic loss. In dismantling the communist structures that had propped up farming for decades, the extent to which the agricultural system was dependent on the state became painfully obvious. In 1991, the average collective farm could buy three to four tractors, compared to two in 1992, and only one in 1993. By 1994, farmers could not even buy a replacement wheel, let alone a tractor.[14]

There are few substantial incentives to motivate people to farm independently. The hope that potential monetary gain would inspire farmers has waned, because thus far, realistic opportunities for increased earnings are negligible. The Yeltsin government was decidedly anti-agrarian and urban biased. The lack of government support is measurable. Agricultural investments declined by 92 percent between 1990 and 1994.[15] National measures passed into law that might help the reform process are often stalled in Moscow and never put into practice. Nonetheless, while a healthy market economy will never succeed without true political support, it is local barriers that are crippling even modest reform advances. These obstacles can be grouped under two main areas, fiscal and sociodemographic.

Fiscal Barriers

In Moshkin, the fiscal barriers to reform are exemplified by the lack of an adequate cash flow in and out of the area. Both the parent farm and individual households are chronically cash poor. Barter and trade have replaced cash payments in a country where inflation is not only a constant threat but a destructive reality. When villagers do collect cash, they quickly buy durable goods or U.S. dollars. Workers often receive payments in kind and, therefore, have little access to cash unless they can sell something at the town market. In addition, the taxes and debt attached to former *kolkhozy* drain most of the loans and credits the farms can secure.

Peasant society has nearly always been characterized by a minimal cash flow; however, the situation has worsened since agricultural reforms began. With inadequate resources, farms are forced to use their meager cash flow for nonwage payments on items such as inputs, taxes, or debts, leaving very little for workers' salaries. When state-subsidized credits ended, farmers were unable to afford the interest rates for loans. They responded in several ways that "affected production and income potential."[16] One way was to reduce livestock holdings.

Meat production in the former Soviet Union was not profitable for years because herds were too large for the available fodder crops, making farms that held a large number of animals continually dependent on government subsidies.[17] Therefore, a component of the reform program included the retraction of government subsidies for livestock raising. Moshkinskoe's solvency was directly affected by these changes in government subsidy policies. Ekaterina decided to eliminate the farm's livestock herd, but soon found that she had to maintain a portion of them because of the villagers' dependence on the parent farm for animal products. In a survey of Moshkin villagers and farm workers, 94 percent of respondents said that they purchased all of their animals between 1993 and 1997 from the Moshkinskoe farm.[18] Despite the unprofitability of livestock raising, it is maintained at some level in order to keep people employed and to provide vital provisions for village residents. Ekaterina discussed this predicament:

> I am not going to invest any more money in animals, and we may even reduce the amount of milk cows we have due to the lack of government support for animal keeping. We will try to increase the quantity and quality from the animals we have rather than increasing the herd size. It's just not profitable to keep them and we have no support from the state anymore. What can we do? But we also have the animal workers to think of. They can't work anywhere else. No one can change easily.

The lack of cash earnings and financial profits is apparently secondary to the informal social obligations traditionally upheld in the village. A 1997 study found that farm managers reported maintaining unprofitable operations for "preservation of jobs, the need to secure foodstuffs for farm residents and hope for future subsidies."[19] While suffering from the absence of subsidies and a negative cash flow, farm directors were forced to develop their agricultural operations and maintain current job levels.[20] Maintaining the minimal functioning level of basic farm operations is currently a challenge. The Moshkinskoe farm cannot buy the supplies necessary to continue operating at a basic level.[21] One morning while riding the village bus to the garage, one of the machinery drivers entered. Valentina Vitalevna, the assistant farm director, asked him, "Do you have petrol for the machinery? The harvest is spoiling in the field! We must hurry. Why is it taking so long?" He answered, "I have very little petrol. I won't be able to work for long." This was one of the countless times I heard that a field was going unplowed or products undelivered because there was no petrol and no cash with which to buy it.

In spring 1999, Ekaterina told me that the cash flow problem had not changed. In fact, the system of barter had been drastically augmented.

> We had, and have, no money to buy equipment. Now we only buy fertilizers, seeds, and spare parts, only the most needed things. We do not usually pay in cash, as we have no cash, and we try to use different connections to sell and buy things. It is like this: We need to buy diesel for the tractors and harvesters, so the plant producing diesel needs, say, paper. The paper plant needs dairy products, so we can exchange milk for paper and then paper for diesel and, voila, we get what we need!

In such a cash-poor environment, trade and barter, such as Ekaterina described, are predictably increasing. With inadequate cash farmers cannot participate in the market. One foreign agricultural consultant from Britain claimed, "Barter will ruin private farming in Russia. The countryside must be monetized." Farmers find barter appealing not only because they are able to obtain goods without cash, but they are also able to avoid taxes. However, their transactional choices are limited to doing business only with those who are willing to trade. Some may avoid barter when possible because the prices can be 1.5 times greater than the cash price. Even individuals who attempt to follow the usual channels for marketing can end up engaged in a complex arrangement to earn cash. For people with little access to cash, however, it is their only option, as explained by a 42-year-old independent farmer:

> I can't do anything simply any longer. I grow and grind my own grain. I produce a fair amount of flour to sell to the bakery. But the

bakery has no money so they pay me in bread, sometimes up to 100 loaves or more. What can I do with 100 loaves of bread? Even my animals won't eat this much bread. And still, I have no money, only bread. So, I opened this small bread shop in order to sell my bread to make money. Now I am a bread seller! I just want to sell my flour, not peddle bread.

With the demonetarization of rural Russia paving the way for an elaborate system of barter, it is difficult to assert that the market economy is being developed under the current reforms.

When cash is obtained through loans or product sales it is immediately depleted by the most basic expenditures. Petrol, diesel, oil, and electricity are the primary regular needs. The operating costs of the farm are over US$2,000 monthly. This amount does not cover salaries or other inputs the farm needs such as fertilizers or machinery parts. After the farm managers use the money they make from selling their goods, they rely heavily on loans and barter to obtain these basic inputs. Even utilities can occasionally be paid for with barter. At least twice during my stay, meat and vegetables were delivered by the Moshkinskoe farm to the electrical plant to be applied to their debt.

Workers' wages were frequently, and always partially, paid in kind. I asked Ekaterina what does she do when there is no money for wages? She answered, "We can also pay them in goods. And if someone really needs something and has no money, we will help them. But, we have to rely on the goods we produce for everything. If we sell our goods we can get money and pay our workers." While workers complain bitterly about the lack of wages, they have no clear alternative. When asked why he bothered to continue working if he hadn't been paid for four months, one man answered, "It's our life! We work. And, we *might* get paid. Besides, they give me food and hay, which I can use. But, I can't buy a car with hay!" This chronic lack of wages, wages that some have called "the most important material incentive," exacerbates the already insufficient rural cash flow.[22]

In addition to unprofitable activities, prohibitive input prices, and barter, village cash flow is influenced by farm debt and taxes. Farms that underwent reorganization assumed, or were burdened with, the debts of the "parent" farm. These debts could be assigned to everything except land, and were highest on machinery and buildings. Even for those who did not take on substantial debt, the process of organizing a farm was still riddled with debt.

Tatyana Pavlovna, the only independent farmer in Moshkin, immediately accrued a large amount of debt when she started up. She previously worked as the chief agronomist for Ekaterina at the Moshkinskoe farm for one year after the reorganization took place. She then realized that "it didn't matter what form of collective farm it was, it was still a collective organization and you don't really work for yourself." She decided to leave the farm and strike out on her own with her husband. On 30 hectares, they grow 18 hectares of cereal grains, 12 of fodder crops, and the home garden is used for vegetables. Understanding her situation made two things very clear: First, the avenues from collective to private farming are so riddled with uncertainty and problems it is no surprise that people are hesitant to attempt the change. Second, Tatyana is one of the more resourceful and persistent people in the village.

> During the first year I just asked the Agricultural Chemicals Organization in Gorodets and they loaned us a tractor for the spring to enable us to seed the plants. But, there was a condition for me. I agreed to buy them a tiller. So, I had to get a loan and I bought the equipment for plowing and harvesting potatoes—a double potato digger actually. So we had to buy this equipment and then they gave us the tractor but we had to pay them for using the tractor and since I had two cows and two calves at home we had to kill them and sell the meat in order to pay for renting the tractor. And then we had to pay back our loan at 50 percent interest per year! Can you imagine? In the beginning we were only able to pay the interest but now we are already paying our second year of the principal. It's already 15 million rubles we've paid in interest. So, it's been three years we have been working only to pay back our loan and the taxes. We earn nothing.

Four independent farmers I interviewed in the region said that every year they rely on loans to pay their taxes and subsequently have to make payments on the loans. One of them, Viktor, said that he cannot pay back his tax loans each year so they just get lumped together with his general loans. This leaves him with an overall loan payment of 300,000 rubles a month.

Taxes were one of the main reasons that rural inhabitants claimed they were fearful of independent farming. Of the 78 workers on the Moshkinskoe farm whom I asked to explain why they did not want to become independent farmers, nearly half said that the burden of taxes was a major deterrent.[23] The reasons cited by these workers for not entering independent farming included:

- 89 percent, insufficient capital
- 44 percent, high taxes

- 39 percent, too risky
- 36 percent, inadequate machinery
- 30 percent, reliant on support from collective
- 17 percent, lack of government support
- 13 percent, too much work
- 7 percent, loss of social benefits

When I asked an independent agricultural consultant at the Rural Consultancy Center in Gorodets why so few people have chosen to become private farmers, she echoed the farmers' concerns:

> Because of the taxation! It's so extreme. Besides, they don't even have the initial capital to start a farm, buy machinery, etc. There are some people who might have their own land, maybe they inherited it or bought it very low/cheap but still they can't farm it privately because they don't have the money to buy even a tractor to cultivate their lands. As for credit, the interest rates are very high. The initial net costs are very high but the prices at the market are very low so it is much easier to survive in the collective enterprise, rather than as a private farmer. Everyone knows this. Only very secure people can become private farmers.

Though very early on in the reorganization process it was possible to obtain discounted loans and subsidies, and occasionally debt write-offs, the reform agencies and banks have moved to wean the farms from this support. Thus, organizational problems surrounding debt and taxation have not been reduced significantly.[24] If anything, inadequate and expensive credit and high taxes have made it more difficult for independent farming to gain a foothold, much less prosper.

Sociodemographic Barriers

Despite the substantive fiscal problems plaguing agricultural reform, it is the collapse of the social safety net that ignites the greatest alarm in villagers. In their minds, harvest yields and the success of the farm as an economic unit are secondary to the social elements and nurturing that the kolkhoz provides. In an early survey, 98.8 percent of peasants said that they could not survive without a "patron-collective" farm.[25] Farm directors also recognize that collective organizations exist today because no reliable alternatives have taken their place. In 1998, one sovkhoz director said,

"Sovkhoz leaders like the workers and can't turn them away. We provide all the necessary things for them. Due to this, the sovkhoz has survived. The most important thing here is not financial support, but spiritual support."

Villagers' concerns are centered on basic quality of life and subsistence as opposed to entrepreneurial work endeavors. Most villagers believe that improved social services, rather than financial bailout, will enhance their overall quality of life.[26] The social services of the village are vital, in part, for the success of the reforms because if villagers are not pleased with the level of services they receive, whether or not it is the fault of agricultural reorganization, they will blame the reform and those implementing change. Inadequate educational and health care services are two of the problems with social services. Despite the decreasing birth rate, child care and education are considered obligatory components of village life. While health care services have never been more than minimal in a small village such as Moshkin, they have deteriorated. This is exceptionally problematic for the large pensioner population, which requires reliable, accessible, and affordable medical care. Improving these social services is made even more challenging by the outmigration of so many young people from the village. Given the current demographic situation, renovation in these areas is unlikely. Despite the fact that, "in accordance with Russian Federation legislation, social facilities previously within the responsibility of agricultural enterprises are to be transferred to the jurisdiction of . . . local administrations," many local governments have yet to accept the responsibility of their new role as social services providers.[27] Thus, many farm managers such as Ekaterina are working to maintain the social infrastructure with the farm's meager resources.

Education

Rural schools and daycare facilities in the Gorodetski *raion* are in a terrible state. Due to low enrollment and dwindling resources, the school in Moshkin closed in 1991, leaving the students to travel seven kilometers to Kovrigino for schooling. Ekaterina organized the transport of the children in outlying villages to school using the farm bus. Unfortunately, when the bus breaks down the children often must wait several days before going back to school. Parents complain that the cost for school supplies has increased while the quality has decreased. They are responsible for buying several of the necessary textbooks but on two occasions some parents could not find the required texts so their children lacked the proper study materials.

At a meeting for the Kovrigino area, the administrative director expressed his concern for the future since there are only 219 students at the school; the eleventh form had only six students. He said that the administration was considering closing the last two forms, because of inadequate enrollment, due, in part, to the fact that many young people begin working while they are in the eighth or ninth forms. He ended on the following note:

> In general, the education provided isn't really good. A lot of parents of our children complain because their children don't get an appropriate education and I'm very worried about the situation at the school because I know that there is work to be done there and the education should be improved. We don't pay for food for pupils and we don't supply them with many of the necessary materials. A lot of parents may ask why, but I tell you, this is our general situation in Russia.

Conditions had not improved as of March 1999. The children had no English instruction and they had history for only part of the year because the teachers of these subjects left the region.[28]

The situation in the local daycare facility (*detskii sad*) is worse. The declining Russian population is no secret.[29] In the Kovrigino territory, the population declined by 22 from January 1997 to January 1998. There were two births in Moshkin during the year that I was there, and eight more in the entire Kovrigino territory. The 1998 report from Moshkin was 28 deaths and 10 births. That puts the overall birth rate in Moshkin at approximately 10 per thousand and the death rate at 56 per thousand. Thus, the village population is declining faster than the Russian national average.

Moshkin's preschool closed years ago, but the women seemed happy with the large, brightly colored building their children subsequently attended in Kovrigino. Again, however, dwindling numbers brought about the unthinkable. In April 1999 it closed. There is presently no daycare facility available for the children in the area. One woman was outraged: "[The communists] would never have left us like this, with no detskii sad— it is a common thing and now we have nowhere for our small children to go. It can't get any worse." Whether things were measurably better during the days of the collective is subordinate to the main argument. Villagers *believe* life was better, that they were cared for, and that there was someone to whom they could look for leadership.

Health Care

Sociologist Galina Radionova said that, in general, it is difficult to say whether social services are better or worse because each individual farm has certain elements that have improved and others that have deteriorated. She did say, however, that post-reorganization health care was definitely worse in all of the villages she visited.[30] Given that health care services in rural Russia have never been satisfactory, the current picture is even more grim.

The situation in Moshkin is no different than that in most rural areas. There is a *fel'dsher* (medical assistant) who has a small office in the *dom kulturi* where the farm offices are located. She is available from 11 AM to 1 PM every weekday, except Thursdays and holidays. Ekaterina assured me that if there was dire need she would come to the village to tend to the ill regardless of the time or day. Despite Ekaterina's assurances, many people complained bitterly that often the doctor would request sick patients to travel to her office in Gorodets, ten kilometers away, rather than make a home visit. Unfortunately, the nearest doctor in Gorodets did not make house calls.

Availability of medicines is a substantial problem. Occasionally, without seeing the patient, a doctor may send a packet with the mail carrier describing the prescription for taking the herbs or medicines enclosed. The only medicines the fel'dsher regularly had in supply at her office were aspirin and a few herbal remedies. She said that other medicines were too expensive for villagers and they could get them in Gorodets if they really wanted them. She complained that many of the peasants would never go to see the doctor anyway. Villagers concurred with her, saying that they usually prefer to treat themselves with a combination of eating a special diet for a few days and some form of herbal remedy.

Several people who needed surgery said they could not afford it. Because these particular surgeries were considered moderately serious, they would have to go to the hospital in Nizhniy Novgorod. One woman needs a hysterectomy and another needs to have a cyst removed. Both will require a hospital stay of 6 to 14 days and a large payment. The woman who needs the hysterectomy told me that it would cost 1,500,000 rubles. She said that she can hardly eat because of these problems and she is resigned to "live as best as I can" until she had the necessary money. When I asked about these kinds of medical problems, an administrator in Kovrigino said that if someone needs an operation and it is life threatening, they will be given the money for it. He was quick to add, "Unfortunately, most people wait too long to see a doctor and it really isn't our responsibility if they haven't been seen by a doctor."

The village of Kovrigino had just purchased an ambulance when I arrived in 1997. Before that time villagers in Moshkin and surrounding areas had to call Gorodets for ambulance service. In that event, the drivers would often not answer the phone, or would never arrive even when summoned. It was also possible that the ambulance drivers would answer and say that they could not come due to weather, lack of gas, or other reasons.[31] While some elements of health care services have ostensibly improved, their dismal state generally leaves people feeling hopeless. One 47-year-old woman poignantly said, "With the medical services we have here it's better to die than to go to the doctor."

Pensioner Population

The impact of agricultural reform on the pensioner population is a social as well as an economic issue. The sheer size and predicament of this population make the situation even more dramatic. Figures show that in 1994, 19.8 percent of the oblast population was aged 60 or over and in the Gorodetski raion the figure was over 30 percent.[32] In January 1998, the Kovrigino administrative territory had a population of 1,420, which included 565 able-bodied workers, and 449 described as non-able-bodied workers. Due to historical demographic realities, it is not unusual for farm populations (covering several villages) to reach levels in excess of 50 percent pensioners. Most of these people have lived their entire lives in the village and are dependent on their pension payments and the paternalistic support of the kolkhoz for food, medical care, and social support. They have little or no hope of leaving the village and want, like most pensioners, to live out the rest of their lives in relative comfort.

At a village meeting in February 1998, Ekaterina was asked about pension payments and other issues surrounding the lives of the elderly villagers. She responded:

> Now, about our pensioners . . . [I]n our region there are a lot . . . and that means we have a lot of work to do about it not only in Moshkin but in Kovrigino as well. But what can we do if we don't have the necessary transportation and the gas money for it? Considering the current situation in our region, I believe still we are doing a good job and still help our pensioners to cultivate their land and we still provide special services for them and these services are very cheap. And if we count all of our expenses we come across a huge sum [for pensioners].[33] But these people spent their whole lives working in our re-

gions on our kolkhozy and farms and that is why we have the responsibility for keeping the pensioners well.

At that same meeting, it was reported that only 54 pensioners out of 121 were receiving their pension payments. Pensions are too low, in general, to provide for even a minimal standard of living, not to mention potential health care needs or disposable income that might help to monetize the community. As one pensioner told me, "Pensioners live better in a graveyard than they do here now."

Due to these circumstances, many pensioners continue to work long past the normal year of retirement.[34] I witnessed, and Ekaterina admitted, how important the work of the pensioners is to the farm. Several women work in the winter sorting potatoes in the storage sheds and elderly men work with the machinery doing repairs or helping younger men with the heavier work. One of the two animal workers on the farm is 67-year-old Stepan. He works with the cows and horses because no one else is willing to do the work. He told me that he and his wife depend on the occasional 10,000 to 20,000 rubles (US$2 to US$4) he receives as well as the grain given to them by the Moshkinskoe farm. He is not as efficient as he used to be, and has "no obligation to work," but he freely admits his love of the animals and his feeling of responsibility to care for them. Lida, a 64-year-old woman, continues to work wherever Ekaterina will allow her. She sorts potatoes, cleans the canteen in the summer, and basically hangs around the office trying to be useful in order to receive a small payment here and there. She receives 234,000 rubles a month (approximately US$40) for her pension, but it doesn't always arrive on time. She is trying to have her pension raised but was told that it will require a lot of paperwork and trips to Gorodets, so she is putting it off until she has time.

Pensioners make up two-thirds of the total number of people who have entrusted, or leased their land, to the Moshkinskoe farm. Ekaterina has only 80 regular workers but is responsible for five times as many people who live in the farm's territory and rely on it for services and assistance. Reorganization models have not made realistic arrangements to deal with the villages' large pensioner populations. Until social support systems are developed in a way that frees the farms from this financial responsibility, pensioners and others will rely on the community collective organizations that have been in place for decades.[35]

Outmigration

All capitalist countries have experienced a gradual reduction of their rural labor force. In the United States, for example, from 1910 to 1987 the percentage of people engaged in farming decreased from 35 percent to 2 percent. This trend is associated with developments in high-technology manufacturing and a higher level of mechanization and automation in agriculture. Despite the large exodus of workers from the Russian countryside, agriculture still accounts for 13 percent of the nation's labor force, which is substantially higher than in more economically advanced nations.[36]

In Russia, agricultural labor potential has been critically reduced over the past decade. For example, in the Gorodetski raion in 1990 alone, the number of rural workers fell by 45 percent.[37] What is most distressing is not the sheer numbers but the fact that the most skilled workers are leaving. Many young, competent people are drawn away from the villages to jobs that were created in the raion and oblast administrations during restructuring. Rather than entering jobs on the farms they have gone to work for rural consultancy centers, raion restructuring administrations, and other more lucrative employment opportunities in sales and civil service. While some report that rural outmigration has stabilized,[38] or even been reversed,[39] the trend seems to be continuing in Nizhegorodskaia oblast.[40]

When I asked Ekaterina about the possibility that there may be a future shortage of capable workers in the village, she seemed resigned to accepting this fate. She told me that 30 percent of the pensioners in the village were already giving their portions of the land to their children as gifts:

> It doesn't worry me but I sincerely hope that most of these younger people will choose to live in the country if they have an acceptable means of living. Of course, the conditions of work and life in the country depend upon the decisions of the government. There are very real and difficult situations for individuals and farmers. This is why the young don't want to be in the country.

Svetlana, a 20-year-old woman who lived in one of the surrounding hamlets and worked in the Moshkinskoe office as a bookkeeper, was studying at the agricultural institute in Nizhniy Novgorod as a correspondent student. She said that she didn't know what she wanted to do yet, but that "if things don't change here I won't stay here. I hope if I have a degree I'll manage to find another job." Her 17-year-old sister, Natasha, lived in a town near Nizhniy Novgorod studying to be a nurse. Natasha came home on weekends and did not plan to move back to the village. I asked Svetlana about her classmates who she said had left the village.

> The majority of people do not stay here to work because the salaries are not paid. It is natural that young people want to be able to afford certain things but if they only pay you 1,000 rubles you cannot afford anything. That's why young people try to go somewhere else.

There were 19 people in my class and I'm the only one who is still here in the village. Most of them went away to study and a lot of girls got married and now have children and some of the men went away to the militia, some serve in the army, some are businessmen. There is no involvement or programs for youth in the villages anymore. In the past we had a Komsomol organization which was responsible for such activities. But now, no one has an obligation so there are no activities.

The cause of this damaging loss of labor from rural areas is evident. Wages are not paid for four to six months; in 1996, wages ranged from 200,000 to 400,000 rubles a month. Because of infrequent and meager payments, there is a "grossly large" number of young workers who are living on subsidiary work connected with basic agricultural enterprises.[41] Some people were increasing the amount of work and attention given to their household gardens in order to generate some surplus for sale in town. More frequently, however, young people were turning away from the farm and spending time scheming over rudimentary business plans and how to quickly earn some cash. Due to the decreasing numbers of workers and the lack of properly functioning machinery, the intensity of individual peasant work is growing. Therefore, a life of arduous labor on a farm is even less appealing than it might have been earlier.

One result of the deterioration of social services and the demographic situation was a feeling of social abandonment. In a sense, the communist system existed to provide social benefits for people, and it enforced a sense of community in general and even more so on a collective farm or in a factory. People lived and worked together and were held together by jobs, homes, and necessity. They had very little to do with the local or national government on a daily basis. Their needs were simple and they were met. Today these needs are not being met and people still feel that the responsibility lies with the government for these basic necessities.

The precise extent to which the current state of social services is correlated with agricultural reorganization is difficult to prove. However, the social welfare dimension of rural Russian life is undeniably inadequate. Without attention given to resurrecting these basic structural elements of village life, any agricultural economic policies will fall short of their intended goals. These elements must be reformed simultaneously in order to keep villagers *in villages*. Without the possibility of a functioning, not to mention thriving, rural community, agricultural reorganization in Russia cannot proceed.

Conclusion

In spite of the hardships faced by Ekaterina, she is decidedly pro-reform and believes that her farm can succeed if the state allows the farms to do their work and follows through with positive reform legislation. She understands that until there is stable political leadership and genuine pro-rural legislation, their economic situation is likely to remain in flux.

One possibility for making advances in production and personal satisfaction on Russian farms would be expanding subsidiary household plots.[42] Their record of sustainability in the past and their historical importance may help bridge the gap between collective and independent farming. Chapter 2 by Lerman and chapter 14 by O'Brien in this volume include empirical data on increasing household plot productivity. Over a decade ago, the household economy, dependent on privately owned livestock and a garden, was seen as the only remnant of the precollectivized system and was, therefore, still used in very traditional ways.[43] The substantial contribution of household gardening to rural household income is no secret.[44] However, the undeniable importance of the coexistence of collective farms and household plots has not been given enough consideration in terms of future potential. There is a historical symbiotic relationship in which the codependency of independent farming and collective farming underscores many of the current crises observed in rural Russia today.[45]

A study in fall 1997 highlighted the continued importance of subsidiary farming for peasant households.[46] In both nonreorganized and reorganized farms, workers' families relied overwhelmingly on their household plots for their main source of income.[47] According to the study, "On the whole, the influence of household plots has grown over recent years, and it generally holds true that the weaker a [large] farm [enterprise] becomes, the more vital become the household plots."[48] This means that peasant farmers, however, will require more and more time to work on their own land. More than half of Moshkin villagers complained that they did not have enough time to work on their household plots. In addition, they usually need some sort of help with planting or tilling. In fact, only 3 percent of those questioned said that they did *not* need help with planting from the kolkhoz. Perhaps a policy aimed at working with both the collectively organized parent farms and subsidiary farms simultaneously would inspire peasants to make further strides toward agricultural reform.

The form in which household subsidiary farming and collective farming can coexist at present is not understood. The extent to which Russia can reasonably rely on production from household farms in this time of economic trouble is questionable.[49] The same infrastructure difficulties that plague the kolkhoz will affect the independent farmer. For these reasons, household subsidiary farming may not be the key to fulfilling the needs of the larger economy and those of the community/collective organization if the kolkhozy are completely ruined and the basic problems of cash flow and social services are not managed.

Despite compelling reasons for Russian villagers to embrace privatized farming, they are fighting to maintain their *communal coherence*. Most of the people in the village mentioned in one way or another that agricultural work is "supposed" (*mnimyi*) to be a collective endeavor. This does not mean that they are against the free market; quite the contrary. Many understand the importance of a market economy in theory; however, they still believe that they should be substantially supported by the state. This is a reflection of the traditional social organization and relationships of village life that have not been adequately assessed or considered in the reform process.[50]

Unfortunately, the attention given to the economic infrastructure of the village has yet to significantly promote a new class of private farmers in rural Russia. The problem is one of scope more than detail. Russian agriculture directly involves a quarter of the population of the Russian Federation so the situation concerns large numbers of people as much as food production and productivity. The collective or state farm has been the "city center," if you will, upon which villagers have relied for their most basic social and material provisions. Focusing too much on the economic productivity of the farm and not enough on methods by which villagers can maintain some sense of community and social well-being will meet with resistance.[51] A more in-depth approach to the way that "cultural attitudes and values influence agrarian structures and policies" must be considered.[52] The models developed need to involve a more bottom-up approach that relates to these vital and inexorable elements. The Nizhniy Novgorod model was successful in implementing the first waves of farm reorganization but has failed to adequately address the multitude of infrastructural and structural problems faced by rural Russia. If villagers are given an alternative to traditional collectives that benefits both their economic *and* their social lives it is likely they will be more supportive than they have been of the current reform efforts.

Notes

1. Portions of this chapter were presented at the American Anthropological Association annual meetings in Chicago, IL, November 1999.

2. This is similar to but distinct from A. P. Chaianov's labor-consumer balance theory, which states that peasants would expend greater effort only if they had reason to believe it

would yield an increase in output. Chaianov, *The Theory of Peasant Economy* (Homewood, IL: Richard D. Irwin, 1966).

3. Ben Eklof and Stephen P. Frank, eds., *The World of the Russian Peasant* (Boston, MA: Unwin Hyman, 1990).

4. Caroline Humphrey, *Karl Marx Collective* (Cambridge: Cambridge University Press, 1983); Marjorie Mandelstam Balzer, "Introduction," *Anthropology & Archaeology of Eurasia* 33, no. 3 (1995): 4–13.

5. This was primarily in Nizhegorodskaia oblast.

6. Donald Van Atta, ed., *The "Farmer Threat": The Political Economy of Agrarian Reform in Post-Soviet Russia* (Boulder, CO: Westview Press, 1993); Stephen K. Wegren, "New Perspectives on Spatial Patterns of Agrarian Reform: A Comparison of Two Russian *Oblasts*," *Post-Soviet Geography* 35 (1994): 455–81.

7. This is noteworthy because the BKHF, together with the International Finance Corporation (IFC), developed, funded, and implemented the Russian agrarian reform program. That they neglected to investigate the opinions of Russian farmers earlier is surprising. Duncan Leitch and Becky Brannan, "Report of the Social Development Consultancy, Nizhnii Novgorod" (FCO/ODA Joint Assistance Unit/BKHF, Centre for Development Studies, Swansea University, UK, January–February 1995).

8. International Finance Corporation, "Monitoring Russian Reorganised Farms" (Moscow, February 1998).

9. Ekaterina explained that she had been "elected by default," that is, no one wanted the job and she felt responsible to try to help the villagers. She could not say no, and the majority of villagers trusted her farming experience and her social commitment.

10. Eight workers relocated, two were fired, and two quit but still live in Moshkin.

11. Inscription beneath the image of Lenin on the flags in all collective farms. Humphrey, *Karl Marx Collective*, 113.

12. This is not to say that Russian peasants are more altruistic than their European or North American counterparts or that they care less about their personal well-being. It is simply that due to historical and political situations, Russian peasants were engaged for so long in collective labor that they naturally came to believe it was the most effective and equitable means of agricultural work.

13. Eklof and Frank, eds., *World of the Russian Peasant*; and Stephen K. Wegren, *Agriculture and the State in Soviet and Post-Soviet Russia* (Pittsburgh, PA: University of Pittsburgh Press, 1998).

14. Vladimir Staroverov, "Antagonisms in Russian Society," in *Russian Society in Transition*, eds. Christopher Williams, Vladimir Chuprov, and Vladimir Staroverov (Aldershot, Hants, UK: Dartmouth, 1996), 123.

15. Karen Brooks et al., *Agricultural Reform in Russia: A View from the Farm Level*, World Bank Discussion Paper #327 (Washington, DC: World Bank, 1996).

16. Wegren, *Agriculture and the State*, 216.

17. William M. Liefert, "The Food Problems in the Former USSR," in *"Farmer Threat,"* ed. Van Atta, 25–42.

18. A total of 178 people were surveyed. Animals include cows, pigs, sheep, and fowl. These animals are purchased young, when they are cheaper, and then raised and slaughtered for meat. The exceptions are dairy cows, which most people keep for years, and hens retained for eggs.

19. International Finance Corporation, "Monitoring Russian Reorganised Farms," 30.

20. In 1996, 605 of 775 farms lost money in Nizhegorodskaia oblast.

21. This situation is far from specific to the Gorodetski *raion*. See Wegren, "New Perspectives on Spatial Patterns of Agrarian Reform," for a similar report from Kostroma oblast, and Brooks et al., *Agricultural Reform in Russia*, for a broader geographic sample.

22. V. A. Nutrikhin, "The Problem of Motives and Incentives in Agricultural Production," in *Social Problems in Rural Areas Under Conditions of Change*, eds. A. Andreas Bodenstedt, Stephan Merl, and Vladimir A. Nutrikhin (Berlin: Duncker & Humblot, 1993), 215–19.

23. This survey was conducted in February 1998. For similar results, see Brooks et al., *Agricultural Reform in Russia*; and Grigory Ioffe and Tatyana Nefedova, *Continuity and Change in Rural Russia: A Geographical Perspective* (Boulder, CO: Westview Press, 1997), 161.

24. Ioffe and Nefedova, *Continuity and Change*, 161.

25. Nutrikhin, "The Problem of Motives and Incentives," 211.

26. A 1991 survey of 1,000 villagers in northern and southern Russia found that 69.1 percent of all respondents selected "social services" as the element of rural life most needing to be changed in order to improve their quality of life. Conversely, only 4.1 percent chose "the economy." David J. O'Brien et al., *Services & Quality of Life in Rural Villages in the Former Soviet Union* (Lanham, MD: University Press of America, 1998).

27. International Finance Corporation, "Monitoring Russian Reorganised Farms," 44.

28. These problems are also skillfully discussed in International Finance Corporation, "Monitoring Russian Reorganised Farms"; Leitch and Brannan, "Report of the Social Development Consultancy"; and O'Brien et al., *Services & Quality of Life in Rural Villages*.

29. Ioffe and Nefedova, *Continuity and Change*, 203; Williams, Chuprov, and Staroverov, eds., *Russian Society in Transition*, 13.

30. Most of her work was done in Nizhniy Novgorod and Oryol oblasts.

31. Ioffe and Nefedova, *Continuity and Change*, 133.

32. Leitch and Brannan, "Report of the Social Development Consultancy."

33. I was never able to have these "expenses" clarified. When pressed, Ekaterina exclaimed, "We help them!"

34. Women can retire and draw a pension at age 55, and men at 60.

35. Alternately, social support could be offered through the farm organizations as long as funding was supplied from some outside source. This might be more desirable as it would keep the raion administrators, already mistrusted, out of the village-level, social security infrastructure.

36. Ioffe and Nefedova, *Continuity and Change*, 106.

37. BKHF Rural Consultancy Center, *Bulletin*, June 1997.

38. Wegren, "New Perspectives on Spatial Patterns of Agrarian Reform," 459.

39. Ioffe and Nefedova, *Continuity and Change*, 279.

40. BKHF Rural Consultancy Center, *Bulletin*, June 1997.

41. Stephen K. Wegren, "Farm Privatization in Nizhnii Novgorod: A Model for Russia?" *RFE/RL Research Report* 3 (27 May 1994): 16.

42. Also referred to as "personal auxiliary farming" (*lichnoe podsobnoe khoziaistvo*). Ioffe and Nefedova, *Continuity and Change*, 80.

43. Humphrey, *Karl Marx Collective*, 9.

44. Van Atta, *"Farmer Threat,"* and Zvi Lerman, Yevgeniy Tankhilevich, Kirill Mozhin, and Natalya Sapova, "Self-Sustainability of Subsidiary Household Plots: Lessons for Privatization of Agriculture in Former Socialist Countries," *Post-Soviet Geography* 35 (1994): 526–42.

45. Ioffe and Nefedova, *Continuity and Change*, 84.

46. International Finance Corporation, "Monitoring Russian Reorganised Farms."

47. In nonreorganized farms, workers' families rely on household plots for an average 47.99 percent of their income, and in reorganized farms, 43.50 percent.

48. International Finance Corporation, "Monitoring Russian Reorganised Farms."

49. Lerman, et al., "Self-Sustainability of Subsidiary Household Plots.

50. L. N. Denisova, *Rural Russia: Economic, Social and Moral Crisis* (New York: Nova Science Publishers, 1995); Leitch and Brannan, "Report of the Social Development Consultancy."

51. O'Brien et al., *Services & Quality of Life in Rural Villages*, makes impressive gains in this area.

52. Wegren, "New Perspectives on Spatial Patterns of Agrarian Reform," 477.

10

The Ethnic Dimension
of Adaptation and Change

CHRISTOPHER MARSH AND JAMES W. WARHOLA

This chapter provides evidence that Russian agriculture has adapted to a market economy in a regionally differentiated manner, with a significant aspect of the variation among regions to be found in the ethnic factor. The ethno-territorial principle of the Russian Federation's political arrangement thus has important consequences for the agricultural reform process, in certain respects serving as an opportunity for regional experimentation yet at the same time presenting certain obstacles to reform.

Given the tremendous diversity of the Russian Federation, comprising upwards of one hundred distinct ethnic groups that account for approximately 20 percent of the country's total population, ethnicity is a potentially powerful and significant factor in any policy domain. When seeking to offer an empirical assessment of adaptation and change in rural Russia, therefore, it makes sense to consider the ethnic dimension of rural reform. Indeed, several studies of agricultural reform and privatization in Russia have found that ethnicity plays a significant role in these processes, insofar as the inhabitants of the "ethnic regions" have been found to exhibit patterns of behavior significantly different from those of the rest of the country. Our purpose here is to explore these issues in greater detail with an explicit focus on the impact ethnicity may have on strategies of adaptation in post-Soviet Russia.

Using quantitative indicators of privatization and agricultural reform as empirical referents for adaptation and change, we explore variations in patterns of adaptive behavior among Russia's regions. A regional level of analysis permits us to categorize Russia's geopolitical entities based on the ethno-territorial principle of Russian federalism, which distinguishes between ethnic (ethnically based) and Russian (non–ethnically based) regions. After a brief background discussion of Russia's federal structure and ethnic diversity, we begin our analysis by comparing the progress that has been made in the areas of privatization and agricultural reform in each of the two groups of regions. In particular, we look at the extent of enterprise privatization, the formation of joint stock companies, and state and collective farm conversion rates. We observe in each case dramatic differences between the relative success reached in the Russian regions and the slow progress in implementing reforms in the ethnic regions.

It appears quite evident from the data presented here that the ethnic regions are more resistant to change than the rest of the country. This begs the question of whether this is just one aspect of a widespread expression of resistance to the post-Soviet system in general. We explore this issue by examining the relationship between indicators of reform and levels of regime support. Contrary to what might be expected, we find that the ethnic regions are in fact *more* supportive of the new regime than are the Russian regions, despite the fact that in the economic realm they are resistant to change. Moreover, statistical analysis indicates that among the ethnic regions, there is a strong *negative* relationship between success in implementing reform and support for the former Yeltsin regime. While we have no definitive explanation for this finding, we conclude with a brief discussion of what seem to us to be the most plausible explanations, particularly those that might lend themselves to further investigation.

Ethno-Territoriality in the Russian Federation

The population of Russia is extremely diverse, comprising over one hundred distinct ethnic groups scattered from the Siberian tundra to the Caucasus and on to the border of Scandinavia. Some of these ethnic groups are quite large, such as the Tatars, who number over five million and comprise 3.75 percent of Russia's total population. Others, such as the Karaims, number only several hundred thousand. In all, there are about thirty million Russian citizens who ethnically are not Russian.

One significant aspect of these different ethnic groups is that many of them live in ethnic communities, as opposed to being assimilated into the greater Russian polity. In several cases, the area of these ethnic communities corresponds to political-administrative boundaries of the Russian Federation. An example of this would be the Republic of Tyva, where the region's population is almost entirely ethnically Tyvan, with most ethnic Tyvans living in the republic (as opposed to living in a neighboring region).

The Russian Federation is comprised of 89 constituent units in all, properly known as the "subjects of the federation." Of these, there are 6 *kraya*, 49 oblasts, 2 administratively autonomous cities (Moscow and St. Petersburg), 21 republics, and 11 autonomous areas (10 autonomous *okruga* and the Jewish autonomous oblast). A crucial aspect of the federation's institutional structure is the ethno-territorial principle in 31 of these regions—the 21 republics and the 10 autonomous *okruga* (the status of the Jewish autonomous oblast is not based on any historical tie to the area).[1] Here the different ethnic groups are given some recognition of their identity through varying degrees of autonomy within the federation. Throughout the rest of this chapter, we refer to this group of regions as the ethnic regions, while referring to the other subjects, which include the kraya, oblasts, and the cities of St. Petersburg and Moscow, as the Russian regions.

On paper, there exist several differences between the ethnic regions and the Russian regions. While governors head the latter, almost all of the republics have their own presidents. In addition to simply calling the regional executives by another title, the ethnic regions also have more political and economic autonomy in certain spheres, such as the retention of export earnings in some republics. In many cases, the ethnic regions have used their ethnic identity and special status as a bargaining tool in negotiating such concessions from the central government.[2]

In those cases in which ethnic identity and geographical boundary correspond to a large degree, as in Tatarstan, Bashkortostan, Tyva, and so on, a sense of political community may exist—either as a spontaneous development or as the product of the promotion of regional elites. Support of such a notion can be gleaned from the remarks of Ingushetiia president Ruslan Aushev, who points out that when visiting Kazakhstan, the Ingush who had gathered there said "Our president has arrived!" He maintains that if Yeltsin had arrived, the people would have instead proclaimed "The president of Russia has arrived."[3] This illustrates the existence of a certain sense of community among the Ingush—both within Ingushetiia and in other parts of the former Soviet Union—and it is highly probable that similar situations exist in other ethnic regions.

The Ethnic Dimension of Adaptation and Change

Numerous interesting and informative studies focus on some of the substantive issues we raise here. Some projects provide case studies of Russia's various ethnic groups from a variety of perspectives, such as Kempton's study of Sakha and Noack's study of Tatarstan.[4] Others explore the many problems facing particular ethnic groups, such as Murashko's study of the retention of native cultures and language among the peoples of the North.[5] These studies are important contributions to the field and help illuminate a variety of issues in the various ethnic regions. Others focus more specifically on the role of ethnic groups in the transition process in general.[6] Such studies are important contributions to the field and help illuminate a variety of issues in the ethnic regions. In addition, there are numerous studies that investigate issues of privatization and agricultural reform, many of which are included in the present volume. However, such studies typically ignore the ethnic dimension of adaptation and change. When some consideration of ethnicity is given, it is usually only done in a coincidental manner, thus failing to discern any federation-wide differences between the ethnic and Russian regions.

Our purpose here is to explore these issues in greater detail with an explicit focus on the impact ethnicity may have on Russia's adaptation to the changes accompanying the post-Soviet transition. We seek, therefore, to develop a generalizable model applicable to Russia as a whole. In so doing, we must take as given certain factors about the ethnic regions, disregard some important differences, and consider simply the differences between the two groups—the ethnic regions and the Russian regions. While there certainly does not exist any one ethnic region that is representative of all the ethnic regions, and what we consider as characteristic of the ethnic regions does not describe accurately any particular region, we propose that this categorization may be helpful in exploring the impact of ethnicity on the reform process while also highlighting some of the politically significant general differences between the ethnic regions and the Russian regions.

The methodology we use here involves comparing the adaptive behaviors of the ethnic and Russian regions. This is a rather simple way of assessing the impact ethnicity may have on the political behavior of a region's populace, but by considering the Russian and ethnic regions as separate groups in a cross-regional quantitative analysis, we can determine if differences exist between the two groups and explore factors to which they may be attributable.

Privatization

The privatization of state-owned enterprises is certainly one of the most challenging obstacles involved in Russia's transition to the free market. It has been accurately described as "the world's most ambitious and rapid program of denationalizing state enterprises."[7] Not only is it a daunting task to privatize such a large number of state-owned enterprises, privatization is perhaps one of the most necessary changes in order to increase Russia's economic productivity and efficiency.

Considering the many factors at work in the privatization process, and the profound significance of ethnicity for Russian politics and governance at the national and regional levels, there are ample grounds for suspecting that the agricultural reform process would include an ethnic dimension as well. In his research on regional variation in privatization, for example, Slider finds that marked and significant differences exist in the pace of privatization among Russia's regions. He finds that several of the ethnic regions were among the slowest to implement voucher privatization. Included in this group were Tyva, Tatarstan, Bashkortostan, and North Ossetiia.[8] In the republics and autonomous regions that achieved high levels of success in privatizing enterprises, moreover, the number of enterprises that had been slated for privatization was low to begin with.[9]

More recent data indicate that variations continue to exist, and that the ethnic regions are slower to implement privatization. Using figures from 1996, by which point the privatization process had made considerable progress, of the almost 5,000 enterprises privatized, the average Russian region privatized 76 enterprises while the average ethnic region privatized only 30 (see Table 10.1).[10] Ethnic republics such as Chuvashiia and Tyva are near the bottom of the list, each privatizing 6 enterprises, while Khakasiia privatized only 5. Russian regions that were more actively en-

Table 10.1

Indicators of Privatization and Agricultural Reform by Regional Grouping, 1996 (means)

Variable	All Regions	Russian Regions	Ethnic Regions
Privatized enterprises	64.2	76.7	29.6
Joint stock company formation	35.3	40.6	22
State and collective farm conversion	59.04	69.7	38.9

Source: All means were computed by the authors using data obtained from *Regiony Rossii*, vol. 2 (Moscow: Goskomstat, 1997). See endnotes 10–11, 15 for statistical notes and sources.

gaged in privatization included Rostov (166), Perm (269), Sverdlovsk (189), and Moscow (176). While there are examples of ethnic republics with relatively high levels of privatization, and Russian regions with relatively low levels, overall the ethnic regions made considerably less progress in privatization.

The privatization of state-owned enterprises is only part of the picture of economic restructuring. Another major issue involves the form of ownership taken by the newly privatized enterprises. In joint stock companies, the charter capital is divided into a specific number of shares of stock and the enterprise is regulated under a multitier management structure. Since one of the main objectives of privatization is to put the ownership and management of enterprises into the hands of the people, the formation of joint stock companies can be considered perhaps the most pro-market type of enterprise restructuring.

Data on the formation of joint stock companies indicate that the Russian regions are again outstripping the ethnic regions. Of the 2,816 enterprises converted from state-owned enterprises into joint stock companies in 1996, the average Russian region privatized 40 enterprises in this manner, while the average for the ethnic regions was only 22.[11] Some examples are Adygeia (1), Kabardino-Balkaria (2), North Ossetiia (4), and Chukotka (3). Russian regions that were most successful in this area were the city of Moscow (469), Moscow oblast (194), Kemerovo (118), and Nizhniy Novgorod (86).

Overall, the ethnic regions appear more resistant to reform than the Russian regions. These regions have a considerably slower pace of privatization, and they convert fewer of their enterprises into joint stock companies. Considering these examples of economic reform and restructuring, the Russian regions seem to exhibit more adaptive behavior than the ethnic regions. Since almost all of the ethnic regions are heavily agricultural, one might suspect that the patterned differences among Russian and ethnic regions might be even more pronounced in the specific policy domain of agricultural reform.

Agricultural Reform

The fact that Russia now receives food aid from the European Union, the United States, and even Hungary reflects the dismal state of Russian agriculture. A recent study, moreover, maintains that outside assistance will continue to be needed for at least the next few years.[12] This clearly reflects the post-Soviet regime's dramatic failure to undergo a successful transition from Soviet agricultural policies and practices to those necessary to make the Russian Federation agriculturally self-sufficient. The fact that the Russian Empire was an exporter of agricultural goods on the eve of World War I further underscores the severity of that failure. If Russia is to recover from the economic dislocations of the transition to the free market, as well as the more general difficulty of overcoming the legacy of decades of highly inefficient Soviet agricultural policies, it must successfully address issues such as agricultural production and privatization that will work for all of Russia, including the ethnic regions.

As with privatization, scholars have reported marked differences between patterns of agricultural reform in the ethnic and Russian regions. For example, Craumer, in his cross-regional analysis of Russian agricultural reform, identifies several differences between patterns of reform in the oblasts and kraya and in the ethnic republics.[13] While the average oblast or krai had only a 29.1 percent retention rate of state and collective farms during reorganization, the average ethnic republic retained 54.3 percent of its *sovkhozy* and *kolkhozy* (state and collective farms, respectively). Of the ten regions that failed to reach a 90 percent re-registration rate, eight were ethnic regions or contained autonomous okruga (the autonomous okruga were not considered separately from their home region in Craumer's study). The rate of re-registration also diverged sharply between the two groups, with 95.6 percent of the oblasts and kraya re-registering during the period Craumer analyzes, while only 86.5 percent of the ethnic republics followed suit.

More recent data indicate that similar trends continued into the following year. The level of success in converting state and collective farms into individual peasant farms, which Craumer maintains is "the ultimate form of farm reorganization,"[14] varied between the Russian regions to the ethnic regions. While the conversion rate for the country as a whole was 59 percent in 1995, the difference in conversion rates between the Russian and ethnic regions continued to widen.[15] The average Russian region had a 69.7-percent conversion rate, while the average ethnic region converted only 38.9 percent of its sovkhozy and kolkhozy. The dramatic difference in conversion rates for the two groups of regions is evident. These findings indicate that the ethnic regions tend to simply retain their status as state and collective farms, rather than converting into individual peasant farms, a form of behavior that is similar to the ethnic regions' lower rate of creating joint stock companies in the privatization process.

Index of Change

In order to develop a broader picture of the adaptive behaviors exhibited by the Russian and ethnic regions, we combine the above indicators to create an index of change.[16] This provides a picture of how much progress has been made in privatization and agricultural reform in each region relative to the federation as whole. Together, these indicators of privatization and agricultural reform act as an empirical referent for adaptive behavior in general.

When the scores for the index of change are visually represented in Map 10.1, it is apparent that there is a general pattern between the Russian and ethnic regions.[17] The regions that scored on the highest level of the index of change were the Moscow oblast, the city of Moscow, Rostov, and Arkhangelsk. Based on their records of privatization and agricultural reform, these regions have made the most progress. These regions are followed closely by the 16 regions at level 4, only one of which is an ethnic region—Tatarstan. It is important to note that of the 20 most successful regions, only one is an ethnic region.

The ethnic regions seem to be rather proportionally represented on level 3, although the ethnic regions did tend to score on the bottom of the range. The ethnic regions in this group included Sakha, Altai Republic, Chuvashiia, and Udmurtiia. More ethnic regions scored on level 2 than on any other level, including Kareliia, Chukotka, Khanti-Mansi, and Dagestan. Finally, of the four regions that scored on level 1, three are ethnic regions (Kabardino-Balkariia, Komi, and Ingushetiia), and only one is not (Magadan).

The indicators of privatization and agricultural reform, both individually and as combined into an index of change, clearly illustrate the patterned differences between the Russian regions and the ethnic regions, which are more resistant to change. Is this phenomenon limited to the economic realm, or is it just one aspect of a more general expression of resistance to the post-Soviet system as a whole?

Ethnicity, Adaptation, and Regime Support

In the analyses above we observed dramatic differences between the relative success reached in the Russian regions and the slow progress in implementing such reform in the ethnic regions. While it appears quite evident that the ethnic regions are more resistant to change than the rest of the country, this raises the question of whether this is part of a more general expression of resistance to the post-Soviet system. We investigate this issue by exploring the variation in levels of regime support among the regions and by examining the relationship between regime support and our index of change.

Map 10.1
Levels of Adaptation and Change in Russia's Regions

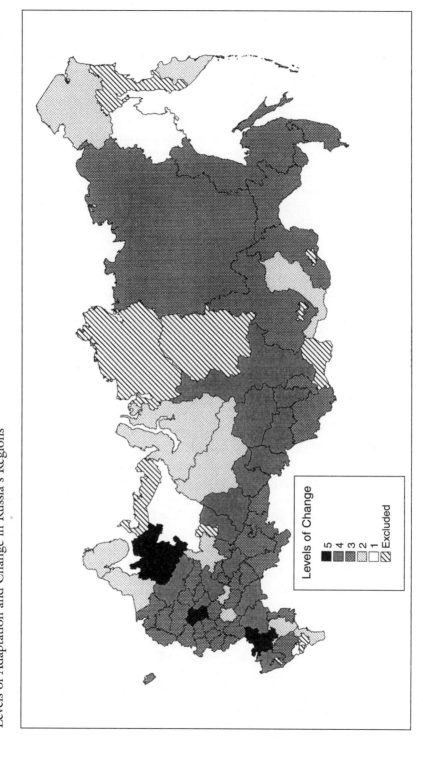

Levels of Change

5
4
3
2
1

Excluded

While many post-communist regimes are little more than ostensibly democratic, popular support for newly democratic regimes is necessary to press ahead through the difficult period of economic reform and democratic consolidation. While support for these regimes may not directly lead to democratic success, their popular support is an important and significant development, insofar as it represents a break with an authoritarian past. For our purposes here, we consider support an adaptive and pro-reform behavior.

Political support is often equated with political legitimacy.[18] From such a perspective, political support involves a relationship between citizens and the government in which citizens cede authority to the government and its institutions that make authoritative decisions in the polity. Citizens, of course, may cede such authority to governments for a variety of reasons. The most common type of political support is specific support, in which citizens hold a given set of attitudes toward an institution based on the fulfillment of certain expectations. In states such as Russia, where the government and its institutions are utterly impotent to provide such basic services as public order, we find it difficult to conceive of regime support as specific support. Instead, such support seems to more closely resemble diffuse support, which is a phenomenon based on the fact that "every citizen will at times disagree with the policies, dislike or distrust the incumbents, or criticize the procedures of political institutions" and leaders.[19] While individuals may disagree with what a government does, many nevertheless continue to cede legitimacy and authority to the government and its institutions. We believe this concept is useful in understanding regime support in post-Soviet Russia, particularly regarding the Yeltsin regime, which consistently received low approval ratings yet was able to retain the support of a majority of the population at the electoral booths despite its ineffectual and unpopular policies. For these reasons, we conceptualize of regime support as diffuse support for the Yeltsin regime.[20]

It is, of course, very problematic to measure regime support in a post-communist environment. While candidates and parties in new democracies rarely have well-defined objectives that would allow for their accurate classification, practically all politicians proclaim democratic ideals, regardless of the particular ideology they actually espouse. Such obstacles compelled us to consider regime support in post-Soviet Russia as support for a candidate that advocated continued economic reform and political liberalization.

Despite the many problems associated with doing so, we operationalized regime support as political support for Boris Yeltsin. While the democratic character of the Yeltsin regime was problematic, there are several reasons that compelled us to use this variable as an indicator of regime support. First, through the events of 1998–99 involving the dismissal and appointment of prime ministers, Yeltsin continually showed that he was willing to play by the rules of democratic politics. He abided by the constitution and followed the rules regarding such procedures, although he most certainly attempted to bend these rules to their breaking point. Second, he played a major role in both liberalizing the economy and further democratizing Russia by such means as holding reasonably clean and fair elections at the national and regional levels, and in several instances by submitting to duly constituted judicial authority when it sought to hold his power in check.[21] Moreover, by resigning the presidency on New Year's Eve 1999, he proved that he was not set on holding onto power until his last breath.

A third reason for using this measure as an indicator of regime support is that in the second round of the 1996 presidential elections, in which Yeltsin faced Communist Party of the Russian Federation candidate Gennady Ziuganov head to head, the choice appeared to be one of continued democratization and liberalization, or a very threatening possibility of retreat to Russia's authoritarian past. As a Russian journalist observed at the time, "Whatever we say of Yeltsin[,] . . . he is still the only guarantor of democracy and the irreversibility of economic reform."[22] While that may or may not have been objectively true, it does appear to have been the perception among significant sectors of the electorate. Finally, support for Yeltsin may very well be the only available means of operationalizing regime support on the regional level of analysis, as it is too early to tell what the meaning of support for a Putin presidency may be. We thus consider the percentage of votes for Yeltsin in the second round of elections a reasonably reliable indicator of regime support (see Map 10.2).

Other scholars have suggested that differences in regime support exist between the ethnic and Russian regions. For example, in discussing nationalist tendencies in Russian politics, Clover states that Ziuganov effectively "models himself a Bashkir nationalist, a Tatar nationalist, and a fierce defender of Kalmykian Buddhism."[23] Clover further maintains that "thanks to his perceived support for self-determination" and his opposition to more exclusionary forms of Russian nationalism, Ziuganov was able to win "handily in non-Russian districts."[24] This is precisely what we would expect, with the ethnic regions exhibiting another form of antireform behavior.

Upon closer examination, however, this relationship may not be as strong as one would expect. A cursory look at the results shows that Ziuganov found little support in the ethnic regions. In the first round of the

Map 10.2
Levels of Regime Support in Russia's Regions

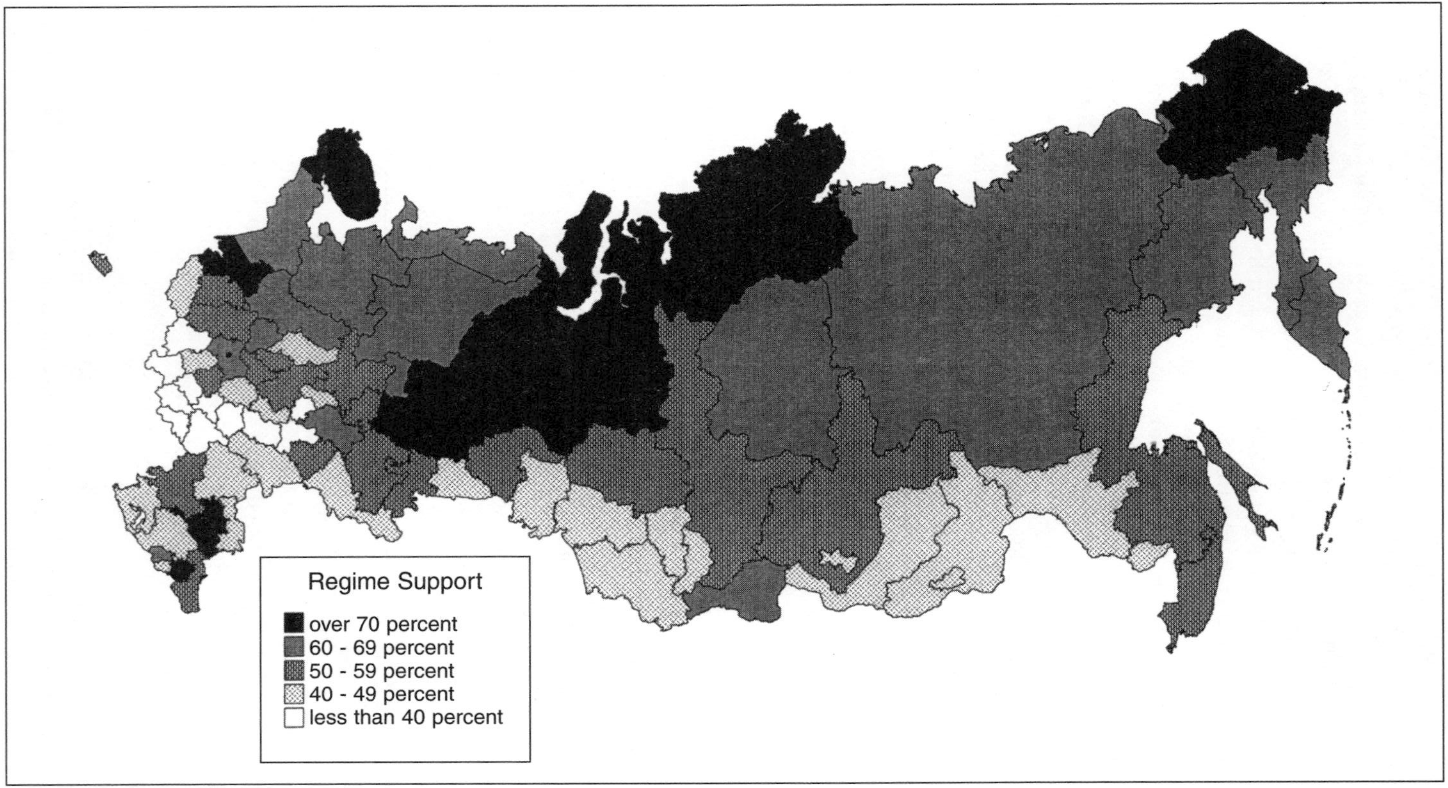

Regime Support

over 70 percent
60 - 69 percent
50 - 59 percent
40 - 49 percent
less than 40 percent

elections, he won in only 4 of the 31 ethnic regions, while in the second round he was able to emerge as the winner in only 6 regions—hardly worthy of the description of "winning handily." Moreover, Clover's assertion that it was Ziuganov's nationalist stylings that helped him emerge victorious is put into question by the fact that in both rounds Ziuganov lost in Tatarstan, Bashkortostan, and even Kalmykia—the very regions that are home to the ethnic groups of which Ziuganov supposedly models himself a nationalist. In fact, of the handful of ethnic regions that did select Ziuganov as the winner, only two of the regions (North Ossetiia and the Chuvash Republic) had populations in which the titular nationality comprised a majority.

This does not disprove Clover's assertions, however, for we have not taken into account voting patterns on the district level. It may very well be the case that in certain districts in which non-Slavic ethnic groups are large, Ziuganov's nationalist stylings did help him emerge as the winner. A cursory examination of voting returns in the ethnic regions, however, indicates that support for Yeltsin was fairly stable from district to district.[25]

The most important question here is whether or not the ethnic regions are less likely to support the new regime than the Russian regions. Given the ethnic regions' slow progress in implementing economic reform, we would expect a priori these regions to be less supportive of the Yeltsin regime. When comparing the average level of support by regional grouping, it becomes apparent that there is indeed a difference in levels of regime support between the Russian and ethnic regions. However, the difference is counterintuitive, as the ethnic regions are *more* likely to support the new regime than are the Russian regions, with the average level of support in the ethnic regions being 58 percent and only 50 percent in the Russian regions. Therefore, despite their resistance to change in the economic realm, the ethnic regions are actually more supportive of the new regime than other regions of the country.

This finding also places the ethnic regions in sharp contrast to Russia's other rural areas where Ziuganov's support was high and Yeltsin was handily defeated in the presidential election. The most cogent analysis of this phenomenon is provided by Orttung and Paretskaya,[26] who clearly show that during the 1996 presidential election Russian society was split between rural and urban areas, with the rural areas more supportive of Ziuganov. The finding here that the ethnic regions, which are also rural, are actually the most supportive of the Yeltsin regime provides further evidence that there exist marked and significant differences in patterns of adaptive behavior between the ethnic and Russian regions.

Our analysis thus far provides seemingly contradictory evidence regarding the impact of ethnicity on patterns of adaptation and change. While the ethnic regions have made considerably less progress in implementing economic restructuring and agricultural reform, this same group of regions was actually more supportive of the Yeltsin regime. Of course, simply comparing statistics from the two groups does not tell us whether or not a direct relationship exists between these two variables. The fact that all of the data presented here are on the same level of analysis, however, permits us to explore this possibility by conducting correlation analyses between the index of change and regime support.

When we correlate the index of change with regime support using all of the subjects of the federation, the result is a weak and negative correlation between these two variables ($R = -.181$, $p = .061$). While this relationship is just outside the bounds of statistical significance ($\alpha = .05$), and therefore no causal relationship can be said to exist, this finding lends some support to the hypothesis that the regions that tend to be more resistant to change are also more supportive of the Yeltsin regime. An interesting question is, then, does this relationship hold true for both the Russian and ethnic regions?

To explore this issue, we correlated the two variables against each other by regional grouping, and discovered another major difference between the ethnic and Russian regions. When the Russian regions were considered separately, the relationship became positive, although still outside the bounds of statistical significance ($R = .148$, $p = .138$). Although statistically insignificant on the .05 level of confidence, this relationship indicates that, for the Russian regions as a group, the regions that have made more progress in implementing reform were also more supportive of the Yeltsin regime—the opposite of the previous finding.

Finally, when the ethnic regions were considered separately the relationship remained negative, increased greatly in strength, and became statistically significant ($R = -.393$, $p = .048$). This means that that the regions that have been the most resistant to change in the economic realm were actually the most supportive of the Yeltsin regime. Moreover, the negative relationship identified in the first set of correlations is most certainly attributable to the negative relationship that exists between these variables for the ethnic regions alone, and does not seem to be characteristic of the relationship between these variables for the Russian regions. The great variation that exists in the relationship between the index of change and regime support is apparent by the differences in the slope lines as illustrated in the scatter plot in Figure 10.1.

Figure 10.1
Correlation Between Regime Support and the Index of Change by
Regional Grouping

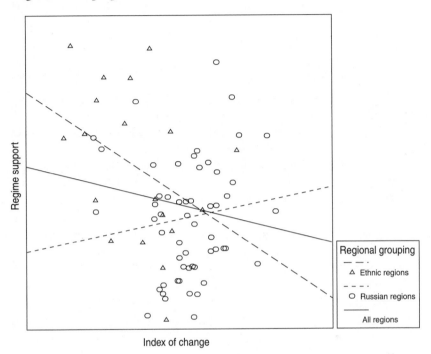

Index of change

Given that the ethnic regions demonstrated greater electoral support for
the Yeltsin regime, and that they clearly differentiate themselves from the
Russian regions in terms of being less given to economic reform, it thus
would appear that the ethnic regions' support for the Yeltsin administration
was for reasons other than its stated, preferred economic policies (e.g., privatized agriculture). This suggests a number of other significant political
questions concerning the overall patterns of development of the post-Soviet
Russian state, which we explore below.

The Political Economy of Center-Periphery Relations

Nearly every study of the processes of agricultural policy formation and implementation since the collapse of the Soviet Union has noted the highly
conflictual and the intensely desultory character of those processes.[27]

Nearly a decade after the collapse of the Soviet Union, and thus into the reform process, the transition away from Soviet-style agriculture is far from complete. Recent scholarly examination of agricultural policy formation and implementation also demonstrates a problematic consistency and clarity in agricultural policy itself, particularly with regard to the realization of the regime's stated goals of fostering a vibrant private agricultural sector.

There can be little question that center-regional politics impinges directly on the larger question of national agricultural policy, and particularly the question of the transition to a more privately oriented agricultural foundation. Three general aspects of center-periphery relations appear particularly important to agricultural policy at the present time, especially as they pertain to the ethnic dimension of that policy.

The first issue concerns the nascent private agricultural sector versus the "rural conservative lobby" (even though the latter may be former sovkhozy and kolkhozy transformed into joint stock companies, they remain nonetheless generally resistant to the emergence of a predominantly private form of agriculture). The question remains whether such a rural lobby is stronger in the ethnic regions than in the Russian regions. While direct evidence on this is difficult to gather, indirect evidence suggests that the opposite is actually the case. While the rural lobby is one of the strongest in the central black-earth area (which strongly supported Ziuganov in the 1996 presidential elections) and in agricultural regions such as Kostroma, Tula, and Volgograd, the agrarians are largely marginalized in the ethnic regions. And as a recent study of the political affiliations of Russia's regional executives found, the executives of the ethnic republics remain largely unaffiliated with any party, bloc, or movement.[28]

A second issue involves the struggle between legislative and executive authority on the national level. This, of course, manifested itself primarily in the form of political conflict between President Yeltsin and the opposition-dominated Duma. Regarding agricultural policy, especially as it pertains to the ethnic regions as distinct from the Russian regions, the picture is quite complicated. First, the Duma's leftist orientation in both the 1993 and 1995 elections would seem to have placed it at loggerheads with the Yeltsin administration regarding the implementation of his (stated) preferences for private agriculture. And in general this was the case. In addition, the Duma appeared to have taken steps to strengthen the regions against the center, at least in part, perhaps, to counterbalance the power of the Yeltsin administration.

In any case, the net result over time may be a reconfigured political landscape in which the regions can to some degree check the power of the center.[29] The ethnic regions' apparently greater reluctance than the Russian regions to bring about a vibrant private agricultural sector may be aided by such a disposition of the Duma. On the other hand, the Yeltsin administration more or less consistently fostered a significant degree of regional autonomy, although as time went on after ratification of the constitution in 1993, Moscow applied increasing pressure upon the regions to engage in bilateral treaties. Also, the Federation Council—the upper house of the Federal Assembly—has clearly assumed a more forceful role in the determination of national policy. This has been especially true since December 1995, when the membership of the Federation Council began to be composed of the popularly elected heads of the legislative and executive branches of government within each of the regions, instead of being appointed by Moscow.[30] This aspect of the transformation of Russian governance, and therefore of reform policy, is certain to be dramatic in the coming years, perhaps in ways that are presently unforeseen.

Finally, agricultural reforms, or the lack thereof, must be considered with respect to the changing pattern of relations between the central government in Moscow and the regions as political units. The question that immediately emerges is, how did the Yeltsin administration dispose itself to the various regions of the federation, both in general terms and with particular respect to agricultural policy? There is no question that the regions, qua political units, have become more restive and assertive vis-à-vis Moscow, perhaps in part because of the changed role of the Federation Council, noted above. And if it is the case that the regions are gaining a more self-confident identity,[31] then this would have enormous implications for the implementation of any sort of coherent national agricultural policy. Yet as noted above, the ethnic regions demonstrated greater support for the Yeltsin administration than the Russian regions, but apparently for reasons other than preferences in agricultural policy. What are we to make of this, particularly the longer-range ramifications of this pattern for both center-periphery relations and for the likelihood of a coherent, workable national agricultural policy? At this juncture much remains to be seen, particularly regarding Yeltsin's successor and the policy pursued in this area by President Putin.

Conclusions and Implications for Further Investigation

Several scholars have recently noted a clear discrepancy between the rhetoric of Boris Yeltsin and his administration (but mostly him personally) concerning the importance of promoting a strong private agricultural sector and the actual policies that emerged from Moscow under his rule. We will proceed from the general assumption that Yeltsin was sincere in his declarations of devotion to the advancement of private agriculture in Russia. The question can be raised as to whether the realization of such policies was hindered by a number of factors, including perhaps Yeltsin's reluctance to alienate regional governments—especially the ethnic regions—which tended to support him in the 1996 presidential election, but which appear to have consistently lagged behind the Russian regions in economic reform. Viewed from the perspective of this uncertainty, it is not surprising that agricultural policy formation and implementation have been conflictual and desultory.

Yet this phenomenon raises again the question of the larger evolving relationship between the various dimensions of conflict over agricultural policy and the Yeltsin regime's handling of center-regional relations. Given the centrality of economic reform to post-Soviet Russia—certainly including agricultural reform—and the extreme urgency of deftly handling centrifugal policy forces in the regions, it stands to reason that some aspects of these conflictual facets of governance have involved agricultural policy. The "negotiative federalism"[32] into which the Russian Federation has evolved since ratification of the 1993 Constitution has certainly provided the framework within which regions have found it possible (and perhaps even desirable) to take their autonomy and use it to craft agricultural policies to their liking irrespective of Moscow's wishes or even the wishes of the fabled "agrarian lobbies." The result, for whatever causal reasons, is that the ethnoterritorial regions have tended to lag in reorganizing their agricultural sectors.

The findings in this chapter also have implications for the future of Russian agricultural adaptation as explored by other authors in this book. Chapter 2 by Lerman provides evidence that those farmers who have undergone a transition to a more market-oriented private agriculture are "better off, happier, and more optimistic than those who have decided to stay attached to the collective farm."[33] This pattern could have clear and strong political implications given the findings of the present chapter: If a socioeconomic chasm develops between those farmers who fit the above description, and those who do not, and this cleavage line happens to coincide with an ethnic cleavage, then the prospect for ethnic-related conflict as well as agricultural stagnation in the ethnic areas would seem to be very present. The analysis provided in chapter 3 by Ioffe and Nefedova also has implications for the findings of the present chapter. If the spatially related factors identified by these authors are significant factors in a successful transition to a more productive agriculture (soil fertility and accessibility to major urban areas), then the ethnic regions of the federation may afford less promise. To the extent that this is the case, the potential for interethnic tensions would seem to increase, driven in part by increasingly differentiated agricultural patterns across the regions.

A number of empirical questions present themselves at this point, useful to guide subsequent research into the question of the relationship between ethnicity and agricultural development in the Russian Federation. These might include:

- Have the regions, particularly the ethnic regions, which supported Yeltsin in 1996 proven in the past to be generally supportive of political parties that have attempted to stymie the emergence of a strong private agricultural sector? What might that suggest for the intersection of national agricultural policy and center-regional relations?
- Is there any correlation between the regions that more heavily supported the Yeltsin administration in the past and the regions that have adopted the "Saratov model" of attempting to foster private agriculture? If so, specifically how might questions of ethnic identity and ethnic-based political considerations be involved in such a connection?
- Is there any specific correlation between the ethno-territorial regions, support for the Yeltsin administration, and geographical location, as the last factor most directly pertains to agricultural considerations (i.e., was support for Yeltsin, and political reform more generally, stronger in the ethnic regions where his agricultural policy preferences were simply less germane to the region's politics because of the region's general unsuitability to agriculture in general, as in the Far North)?

The above questions merely underscore the complexity of the complicating factor of ethnicity in the Russian Federation's transitional period, regarding both the establishment of a more democratic political order, and in establishing a post-Soviet agricultural system that works suitably for the federation.

Notes

1. *Constitution of the Russian Federation*, Chapter 3, Articles 65, 66, and 67.
2. Ibid., Chapter 3, Article 66.

3. "Interview with Ingushetiia President Ruslan Aushev," *EWI Russian Regional Report* 4 (11 March 1999), available at *www.iews.org/rrrabout.nsf.*

4. Daniel Kempton, "The Republic of Sakha (Yakutia): The Evolution of Centre-Periphery Relations in the Russian Federation," *Europe-Asia Studies* 48 (1996): 587–613; Christian Noack, "Tatarstan—Ein Modell fuer die Erneuerung Russlands?" *Osteuropa* (February 1996): 134–49.

5. O. A. Murashko, "Etnoekologicheskii refugium: kontseptsiia sokhraneniia traditsionnoi kul'tury i sredy obitaniia korennykh narodov severa," *Etnograficheskoe obozrenie* 5 (1998): 83–94.

6. For example, works that focus on ethnicity in general include Roman Szporluk, ed., *National Identity and Ethnicity in Russia and the New States of Eurasia* (Armonk, NY: M. E. Sharpe, 1994); Graham Smith, "The Ethno-Politics of Federation without Federalism," in *Russia in Transition: Politics, Privatization, and Inequality*, ed. David Lane (New York: Longman, 1995), 21–35; James W. Warhola, *Politicized Ethnicity in the Russian Federation: Dilemmas of State Formation* (Lewiston, NY: Edwin Mellen, 1996); and Gail Lapidus and Edward W. Walker, "Nationalism, Regionalism, and Federalism: Center-Periphery Relations in Post-Communist Russia," in *The New Russia: Troubled Transformation*, ed. Gail Lapidus (Boulder, CO: Westview, 1995), 79–113.

7. Darrell Slider, "Privatization in Russia's Regions," *Post-Soviet Affairs* 10 no. 4: 367.

8. Ibid., 379.

9. Ibid.

10. The data on the number of enterprises privatized in 1996 are from *Regiony Rossii*, vol. 2 (Moscow: Goskomstat, 1997), 610–12. The figures presented were calculated by comparing the means of the two groups. Using Levene's test for equality of variance (assuming equal variances), the significance of this difference was .136 (F = 2.275).

11. The data on the number of joint stock companies formed in 1996 are from *Regiony Rossii* 2, 450–52. The figures presented were calculated by comparing the means of the two groups. Using Levene's test for equality of variance (assuming equal variances), the significance of this difference was .303 (F = 1.074).

12. "Russia's '99 Grain Harvest Falls 11% Short of Needs," *Johnson's Russia List* 3571 (19 October 1999), available at *www.cdi.org/russia/johnson/3571.html##9.*

13. Peter Craumer, "Regional Patterns of Agricultural Reform in Russia," *Post-Soviet Geography* 35 (1994): 329–51.

14. Ibid., 343.

15. The data on the conversion rates of state and collective farms were calculated using statistics on the number and type of farms in Russia as of January 1996. The statistics used are from *Regiony Rossii* 2, 577–79. The comparative figures presented were calculated by comparing the means of the two groups. Using Levene's test for equality of variance (assuming equal variances), the significance of this difference was .001 (F = 11.241).

16. The index of change was constructed by computing the z-score for each of the variables and then summing the scores. Several cases were excluded from the index because of missing data for one or more of the variables.

17. The scores for the index of change ranged from 4.35 to –3.03. The measure of dispersion used in creating the five-level scale used here is simply the range divided by the number of levels, with each level then representing 20 percent of the range (though not necessarily 20 percent of the cases). While not representing absolute levels that are comparable cross-nationally, this does accurately illustrate the varying levels of adaptation and change among Russia's regions.

18. David Easton, *A Systems Analysis of Political Life* (New York: Wiley, 1965); and Easton, "A Re-assessment of the Concept of Political Support," *British Journal of Political Science* 5 (1975): 435–57.

19. Gregory Caldeira and James Gibson, "The Legitimacy of the Court of Justice in the European Union: Models of Institutional Support," *American Political Science Review* 89 (June 1995): 357.

20. A more detailed analysis of factors relating to regime support in Russia appears in Christopher Marsh and James W. Warhola, "Ethnicity, Modernization, and Regime Support in Russia's Regions Under Yeltsin," *Nationalism and Ethnic Politics* 6, no. 4 (winter 2000): 23–47. Our discussion of regime support presented here draws heavily from that work.

21. Thomas F. Remington, Steven S. Smith, and Moshe Haspel, "Decrees, Laws, and Inter-Branch Relations in the Russian Federation," *Post-Soviet Affairs* 14 (1998): 287–322.

22. Oleg Moroz, *Literaturnaia gazeta* 46, no. 10 (1995), quoted in Richard Sakwa, *Russian Politics and Society* (London: Routledge, 1996), 171.

23. Charles Clover, "Dreams of the Eurasian Heartland," *Foreign Affairs* 78 (March/April 1999): 12.

24. Ibid.

25. Electoral results can be found in *Tsentral'naia izbiratel'naia komissiia Rossiiskoi Federatsii, vybory prezidenta Rossiiskoi Federatsii 1996: elektoral'naia statistika* (Moscow: Ves' Mir, 1996). The comparative figures presented were calculated by comparing the means of the two groups. Using Levene's test for equality of variance (assuming equal variances), the significance of this difference was .077 (F = 3.209).

26. Robert Orttung and Anna Paretskaya, "Presidential Election Demonstrates Rural-Urban Divide," *Transition* 2 (September 1996): 45–49.

27. See, among others, Stephen Wegren, "Russian Agrarian Reform and Rural Capitalism Reconsidered," *Journal of Peasant Studies* 26 (October 1998): 82–111; Wegren and Vladimir Belen'kiy, "The Political Economy of the Russian Land Market," *Problems of Post-Communism* 45, no. 4 (1998): 56–66; Wegren, "The Politics of Private Farming in Russia," *Journal of Peasant Studies* 23, no. 4 (1996): 106–40; and Donald Van Atta, ed., *The "Farmer Threat": The Political Economy of Agrarian Reform in Post-Soviet Russia* (Boulder, CO: Westview Press, 1993).

28. "Political Affiliations of Russia's Governors: A List," *EWI Russian Regional Report* 4 (29 April 1999), available at *www.iews.org/rrrabout.nsf/pages/governors+party+affiliation.*

29. James W. Warhola, "Is the Russian Federation Becoming More Democratic? Moscow-Regional Relations and the Development of the Post-Soviet Russian State," *Democratization* 6 (summer 1999): 42–69.

30. See Federal'nii Zakon, "O poriadke formirovaniia Soveta Federatsii federal'nogo sobraniia Rossiiskoi Federatsii," No. 192-F3, signed into law on 5 December 1995. Available via the Federation Council's official Internet site at *www.council.gov.ru/zd/zd.html.*

31. See Jerry Hough, "The Political Geography of European Russia: Republics and Oblasts," *Post-Soviet Geography and Economics* 39, no. 2 (February 1998): 63–95.

32. N. Mescheriakova, ed., *Natsional'naia politika Rossii: istoriia i sovremennost'* (Moscow: Russkii Mir, 1997), 431.

33. See chapter 2 by Lerman in this volume.

11

What Turns the *Kolkhoz* into a Firm?
Regional Policies and the
Elasticity of Budget Constraint

MARIA AMELINA[1]

Students of Russian agricultural reform have been struck by the institutional resilience of collective farms.[2] Between 1991 and 1997 the former *kolkhozy* and *sovkhozy*, transformed into joint stock companies and now largely owned by their employees, showed declining profitability (see Table 11.1) and low and falling efficiency.[3] Yet, almost a decade into the reforms, their numbers have not decreased. They continue to be the dominant agricultural producers, generating half of the country's agricultural output and controlling more than 80 percent of agricultural land.

This chapter examines the staying power of the former collective farms on the basis of the results of an empirical study of the relationship between regional (oblast) level agricultural policies and the propensity of collective enterprises to restructure in two Russian oblasts. The study demonstrates that the decision by enterprise managers to pursue restructuring has depended on the institutional environment created by the agricultural policies of regional governments—specifically, whether regional governments reconstituted Soviet-type financing of agricultural enterprises at a time when federal policies were moving away from direct support of agricultural producers and toward promotion of market-based transactions.

264

Table 11.1

Characteristics of Collective Enterprises, 1991, 1994, and 1997

Indicator	1991	1994	1997
Number of collective enterprises (thousands)	26.9	26.9	27.0
Unprofitable collective enterprises (%)	5	5	82
Share of national agricultural production (%)	68.8	54.5	49.9
Control of agricultural land (%)	91.2	82.8	80.4
Average size of landholdings per enterprise (hectares)	4,200	3,300	2,900

Sources: Calculations based on Goskomstat, *Statistical Bulletin* 37, no. 8 (October 1997); *Sel'skoe khoziaistvo v Rossii, 1998* (Moscow).

The Disappointment of Federal Reforms

From 1990 and until the return of a more centralized approach to agricultural financing in 2000 the federal government was pursuing pro-market agricultural reforms composed of two complementary strategies. One was a consistent effort at distancing itself from collective agricultural production. The government achieved this goal by curtailing its direct involvement in financing, management, and ownership of former collective farms. Federal financing for agriculture declined from almost 11 percent of gross domestic product (GDP) in 1992 to about 1 percent in 1997.[4] By 1997, the state owned less than 10 percent of both agricultural land and agricultural enterprises.[5] Direct state control of agriculture has markedly diminished as well after pricing of the majority of agricultural inputs and products has passed from the state to the market.[6]

The second strategy employed by the federal government was to promote the development of efficient profit-oriented individual farming capable of replacing inefficient collective producers as dominant actors in Russian agriculture. To achieve this objective the federal government (vociferous objections of the Duma notwithstanding) started to create a legal framework for the existence and operation of independent private farms. The assumption of reformers was that once an adequate legislative base was in place, the invisible hand would sweep away inefficient collectivist structures and establish individual farmers as the prevalent type of agricultural producers. The Presidential Decree of 1991 turned ownership of collective farms over to their employees, encouraging these new owners to

Table 11.2

Characteristics of Independent Farms and Private Plots, Selected Years, 1991–97

Indicators	1991	1994	1996	1997
Share of national agricultural production (%)	—	1.7	1.9	2.2
Control of agricultural land (%)	0.6	4.8	5.2	5.7
Average size of plots (hectares)	—	42	43	44
Number of producers (thousands)	4.4	270	280	278.6

Note: In 1993, some privately held plots were reclassified as plots for home construction, which led to a decrease in the total number of plots in this category.
Sources: Calculations based on Goskomstat, *Statistical Bulletin* 37, no. 8 (October 1997); *Sel'skoe khoziaistvo v Rossii, 1998* (Moscow).

dismantle collective enterprises and distribute land and property shares among themselves. Those who did not want to farm as individuals were given the right to sell their land entitlements to more enterprising shareholders at freely negotiated prices.[7] The Presidential Decree of 1993 broadened rights to trade land shares, including the right to sell, mortgage, rent, and exchange land.[8]

However, despite these and other efforts to level the playing field between the collective and independent farmers, performance and growth of independent farming proved disappointing. In 1997 independent farms produced an unimpressive 2.2 percent of national agricultural output (Table 11.2). After an initial period of growth, the reported number of closures surpassed the number of newly created private farms.

These developments provoke a number of questions. What allows a post-Soviet collective farm to continue as a productive unit despite the efforts of federal reformers to promote price liberalization and expansion of independent farming? In cases where collective farms are actually changing their behavior, what are the patterns of change and on what do the dynamics of change depend?

This chapter has three main sections. The first examines key determinants of oblast-level agricultural policy, and offers a general conceptualization of the institutional environment that results from the efforts of regional governments to reconstitute Soviet patterns of coordination in the sector. The concept of an elastic budget constraint under which collective agricultural enterprises operate in one of the oblasts of the study is introduced as a particular transitional phenomenon, distinct from the soft budget constraint of socialism or the hard budget constraint of capitalism.

Commodity crediting schemes are identified as the critical organizational mechanism through which an elastic constraint materializes at the subnational level. A discussion of the scale, scope, and divergent effects of distribution practices associated with the implementation of commodity crediting arrangements in the two oblasts concludes the section. The second section presents empirical evidence of the impact divergent subnational agricultural policies have on the behavior of agricultural producers in each oblast. The study shows that the behavior of collective enterprises in the more interventionist oblast is characterized by a high level of dependence on the provincial government for financial and other resources combined with little market-oriented restructuring, while in the oblast free of government coordination, enterprises are undergoing more radical market-oriented changes. The concluding section summarizes the variables identified as instrumental in the government's decision to embrace or delay reforms and discusses the implications of these findings for strategizing reforms at the subnational level.

Institutions and Structures

Institutional Modifications: An Elastic Budget Constraint

The institutional context created by the obligation of the socialist state to finance producers regardless of viability has been famously described by Kornai and termed a soft budget constraint.[9] Contrary to the habitual usage of the term, for Kornai "soft" does not mean unconditional or unrestrained. In the land of shortages, untimely deliveries, and widespread inefficiencies, managers were savvy enough to understand that material shortage was a fact of life. What Kornai described was a complex bargaining process based on an imprecise mix of the plan, political clout, economic returns, social responsibilities, and ideological priorities. Both sides, the government and enterprise managers, understood the realm of the possible and tried to capitalize on the cards they were holding at a particular point in time, be it provision of social services to their employees, high profile of the enterprise, particular need for inputs, and particularly high output, among others.

Since the game was perceived as recurrent and long term, both sides took into consideration the needs of the other. If the government needed resources for some other purpose one year, the managers realized that treating these needs with understanding in the bargaining process could secure better treatment in the next round of bargaining. What appeared to be permanent was the long-term guarantee that the state as the owner of the enterprises was ultimately responsible for the financing of all production. Therefore, some resources were bound to be granted. Furthermore, there was no legal way of obtaining financing anywhere else. And state financing, while not being unconditional, was conditioned on the mix of variables described above in which the hierarchy of ingredients changed over time and productivity and efficiency usually occupied a low position. Bankruptcy was not even a theoretical possibility and the existence of the enterprise was secure.

After the end of socialism, unconditional state support disappeared. Explicit curtailment of direct federal financing sent the vast majority of collective agricultural producers into a tailspin, which, in accordance with the design of the reformers, was to result in a painful but unavoidable restructuring. This restructuring was forestalled when local governments in a number of oblasts chose to reconstitute resource-distribution structures in the new environment. The attempt by regional governments to substitute regional agricultural policy for curtailed federal support raises three linked questions: Why would regional governments pursue such a policy? Why would enterprise managers participate in regional attempts to coordinate production and financing in the agriculture sector? What is the institutional environment that results, that is, how is the Soviet soft budget constraint transformed in this new context?

A regional government can choose to support agricultural producers to keep its skills in resource distribution current and valid, thereby diminishing competition from newcomers who are not familiar with the distribution schemes. Part of this skill mix and part of the old socialist design is to distribute financial resources in return for the commitment of the managers to provide social services to their employees and other noneconomic as well as economic obligations. The new part of the government's incentive to reconstitute the system is to solicit political support from the agrarian lobby and rural population come election time. Another new twist in the distribution design is that the government can manipulate the distribution system so as to generate returns for itself. While this is not a new phenomenon, the ability of the provincial government to create public, private, or mixed entities that can legally (but not necessarily transparently) put these resources to private and public use at the government's discretion is a post-socialist development.

Meanwhile, collective enterprise managers may also derive benefits from participation in the redistribution design. Almost all of them are poorly prepared for operating in the market in general and for restructuring their enterprises in particular. Restructuring would mean turning the multipurpose structure of a socialist enterprise that produced agricultural output, provided social benefits, and served as an embodiment of an ideological stance into a profit-maximizing firm. It is reasonable to expect a rational manager to seek to avoid this formidable task (vastly increased by macroeconomic uncertainties during the transition period). The managers, therefore, accept the rules offered by the local government and continue to participate in the direct distribution system.

The distribution of power among the political and economic actors, however, is radically different from the Soviet prototype. The main difference is the long-term uncertainty of government actions. The government is not the owner of the enterprises and, therefore, is not obliged to provide financing. Furthermore, the new use of redistribution as an officially sanctioned money-making opportunity makes the government periodically harden the budget constraint and act as a tough debt collector. Under these circumstances, the bargaining position of enterprise managers is much weaker than in the Soviet scheme. If the government changes, newly elected administrators may decide not to invest in the preservation of the redistribution scheme and let it collapse. The only guarantee managers have that the redistribution system will continue is the expectation that the benefits regional governments derive from these arrangements provide an adequate incentive to strive to reproduce them.

From the perspective of the goals of agricultural reforms, the result is a vicious circle. Inability to obtain financing from commercial sources without restructuring narrows the choice of creditors for the manager to the one creditor that continues to finance with little regard for profitability or efficiency—the regional government. Yet, the managers do not have sufficient incentives to restructure as long as the possibility of direct financing uncoupled from their restructuring effort continues to exist. Therefore, they continue to muddle through in the context of institutional arrangements that do not let collective producers collapse, yet also do not offer incentives for transformation into efficient market-oriented producers.

To distinguish subnational state intervention from its Soviet prototype, the phenomenon of post-socialist reconstitution of the soft budget constraint is called an *elastic budget constraint*. The word "elastic" is used to designate two features, both of which are inflected by the profound uncertainty of the post-Soviet institutional environment for agricultural producers. The first is the flexibility the provincial government has in deciding whether to support both the redistribution structures and the producers involved in the system. The second aspect of the elasticity of the budget constraint is that, as with an elastic band, after the periods of tightening the arrangement is expected to settle back into softness. In contrast to the Soviet past, the return to a soft constraint is not a legal certainty. However, a strong possibility of soft financing in combination with the high costs of restructuring makes the enterprise management follow the elastic lead of the subnational government. As seen in the following empirical discussion, in the oblast where the distribution scheme has been reconstituted, agricultural producers perceive tightening of the budget constraint as temporary episodes, not as departures from the model and, therefore, do not radically change their managerial practices.

Mechanisms that allow local governments to sustain their role as the main players in agricultural management and financing as well as the specific benefits that they expect to extract from the exercise are discussed below.

Structural Modifications: Costs and Benefits of Commodity Credits

The mechanism that has been used in a number of provinces to reconstitute a Soviet-type system of coordination in the agricultural sector is called *commodity crediting*.[10] Figure 11.1 illustrates how commodity crediting works.

The food corporation is a parastatal that organizes resource distribution among agricultural producers and input providers, collects commodity credits from agricultural producers in cash or in kind, and stores and disposes of food commodities that it accumulates as in-kind payments. As shown in the next section, the scope of responsibilities of food corporations in different oblasts varies greatly. There are, however, some general characteristics. Food corporations sign agreements with input providers to deliver inputs to agricultural producers at the time of sowing. In return input providers are granted a tax forgiveness from the government equal to the size of input deliveries to the agricultural producers at pre-specified prices. Agricultural producers, meanwhile, have a contractual obligation to repay the food corporation after harvest, either in cash or in kind.

Commodity credits were first introduced by the federal government in 1995 but abandoned in 1997 because of the distortionary influence of the pre-announced procurement prices on price formation of agricultural commodities.[11] Another reason for the abandonment of commodity credits at the federal level was the dismal repayment record, as collective enterprise managers continued to perceive state credits as soft.[12] It was precisely

Figure 11.1
Commodity Credits Delivery Scheme

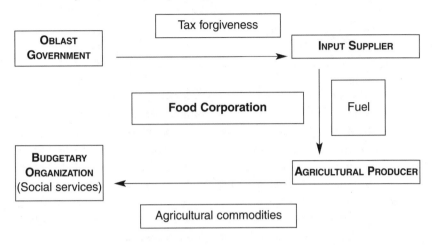

these reasons that inspired some oblast governments to expand commodity crediting in their oblasts. Commodity credit schemes gave the oblast government an opportunity to intervene both in agricultural price formation and farm financing in a recognizably path-dependent socialist, yet sustainable, way.[13]

The pivotal bargaining point in the commodity crediting arrangement is the level of enforcement of credit repayment. There are two important levers that allow the oblast government, the key player in the commodity credit scheme, to manipulate the system so that its long- and short-term economic, social, and political goals are adequately met. First, the government decides how binding the repayment requirement is going to be in a given year. Second, it can establish whether the commodity prices—at which barter commodity payments are accepted—are going to be below, equivalent to, or above market prices.

The actual use of these levers by regional governments reflects the balance of political, social, and economic priorities. If the government is more interested in solidifying or increasing its popularity with the agrarian heavyweights and those sectors of the rural population that stand to benefit from the government largesse, commodity credits may be forgiven completely or partially through an explicit arrangement or by nonenforcement of repayment. If the government's need for financial resources is stronger than its need for rural support, it will make an effort to enforce credit repayment. The second lever, control over pricing in commodity crediting, plays a role similar to that of payment enforcement with the additional advantage of being both less transparent and less explicit. If the government preserves or recreates its role as a monopsonist in the commodity market, it can distort commodity pricing by enforcing repayment of commodity credits at artificially low internal prices. In this case, the oblast government stands to make significant financial gains by selling the commodity outside of the oblast.

What specific types of benefits do provincial governments extract from the preservation of the redistribution arrangement, such that these systems led by oblast governments are perceived as stable ten years into the reforms? What makes the agricultural sector particularly amenable to a redistribution-based scheme long past its federal endorsement? Finally, what are the circumstances that tip this path-dependent, post-Soviet arrangement in the direction of more radical reforms?

The benefits an intervention-minded subnational government expects to extract from participation in the distribution of resources in agriculture can roughly be divided into three categories: economic, social, and political. The first set of benefits is economic. As discussed above, local government gains from engagement in the distribution of material flows if repayment is enforced or prices inflated. Furthermore, nontransparency of the commodity credit scheme and of the flow of commodities that passes through the food corporation allows local governments to direct resources to nontransparent goals and in nontransparent amounts.

The second set of benefits is related to social service provision. Social services covered by the arrangement are of two types. First, collective enterprises, following the Soviet model, continue to secure the livelihood of their employees regardless of their performance. Access to inputs decoupled from their financial performance allows collective farms to subsidize individual production of their employees/shareholders, thus multiplying the effect of the subsidy associated with commodity crediting.[14] The second benefit pertaining to social services is alleviation of the burden of providing budgetary organizations (e.g., schools, hospitals, and prisons) with foodstuffs, a domain in which the role of local government has increased since socialism. Deliveries of foodstuffs that collective agricultural producers make to these organizations are counted toward commodity credit repayment.

A third set of benefits local governments may derive from commodity crediting is related to the second. By providing social services via collective enterprises to collective farm employees and to social-service budgetary organizations, the government minimizes the short-term costs of restructuring and diminishes the threat of competition from administrative teams more skilled at managing provision of social services directly. The arrangement keeps the skills set of provincial governments useable and current, and thus extends their political life. Transition to a market- and regulation-based economy and public management styles would make these skills outdated and irrelevant.

Singling out three sets of benefits helps in understanding the reasons behind the preservation of Soviet-style distribution at the subnational level, but does not help in understanding why the redistribution mechanisms have demonstrated both longevity and sustainability in agriculture more than in other sectors. Re-creation of Soviet-type subnational allocation of resources in agriculture is made possible by a number of characteristics of the material organization of agricultural production. The main such characteristic is low complexity of inputs, and, in the case of crop production, the discrete need for inputs twice a year at planting and harvesting. As was demonstrated by Blanchard and Kremer, in the short run, transition in industries with high complexity of inputs is more costly to reconstitute.[15] In the case of agriculture, particularly of crop production, the number of inputs needed to resume the production cycle is low; therefore, the task of coordination of resource distribution among agricultural producers and input providers is simplified and, as this research shows, can be managed at the subnational level.

Finally, it is important to establish whether particular characteristics of a given oblast will make it more or less likely to re-create Soviet-type interventionist practices. It is safe to assume that the level of involvement of a local government will largely depend on the expected political and economic returns from this involvement. In this case, an argument can be made that administrative systems of distribution and coordination will be more likely to play a prominent role in more agriculturally endowed regions where political and economic returns from adapting the old system to meet current needs are perceived to be high. Alternatively, the governments of the regions with lower expected political and economic returns from agriculture are more likely not to invest in trying to salvage the old system. Therefore, agriculturally less-endowed regions will make less effort to re-create a Soviet model of distribution and will promote (or simply allow) the emergence of market-oriented exchanges *faster* then their agriculturally better-endowed counterparts.

It is also important to assess which agricultural characteristics of a region are more likely to make it a fruitful ground for commodity crediting. Highly centralized distribution is achieved much easier with grain, a bulk wholesale commodity, than with milk and vegetables, both retail agricultural goods. In addition, meat and dairy production requires inputs such as fodder and fuel for heating shelters for livestock continuously throughout the year rather than twice a year at harvesting and sowing, which makes meat and dairy production much more difficult to manage and coordinate.

Agricultural Production
and Agricultural Policies at the Oblast Level

These hypotheses were studied in two Russian oblasts, Leningrad and Saratov. These oblasts were chosen for this study because of their geographical location and product mix. Leningrad oblast is located in the northwestern region (Map 11.1) and typically produces vegetables, meat, and dairy products. Saratov oblast is located in the central Volga region and is a representative black-earth, grain-producing province (Map 11.2).

Within each oblast, one *raion* (district) was chosen for a more focused qualitative and quantitative analysis.[16] Both Vsevolozhsk raion in Leningrad oblast and Engels raion in Saratov oblast are located in peri-urban areas, adjacent to the oblast capitals (see Maps 11.1 and 11.2). Peri-urban locations have been shown to be the locus of more dynamic changes in agricultural production in Russia, and the first to register new ownership patterns. As a result, these regions were expected to be the first to demonstrate shifts to market-oriented production.[17] (See the discussion of spatial factors in agricultural revival in chapter 3 by Ioffe and Nefedova in this volume.)

Leningrad and Saratov oblasts differ dramatically in terms of the role of agriculture in the oblast economy, the agricultural policy orientation of the oblast government, and the role of the food corporation. This section examines how these different characteristics interact and the outcomes of these interactions in terms of production environment and incentives.

Saratov is part of an area known as the grain basket of Russia. In 1997, agricultural production accounted for 14 percent of the oblast's GDP, twice the national average. The rural population made up one-third of the population of the oblast (32 percent), 5 percent higher than the national average. In contrast, Leningrad is largely an industrial oblast. St. Petersburg, a separate administrative unit, is included in the GDP estimates for Leningrad oblast. This is a necessary adjustment, because the GDP of the city of Saratov is part of the Saratov oblast GDP. The combined agricultural output of Leningrad oblast and St. Petersburg accounts for 3 percent of oblast GDP. Rural residents comprise less than 10 percent of the oblast's population, 17 percent below the national average.[18]

Map 11.1
Leningrad Oblast

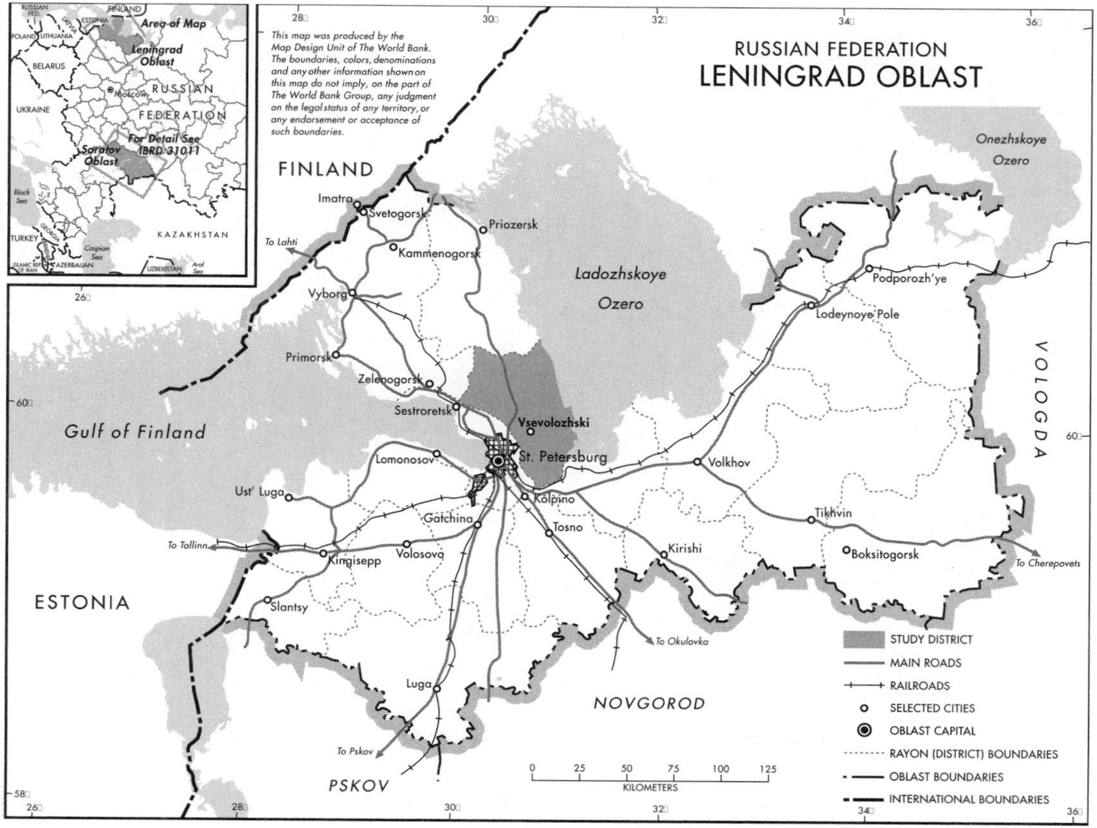

RUSSIAN FEDERATION
LENINGRAD OBLAST

VOLOGDA

Onezhskoye Ozero

To Cherepovets

Podporozh'ye

Ladeynoye Pole

Boksitogorsk

Tikhvin

Ladozhskoye Ozero

Volkhov

Kirishi

To Okulovka

NOVGOROD

Priozersk

Vsevolozhski

St. Petersburg

Kolpino

Tosno

Kamennogorsk

Svetogorsk

Imatra

Zelenogorsk

Sestroretsk

Lomonosov

Gatchina

Volosovo

Luga

To Pskov

FINLAND

To Lahti

Vyborg

Primorsk

Kingisepp

Slantsy

PSKOV

Ust' Luga

To Tallinn

Gulf of Finland

ESTONIA

STUDY DISTRICT
MAIN ROADS
RAILROADS
SELECTED CITIES
OBLAST CAPITAL
RAYON (DISTRICT) BOUNDARIES
OBLAST BOUNDARIES
INTERNATIONAL BOUNDARIES

0   25   50   75   100   125
KILOMETERS

This map was produced by the
Map Design Unit of The World Bank.
The boundaries, colors, denominations
and any other information shown on
this map do not imply, on the part of
The World Bank Group, any judgment
on the legal status of any territory, or
any endorsement or acceptance of
such boundaries.

Area of Map
Leningrad Oblast

RUSSIAN FEDERATION

KAZAKHSTAN

For Detail See
IBRD 31011

Leningrad Oblast

FINLAND
ESTONIA
LATVIA
LITHUANIA
POLAND
BELARUS
UKRAINE
MOSCOW
Black Sea
TURKEY
GEORGIA
AZERBAIJAN
Caspian Sea
Aral Sea

Map 11.2
Saratov Oblast

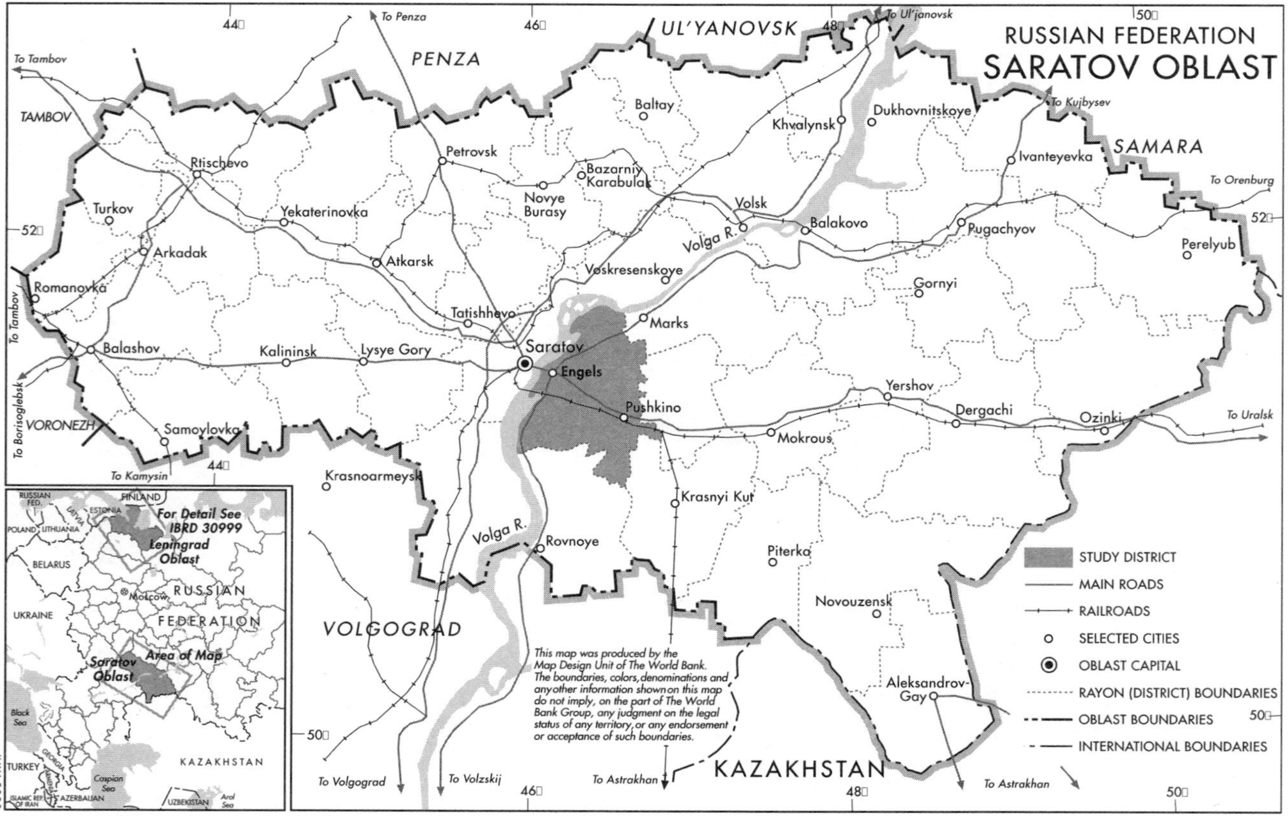

RUSSIAN FEDERATION
SARATOV OBLAST

STUDY DISTRICT
MAIN ROADS
RAILROADS
SELECTED CITIES
OBLAST CAPITAL
RAYON (DISTRICT) BOUNDARIES
OBLAST BOUNDARIES
INTERNATIONAL BOUNDARIES

This map was produced by the
Map Design Unit of The World Bank.
The boundaries, colors, denominations and
any other information shown on this map
do not imply, on the part of The World
Bank Group, any judgment on the legal
status of any territory, or any endorsement
or acceptance of such boundaries.

SAMARA

ULYANOVSK

PENZA

TAMBOV

VORONEZH

VOLGOGRAD

KAZAKHSTAN

To Ulyanovsk
To Kuibysev
To Orenburg
To Uralsk
To Astrakhan
To Penza
To Tambov
To Borisoglebsk
To Kamyshin
To Volzskij
To Volgograd
To Astrakhan

Perelyub
Ivanteyevka
Pugachyov
Ozinki
Dukhovnitskoye
Gornyi
Dergachi
Yershov
Khvalynsk
Balakovo
Mokrous
Volsk
Novouzensk
Aleksandrov-Gay
Baltay
Bazarnyi Karabulak
Veskresenskoye
Marks
Pushkino
Krasnyi Kut
Piterka
Novoye Burasy
Saratov
Engels
Rovnoye
Petrovsk
Tatishhevo
Volga R.
Atkarsk
Yekaterinovka
Lysye Gory
Kalininsk
Krasnoarmeysk
Rtischevo
Arkadak
Balashov
Samoylovka
Turkov
Romanovka

RUSSIAN FED.
FINLAND
ESTONIA
LATVIA
LITHUANIA
POLAND
BELARUS
UKRAINE
MOLDOVA
ROMANIA
GEORGIA
ARMENIA AZERBAIJAN
TURKEY
RUSSIAN FEDERATION
KAZAKHSTAN
UZBEKISTAN
Moscow
Black Sea
Caspian Sea
Aral Sea

For Detail See
IBRD 30999
Leningrad
Oblast

Saratov
Area of Map
Oblast

Another indicator of the relative importance of agriculture compared to other sectors is the oblast's agricultural trade balance. Leningrad imports about half of its dairy and meat products and almost all of the food grain and fodder consumed in the oblast. Saratov produces enough of all basic foodstuffs to satisfy the needs of its population and is one of the federation's major exporters of grain and sunflower seeds.[19]

The different roles agriculture plays in the economies of the two oblasts correspond to very different financing of agricultural production by the regional governments.[20] In Saratov, the oblast government maintains high levels of both budgetary and extrabudgetary subsidization of collective agricultural producers. Twenty percent of the budgetary expenditure of the oblast is spent on the support of collective enterprises.[21] In Leningrad, even if the St. Petersburg budget is not included in the calculation, the level of direct oblast support to agriculture is much more modest. In 1997, it stood at 6.6 percent of oblast expenditures. If the St. Petersburg budget is included in the calculation, the share of agriculture falls to less than 1 percent.[22]

Sustainability of direct oblast-level subsidies to agriculture, however, is problematic because of a severe contraction of regional budget revenues.[23] It is in this context that commodity crediting has been introduced in the two oblasts.

Both Leningrad and Saratov oblasts have oblast-level food corporations.[24] However, the share of inputs they provide, the share of output they accumulate, the price-making power they possess, and even the titles they hold differ greatly. The sizes of commodity credits in both oblasts are carefully guarded secrets and data are not available either directly from the food corporations or from the oblast administrations. However, indirect sources, including regional legislation, interviews with wholesalers who deal in agricultural commodities, and interviews with oblast government officials allowed us to assess the role of the two corporations in agricultural transactions with some level of certainty.

Interviews with independent wholesalers and managers of the food corporation in Leningrad oblast—which together with the federal food corporation of which it is a branch, was renamed as the Oblast Agency for the Regulation of the Food Market—show that in Leningrad the corporation controls approximately 10 percent of the vegetable and dairy markets. Small-scale individual production and retail sales of these commodities make higher levels of control difficult to achieve and are not actively sought by the oblast-level corporation.[25] There are no signs of collusion between the Leningrad corporation and the oblast administration. Neither the wholesalers nor the collective enterprise managers reported any efforts on the part of the oblast government to preclude the export of agricultural commodities from the oblast or to tie these measures to arrears on commodity credits or other debts to the oblast government.

The situation is different in Saratov oblast. The food corporation is an independent entity not affiliated with the federal food corporation. Its role ballooned after an assertive and interventionist governor with professional roots in Soviet agricultural management came to power in Saratov in 1996. The legal powers of the Saratov Oblast Food Corporation are vast.[26] A few of the conflicting tasks of the corporation include meeting the vague "needs of the oblast in foodstuffs," intervening in the market if food price fluctuations appear to be destabilizing or if *other* market players behave in a noncompetitive manner, facilitating agricultural producers' access to markets, giving credit to agricultural producers against their food deliveries to the oblast food fund, and conducting export-import transactions. To achieve these multiple conflicting goals, the corporation is allowed to use "*material'nie resursi oblast'*," the ill-defined "material resources of the oblast," which legally facilitate and improve access to both state and private financing. The corporation is allowed to sell and buy agricultural inputs and outputs both inside and outside the oblast. The corporation can use its revenue to increase its own capital and/or to purchase shares in other entities without making any obligatory remittances to the budget or having to make explicit reports on the use of funds. The operating expenses of the corporation are covered by the oblast budget.

The corporation is also used as a debt collection agency in the event economic and political imperatives drive the oblast government to harden the budget constraint of the enterprises to which it supplies credits. The corporation in Saratov oblast is charged with debt collection from collective agricultural producers not only for itself, but also for the oblast and federal budgets; extrabudgetary funds for gas, electricity, and fuel companies; and the equipment leasing agency.[27] In a particular year, if the oblast government decides that it is in its interest to enforce debt repayment, then grain sales are not allowed outside the oblast without clearance from the corporation. Agricultural producers transporting grain without the full set of documents confirming that debts to a list of agencies have been fully repaid are charged with theft. These trade restrictions are in violation of the constitution, which proclaims Russia to be a single economic space, but until the launching of efforts at recentralization by the Putin government in 2000, the federal government had no effective means of contesting such a violation.

The vaguely defined but expansive powers of the food corporation, and the significant year-to-year discretion it enjoys in using them, are key components of the institutional environment that I refer to as an elastic budget constraint. The uncertainty of hard-soft variations in credit and repayment regimes, combined with the continued dependence on the goodwill of the oblast government to ultimately return to a regime of soft credits, distinguishes an elastic budget constraint from both the ideologically unambiguous soft budget constraint of socialism on the one side or the market-induced, hard budget constraint of commercial financing on the other.

The variations in the nature of the constraint in Saratov oblast were found to depend on a wide range of possible factors and needs of the oblast government. In 1997, the governor of Saratov decided to participate in the national presidential elections and needed finances for the venture. The oblast government demanded that collective agricultural producers repay their commodity credit debts to the corporation. According to estimates by experts from Saratov wholesale firms, in 1997 the food corporation handled 4.8 million tons of the 6.2 million tons of grain produced in the oblast.[28] Official estimates are much smaller, on the order of 10 percent of the harvest.[29] At the same time, the oblast government openly expressed its desire that the food corporation fully monopolize grain production in the future. The document "Concepts and Program for the Development of the Agroindustrial Complex in 1997–2000" goes further, placing the desired market share for transactions carried through the corporation at 90 percent of total grain sales.[30]

The mechanism used by the oblast-level corporation in Saratov to gain revenue through price distortions includes paying lower prices for higher-quality grain. Because grain evaluation and classification are done in-house by the corporation's specialists, grain of higher quality can be classified as fodder-quality grain, thus substantially lowering its price. The task is made easier by using a skewed grain classification that allows for a large fluctuation in prices. In 1997, for example, third-class soft wheat was priced at 650 rubles per metric ton, while fifth-class soft wheat was priced at 350 rubles per ton. There was no fourth-class soft wheat![31]

Patterns of Managerial Adaptation

What relationship do differences in oblast agricultural policy have to differences in the extent and nature of post-Soviet restructuring of agricultural enterprises in each oblast? More specifically, how have the managers of the joint stock companies reacted to a de facto reintroduction of central controls in one oblast and to a more laissez-faire regime in the other? How do their managerial strategies change under the influence of market-based hardening of the budget constraint in Leningrad oblast, and post-Soviet, access-based control in Saratov oblast?

An analysis of collective enterprise–level data captures the difference in the elasticity of constraints imposed by the oblast government on the collective enterprises in Vsevolozhsk raion of Leningrad oblast and in Engels raion of Saratov oblast. Since federal policies are the same in both oblasts, the difference in the economic regime faced by enterprises reflects the oblast's modifications of these policies. To compare oblast-level modifications, I first discuss differences in managerial behavior and then present enterprise-level data aggregated by raion to show the actual effect the difference in provincial agricultural policies has on enterprise performance.

Not surprisingly, the attitudes of collective farm managers to the regional government in general and their agricultural policies in particular depend on the level of the government's involvement in the affairs of the enterprise. Whether the assessment of state involvement is positive or negative, the strength of managers' reactions depends on the intensity of these interventions. In Saratov oblast, interventions are direct and pervasive. In Leningrad oblast, the government is perceived as a peripheral rule setter but not consulted or contended with in day-to-day managerial decision making.

Differences in constraints are manifested in divergence in managerial attitudes to labor and other assets and are translated into divergence in strategic paths for enterprises. Here I present examples of the role of the government in the management of indebtedness, labor, and capital assets as perceived by collective farm managers.

Indebtedness

In Engels raion, state interventions are sometimes welcomed by enterprise management ("I approve the return of the command methods. There is no disarray, no chaos with the command methods"), often resented ("The government and the corporation have complete power over us. . . . [T]his is a hybrid of primitive communal life with capitalism." "We are in a vicious circle and they will not let us out"), but are not challenged. The managers realize that the involvement of the state will guarantee their survival ("They want to keep us in this [dependent] state. They will not let us die"). Despite these ambivalent feelings toward the oblast government role in agriculture and the commodity crediting scheme, managers admit to not having sufficient political and business savvy to avoid the temptation of re-lying on state-provided credits, even at the steep price of losing control over their output: "Those who know how to trade are financially inde-pendent and they survive." This comment was made in reference to the only profitable enterprise in Engels raion. The manager of Berezovka has outstanding entrepreneurial skills and finds new sales channels all over Rus-sia and abroad. A network of buyers and a well-managed cash flow allow this particular manager to avoid price controls imposed by the food cor-poration and built into oblast-level commodity credit, and to use the ben-efits of low-interest-rate state financing. In 1997, Berezovka was the only joint stock company in the raion to have commodity credits repaid on time and to sell the bulk of its grain outside of the oblast.

Since federal-level laws and regulations allow and promote market trans-actions, even while the oblast government continues to provide seasonal financing, an entrepreneurial enterprise manager with good initial con-ditions is capable of reaping the benefits of both systems, using regional subsidized credits in combination with national market opportunities for sales. It appears, however, that entrepreneurial savvy is not widely spread among the managers of Engels raion. Other joint stock companies did not escape the vicious circle of increasing indebtedness and dependency on oblast-level financing. (See chapter 15 by Kalugina in this volume for a dis-cussion of the different strategies of enterprise managers in dealing with the new set of economic, social, and political constraints introduced by agrarian reforms.)

The majority of the managers, however, continue to depend on com-modity credits and other soft, state-sponsored repayment arrangements. With the elastic repayment scheme, there is an unofficial hierarchy of the "softness" of debts: Enterprise managers emphasize repayment of some obligations while ignoring others. Enterprise managers in Engels raion consider arrears to the social funds (consisting of health, employment, and social security funds) and tax payments to be their least important priori-ties. In 1997, six managers in Engels enterprises admitted they had not paid on either of these items for more than two years! They justified this position on the grounds that they provide social services to their employ-ees and entire villages anyway, so paying in to the social funds would mean paying twice. "I am a head of a commune. Whether you are a farmer or a worker, you come to me. Wedding, funeral, a boy is sent off to the army—I provide finances for that."

This attitude to indebtedness contrasts strongly with the situation in Vsevolozhsk. Even though enterprises in Vsevolozhsk are much less indebted than enterprises in Engels (see financial outcomes below), the managers of the most indebted and the least profitable enterprises realize that their existence is threatened since past indebtedness disqualifies them from commercial credits. To deal with the problem, three Vsevolozhsk managers described a scheme they were working on. According to the scheme, the manager, with a core of hardworking employees, starts a new agricultural firm using the original enterprise's most productive assets and leaves the debt with the shell of the old company. These radical strategies, which are similar to those pursued in other sectors during the economic transition in Russia, indicate how binding and behavior-defining the budget constraint is in Vsevolozhsk.

Hiring and Firing

The different institutional environment in the two oblasts also reflected directly on hiring and firing decisions at the enterprise level. In Engels raion, firings were seen as socially difficult and economically nonproductive. In Vsevolozhsk raion, they were regarded as an unpleasant but unavoidable economic necessity.

In Engels raion enterprises, the managers admitted that they had too many workers since the size of livestock herds had diminished. However, they could not foresee firings, because theft by fired workers would be even more difficult to control than that of employees. Furthermore, the right to subsist off the joint stock company is perceived as an entitlement and a fired worker is expected to continue to be a cost to the enterprise without "paying" for subsistence with his or her labor. As one manager said, "I cannot fire everybody I want. They live here. . . . Say, I fire them for drinking. . . . They [other employees] will feed him [and his family] anyhow with the food from the farm." The boundaries between the enterprise and the village in Engels raion continue to be ill defined and the enterprise cannot easily cut off "free riders."

Seven Vsevolozhsk enterprise managers said that they were anticipating firings, despite a tradition against such a move. Contrary to the tradition, their attitude to departing employees was anything but paternalistic. Three of the Vsevolozhsk managers expressed resentment of the fact that departing shareholders under law carry no responsibility for repayment of the accumulated enterprise debt of which they legally were shareholders, a far cry from the relationship with the employees of Soviet collectivist agriculture.

Despite the overall decrease in the number of permanent workers, one category of employees has grown in Vsevolozhsk, but not in Engels raion

Table 11.3

Number of Employees Working in Canteens and Sales, Collective Enterprises in Vsevolozhsk and Engels Raiony, 1994–97

Vsevolozhsk				Engels			
1994	1995	1996	1997	1994	1995	1996	1997
6.3	7.7	8.3	10.3	4.75	3.6	3.9	4.0

Source: Financial statements of collective producers filed with departments of agriculture of Vsevolozhsk and Engels raiony, winter 1999.

enterprises. These are workers employed in the newly developing marketing end of the business, and are listed in the category "salespeople and canteen workers" (Table 11.3). Since the number of canteen workers did not increase over the four years of the study, sales and marketing staff accounted for the higher numbers in the category. In Engels raion, four enterprises did not have a single person designated to deal exclusively with sales, while in Vsevolozhsk all enterprises had employees who were assigned exclusively to sales departments.

The numbers presented in Table 11.3 do not include the increase in employees with higher education involved in marketing. Those employees were accounted for under the category "specialists." In Vsevolozhsk, all managers said they had hired new full-time employees to deal with sales and marketing or had redeployed existing employees into marketing. Engels raion managers claimed they were still carrying out most of the marketing themselves since the enterprise dealt mostly with the government, a traditional relationship that does not require new skills.

Capital Assets

Interviews with managers indicated that declines in capital assets in Engels raion enterprises reflect depreciation and nonreplacement rather than strategic divestment, while in the Vsevolozhsk enterprises, managers were strategically selling assets or replacing unproductive equipment.

Landholdings

Managerial attitudes regarding the reduction of landholdings differed. Prior to the adoption of Saratov oblast's Law on Land in December 1997, managers in Engels raion had no interest in selling land as a means of reducing their growing liabilities, even if such an option had legally existed.[32]

An official from the Land Committee reported that there were no sales of collective land two years after the oblast's Law on Land was enacted.[33] The land was also rarely rented to anyone other than farm employees. De facto controls over grain prices introduced by the oblast government made land a risky asset of uncertain value for sellers as well as for buyers.

Despite the lack of a federal- or oblast-level land code, enterprise managers in Vsevolozhsk raion were actively searching for ways to sell valuable land in the suburbs of St. Petersburg. This was done to diminish debt and to take companies off the *kartoteka*, a list of debtor enterprises whose bank accounts have been frozen for nonpayment. Two of the enterprises in Vsevolozhsk actually secured permission from oblast authorities to carry out such limited sales. Five of the nine Vsevolozhsk managers interviewed had sold some assets to pay debts and six were renting out unused facilities to improve cash flow.

Tractors

In both *raiony* tractor fleets have shrunk since Soviet times by approximately one quarter. In Engels raion, the depletion of tractor fleets represents amortization rather than strategic divesting. Four enterprise managers in Engels raion expressed a belief that, under the new leadership, the oblast government would supply them with new tractors or at least arrange for the use of equipment for harvesting. There was also an understanding among the managers that payment for such support is the loss of control over the harvest. One of the enterprise managers put it simply: "They better bring new tractors in; we do not own our grain anymore anyhow."

In the Engels raion, district or provincial authorities coordinate vertical interactions among enterprises. After the election of the new governor in Saratov, a Soviet-type district coordination headquarters was set up every year at harvest time. The headquarters mandated that the more efficient enterprise managers who finished harvesting must send their equipment to the laggards. The new private status of enterprises and the private nature of the assets shipped around the oblast did not seem to be part of the discussion. More importantly, the oblast-level price controls and continuing managerial involvement of the oblast administration made managers in Engels raion reluctant to show initiative and incur coordination costs to cooperate privately with other joint stock companies in the use of equipment. In Vsevolozhsk, by contrast, all managers who were interviewed claimed they had stopped counting on the state as a supplier of equipment or as a hands-on coordinator ("The state is no longer important in the production process." "We learned to rely only on ourselves"). Five managers gave examples of specific instances when their enterprises cooperated with other collective producers in pooling resources for the purchase of combines, hay compressors, and seedling-growing technologies. The district-level government acted as a mediator in finding foreign suppliers and guaranteeing credits and did not directly intervene in enterprise management.

Livestock

While making no effort to diminish their assets in crop production, enterprise managers in Engels were looking to reduce livestock holding. Between 1994 and 1997, the size of the herd in Engels was halved. The curtailment of state subsidies for fodder gave managers an incentive to decrease the size of their herds. As the food corporation was not involved in the livestock or dairy subsectors, the cost of production proved too high. In 1997, if an enterprise manager decided to reduce an unproductive herd (i.e., slaughtering animals), he was likely to receive a radiogram from the oblast administration forbidding him from continuing with this cost-saving strategy. (Copies of such radiograms were shown to the interviewer during the field study in summer 1997.) Furthermore, the enterprise managers were directed to sell milk to the formerly state-owned, parastatal dairy processors at below market prices. This de facto price control mechanism prevented managers from increasing the profitability of dairy operations, and little investment was made in herd improvement. Some managers resorted to passive resistance against state control; one veterinarian admitted to writing false reports on livestock disease to justify the slaughter of a part of an unproductive herd. These post-Soviet practices of responding to excessive control by illegal evasion of government demands allows for survival, but are not conducive to the pursuit of long-term restructuring strategies.

In Vsevolozhsk enterprises, the size of the herd stabilized in 1996, as managers attempted to raise the value of their herds and transform them into profitable assets. Five managers said they were purchasing higher-yield breeds and designing barter schemes in cooperation with other enterprises to procure and share high-breeding heifers. There are also instances of cooperation with successful individual farmers in cattle breeding. One reason for this proactive stance mentioned by the collective enterprise managers is lack of managerial control by the provincial government over sales channels or livestock product prices. None of the collective farm managers reported any pressure from the local government to sell their products to former parastatal processors.

Attitude Toward Private Investment

In Vsevolozhsk enterprises, the demand for new sources of financing is demonstrated in the managers' attitude toward third-party investments. Seven out of nine managers interviewed were searching for outside investors, while two actually had ongoing projects with domestic and foreign investors. In Engels raion enterprises, only 2 out of 12 managers said they would welcome outside investment. One was the head of the only profitable enterprise in the raion while the other was a former independent farmer who was explicitly invited by the oblast government to take over a badly mismanaged farm. One Engels raion manager voiced his concern succinctly: "We have to try to become profitable by ourselves. An investor will come in and fire everyone." Engels raion managers realize how much inefficiency is built into the enterprises they manage and fear market constraints and competition.

In Engels raion, enterprise managers felt more constrained and controlled by the state, first by the de facto confiscation of grain, and second by local price controls on grain and milk. There was little effort to invest in new facilities beyond small processing ventures to generate untaxed cash. Nor was there an effort to pool resources and cooperate with other enterprises in larger investment projects as was the case in Vsevolozhsk. In Engels raion, no visible effort was made to sell assets to generate cash. The strategy chosen by managers under these circumstances was to continue to rely on the state to provide equipment necessary for survival and not to repay the debt to the state as long as the oblast government does not extract it forcefully by forbidding the enterprise to sell grain outside of the oblast.

Looking at these examples of asset management it is possible to discern the distinctive effects of oblast policies on the management decisions of collective agricultural producers. In the less interventionist oblast, collective agricultural enterprise managers are making an effort to decrease holdings of unproductive loss-generating assets and are searching for creative ways to finance the acquisition of more productive assets. In the more interventionist oblast, the realization that governmental discretion may change the rules of the game stunts the search for creative use of existing assets and for channels to acquire more productive assets. These divergent attitudes to asset use and accumulation add to divergence of paths among enterprises exposed to different economic environments promoted by different regional governments.

Financial Outcomes:
The Impact of Different Regimes of Budgetary Constraints

How do these differing managerial orientations show up in terms of the financial outcomes of collective farms? This section examines the balance sheets and income statements of collective agricultural enterprises in the two raiony to assess whether differences in managerial attitudes and behavior translate into demonstrable and regular differences in financial outcomes.

Few agricultural enterprises in either raion included in the study are capable of financing their own operations. Between 1994 and 1997, the ratio of sales to profits fell for all 22 enterprises in the sample. In 1994, out of 9 mixed-product, collective agricultural producers in Vsevolozhsk, only 1 was generating losses.[34] The number of loss-making enterprises grew to 6 in 1997. Most joint stock companies in Engels raion were already unprofitable in 1994, as 9 out of 12 generated losses. In 1997, a bumper crop year, only 1 enterprise showed profits, despite a steep increase in grain production.[35] On average, the proportion of unprofitable enterprises in Vsevolozhsk was 16 percentage points lower than the national average of 82 percent (Table 11.4), while Engels raion enterprises performed approximately 10 percent worse than the national average.

The relative decline in profitability—the ratio of profits to sales—in the two districts is different as well. Table 11.5 shows that in Vsevolozhsk, the average profitability for the district turned negative for the first time in 1996 and continued negative in 1997. In Engels raion, the average profitability of the enterprises was extremely negative already in 1994 (−39 percent) and deteriorated further in 1996, with sales covering only half the

Table 11.4

Profitability of Collective Enterprises in Vsevolozhsk and Engels Raiony, 1994 and 1997

	Vsevolozhsk		Engels	
	1994	1997	1994	1997
Number of enterprises	9[a]	10	12	12
Profitable/unprofitable enterprises	1/8	4/6	3/9	1/6
Enterprises with zero profits				5

[a] One enterprise was not under the jurisdiction of the Department of Agriculture in 1994–95. It started filing reports with the department in 1997.
Source: Financial statements of collective enterprises filed with the departments of agriculture of Vsevolozhsk and Engels raiony, winter 1999.

Table 11.5

Average Profit Margins of Collective Enterprises in Vsevolozhsk and Engels Raiony, 1994–97

	1994	1995	1996	1997
Vsevolozhsk	0.9	0.06	−0.27	−0.27
n =	9	9	10	10
Engels	−0.39	−0.52	−1.94	−0.44
n =	12	12	12	12

Source: Financial statements of collective enterprises filed with the departments of agriculture of Vsevolozhsk and Engels raiony, winter 1999.

costs of production. In 1997, however, many Engels raion enterprises showed an improvement in profit margins, the result, first, of a bumper grain crop and, second, of steeply increased subsidization of agriculture by the provincial government.

The changes in profitability shown in Table 11.5 were not driven by changes in sales, except for 1997 in Engels raion. Figure 11.2 presents an index of sales from 1994 to 1997 adjusted by the consumer price index.

While sales in Engels raion increased only in 1997, the cost of production grew consistently between 1994 and 1997. Figure 11.3 shows the difference in the rate of increase in variable costs between the two districts adjusted by the consumer price index. The variable costs used in these calculations are the sum of fuel, fodder, seed, fertilizer, gas, and electricity.[36]

Figure 11.2

Real Sales Index, Collective Agricultural Enterprise Products, Vsevolozhsk and Engels Raiony, 1994–97

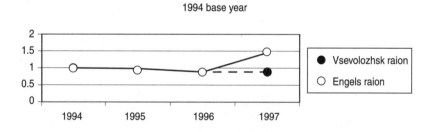

Source: Financial statements of collective enterprise producers filed with departments of agriculture of Vsevolozhsk and Engels raiony, winter 1999.

Figure 11.3

Real Variable Cost Index of Agricultural Inputs, Vsevolozhsk and Engels Raiony, 1994–97

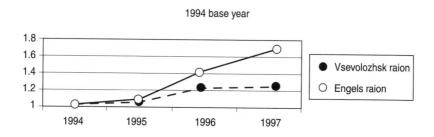

Source: Financial statements of collective enterprise producers filed with departments of agriculture of Vsevolozhsk and Engels raiony, winter 1999.

Ratios of expenditures to sales in Table 11.6 demonstrate that, on average, the enterprises in Engels raion were not capable of covering their increasing variable costs with revenue. Even in the bumper crop year of 1997, with a 45-percent increase in sales, these enterprises did not generate sufficient revenue to cover the sum of major variable costs incurred by a collective enterprise (first line in Table 11.6). If we include total expenditures of the enterprises in the calculation, the expenditures of the joint stock companies in Engels raion exceeded sales by a factor of two to three (second line in Table 11.6).

Table 11.6

Ratio of Cost of Production to Sales, Collective Enterprises in Vsevolozhsk and Engels Raiony, 1994–97

	Vsevolozhsk				Engels			
Expenditures/Sales	1994	1995	1996	1997	1994	1995	1996	1997
Variable costs (fuel, fertilizer, seed, fodder, gas, electricity)/sales	0.51	0.55	0.66	0.65	0.93	1.20	1.69	1.01
Total costs/sales	0.98	1.01	1.36	1.31	2.07	2.21	3.29	2.56

Source: Financial statements of collective enterprise producers filed with departments of agriculture of Vsevolozhsk and Engels raiony, winter 1999.

Table 11.7

Current Liabilities to Sales by Type of Liability, Collective Enterprises in Vsevolozhsk and Engels Raiony, 1994–97

	Vsevolozhsk				Engels			
	1994	1995	1996	1997	1994	1995	1996	1997
Current liabilities/sales	0.35	0.45	0.95	1.09	1.09	1.17	3.59	2.47
Short-term nonbank credits	0.15	0.13	0.24	0.12	0.09	0.36	1.33	0.54
Short-term bank credits	0.05	0.03	0.03	0.01	0.43	0.02	0.06	0.05
Accounts payable	0.22	0.35	0.78	0.97	0.57	0.79	2.20	1.91

Source: Financial statements of collective enterprise producers filed with departments of agriculture of Vsevolozhsk and Engels raiony, winter 1999.

In Vsevolozhsk, these indicators look relatively much healthier. Enterprises use half of their sales to cover their variable costs, with this ratio decreasing to 1.3 if all expenditures are taken into account. These numbers are nowhere near sustainability in Engels raion and indicate a need for restructuring in Vsevolozhsk. The continuous operation of enterprises in Engels raion with such high expenditure-to-sale ratios can be explained only if some of the expenditure is financed externally and/or if a large portion of the financing does not have to be repaid.

Current Assets, Current Liabilities, and Who Ultimately Pays

Both sides of the balance sheet in Russian agricultural reporting are fairly reliable sources of information about enterprises: Since liabilities to the state (the budget and the social funds) are already known to the state, enterprises have no incentive to distort them. The same logic (pointed out by collective farm accountants) applies to the joint stock company's liabilities to suppliers: Distorting the accounts payable records would mean complex coordination with suppliers. Relative reliability of some sections of the balance sheet prompted a more detailed analysis of these sources.

Table 11.7 shows that the current liabilities accumulated by the joint stock companies in both raiony were large and growing, but in Engels raion they were much higher. The ratio of current liabilities to sales in Engels raion enterprises on average was almost three times higher than in the Vsevolozhsk enterprises. In Vsevolozhsk, the ratio rose from one-third of sales to 100 percent of sales between 1994 and 1997, while in Engels raion, the ratio was already above unity in 1994, increased to 3.59 in 1996, and then fell by one point in 1997.

Up to 1997, the level as well as the rate of increase of indebtedness was higher in Engels raion than in Vsevolozhsk. A sharp decrease in liabilities to banks in 1994 (short-term bank credits dropped from 0.43 to 0.02 between 1994 and 1995) in Engels raion was the result of a write-off of centralized credits by the federal government, and is not relevant to this discussion. The decline in indebtedness in Engels in 1997 was driven by two factors. The first was the effect of the abovementioned bumper grain crop and increased sales. The second was the policy of forcing repayment of some of the credits granted by the oblast.

Apart from the difference in the overall level of indebtedness, the most distinct difference in the shares of liabilities to sales by creditor type in the two districts is the year-to-year rate of change in nonbank credits. Short-term nonbank credits for Vsevolozhsk fluctuated between 12 percent and 24 percent of sales, while in Engels, current liabilities increased to 3.59 times sales in 1996 and then decreased to 2.47 times sales in 1997. Part of the decrease in liabilities was driven by the good grain harvest, but it also reflects priorities in debt repayment. Upon closer analysis of the flow of liabilities in Engels in 1997, short-term nonbank credits was the only category that appeared with a negative sign, meaning an actual repayment of credit. In 1997, collective enterprises in Vsevolozhsk chose to reduce their liabilities to workers and their indebtedness to the social funds as a top priority, while Engels enterprises compensated for their repayment of nonbank credits by accumulating a larger debt to the social funds.

What does the 1996 increase in short-term nonbank credit in Engels raion actually mean? Why was it followed by a sharp decrease in short-term nonbank liabilities in 1997? The available data do not provide a more detailed breakdown of nonbank credits, but, according to the accountants of the joint stock companies, the greatest share by far of the nonbank credits were commodity credits. The steep increase in nonbank credits among Engels enterprises coincided with the election of the new governor in 1996 and with the shift in the oblast-level agricultural policy back to hands-on participation. Credit repayment is an expected effect of the enforced repayment campaign conducted by the Saratov oblast government described in the previous section.

The sporadically enforced repayment combined with increased state financing is the manifestation of an elastic budget constraint in action. In period 1, the state credits input supplies, with the enterprise accumulating debt to the creditor-state. In period 2, guided by political and economic imperatives exogenous to agriculture, the government may choose to enforce the repayment of input credits. This enforcement, however, does not signal a change in paradigm, since the government does not stop supplying inputs to producers. Because the budget constraint does not change, the ratio of costs to sales does not decrease (see Figure 11.3), and the repayment of credits to the state is compensated by the nonpayment to other creditors and even by nonpayment of other liabilities to the state.

This comparative study of changes in expenditure patterns illustrates the extent to which post-reform behavior of enterprises is affected by oblast policies. Local governments can either choose to be involved in price manipulation and production decisions of collective enterprises or to follow the noninterventionist pattern foreseen in federal reforms. The reaction of enterprise managers in both cases is rational. Aware that they are operating in the context of continuous state control, managers in regions with a more interventionist agricultural policy seek to avoid restructuring that would allow them to cut variable costs but would imply painful short-term decisions. They also react to the elasticity of state financing by refraining from costly investments that could be feasible if the ability to sell the output to the highest bidder were ensured.

In a more laissez-faire environment, the diminished financial and managerial involvement of the oblast government forces managers to make tough decisions about cost cutting and to engage in deeper restructuring. The difficult decisions about cost cutting in capital assets and indebtedness have been followed by admittedly the most difficult decision of all, the decision that affects the social contract with employees: hiring, firing, and changes in compensation practices. There were signs in Vsevolozhsk that the managers were starting to make tough decisions to let redundant workers go. In Engels raion, meanwhile, labor relations were still based on Soviet-type paternalistic dependence between employees and managers, and the preservation of the social safety net for all employees regardless of their productivity.

Unfortunately, accounting reports cannot be credibly used for an assessment of a collective enterprise's capital assets. Joint stock companies' assets were indexed to inflation according to a federally approved formula. All interviewed accountants claim that indexation severely distorted the accounting value of fixed assets, which makes it difficult to supplement the qualitative data presented above with quantitative analysis.

Conclusions

This analysis has shown a connection between oblast-level agricultural policies and patterns of restructuring adopted by enterprises. Two basic patterns of post-Soviet transformation of the agricultural sector at the regional level were identified. In the more interventionist Saratov oblast, the government succeeded in reconstituting a Soviet-style model of direct involvement in resource distribution. Collective agricultural producers are included in the redistribution scheme, which provides a host of social, financial, and political benefits to the oblast government, a safety net for collective farm employees/shareholders, and short-term survival of collective farms in their pre-reform configuration. The costs of this model are lost budgetary revenues and delayed restructuring of Saratov agriculture.

The interventionist system is sustained through a mechanism of commodity crediting. Under this distribution scheme, collective agricultural enterprises continue to receive financing regardless of their profitability or viability. In return they continue to provide a number of social services to their employees, thus allowing the regional government to delay urgently needed restructuring of the provision of these services in rural areas as well as providing a number of other benefits to the oblast government. Enterprise managers, fearing high costs of restructuring and displacement by a managerial team more skilled in market-based transactions, accepts the rules of the game despite legal uncertainties of direct state financing in post-Soviet times. Therefore, when the local government decides to use its right to enforce credit repayment by now privately owned joint stock companies, the managers see this situation as transient and do not fundamentally change their behavior.

These intermittently soft and hard budget constraints, based on the expectation that the episodes of credit repayment enforcement will be followed by a weakened repayment constraint despite the lack of a clearly defined legal or ideological obligation of a provincial government to sustain such an arrangement, has been called an elastic budget constraint. An elastic budget constraint refers to the situation just described, in which enterprise managers expect that commodity credits will be soft in the long run and thus adopt muddle-through restructuring strategies. It also allows the provincial government to use the same institutional lever to pursue both political and economic needs, deciding at the beginning of each season which imperative is dominant and hardening or softening the repayment constraint on the enterprises. The imperative determines the repayment constraint, not borrowers' financial or economic viability.

Agricultural policies in the Leningrad oblast were found to be less interventionist. The government released direct control of agricultural production and did not invest in the re-creation of a socialist-type coordination of agriculture in a region where agriculture constituted a smaller share of GDP and where a smaller share of the rural population was involved in agriculture. Enterprise managers, in turn, have responded to the perceived hardening of the budget constraint with radical restructuring strategies, including more drastic and unpopular cost-cutting measures, a search for synergetic cooperation with other agricultural producers, and a more concerted search for sales outlets.

Together with differences in the importance of agriculture in the oblast economy and employment structure, the study noted other characteristics of regions that could be important determinants of the level of state interventionism in regional agriculture. One is the nature of agricultural commodities produced in the oblast's territory. In Leningrad oblast, meat, dairy, and vegetables are the dominant commodities. The first two require a continuous rather than intermittent supply of inputs, as is the case with grain produced in Saratov. Further, vegetables are easily sold as retail goods, whereas grain is sold to wholesalers, and is more amenable to centralized distribution. Therefore, one can hypothesize that the re-creation of resource redistribution at the subnational level along the lines of a Soviet redistribution scheme, where economic and political benefits are not separated, is more easily achieved in situations where complexity of inputs is low, the need for coordination is discrete rather than continuous, and where primary products are naturally sold wholesale rather than retail.

Variables identified in this chapter determine the propensity of a subnational government to accept national-level policy changes and of enterprises to reform. These variables need to be taken into account when national-level agricultural reforms and their implementation are designed. This study allows us to conclude that the fastest and more successful reformers may not be the oblasts that are better endowed for agricultural production, but the ones that create a more level playing field for different types of agricultural producers. Between 1997 and 1999, the number of independent farmers in Saratov oblast actually decreased, while in Leningrad oblast, which has a much poorer agricultural endowment, the number of independent farmers has been consistently growing.[37]

To have a chance to succeed, any national policy and external assistance to the development of new agricultural institutions in Russia must take these divergent incentives and patterns of restructuring into account. It is also important to undertake a broader, nationally representative study to assess if the observed patterns show regularity at the national level.

Notes

1. Views expressed in this paper are mine and do not reflect the positions of the World Bank, its executive board of directors, or any of the countries it represents. Funding from the Harvard Institute of International Development and from the Research Group of the World

Bank are gratefully acknowledged. I thank Zvi Lerman and Stephen Wegren for detailed and very helpful comments on earlier drafts of this chapter. Lessons learned from Stephen Collier in the course of the work on this chapter go beyond direct benefit to the final product.

2. The terms "collective producers," "collective farms," and "collective enterprises" are used interchangeably and denote large-scale, post-Soviet agricultural producers. The vast majority of Soviet collective producers were transformed into joint stock companies, and the term legally describes 21 out of 22 collective enterprises in the sample.

3. For discussion of the efficiency of collective farms, see David J. Sedik, Michael Trueblood, and Carlos Arnade, "Corporate Farm Performance in Russia 1991–1995: An Efficiency Analysis," *Journal of Comparative Economics* 27 (1999): 514–33.

4. Douglas Galbi, *The Significance of Credits and Subsidies in Russian Agricultural Reform*, World Bank Policy Research Working Paper (Washington, DC: World Bank, 1995); Y. Gaidar et al., eds., *Ekonomika perechodnogo perioda* (Moscow: Institute of Economy in Transition, 1998).

5. On state ownership of agricultural land, see Csaki Csaba and John Nash, *The Agrarian Economies of Central and Eastern Europe and the Commonwealth of Independent States*, World Bank Discussion Paper No. 387 (Washington, DC: World Bank, 1997), 104. On the share of state-owned agricultural enterprises, see *Sel'skoe khoz'aistvo v Rossii*, official ed. (Moscow: Goskomstat, 1998), 81.

6. Daniel Berkowitz, David N. De Jong, and Steven Husted, "Quantifying Price Liberalization in Russia," *Journal of Comparative Economics* 26 (1998): 735–60.

7. Presidential Decree, "On Immediate Measures for the Implementation of Land Reform in the RSFSR" (Moscow, 27 December 1991); Resolution of the Government of the Russian Federation No. 86, "On the Procedure for Reorganization of State and Collective Farms" (Moscow, 29 December 1991); Resolution of the Government of the Russian Federation No. 708, "On the Procedure for Privatization and Reorganization of Enterprises and Organizations of the Agro-Industrial Complex" (Moscow, 4 September 1992); Presidential Decree No. 1767, "On Regulations of Land Relations and Development of Agrarian Reform" (Moscow, 27 October 1993).

8. For more detail on the legal framework of the reform process, see Karen Brooks and Zvi Lerman, *Land Reform and Farm Restructuring in Russia*, World Bank Discussion Paper No. 233 (Washington, DC: World Bank, 1994); and Karen Brooks et al., *Agricultural Reform in Russia: A View from the Farm Level*, World Bank Discussion Paper No. 327 (Washington, DC: World Bank, 1996).

9. Janos Kornai, *Economics of Shortage* (Amsterdam: North-Holland, 1980); Janos Kornai, *The Socialist System: The Political Economy of Communism* (Princeton, NJ: Princeton University Press, 1992).

10. For a more detailed discussion of commodity crediting, see Maria Amelina, "False Transformations: From Stalin's Peasants to Yeltsin's Collective Farmers" (Ph.D. diss., Fletcher School of Law and Diplomacy, Tufts University Medford, MA, 2000).

11. Resolution of the Russian Government No. 1121 (Moscow, 3 October 1994, amended 3 December 1994 and 26 January 1995); Resolution of the Russian Government No. 1224, "On the Creation of the State Enterprise called 'The Federal Agency for the Regulation of the Food Market' Subordinate to the Ministry of Agriculture of Russia" (Moscow, 26 September 1997).

12. For details on the performance of federal and regional state crediting, see Eugenia Serova, "Developments in the Agricultural Sector," in *Russian Economy: Trends and Perspectives, Monthly Reports, 1996–1999* (Moscow: Institute for the Economy in Transition, 1999). Federal commodity crediting was reintroduced in 1999, a time frame that is outside of the scope of this study.

13. The concept of path dependency is used here in the same sense it was used by Paul David, when he traced the standardization of a suboptimal keyboard to a sequence of historic events and decentralized decisions that determined the inefficient outcome: "A *path-dependent*

sequence of economic changes is one in which important influences upon the eventual outcome can be exerted by temporally remote events, including happenings dominated by
chance elements rather than systemic forces. In such circumstances 'historical accidents' can
neither be ignored, nor neatly quarantined for the purpose of economic analysis; the dynamic
process itself takes on an *essentially historical* character." David, "Clio and the Economics of
QWERTY," *American Economic Review* 75, no. 2 (1985): 332–37. I thank Karla Hoff for
this reference.

14. For a detailed discussion of the mechanisms used by the collective farms to subsidize
individual production of their employees, see Maria Amelina, "Why Do Russian Peasants
Remain in Collective Farms? A Household Perspective on Agricultural Restructuring," *Post-
Soviet Geography and Economics* 41 (October–November 2000), 483–511.

15. Oliver Blanchard and Michael Kremer, "Disorganization," *Quarterly Journal of Economics* 112, no. 4 (1997): 1091–126.

16. At the administrative level, the qualitative data include a series of structured interviews
with provincial and district-level officials involved in designing and implementing agricultural
policies. Among those interviewed were executives in charge of the food corporation in Engels raion, and the head of the oblast-level food corporation in Leningrad oblast. Additional
interviews were held with the heads of raion administration, accountants, and managers in
raion departments of agriculture, and directors of raion land committees. These interviews
were complemented by data on the legal, political, and institutional infrastructure at the
oblast level as it evolved between 1992 and 1998. Oblast-level quantitative data cover the
same time span (1992–98) and include agricultural production indicators and data on budgetary and extrabudgetary financing of agriculture.

The enterprise-level subset of data includes financial and production data for all the mixed
(crop and dairy) joint stock companies located in the Vsevolozhsk and Engels raions. A total
of 22 collective enterprises were included in the survey for this study: 10 in Vsevolozhsk raion
and 12 in Engels raion. The departments of agriculture of each raion provided production
and financial data. The data cover the 1994–97 fiscal years. Quantitative data were supplemented by open-ended structured interviews with the enterprise managers. In two cases
where the manager was not available for the interview, a deputy manager and a chief accountant were interviewed instead.

Additional information was collected through structured interviews with other actors involved in agricultural trade and financing, such as grain wholesalers and banks with a history
of lending to agricultural producers (SBS-Agro in Vsevolozhsk raion and Pokrovskii bank in
Engels raion). Experts from the oblast administration were asked to provide legal materials
and comments regarding oblast-level agricultural policymaking.

17. For more detail on the geographical characteristics of agricultural patterns in Russia,
see chapter 3 by Grigory Ioffe and Tatyana Nefedova in this volume and their book, *Continuity and Change in Rural Russia* (Boulder, CO: Westview Press, 1997).

18. Materials prepared for the meeting of the administration of Saratov oblast, October
1998, 55–59; *Sel'skoe khoziaistvo v Leningradskoi Oblasti* (St. Petersburg: Peterburggoskomstat, 1997), 8; *Sel'skoe khoziaistvov Rossii* (Moscow: Goskomstat, 1998).

19. *Sel'skoe khoziaistvov Leningradskoi Oblasti* (St. Petersburg: Peterburggoskomstat,
1997), 99; *Koncepcii razvitija agropromishlennogo kompleksa v Saratovskoi Oblasti na 1997–
2000 gg.* (Saratov, 1998).

20. See Amelina, "False Transformations."

21. Budget Committee of the oblast Duma, Saratov, summer 1999; database of Saratov
oblast Ministry of Economy, Investment Policy, and International Relations, Saratov, summer
1999.

22. *Vestnik pravitel'stva oblasti*, no. 23 (St. Petersburg: Peterburggoskomstat, Department
of Budgets, 29 June 1996), no. 36 (30 September 1997), and no. 18 (20 June 1998).

23. For more detail on fiscal contraction at the subnational level, see Lev Freinkman, Daniel Treisman, and Stepan Titov, *Sub-national Budgeting in Russia: Preempting a Potential Crisis*, World Bank Technical Paper No. 452 (Washington, DC: World Bank, 1999).

24. Resolution of the Governor of Saratov Oblast (Saratov, 11 November 1997); Resolution No. 502-p of the Mayor of St. Petersburg, "On St. Petersburg Food Corporation" (St. Petersburg, 19 May 1995); Order of the Federal Food Corporation No. 518, "On the Creation of Leningrad Oblast Affiliate of the Food Corporation" (Moscow, 26 October 1996).

25. Interview with Yuri Priochod'ko, chairman of the Oblast Agency for the Regulation of the Food Market, St. Petersburg, summer 1999.

26. Resolution of the Governor of Saratov Oblast (11 November 1997).

27. Decree No. 587 of the Government of the Saratov Oblast (Saratov, 23 July 1997).

28. Interviews with Saratov wholesalers, Saratov, winter 1999.

29. Alexei Kalamin, "Agricultural Policies in the Saratov Oblast, 1991–1999," report prepared for the World Bank, Saratov, 1999.

30. Government of Saratov Oblast, "Concepts and Program for the Development of the Agroindustrial Complex in 1997–2000" (Saratov, 1998), 28.

31. Decree No. 464-p of the Governor of Saratov Oblast, "On the Sales of the 1997 Grain Harvest" (Saratov, April 1998).

32. "Law on Land of Saratov Oblast" (Saratov, 11 December 1997).

33. Interview with Mr. Ovs'annikov, deputy head of the Engels Land Committee, Saratov, 1999.

34. For Engels raion, the 1997 balance sheet data were incomplete; thus, 1996 data were used instead.

35. The number of joint stock companies in the Vsevolozhsk raion in 1994 was one less than in 1997 because one enterprise that was reporting to another ministry in 1994 was transferred into the jurisdiction of the raion Department of Agriculture in 1995.

36. Inputs used to approximate variable costs exclude labor costs for two reasons. First, the permanent nature of labor arrangements in the joint stock companies puts labor costs in the category of fixed rather than variable costs. Second, the complicated system of payments makes balance-sheet information a poor approximation of true labor costs.

37. For data on the number of individual farmers in Leningrad oblast, see *Sel'skoe khoziaistvo Leningradskoi Oblasti* (St. Petersburg: Peterburggoskomstat, 1997), 30. For the number of individual farmers in Saratov oblast, see *Oblasti v cifrach i faktach, sbornik oblgoskomstata ogranichennogo pol'zovanija* (Saratov: Oblgoskomstat, 1995), 5.

12

Reorganization and Its Discontents: A Case Study in Voronezh Oblast

JESSICA ALLINA-PISANO[1]

Introduction

While agrarian reforms of the early 1990s produced a slight if perceptible shift toward market-oriented production in the Russian countryside, they simultaneously generated a source of opposition to those changes. Reform initiatives emphasized privatization of production factors and the independence of individual people and enterprises in a context of presumed equilibrium. These initiatives, amid a shifting terrain of political and economic relations, produced outcomes that conflicted with many of the needs of producers and managers alike. Reform resulted in deepening inequalities in the countryside, ossifying social hierarchies while rending the networks of interdependence that were sources of support, incentive, and protection. Producers did not actively resist reform; rather, they went about the business of survival. Their responses to reorganization, and their strategies for persisting in their livelihoods, illuminate some of the flaws in reform policy. Through a case study of the experience of a single farm in the center of the largest of southwestern Russia's central black-earth regions, this chapter explores the intentions, process, and results of the reorganization of collective farms.

Reorganization of collectivized agriculture was meant to accomplish three fundamental, related tasks: improve production efficiency, establish a rural class of independent property owners, and render production and distribution processes transparent to the state and outside investors. In this chapter, I suggest that in attempting to transfer ownership of the means of production to private citizens rather than ensuring fair access to those means, and in undertaking to improve the efficiency of individual enterprises instead of production and distribution networks, reorganization undermined its own aims and ultimately helped to create an environment hostile to further reform.

In agriculture as in other sectors of the Russian economy, the transfer of resources away from state entities and into the hands of individual citizens—in this case members of agricultural collectives—was to be the foundation of a market-based economy. The reorganization of collective and state farms dictated that land and other assets were to be divided among their members. In theory if not in practice, members could choose either to exit the collective with their individual shares or to pool their resources as joint stock companies, limited liability partnerships, or privately held agricultural producers' cooperatives. If before reorganization farm property belonged at once to no one and everyone, after reorganization every hectare of cultivated land and every ruble of enterprise assets would have an owner.

Implementation of reorganization was left to local officials: District-level bureaucrats and *kolkhoz* chairmen generally stood to lose by a successful transfer of the state resources they controlled to individual farm members. As noted in chapter 7 by Macey, unlike other major efforts at land reform earlier in the century, in particular the Stolypin-era reforms and collectivization, Moscow did not dispatch cadres to the countryside to oversee and secure the implementation of reorganization.[2] While reorganization was certainly a reform issued "from above," its enactment depended to an almost unprecedented extent on the cooperation of members of the local rural elite.

The view that reorganization of individual enterprises could transform Russian agriculture overlooked two important features of collectively organized rural life. First, in an economy plagued by chronic shortage of machinery and inputs, access to the means of production was and continues to be of greater importance than outright ownership.[3] Reorganization as privatization placed concerns about use at the margins, and in doing so defeated its own aims. Second, the inefficiency of collective farms proceeded at least in part from the extent to which each enterprise was embedded in a poorly functioning, broad network of production, processing, and distribution relationships without which it could not survive.[4]

Reorganization targeted the individual enterprise while production networks received comparatively little attention. Legislative and administrative changes dissolved ties among enterprises together with the command system that had established those relationships, with no obvious replacement at hand. The logic of reform suggested that production and distribution ties, like markets themselves, would spring up like Minervas from emptied fields.[5]

Rather than attend to the myriad underlying difficulties in relationships within and among Russian agricultural and processing enterprises—information asymmetries, high transaction costs, incomplete markets, adverse selection, and environments of pervasive risk and moral hazard—reorganization focused on the declaration of private ownership of the means of production as a vehicle for achieving its ends.[6] However, reorganization policy did not specify a mechanism for establishing a new property regime in the face of these problems and amid rapid political, social, and economic change.[7] Instead it prescribed a thin set of institutions that were expected both to accomplish and to accommodate profound transformation. Furthermore, reorganization's emphasis on efficiency as an end in itself, at the expense of a commitment to substantive distributive concerns, ensured that inequitable distribution of production factors before reorganization was unlikely to be resolved by reorganization.[8]

A growing body of literature on property rights in the context of agrarian change in post-socialist countries suggests that under conditions similar to those in rural Russia, ownership categories neither help us to understand the local realities of property relations nor necessarily determine particular economic outcomes. Scholarship examining enterprise reform in the Chinese countryside and Katherine Verdery's work on "fuzzy" property rights in reorganized Transylvanian agricultural collectives illustrate the complex and intertwined political, social, and economic relationships that govern the use and disposition of material factors in post-socialist agricultural production.[9] In these contexts, power vested in local social and political structures can be more significant than legal ownership as such in the distribution of goods. In this chapter, I emphasize that relationships among persons in relation to things are more important both to the people involved and for productivity than the reform of property relations under reorganization, which emphasized relationships between persons and things.

Much of the scholarly work on the reorganization of Russian collective farms focuses either on the creation of small-scale private farms (*fermerskie khoziaistva*) on the territory of reorganized collectives or on the essentially unchanged institutional aspects of former collective and state farms.[10] Rural transformations involving individual farmers have received much attention; otherwise change is presumed not to have occurred at all. I show how change precipitated by and accompanying reorganization neither created a new class of rural owners nor maintained the status quo, but rather deepened existing inequalities by further concentrating power in the hands of local elites.

Both the policy and scholarly literatures on the subject of privatization and economic reform in post-Soviet countries take for granted that the proper functioning of market mechanisms and the development of a market-based economy depend on private ownership of the means of production and the separation of individual enterprises from production and distribution networks established by the state.[11] The orthodoxy that individual, independent, private ownership is a necessary or even sufficient condition for efficient production has gone largely unchallenged in the study of former Soviet states. This chapter, based on the experience of a former collective farm in Voronezh oblast and drawing on the insights of scholars working in other post-socialist contexts, presents a rather different picture. Tracing the mechanisms by which the aims of reorganization manifested themselves in outcomes directly contradictory of its goals, I will show that a single-minded emphasis on individuals and ownership over networks and use rights undermined efficiency, independence, and transparency.

Research Methodology and Geographic and Economic Context

This chapter is part of a larger study that included over two years of field research in southwestern Russia and eastern Ukraine. I gathered much of the material presented in this chapter in August and September of 1998, while I lived on the territory of a collective in Voronezh oblast. The experience of that collective, which for the purposes of this chapter I shall call "Chayanovskoe," is at the heart of this chapter.

I have chosen to tell the story of reorganization on a particular collective because some of the important nuances of the process easily might be lost in a meta-narrative encompassing the experience of multiple enterprises. While this chapter represents a single case study, my observations and conclusions are informed by extensive work in the region and exposure to a number of collective agricultural enterprises with varied management strategies and degrees of material success.[12]

Former collective farm Chayanovskoe is an appropriate subject for this study not because it is in some way unusual, but rather because it is in many respects typical. In addition to its roughly median levels of production for both its district and for the Voronezh region as a whole, its social hierarchies and economic conditions are representative of those that informed attempts to transform property relations throughout the country.[13]

Evidence presented here draws on ethnographic and statistical material gathered in the course of on-site fieldwork on the collective and in *raion* center administrative offices; national and local press reports, primarily interviews published in the newspaper of the district in which the collective is located; and published and unpublished statistical data obtained from the regional offices of Goskomstat.

During my stay on Chayanovskoe, most of my conversations with raion and farm administrators were formal interviews. Therefore, their comments appear in the text as direct quotations. Conversations with all other members of the collective took place in the course of informal meetings, with both parties asking questions. I spoke with approximately 50 of the 350 people living on the collective: shareholders and hired employees; administrators and rank-and-file workers; recent arrivals and lifelong residents; summertime and permanent residents; pensioners and schoolchildren; and teachers, childcare workers, and medical personnel. While all informants were aware that many of my questions were asked in connection with my research, there was rarely an explicit understanding that our conversation constituted a personal interview. Therefore, I report the impressions I formed from these encounters without reference to specific individuals, identifying only the general social group of informants where applicable.

What follows is a brief description of Chayanovskoe with emphasis on its geographic location and its production, distribution, and social infrastructure. I hope that this context helps the reader judge for herself the character of the political processes that took place on the enterprise as well as the usefulness of my conclusions beyond the narrow geographical scope of this paper.

"Chayanovskoe"[14]

The land on which this former kolkhoz sits lies several hundred kilometers south of the provincial city of Voronezh. The area was first settled in 1615, when fugitive serfs from the regions of Kostroma and Tambov sought shelter in the area's backwoods along the Don. Fertile soil and abundant wildlife, combined with the relative security of this spot surrounded by hills, forest, and water made the location attractive for these families. Around 1700, a village formally was established on the site when Tsar Peter I exiled ten families to the region for their insurgent activity during the Turkish war. The new arrivals settled to the east of the original settlement, on the spot where the farm administration buildings now stand. Despite frequent intermarriage, over the next two centuries the village developed as two separate societies. The old and new settlers (*starozhily* and *novozhily*) each had their own elders (*starosta*) and spoken dialect. The collectivization drives of the 1930s established two farms on the land around the village. The families of the original settlers became members of a collective farm named after the Twentieth Party Congress. Families of later settlers were members of a collective farm named after Lenin. Eventually, the two collective farms joined as one kolkhoz named Chayanovskoe.[15]

Unlike many collective agricultural enterprises that are located between villages or in the midst of a number of settlement points, the farm draws its membership from a single village. Its population has fluctuated in past years but hovers at about 350 inhabitants. During 1992, the year in which reorganization took place, as many pensioners and disabled people as able-bodied adults of working age lived in the village.[16]

A paved road leads from the village and collective farm to the federal highway that runs to Voronezh and Moscow to the north and Rostov to the south. The proximity of this highway and the quality of the road that connects it to Chayanovskoe allow truckers easy access to the village. Residents periodically trade potatoes and other goods for coal brought by trucks from the south. The road allows convenient exit from the farm for those who have access to transportation. Villagers reach the district center by bus, at considerable expense for those who travel frequently. In the district center, villagers sell dairy products and baked goods and make major purchases. Residents may purchase staples—oil, matches, salt—at one of the two stores in the village. Bread and a limited selection of other goods are delivered to the village twice a week.

The abundant fish and fowl that inhabit the river, marshes, and lakes south and west of Chayanovskoe supplement the diet of many villagers. A cultivated forest to the east provides opportunity for acquisition of wood and shelters the village from cold winds from the steppe. The nearest neighboring village lies three kilometers away as the crow flies, on the opposite bank of the Don. During the winter, individual villagers cross the frozen river to conduct trade with their neighbors.

All members of the community live in private houses, many of which date to early in the century. Not all houses have running water or electricity and few have telephones.[17] The residence of the farm chairman boasts an indoor plumbing system, but his is the exception.[18] Recently, the enterprise has begun to install gas lines. The district began to switch to natural gas in 1993, but limited financial resources have slowed the program considerably. On Chayanovskoe, the cost of running a gas line from any private home to the main costs hundreds of dollars or more, making this form of heating prohibitively expensive for nearly everyone in the village.

The production infrastructure of the enterprise has fared scarcely better than that of the village. Like many collective agricultural enterprises, Chayanovskoe suffers from a chronic shortage of machinery and spare parts. Its equipment has seen better days—the last time the farm acquired a combine was in 1988.[19] The irrigation system was built during the 1980s, and its functioning has declined markedly since then.

The current arable landholdings of Chayanovskoe are comparatively small for the district, comprised of shares totaling 2,778 hectares plus 161 additional hectares formerly cultivated by the collective that now must be leased (without charge) from the district administration. Of the farm's approximately three thousand hectares, about 180 hectares each are used for pasture and hayfields. In recent years, a growing cluster of dachas built by townspeople has begun to encroach upon the land villagers use to grow produce for their own use (*lichnye podsobnye khoziaistva*). Under reform legislation, the district land committee has granted these plots to residents of the district center and other semi-urban areas.

The quality of the soil on Chayanovskoe is noticeably poorer than in neighboring collective farms. In good years, the farm compensates for the slight sandiness with extra expenditures on chemical fertilizer, which it obtains from a plant in a neighboring district. Its main crops are grain, feed corn, sunflowers, and sugar beets. The enterprise also has been producing seed corn since 1988 and more recently has begun cultivation of seed wheat. Chayanovskoe supplies seed corn to 15 other enterprises in the Voronezh region in addition to enterprises in Lipetsk, Ulianovsk, and Belgorod oblasts. Financial constraints have led to short-term compromises in crop rotation that pose long-term risks. For example, in order to maximize profit, the enterprise now plants sunflowers every other year instead of every five or seven years.[20] Such adjustments notwithstanding, over the years since the collapse of Soviet power the livestock holdings and cultivation patterns of Chayanovskoe have not changed appreciably.

The past seven years have seen a steady decline in farm production. A constant lack of cash is one of the most persistent and serious problems. The enterprise is able to exchange its products for inputs for the next growing season, but there are few opportunities to make cash sales. The chair of Chayanovskoe described the situation: "That's the biggest question. There are resources, but no cash. . . . [I]t's an absurd situation, and difficult to explain. We can't even explain it to ourselves. Why? There is production of consumer goods. But production is realized in other goods. It doesn't pay in cash."[21] In recent years, the collective has faced difficult financial choices at harvest time. Low grain prices and high prices on petroleum products have exacted a heavy toll on production. The cost of the fuel necessary to run a combine can exceed the market worth of the grain it harvests. Each summer, the administration of Chayanovskoe compares the calculated cost of bringing in a crop with an estimate of its current value. Some years, grain is left standing in the fields.

Purposes and Procedures of Reorganization

The stated aims of reorganization—improved production efficiency, the creation of a rural class of property owners, and transparency in production and distribution processes—were linked to one another and to a pair of assumptions: first, that individual ownership was key to an efficient use of resources; and second, that the system of collectivized agriculture could be reformed successfully by focusing on the problems of individual enterprises. By dividing title to collective farm resources among its members, enterprises could fulfill two of the aims of reorganization at once. Workers would become owners; with the financial incentives believed necessary for hard work in place, collectives would function more effectively.

Of reorganization's three goals of efficiency, independence, and transparency, the primary aim was improved production efficiency.[22] This need was clearly stated in federal legal guidelines. In December 1991, the Russian government issued a set of instructions for the reorganizing of collective and state farms. Reorganization was to take place "[i]n the interests of increasing the efficiency of agricultural production and the creation of conditions for entrepreneurship in the countryside."[23]

The incentives that reorganization was meant to produce were to have a subsidiary political function. Before its implementation, reorganization was widely perceived to be an instrument of independence for the rural population. The local press in Voronezh oblast voiced this perception, at times with slight irony: "[W]ill privatization allow the villager to feel like the master (*khoziain*) of the land on which he is fated to live and work? Probably it will. It will force the peasant to become his own master more quickly, for it will bring with it the incomparable joy of free labor."[24] The parceling of land plots and other assets of collective and state farms would provide agricultural workers the opportunity to transform a state of subjugation into a state self-reliance.

Mainstream policymakers believed that formalizing the new property relations would foster a strong sense of personal ownership and agency: "[T]he process [of documenting land shares] . . . will show peasants that they are creating their own, non-state, private enterprise."[25] Reorganization was expected to lead to a sense of independence and control: In Chayanovskoe's district, the local press proclaimed, "each will know that he is an owner, he'll approach everything more thriftily (*po-khoziaiskii*), he won't tolerate scofflaws, no-shows, loafers (*narushitelei, progul'shchikov, lodyrei*)."[26] The creation of a rural property-holding class was to serve the state as well as agricultural workers: In the eyes of one representative of the Russian state land committee, "[a] broad stratum of [land]owners is the foundation of stability for the entire state."[27]

Finally, reorganization was expected to render transparent an increasingly opaque system of production. The then first deputy chair of the State Committee on Land for the Russian Federation put it this way: "What's even more important is clarity, 'transparency' of land tenure . . . [so that the authorities will know] whom and what to tax. . . . This will give the state the chance to control the land market, regulate the 'rules of the game' in the interests of the entire society."[28] At the national level, analysts of reform envisioned reorganization as "not the splintering of agriculture, but a choice of rational dimensions and organizational-legal forms of agricultural enterprises."[29] To that end, the process of reorganization included strict protocols regarding the timing and form of the transformation of collective farms into independent private enterprises.

Procedures

In carrying out reorganization, Chayanovskoe adhered precisely to the procedure outlined by federal legislation.[30] Despite compliance with policy, however, the process of implementation contradicted and undermined the democratizing aims of reorganization. Reorganization was conceptualized and presented by local leadership as a project to be carried out by farm management, not by the entire collective. The chief economist of a nearby collective farm described the process as follows: "Soon there'll be a general meeting of the collective at which we—I'm speaking as a member of the leadership cadres, kolkhoz administration—will announce that we are removing ourselves from our posts and the collective farm ceases to exist."[31]

The only part rank-and-file workers were to play in the process was to give their consent. Social and economic inequalities in the countryside, however, made that consent meaningless: Under existing conditions, consent could not be given freely and as such was impossible by definition. A technician on a farm near Chayanovskoe summed up the situation: "I understand that they took the land legally,[32] of course, without asking the peasant anything [about it]. . . . They operate according to the letter of the law but not according to the letter of consent. That isn't right. And is it really possible that no one understands that conflicts are unavoidable in such a situation?"[33] The process of reorganization as dictated by law afforded those with power plenty of opportunity to acquire even more, while it provided most people the illusion of agency in the form of practically irredeemable share certificates.

The first step in the reorganization process, required by federal government regulations to be executed by 1 March 1992, was registration of the kolkhoz as a commercial entity. In theory, members collectively could choose among a number of different forms of organization for the farm, including closed and open joint stock companies (AOZT and AO), limited liability partnerships (*tovarishchestva*, or TOO), and agricultural producers' collectives (SPKh).[34] The law permitted individuals who chose to leave the collective to establish yeoman farms, a practice that was largely discouraged by both district officials and collective farm managers.

The primary difference between the two most commonly chosen forms of organization, AO and TOO, concerns the relationship of ownership to labor. Joint stock companies issue stockholder certificates that may be sold to individuals who do not work on the enterprise. Shares in limited liability partnerships may be inherited or sold to members of the enterprise or the enterprise itself, but they may not circulate outside of the enterprise. Joint stock companies allow a separation of ownership from labor and are prone to concentration of ownership among individuals outside of the enterprise. In such cases, members of the collective become hired workers with no stake in the company and no voice in its management. Under conditions of economic crisis, limited liability partnerships, on the other hand, tend toward increasing concentration of ownership of assets in the hands of a few members of the community, usually the director (chairman) or other enterprise administrators. That limited liability partnerships were not immediately subject to some kinds of taxation also made them an attractive choice of organizational form for farm managers.[35]

The reorganization of Chayanovskoe, as for most if not all of the other collective farms in its raion, was less a process requiring active participation of the community than a legal change carried out by fiat but requiring the formal consent of the collective. The process of choosing an organizational form happened as follows: The district administration made a recommendation of organizational form to each enterprise's reorganization commission (which included both farm chairman and a representative of the district administration).[36] The commission then proposed that form at the general meeting of the membership, and the labor collective immediately voted on it, yea or nay.

On 2 March 1992, members of Chayanovskoe gathered to vote on the reorganization of their enterprise. The commission charged with overseeing the reform process on the enterprise proposed to reorganize Chayanovskoe as a limited liability company. According to farm records and in keeping with a long tradition of relegating dissent to the margins of political life on the collective farm, the collective voted unanimously to do so. Over 80 percent of the collective and state farms in Chayanovskoe's district also reorganized as limited liability partnerships.[37]

The same records testify that in 1992, the membership of Chayanovskoe unanimously passed every motion related to enterprise reform. Minutes of the meeting show that of its 357 members, 238 attended the meeting—precisely 66.7 percent of the kolkhoz population, the same proportion needed to approve changes in the legal status of the farm. According to attendance records, the same number purportedly attended every meeting in 1992 that required a vote on some aspect of the reform process. It is unclear how many members actually attended. As the farm chairman pointed out, although he tried to select a meeting time convenient for all members of the collective, "you can't invite everyone"[38] to the general assembly.

The second step in the reorganization process was selection of a type of collective ownership. According to the provisions of the 1991 Land Code of the Russian republic (RSFSR), intact *kolkhozy* and other agricultural enterprises could transfer their land into collective joint ownership (*sovmestnaia sobstvennost'*) or collective shared ownership (*kollektivno-dolevaia sobstvennost'*). Collective joint ownership meant that enterprise land would be owned collectively, without definition of shares. Where apportionment of shares under collective joint ownership does occur, the size of shares is governed by a district mean. Chayanovskoe chose collective shared ownership, which allowed quantitative specification of each member's land share. Under collective shared ownership, the enterprise labor collective determines the size of the share of each member, provided individual shares do not exceed the maximum size of land allotted for yeoman farms.[39] The latter measurement is determined at the regional level of administration.[40] Neither collective joint ownership nor collective shared ownership provides for the identification of individual land shares as concrete plots of land. Both types of ownership permit apportionment of land shares only under a narrow set of circumstances, usually upon exit from the collective.

In March 1992, whether Chayanovskoe and its neighbors would continue to function as collective farms or substantively change their system of property relations was not yet clear. What was clear was that once again, beneath the veneer of a democratic procedure, the future of the members of Chayanovskoe had been decided for them.

Wages of Independence: Crop Failure, Downtrodden Workers, Black Markets

Despite adherence to the letter of the law, the process by which reorganization took place on Chayanovskoe and other collectives inverted its stated goals. Reorganization was supposed to cultivate independence on the part of agricultural workers, but its implementation required minimal active participation on the part of members of the collective. Reorganization was intended to produce transparency in the operation of agricultural enterprises, but very little information about the policy and its anticipated effects was made available to the general rural population. Finally, reorganization was meant to goad enterprises into efficient production, but implementation of the policy required disruption of the already delicate and precarious cycle of cultivation.

If the primary aims of reform were to improve the efficiency of collective agricultural enterprises, create a self-reliant class of peasant owners, and render rural economies transparent to the outside, the results were to depress production levels, further disenfranchise rural residents, and drive almost all transactions into the barter economy, rendering them opaque to all but their agents. Certain of these outcomes were direct results of the implementation of reorganization. Others resulted from economic conditions independent of reorganization policy. A third category was the fruit of sins of omission—conditions worsened by what reorganization should and could have done but did not.

In the three years following reorganization, every district of Voronezh oblast experienced steep declines in net production of grain. Between 1993 and 1995, the harvest for the region dropped from 35,956,500 quintals (1 quintal = about 100 kg) to 15,528,400.[41] Nationwide, the pattern was similarly dismal: Grain production fell from 106,900 million tons in 1992 to 81,300 million tons in 1994.[42] Contrary to the expectation that private cultivation would expand as collective production diminished, household production of wheat, potatoes, and vegetables also declined during the same three-year period. Net production of potatoes in household plots dropped from 8,958,600 quintals in 1993 to 4,432,800 quintals in 1995. Overall livestock holdings also markedly declined during that period, often by as much as 30 percent. Only the dairy cow herd did not experience precipitous decline, decreasing steadily but gradually between 1991 and 1995, from 498,700 head region-wide in 1991 to 459,000 in 1995. However, the deteriorating conditions were reflected in dairy production. In the district where Chayanovskoe is located, milk production per cow per year dropped from 3,014 kilograms in 1991 to 2,544 kilograms in 1995.[43]

Changes in production efficiency—the main target of reorganization—resulted from all three of the causal categories mentioned above. The process of reorganizing collectives, especially for those that lost members and resources to private farming (fermerskie khoziastva) and newly established agricultural cooperatives, constituted a disruption in the work of cultivation. For struggling enterprises, setbacks early in the season could prove difficult to recoup. Contributing to the problem were conditions of general economic decline precipitated by the macroeconomic reforms instituted in January 1992. The precipitous lifting of price controls on most goods, and the severe price disparities that immediately resulted, made agriculture even less profitable than before. Finally, agricultural enterprises made a formal break from the Soviet system of production relations when they declared themselves to be independent commercial entities free to select their own partners in trade. Rapid dismantling of the command system at the district level meant inefficient production and trade at the enterprise level, leading to sharp declines in production.[44] Reorganization's emphasis on reforming individual enterprises, with no attention to networks of production and distribution, not only did not improve the situation, but also drew valuable human and material resources away from the task of developing new exchange infrastructures.

Despite its formal provision of private ownership, reorganization played both a direct and an indirect role in undermining the independence of rural populations. With the increasing economic and political isolation of individual enterprises, rural social structures underwent a transformation resembling a cart wheel in motion losing its rim: Their protection and ties gone, agricultural workers had no choice but to cast their lot with their leadership, like spokes clinging to the center, their wheel spinning out of control over rough ground. Declines in production meant that many of the lines of interdependence that support household and enterprise economies became lines of mere dependence. The flexible quid pro quo that sustains Chayanovskoe came to resemble a precarious entitlement system that requires workers to be on good terms with managers as much as possible at all times. With his control of inputs for household production, his connections with district administration, his ability to conduct informal large-scale transactions for fuel, sugar, and other commodities on behalf of the enterprise, the chairman of a farm literally holds the fate of its workers in his hands. As every villager learns, "*lushche molchi ili poddakivai*"—"it's better to keep silent or 'say yes sir.' "[45]

The final aim of reorganization—the creation of transparent markets—met with a similar fate for similar reasons. Agricultural enterprises adapted to isolation and the cash and input shortages caused by production declines by seeking out partners for trade both with the assistance of district administrations and through previously existing commercial relationships. This led on the one hand to the reproduction of a system resembling a command economy at the local level, and on the other, a restrictive and inefficient shadow economy. The rapid growth of barter transactions was a direct result of the instantaneous breakdown of production relationships among enterprises that had existed under Soviet rule combined with the chaos engendered by macroeconomic reform in 1992. Without reliable access to efficient networks, cash, or all of the means of production, collective enterprises were forced to cultivate informal ties and in-kind exchanges. In 1998, 50 percent of all enterprise transactions on Chayanovskoe were conducted on the basis of pure barter or *vzaimoraschet*, an accounting system that allows the cancellation of mutual debts through in-kind transactions, often involving a third or fourth partner.[46] While such transactions appear in the enterprises' accounting records, they produce no cash. Reorganization, together with other reforms, not only encouraged the development of opaque markets, but also divorced the economy from the state at the regional and federal level in ways the Russian government never intended, namely depriving the state of its power to extract rents from the population.

Responses to Reorganization

With its failure to spur efficient production, create an independent rural property-holding class, or render transparent agricultural activity, reorganization elicited two main responses from the members of Chayanovskoe and their neighbors: indifference and resentment. Their main response was indifference. Reorganization had had little effect on workers' understanding of their role in the economic and social life of the enterprise or on their day-to-day activities. The members of Chayanovskoe did not point to any particular significance of reorganization because, as they put it, there was none. Reorganization seemed to them a formal exercise that produced a class of owners before the law but that in truth gave few of them real advantages.

Members of the rural elite articulated resentment of the process. The director of Chayanovskoe and local raion administrators regarded reorganization as an alien project foisted upon the enterprise by outside forces. Those who expressed indifference saw no real meaning in this reform of property rights[47]; those who stressed the policy's origins in the federal government distanced themselves from responsibility for its outcomes. Chapter 4 by Wegren and Belen'kiy in this volume includes a general discussion of the different reactions of rural elites to reform.

One of the central reasons for members' indifference toward reorganization was that collective shared property gave shareholders no real sense of ownership. Under reorganization, each member was allocated a land share (in this instance 5.67 hectares), to be apportioned in theory only. Members of the collective received shareholders' certificates, but shareholders working enterprise land could realize their claim in concrete terms only if they risked leaving the collective. Only upon application to the district land committee would a shareholder intending to establish his or her own private farm receive information about the location of the lot in question.[48] All others simply knew that some plot of collective land belonged to them personally and would be identified if they relinquished their claim to membership in the collective. Few on Chayanovskoe took the irrevocable step of leaving the enterprise and applying for a land parcel. For nearly all members of Chayanovskoe, exit from the kolkhoz was neither a viable nor a necessarily desirable option.[49]

For those who chose neither to establish small-scale farms of their own nor to lease their land shares to such farms, any growth in their asset shares was virtually invisible. Asset shares could generate dividends only when the enterprise generated profit, and the overwhelming majority of agricultural enterprises in Voronezh region were unable to do so. In 1992, economic conditions across Russia were such that most enterprises could hope only to remain solvent. By 1998, over 80 percent of the farms in the oblast were bankrupt. Reorganization endeavored to improve production efficiency by providing incentives for individuals to work, but in such an economic climate, the expectation of incentives in the form of dividends—even dividends to be reinvested in the enterprise—was unrealistic. Irina Koznova writes that "[i]t should be noted that for the majority, so far property means the materially expressed situation, 'I'm an owner because I receive dividends on my shares.' If there are no dividends, people don't feel like owners."[50] The incentives private ownership was meant to generate were themselves dependent on circumstances beyond the control of any one enterprise, much less any single individual. For this reason, the lack of a systemic approach in reorganizing collective and state farms greatly limited the reform's possible impact.

Both village intelligentsia and unskilled laborers concluded that the reorganization process itself did not provide for the fundamental, equalizing change in power relations it was intended to produce. Nominally held private property did not transform villagers' control over their economic or social status. In the absence of such a change, there was no compelling reason for interest in reorganization. Indifference was a reaction to the failure of reorganization to produce any improvements in their lives.[51]

Administrators attributed workers' indifference to reorganization to a lack of information or intellect. Both enterprise management and district officials tended to hold shareholders responsible for their own discontent, asserting that the impact of reorganization as such depended on people's understanding of the concept of land ownership. The chairman of Chayanovskoe shared this view: "Everything depends on the level of personal interest, the level of understanding of this question. Maybe [they] didn't explain 'why' to every person . . . but maybe every person didn't ask the question."[52] A local newspaper reporter commenting on the dynamics of reorganization in a nearby enterprise explained the quiescence of members in the same terms: "[W]e can only assume that the rank-and-file workers had a weak understanding of what role had been delegated to each of them as stockholders, what their rights and responsibilities would be."[53]

The contrast between managers' and workers' explanations points to a fundamental difference in the way social position mediated perception of the reform process. Administrative elites at the enterprise, district, and regional level also ascribed shareholders' lack of interest in reform to simple ignorance, but the view that no change had or could come of reorganization persisted among both highly educated and less educated workers. Power, not literacy or information, was the most obvious mediator of individuals' interpretation of the reorganization process.

Indifference toward reorganization existed alongside an entirely different and seemingly opposed belief: that far from being a meaningless policy, reorganization had been forced upon the countryside in an "incoherent, destructive experiment."[54] Administrators in and around Chayanovskoe's raion regarded reorganization as a legislative matter in which they were reluctant but compelled to participate. To illustrate this point, the chairman of Chayanovskoe described reorganization as a process that had been "forced upon the enterprise from above."[55] The head of the district agricultural department described reorganization in similar terms, as a decision-making process that did not include the very people it was meant to affect: "The further fate of collective farms is practically predetermined [*predreshena*]."[56] A specialist on Chayanovskoe characterized Soviet reforms of recent decades as intra-enterprise restructuring but placed the reforms of the 1990s in a broader context, regarding reorganization as a process exogenous to the collective.[57] The newspaper of a nearby raion announced: "Village laborers in the middle of the bitter winter season found about how their dear old collective farm in its former appearance no longer suits the government—the government insists on reorganization. Into what, how, why—those questions are for later. For now please allow the collective farm to change its status in accordance with the law."[58]

If administrators at the local level interpreted reorganization as a coercive project of the central state, federal officials had given them occasion to do so. As Sergei Nikol'skii has noted, the timing of the official introduction of reorganization on 27 December 1991 recalled Stalin's inauguration of collectivization on the same day in 1929.[59] Government officials probably chose the anniversary to mark the end of 62 years of collectivized agriculture, but in retrospect the launching of the reorganization program took on an ironic complexion, resembling recapitulation rather than closure.[60]

Although local elites responded to reorganization with measured indifference or resentment, they were the winners in the process. Under reorganization, land and material resources ceased to be the property of the state and nominally became the property of enterprise members. Farm managers and district administrators—as gatekeepers to the exercise of enterprise members' ownership rights—gained de facto ownership of land and with it, the autonomy and economic incentive to persist in their new roles as leaders in a quasi-feudal system. Legal provisions for the disposal of land shares were oriented toward the consolidation of power in the hands of local elites: V. Bachmashnikov, the head of the national farmers' association, later remarked that the peasant "transfers rights to land shares only to the directors-chairmen, that is to juridical persons, but rank-and-file people once again are proletarianizing, turning into voiceless cattle."[61]

Rank-and-file workers reacted to reorganization by ignoring it. Most members of Chayanovskoe directed their attention to the most imminent and important problem at hand: developing and maintaining the networks of exchange that would allow them to continue to cultivate the land to which they did have individual access—their garden plots.

Interdependence of Enterprise and Household Economies: The Necessity of Ties

If reform of property relations in the enterprise provoked indifference, the problems reorganization specifically did not address—access to inputs and networks of exchange—were the main concerns of Chayanovskoe's members. Ownership did not guarantee households access to the means of production. In the wake of reorganization, agricultural workers found themselves trapped in a system of labor relations that bound household and enterprise together. Seven years after reorganization, even bankrupt collectives continue to exist because their members' households cannot survive without them. Likewise, individual enterprises depend on one another for inputs, processing, and distribution, but reorganization's exclusive focus on individual enterprises led to neglect of important linkages among them. In an environment of information asymmetry, transaction costs are high; without reform of networks, individual enterprises cannot hope to function more efficiently. Both households and enterprises were left with no better choice than to persist in production relations that allow little room for risking further change.

In the years following reorganization, access to garden inputs and trading relationships grew increasingly important for households on Chayanovskoe. Consistently declining production at the enterprise level meant that individual access to the means of production became gradually more and more crucial to villagers' survival. Reorganization did not make the collective's resources available to villagers, either corporately or individually. Neither land nor other asset shares are concretely identified until and unless an individual leaves the collective. Ownership of shares did not give villagers any direct access to specific, tradable, or renewable commodities.

Prior to reorganization and the macroeconomic reforms that accompanied it, the members of Chayanovskoe could rely on cash and in-kind salaries from the kolkhoz to satisfy their basic needs. Now, the members of Chayanovskoe may best be described as subsistence farmers on small plots, dependent on the collective farm for the garden inputs they receive as wages in kind. Wages are typically two to four months late. The cash value of in-kind payments is subtracted from the sum of wages owed the employee. When, as in the inflation that followed the currency devaluation of

August 1998, prices rise and theoretical wages remain constant, wages lose value, even if measured in grain, livestock, textiles, or building materials instead of cash. Inflation effectively can liquidate the wage arrears that employees had thought of as their savings.

Wage delays create a dangerous gap between allocation of wages in theory and receipt of goods in kind. As in many villages, cash is used to pay only for soap, matches, bread, and utilities. All other exchanges take place using some form of reciprocity in kind. Labor for goods transactions provide some of the raw materials necessary for individual households' private agricultural production: livestock, feed, and building materials. With a short growing season, the timing of payment is of paramount importance. To an even greater extent than their dacha-going seasonal neighbors, villagers survive almost exclusively on what they grow in their private plots during the summer months. The absence of appropriate and timely inputs greatly limits the production capacity of village households.

The relationship between work on the collective and inputs for private production explains one of the central paradoxes of contemporary rural life in Russia. Like villagers throughout the region, the employees of Chayanovskoe work at least two shifts every day: one for the kolkhoz and one for the household. This is true even of the household of the farm chairman. Particularly during the summer, when employees typically work 12-hour days on the enterprise, such constant labor is exhausting. Whatever its duties on the collective, each household must grow its own potatoes, cultivate and preserve its own vegetables and fruit, and engage in the many other tasks required to ensure a steady food supply throughout the long winter. This activity typically takes place in the early morning, before the salaried workday begins, and later in the evening, after Chayanovskoe's workday is over. Given such a schedule, it might be difficult to understand why so many villagers continue to work a second job that no longer pays a salary. Indeed, many villagers have stopped working for the collective: At times, as many as half of the adult population of the village that serves Chayanovskoe is engaged in other activity or employment. For those who continue to put in long and thankless hours, the garden inputs they receive as payment provide an economic justification for their work on the collective.[62]

Exchanges of labor for wages paid in kind are the most explicit and codified among the web of transactions within the community; others are more flexible and at times ad hoc arrangements between farm management and workers.[63] The constant movement of resources around the village through exchanges among households and between households and the enterprise results in a mutual dependence of all members of the community. These transactions include borrowing as well as permanent exchanges of goods and services. One household might offer to share part of a butchered pig and in return would expect help digging a pit latrine. At the center of this set of transactions is the collective: For some employees, access to machinery, fuel, and other collectively held property provides further opportunity for informal transactions. The entire system operates on an implicit understanding of community and mutual dependence.[64]

Chayanovskoe generates no profit, producing only inputs sufficient for the following year's growing season. Its production levels are dependent not only on households' demand for inputs, as this need drives the labor supply, but also on the solidity and extent of its ties with other enterprises. In the absence of a viable cash economy, barter runs the business. Sugar, oil, fuel, coal, and machinery parts normally are obtained from other enterprises in exchange for seed, animal feed, potatoes, and sugar beets. Some trading relationships develop out of ties that existed under the command system, but many are entirely new. For the enterprise, establishment of and gaining access to external distribution networks consume much of the chairman's time. Partnerships can be risky, and farm managers must spend a great deal of time and energy searching for reliable partners.

In September 1998, for example, Chayanovskoe encountered a typical problem: One of its grain debtors refused to make payment.[65] Transactions between enterprises often take place on the basis of personal contacts, but the relationship in question was an official one. The formal character of the relationship meant that there were no personal ties to guarantee fulfillment of the contract. As the district head of agricultural administration put it, the pressure (*davlenie*) that formerly ensured compliance in official transactions had given way to "pure partnership relations."[66] The chair of Chayanovskoe summed up the situation: "For us this is not a very good time in terms of the dependability of business partners. You have to work with your own people . . . people who are tried and true, and you do your best to avoid deception, and secondly all other kinds of unpleasantness."[67]

Enterprises in the district do receive help in identifying possible trading partners, but the reliability of such partners must then be evaluated through personal contacts. In Chayanovskoe's raion, a member of the district administration acts as a broker, periodically contacting farm chairpersons with news about prospective business transactions. On Chayanovskoe, the chairman records this information in a log that he makes available to farm specialists (agronomist, veterinarian, etc.), who may establish partnerships on an independent basis. Alternatively, specialists may contact the district administration directly. This system supports personnel searches as well.

New arrivals in the district can contact the district agricultural department to inquire about enterprises seeking employees. Although the dismantling of the command economy should have separated the state from commerce, local government remains actively involved in the choice and location of business partners. As the chairman of Chayanovskoe characterized the institutional role of the district government, "the agricultural department of the local administration plays the role of an advertising agency."[68]

The net effect of exchange relations within and between enterprises strikes a triple blow at the central goals of farm reorganization. Both individual households and enterprises produce not what they might most efficiently achieve in an ideal situation, but what they need to survive in a climate of permanent scarcity and uncertainty. Instead of becoming independent producers, members of Chayanovskoe remain tightly bound to the slowly disintegrating carcass of Russia's agroindustrial complex. Finally, commercial exchanges are funneled through an inscrutable, idiosyncratic world of informal transactions rather than a transparent commodity market. Chapter 11 by Amelina provides further discussion of the impact of these relationships on reform.

Conclusion: Innovation in Spite of Reform

Reorganization of collective and state farms was meant to spur efficiency in agricultural production, create a rural class of independent landowners, and render transparent to the state the processes of production and distribution. Instead, reorganization helped create conditions for subsistence cultivation, loss of autonomy for enterprise members, and an opaque, improvised system of exchange. The strengthening of already rigid social and economic hierarchies did nothing either to encourage support for reform or to provide conditions under which efficient, independent, and transparent production processes could become a reality.

Reorganization as it was implemented at the enterprise level was a fundamentally undemocratic process. Those most affected by the reform had little or no opportunity to participate in choosing an organizational form most appropriate for their enterprise. Both the implementation of the policy and the initial decision to reorganize agricultural collectives were far removed from kolkhoz members. A driver for another collective farm in Chayanovskoe's district commented on the process: "Right now, academics sitting there in Moscow are, once again, deciding our fate. What gives them the right? Why can't *kolkhozniki* decide for themselves?"[69]

Despite reorganization's failure to meet its goals, members of Chayanovskoe managed to find ways to keep producing food for their families, maintain a minimal degree of independence from the kolkhoz, and conduct trade at the household level. By widespread tacit agreement to conduct barter according to market prices, members of the enterprises circumvent local power discrepancies, temporarily solve the problem of cash shortages, ensure a necessary level of trust among contracting parties, and minimize transaction costs. The in-kind transactions that run Chayanovskoe's economy may represent nothing more than a transitional equilibrium. Nonetheless, they together constitute an efficient and in many cases ingenious adaptation to some of the problems of survival posed by the rocky and painful transition to a market economy. These adaptations are the subject of the chapters in the next section of this book.

Notes

1. This material is based on work supported by a National Science Foundation Graduate Research Fellowship. Any opinions, findings, conclusions, or recommendations expressed in this chapter are mine and do not necessarily reflect the views of the National Science Foundation. Fieldwork for this chapter was supported by a research fellowship from the Yale Center for International and Area Studies at Yale University. I extend my sincere thanks to the director of the Chayanovskoe collective for his generosity with his time as I struggled to understand the day-to-day realities of life and work on the collective. Finally, I would like to thank all those who read and provided comments on drafts of this chapter, including the anonymous readers at the Woodrow Wilson Center Press. Responsibility for any remaining errors or shortcomings, of course, is entirely mine.

2. For accounts of the use of mobilizing and supervisory cadres during earlier attempts at land reform, see George Yaney, *The Urge to Mobilize: Agrarian Reform in Russia, 1861–1930* (Urbana: University of Illinois Press, 1982); and Lynn Viola, *The Best Sons of the Fatherland: Workers in the Vanguard of Soviet Collectivization* (New York: Oxford University Press, 1987).

3. This view is borne out both by the literature on property rights in the Chinese transition and some of the literature on sharecropping, as well as the articulation by Russian cultivators themselves, that outright ownership of land is not important so long as they have reliable access to it. That idea emerged repeatedly in my hundreds of conversations with Russian and Ukrainian agricultural workers; only private agricultural entrepreneurs (*fermery*) expressed a need for ownership of land as an incentive for its improvement. China scholars have found that access to production factors can lead to their diversion and accumulation by those with social or political power, even if legal ownership of those factors belongs to others. See, for example, Nan Lin and Chih-Jou Jay Chen, "Local Elites as Officials and Owners: Shareholding and Property Rights in Daqiuzhuang," in *Property Rights and Economic Reform in China*, eds. Jean C. Oi and Andrew G. Walder (Stanford, CA: Stanford University Press, 1993), 145–70. Theoretical work on sharecropping suggests that contracted access to resources can produce certain efficiency benefits: Cheung (1969, cited in Stiglitz) argued that sharecropping minimizes transaction costs, while Joseph Stiglitz found that sharecropping increases incentives. Stiglitz, "Rational Peasants, Efficient Institutions, and a Theory of Rural Organization: Methodological Remarks for Development Economics," in *The Economic The-*

ory of Agrarian Institutions, ed. Pranab Bardhan (Oxford: Clarendon Press, 1989), 18–30. For detailed empirical support for the contention that sharecropping can be an efficient solution to the problem of resource combination, see Naresh Sharma and Jean Dreze, "Sharecropping in a North Indian Village," *Journal of Development Studies* 33 (1996): 1.

4. Gavin Kitching provides a clear description of local processing networks in "The Development of Agrarian Capitalism in Russia 1991–1997: Some Observations from Fieldwork," *Journal of Peasant Studies* 25 (1998): 3. Although there is ample evidence to suggest that collectivized agriculture often is less efficient than other forms of agricultural organization, there is no general agreement as to what characteristics of the kolkhoz are most directly responsible for periodic declines in efficiency. Reorganization targeted property rights, but many scholars and observers have found that subsidies and procurement prices were more important determinants of productivity levels in Soviet and Soviet-model agriculture. See, for example, Ronald A. Francisco, Betty A. Laird, and Roy D. Laird, eds., *The Political Economy of Collectivized Agriculture: A Comparative Study of Communist and Non-Communist Systems* (New York: Pergamon Press, 1979); Zhores A. Medvedev, *Soviet Agriculture* (New York: Norton, 1987); and Stephen K. Wegren, *Agriculture and the State in Soviet and Post-Soviet Russia* (Pittsburgh, PA: University of Pittsburgh Press, 1998). James K.S. Kung and Louis Putterman address this question by asking why Chinese agriculture exhibited gains in productivity both during collectivization (1954–58) and decollectivization (1979–84). While the contexts of Chinese agrarian reform are not identical to Russia's, their findings do suggest that formal property rights—and the incentives various property regimes are thought to engender—are not determinative of productivity levels in all settings. Kung and Putterman, "China's Collectivization Puzzle: A New Resolution," *Journal of Development Studies* 33 (1997): 6.

5. Russian commentators have used this analogy to capture reformers' assumption of a tabula rasa where the countryside is concerned. One writer has described land reform in precisely these terms, as a process conducted with no regard to context, as if on an empty field (*kak budto na chistom pole*). A. Mordvintsez, "Slezy zemli," *Trud,* 24 January 1995, 6.

6. I describe these issues later in this chapter. For example, information asymmetries arose both among enterprises and within them, as enterprise managers struggled to obtain information about local and regional markets and agricultural workers remained incompletely informed about the laws governing enterprise reorganization.

7. While reorganization policy has its roots in neoclassical economics, endogenous theories of institutions exhibit a similar problem. These theories do not specify processes by which change might occur; they assume that economies deemed ready for change will beget it. See Bardhan, ed., *The Economic Theory of Agrarian Institutions.* Bardhan's critique of Marxist approaches resonates on the issue of obstacles to change: "Under a set of informational constraints and missing markets, a given agrarian institution (say, sharecropping) may be serving a real economic function; and its simple abolition, as is often demanded on a radical platform, without taking care of the factors that gave rise to this institution in the first place, may not necessarily improve the conditions of the intended beneficiaries of the abolition program" (p. 7).

8. Karla Hoff and Andrew B. Lyon have argued that in conditions of imperfect information and missing markets, efficiency depends on distribution of wealth. Hoff and Lyon, "Collateral, Asymmetric Information, and Pareto-Improving Labor Taxation," Working Paper 92-13 (College Park, MD: University of Maryland, Department of Economics, 1992). See also Karla Hoff, Avishay Braverman, and Joseph E. Stiglitz, *The Economics of Rural Organization: Theory, Practice, and Policy* (New York: Oxford University Press, 1993), 15.

9. See, most notably, Jean C. Oi and Andrew G. Walder, eds., *Property Rights and Economic Reform in China* (Stanford, CA: Stanford University Press, 1999); and Katherine Verdery, "Fuzzy Property: Rights, Power, and Identity in Transylvania's Decollectivization," in *Uncertain Transition: Ethnographies of Change in the Postsocialist World,* eds. Michael Buroway and Katherine Verdery (Lanham, MD: Rowman and Littlefield, 1999), 53–82.

10. See, for example, Frank Durgin, "Russia's Private Farm Movement: Background and Perspectives," *Soviet and Post-Soviet Review* 21 (1994): 1; Erik Mathijs and Johan Swinnen, "The Economics of Agricultural Decollectivization in East Central Europe and the Former Soviet Union," *Economic Development and Cultural Change* 47, no. 1 (1998): 1–26; Donald Van Atta, ed., *The "Farmer Threat": The Political Economy of Agrarian Reform in Post-Soviet Russia* (Boulder, CO: Westview Press, 1993); and Stephen K. Wegren, "Rural Reform and Political Culture in Russia," *Europe-Asia Studies* 46 (1994): 2.

11. Proponents of both neoliberal reform programs and gradualist or evolutionary approaches to economic reform subscribe—if only implicitly—to this view. In the literature, the question rarely is whether or why to ensure the establishment of private property rights in transition settings, but how. Examples include Maxim Boyko, Andrei Shleifer, and Robert Vishney, *Privatizing Russia* (Cambridge, MA: MIT Press, 1995); Jeffrey Sachs, *Poland's Jump to the Market Economy* (Cambridge, MA: MIT Press, 1993); and Peter Murrell, "What Is Shock Therapy? What Did It Do in Poland and Russia?" *Post-Soviet Affairs* 9 (1993): 2.

12. This fieldwork included visits to approximately thirty former collective farms in five districts (*raiony*) of Voronezh oblast between 1998 and 2000.

13. Using the typology provided by Kalugina in chapter 15 of this book, Chayanovskoe fits most closely model two, enterprises that are characterized by compensatory and adaptive economic strategies. For an assessment of the agricultural sector, public infrastructure, and demographic characteristics of the 32 raiony of Voronezh oblast, see *Goroda i raiony Voronezhskoi oblasti*, vol. 3 (Voronezh: Voronezhskii oblastnoi Goskomstat, 1996).

14. All place names below the regional level have been changed to protect the identity of those who were kind enough to share their thoughts with me and who took on certain risks by doing so. Place names in printed sources have not been changed.

15. As told by Chayanovskoe librarian and village historian in interview by author, 23 August 1998. A similar account appears in V. Zagorovskii, *Istoricheskaia toponimika Voronezhskogo kraia* (Voronezh: Izdatel'stvo Voronezhskogo Gosudarstvennogo Universiteta, 1973).

16. Unpublished enterprise statistics. In 1992, there were 174 able-bodied adults, 163 pensioners, and 12 disabled persons living in the village. This age distribution is representative of the oblast as a whole, in which 55 percent of the population is of working age. For regional level statistics, see *Regiony Rossii 1998* (Moscow: Goskomstat, 1998), 2:205.

17. In 1997, 21.5 percent of rural families in Voronezh oblast had access to a home telephone line, compared with 53 percent of urban families in the region. The oblast ranks 29th (of 80) among administrative regions of the Russian Federation in household access to a telephone. See *Regiony Rossii 1998*, 2:581.

18. This state of affairs is typical for Russian villages. In 1998, 22 percent of rural communities in Russia possessed a piped-in water supply, and only 3 percent had a plumbing system. This compares to 86 percent and 63 percent, respectively, for urban settlements (*poselki gorodskogo tipa*) and 96 percent and 93 percent for cities. See *Rossiiskii statisticheskii sbornik 1998* (Moscow: Goskomstat, 1998), 252.

19. Figures for machinery acquisition by collectives in a neighboring raion show the same pattern. Between 1989 and 1998, collectives in that raion experienced a net loss of 22 percent of their combined tractor fleet. Likewise, the load for each grain combine during that period increased from 146 to 209 hectares. Unpublished statistics obtained by the author from the economic division of the Liskinskaia district administration, Voronezh oblast.

20. Such changes in crop rotation can cause serious soil degradation in a relatively short time. Two consecutive years of planting sunflowers in a single field, for example, will ruin the land for cultivation of other crops for several years.

21. Chayanovskoe chairman, interview by author, 8 August 1998.

22. Stephen K. Wegren suggests that reorganization had a primarily political, not economic, purpose. See Wegren, *Agriculture and the State*. Wegren concludes that "farm privatization was waged as a political campaign to undermine the economic and political power of the old rural elite, the farm managers" (p. 107). If this is true, reorganization failed utterly.

As I argue later in the chapter, the process served both to increase the political power of farm managers relative to farm workers and to strengthen the social and economic hierarchies that govern production relations.

23. Russian government resolution No. 86, "O poriadke reorganizatsii kolkhozov i sovkhozov" (29 December 1991).

24. *Liskinskie izvestiia*, 10 October 1991, 5.

25. V. Uzun, ed., *Sotsial'no-ekonomicheskie posledstviia privatisatsii zemli i reorganizatsii sel'skokhoziaistvennykh predpriiatii 1994–96* (Moscow: Entsiklopediia rossiiskii dereven', 1997), 37.

26. Interview of a kolkhoz chief economist in *Maiak pridon'ia*, 21 January 1992, 3.

27. *Trud*, 15 February 1996, 2.

28. *Trud*, 16 October 1995, 5.

29. *Sotsial'no-ekonomicheskie posledstviia privatisatsii zemli*, 7.

30. Legislation governing the process included Russian government Resolution No. 86, "O poriadke reorganizatsii kolkhozov i sovkhozov," 29 December 1991; government Resolution No. 708, "O poriadke privatisatsii i reorganizatsii predpriatii i organizatsii APK," of 4 September 1992; and Russian Federation Law, "O predpriatiiakh i predprinimatel'skoi deiatelnosti," 25 December 1990.

31. *Maiak pridon'ia*, 21 January 1992, 3.

32. Under reorganization, all acreage on a collective exceeding the product of the number of shareholders times the district norm (in this case 5.6 hectares) was designated as reserve land to be administered by the district administration and no longer cultivated by the collective except under lease.

33. *Maiak pridon'ia*, 14 January 1992, 3.

34. Later, solvent enterprises that wished to return to their former status as collective farms were permitted to do so.

35. It seems not unlikely that the popularity of the choice of TOO might be explained in part by linguistic resonance: In contrast to the AO, or *aktsionernoe obshchestvo*, "*tovarishchestvo*" carries strong Soviet overtones. The familiarity of the name, if not the concept, may have played a role in decisions to reorganize into limited liability partnerships.

36. Interview by author of surveyor in raion land tenure office, 9 September 1998. Subsequent interviews with land tenure officials in four other districts of Voronezh oblast document the same process at work in those districts.

37. This form of collective organization has since been declared invalid. In 1998, Chayanovskoe and other collectives in the district were in the midst of registering for the third time in the past seven years, this time simply as a commercial organization.

38. Chayanovskoe chairman, interview by author, 10 September 1998.

39. Land Code of RSFSR (1991) S1/Ch1/A8-10.

40. Land Code of RSFSR (1991) S1/Ch5/A36.

41. *Goroda i raiony Voronezhskoi oblasti* (Voronezh: Voronezhskii oblastnoi goskomstat, 1996).

42. *Sel'skoe khoziaistvo Rossii* (Moscow: Goskomstat, 1995), 216.

43. *Goroda i raiony Voronezhskoi oblasti* (Voronezh: Voronezhskii oblastnoi goskomstat, 1996).

44. It is possible that some fluctuation in production levels is due to changing incentives to underreport production. Given the decreasing power of the state to requisition crops, one might expect that farms would feel freer to conceal the production of goods, especially goods that easily could be traded or sold to private commercial entities. However, the fact that state subsidies for collective farms were directed primarily toward successful enterprises suggests that it is unlikely farms would engage in behavior that might limit their chances for financial support.

45. The reality described by this folk saying and its use in the context of contemporary agrarian change reveal the thin meaning of worker "consent" to reorganization. The large body of literature on subaltern studies and the work of James C. Scott have explored how relationships of domination produce particular social narratives and how people resist without challenging hegemonic discourse. See, for example, Ranajit Guha and Gayatri Chakravorty, eds., *Selected Subaltern Studies* (New York: Oxford University Press, 1998); Ranajit Guha, *Dominance Without Hegemony: History and Power in Colonial India* (Cambridge, MA: Harvard University Press, 1997); James C. Scott, *Weapons of the Weak: Everyday Forms of Peasant Resistance* (New Haven, CT: Yale University Press, 1985); and James C. Scott, *Domination and the Arts of Resistance: Hidden Transcripts* (New Haven, CT: Yale University Press, 1990). On approaches to the study of consent in social scientific inquiry, see Ian Shapiro and Alexander Wendt, "The Difference That Realism Makes: Social Science and the Politics of Consent," *Politics and Society* 20 (1992): 2.

46. Chayanovskoe chairman, interview with author, 9 August 1998.

47. Wegren cites similar reasons for indifference on the part of agricultural workers in Bryansk oblast. See Wegren, *Agriculture and the State*, 80.

48. Districts in Voronezh oblast vary on this point. Some districts made maps of land to be apportioned for private farming available to applicants in advance of their final decision to leave the collective.

49. This was true on a national level as well. The barriers to exit were considerable. Of those who remained on collective enterprises, pensioners without family most frequently sold their land shares. Others preferred to lease their land, or most often, to sell the land to the collective. See, for example, *Trud*, 10 October 1995.

50. Irina Koznova, "Traditsii i novatsii v povedenii sovremennykh krest'ian," in *Identichnost' i konflikt v postsovetskikh gosudarstvakh*, eds. M. Olcott, V. Tishkova, and A. Malashenko (Moscow: Moskovskii Tsentr Karnegi, 1997), 359–82.

51. The failure of transformed property relations to effect significant and positive change did not go unnoticed at higher levels of government. In 1995, the then first deputy chair of the State Committee on Land for the Russian Federation observed that "the current landholders, for all intents and purposes, are the bureaucrats of the agro-industrial apparatus. . . . Why? The chairman [management] and often the local administration did not want to change anything. And the Russian government didn't have enough persistence to protect the rights that had been proclaimed." In this instance, the excessive discretion exercised by local officials was to blame for the failure of reorganization to achieve its aims. With collective farm chairpersons and chiefs of agricultural administration overseeing reorganization, it was impossible to escape conflicts of interest in the implementation of reform. The result, therefore, was "not reorganization, but a facsimile thereof." In V. Alakoz, "Zemlia do vostrebovaniia," *Trud*, 16 October 1995, 5.

52. Chayanovskoe chairman, interview by author, 10 September 1998.

53. *Maiak pridon'ia*, 11 September 1993, 2.

54. *Trud*, 24 January 1995, 6.

55. Chayanovskoe chairman, interview by author, 10 September 1998.

56. *Maiak pridon'ia*, 28 January 1992, 1.

57. Chayanovskoe chief agronomist, interview by author, 9 August 1998.

58. *Liskinskie izvestiia*, 11 January 1992, 1.

59. S. A. Nikol'skii, "Kollektivizastsiia i dekollektivizatsiia: sravnitel'nyi analiz protsessov, posledstvii i perspektiv," in *Krest'ianovedenie 1997: teoriia, istoriia, sovremennost'*, eds. V. Danilov and T. Shanin (Moscow: Aspekt Press, 1997), 223–40.

60. The experimental character of the collectivization process is also frequently attributed to the reforms of the 1990s, not only by reporters and scholars, but also by villagers, who complain of once again being the objects of experimentation by the state.

61. Interview with the head of the Russian national private farmers' association (AKKOR), in *Literaturnaia gazeta*, November 1995, 10.

62. Kitching speculates that this relationship explains why workers remain on worse-off collectives. The example of Chayanovskoe—whose director exhibits the characteristics of "strong leadership" that Kitching argues are determinative of relative success—suggests that this is true for other collectives as well. Kitching, "The Development of Agrarian Capitalism," 3. For a discussion of the economy of private plot production and an argument about its relationship to declining collective cultivation, see Gavin Kitching, "The Revenge of the Peasant? The Collapse of Large-Scale Russian Agriculture and the Role of the Peasant 'Private Plot' in that Collapse, 1991–1997," *Journal of Peasant Studies* 26 (1998): 1.

63. For example, during my stay at Chayanovskoe, I lived in the home of a pensioner. Since I was a guest of the enterprise, arrangements were made between the director of the enterprise and my host. In exchange for housing me, my host received a promise from the enterprise director that she would not go without coal during the coming winter.

64. This notion of community can manifest itself in negative ways, as in behavior that stems from the understanding that "*vse vokrug kolkhoznoe, vse vokrug moe*," "everything around is the kolkhoz's, so everything around is mine."

65. Daily meeting of Chayanovskoe's managers and specialists (*planerka*), 21 August 1998. As the chairman put it, the enterprise's debtors "don't want to pay up."

66. Raion head of agricultural administration, interview by author, 9 September 1998.

67. Chayanovskoe chairman, interview by author, 21 August 1998.

68. Ibid.

69. *Maiak pridon'ia*, 16 January 1992, 3.

Part Three

Household and
Village Adaptation to Change

13

Adapting to Neglect: The Russian Peasant in the 1990s

ETHEL DUNN

This essay, like " 'They Don't Pay Attention to Us!' The Russian Peasant Today," written in 1992,[1] assesses how the peasant reacted in the 1990s to a market economy which is supposed to replace collectivized agriculture. My task here is to put a face on Russian peasants, farmers, women, and the rural elderly and disabled. To do this, I have used, besides scholarly books and journals, the Russian press, treating the press like the ethnographic resource it is.

I have previously argued that the Russian peasant is female, since what is produced both on the private plot and in large part on *kolkhozy* and *sovkhozy* is the result of manual female labor.[2] According to Bridger, two-thirds of the new private farm families are from urban areas, and in most cases, the farm is in the husband's name. "In some regions the proportion of rural people taking on private farms was less than 10 percent."[3] However, farmers recognize that women are essential to their operations, and bachelors are accustomed to placing advertisements in the Russian press, not for women workers, but for wives. This division of labor between husbands and wives is traditional: The men use machinery, the women work the private plot by hand.[4] What is produced has become increasingly important as a source of food for families. Even in relatively well-off Moscow, women needing to feed their families or supplement the family income as they become unemployed, spend time at their dachas working in their gardens,[5] although there is a clear preference for trades and skills which are not so labor intensive.

A detailed account of life in the provincial city of Voronezh in late 1998 shows how people are adapting to a lack of money from salaries. An official in the office of Gazstroi (a construction company), Natalia Lugarkina, says that she and her husband canned and laid in about the same amount of vegetables and staples as in 1997: 60 three-liter jars of tomatoes, about 50 jars of cucumbers, 2 sacks of potatoes, a bag of flour and of sugar, several jars of stew, a barrel of sauerkraut, and 40 jars of stewed fruit. They also pitched in on the rural gardens of her mother and sister. The rural connections of city residents are an important element in survival tactics in the late 1990s. In times of crisis, relatives gravitate toward the village, and in better times, rural people visit their urban relatives. People who have a little money are not spending it on clothes and leisure activities but are thinking of cars and trucks as a way to market excess produce.

Alexander and Elena Shishkin, who live on the Maslovskii *sovkhoz*, have 18 biological children (9 boys and 9 girls).[6] The family is said to live by their Christian principles. Alexander works as a driver for the fire department for 1,000 rubles a month. They feed themselves from their private plot, on which they keep 2 cows, 2 calves, 4 piglets, and 15 chickens. The 400 buckets of potatoes they needed for the winter came mostly from the private plot. Over the last three years they have had little financial aid for the children, although the previous governor of Voronezh oblast gave them a grant of 16 million old rubles, and the new governor gave 18 million new rubles. Alexander says that every bit of aid helps, but mostly they rely on themselves, and they are making it.

Mrs. Lugarkina and the Shishkins are adapting by providing much of their own food. Sergei Poriadin, through hard work and a bit of luck, began to live differently. When he lost his job, his wife left him. He now lives with his pensioner mother and a disabled younger brother. He tried to find work at other factories, but they were giving workers unpaid leave, or closing, or not paying wages at all, so he took on odd jobs, such as digging a trench 50 meters long by 1.5 meters deep by 50 centimeters wide for 50 rubles. His mother helps out by spinning wool for a neighbor in exchange for a sack of potatoes. Then Poriadin met Vitalii Zhukov, a former administrator at a communications enterprise, who hired him as a helper and organized three employment cooperatives for more than 300 unemployed freight handlers, bookkeepers, and household workers. Women who sit with the sick earn 100 rubles a month or 10 rubles an hour as baby-sitters, and frequently work for their suppers.[7]

Rural women, whether they are native to the agricultural enterprise, former urban residents, or migrants from non-Russian republics of the former Soviet Union, are frequently underemployed or employed in occupations that do not utilize skills acquired through education and experience. According to Bridger, at the beginning of the 1990s, rural unemployment was relatively low: "[A]t the time of the major farming reorganization in 1992, around one-sixth of Russia's official unemployed lived in rural areas. As in the cities, over 70 percent were women, yet less than 1 percent of Russia's unemployed women at this time were former farm workers." Bridger states that "the major direct cause of official unemployment in the countryside was the collapse of the rural service sector and problems with rural industry."[8] If this really is the official view of unemployment among rural women, it ignores the crucial role that women have in work on the private plot, because in many areas of the Russian countryside the rural service sector and rural industry are practically nonexistent. Under these conditions, women trained as teachers or medical workers, for example, will find themselves working as livestock handlers, and they have fewer and fewer avenues for redress of complaints about working conditions or other problems.

In Soviet times, people wrote to newspapers and magazines to complain, and they still do, but there is a certain lack of incentive to speak up, having to do with the fact that if people complain, they run the risk of losing their housing and their jobs. As Bridger says, "such a situation can scarcely be regarded as progress. . . ."[9] One journalist reported in 1990 that a farm chairman told him that "we've got democracy now so I don't have to ask anyone's permission. The district Party committee used to order me to respond to criticism so I responded, but now I don't owe anybody anything."[10] A recent example of bureaucratic nerve is illustrated by the case of a woman *fel'dsher* (medical assistant) who resettled from Kirgiziia with her husband in a village in Belgorod oblast. She was immediately given work and housing in the same building as the medical facility. In 1998, a new administrator tried to extract payment for heating and light for the entire building from her, and the expenses were only picked up again by the rural administration when the newspaper *Sel'skaia nov'* protested.[11] The incident seems minor compared to the case of the director of the Nechaevskii Joint Stock Company in the Mokshanskii *raion* of Penza oblast, who turned off the water to the child-care facility, the school, and the hospital in the village of Nechaevka, on the grounds that they had not paid him enough money. People were reduced to melting snow or carrying water from the railway station 1.5 kilometers away. The matter was resolved by having the Ministry for Extreme Situations remove the stoppers on the line. The director is no stranger to the area: He graduated from the village school in 1966, and his children studied there as well.[12]

Sel'skaia nov' also aided a woman in Kirov oblast, who wrote that she needed a hearing aid and she was unable to get one. The newspaper intervened on her behalf, and learned that the woman did get the free hearing aid that she needed. Another woman in Orel oblast wrote that the Agricultural Professional-Technical School where her son studies has not paid his stipend for many months. *Sel'skaia nov'* asked the local administrators to look into the situation and was subsequently informed that all the monies were paid. Another woman in Samara oblast who is old and ill asked for help getting a telephone (which she is entitled to have free). Again the journal intervened, and the local authorities complied.[13] A jobless rural woman in Voronezh oblast with two children who was unable to feed and clothe them was given a job in the House of Culture as a technical worker and a 12-*sotki* plot of land, and clothing from the resources of the Talovskii raion administration, as well as food (stew meat, groats, vegetable oil, sugar, and flour).[14] *Sel'skaia nov'* even sent a rural library in Stavropol *krai* some issues when the library was not given funds in 1996 to continue its subscription for local readers who are no longer able to subscribe.[15]

Unfortunately, a system of redress that is based on intervention on a case-by-case basis still leaves the majority to their own devices, and as has already been suggested, women are adapting to underemployment and unemployment by concentrating on feeding their families from the produce of private plots. Bridger, basing her opinion on fieldwork in 1993, suggests that it is generally easier to expand the size of the private plot than to start up a small farming operation. One poor woman told her: "I have three children and a large plot. And I don't manage. I don't manage. And it upsets me a lot."[16] I agree with Bridger that just having the land is not "an infallible safety net against the ravages of soaring inflation,"[17] or, indeed, that private ownership of land will solve the problems of Russian rural life. According to Bridger, who cites the 1989 census, in the 15 central Russian regions, between 30 percent and 40 percent of the rural population were pensioners. Most farm administrations tried as best they could to meet the obligation to help elderly women maintain themselves, but many elderly women in the mid-1980s were reduced to making homebrew in order to have a medium of exchange for handymen to help them maintain their houses and plow their plots.[18] Even younger women are reduced to writing appeals to newspapers and magazines for clothes for their children who, for the lack of them, sometimes cannot attend school.[19] In the late

1990s, the situation is no better, because the state frequently fails to pay grants and subsidies to which citizens are entitled by law. For instance, a young army recruit from a village in Murmansk oblast was sent to Groznyi (during the war with Chechnya) after he signed a contract promising him benefits that he hoped to use to put himself through a police training school. When he returned to his unit in St. Petersburg, the military commander told him that the contract was worthless. *Sel'skaia nov'* intervened, and some money was found in the army's budget. Money was also found for a woman in Vladimir oblast, whose sole income was derived from a subsidy for her child.[20]

When the economy operates without money, produce from the private plot or the farm can be an important source of income. As Tables 13.1 through 13.4 show, Russians do not eat well. Historically, there has been a significant difference between the nutrition of urban and rural residents. The data in Table 13.3 for 1996 show that in many respects, the rural resident appears to eat better than the city dweller. There are, however, a number of products (e.g., fish, meat, and berries) that are marketed rather than consumed by the rural resident, who does not have the money to purchase them. Malnutrition is endemic, and probably has been for a long time. Wheatcroft has written about the food supply for Russia and the Soviet Union from 1900 to 1960. The total daily caloric intake in 1900–13 was 2,964; most of it classified as vegetable. By 1960, the total had risen only slightly to 2,978, but the amount of animal protein had nearly doubled, from 342 to 675 calories per day.[21] I have argued for years that the issue of meat consumption in the Soviet Union and Russia was not a nutritional but a political issue—the more meat consumed, the wealthier the individual felt and the nation appeared. Sugar seems to be a substitute in the absence of meat (compare consumption recommendations in Tables 13.1, 13.2, and 13.4). By 1989 and 1990, as seen in Table 13.3, individual meat consumption had nearly caught up with the established recommendation, but then a decline set in. In 1995, animal protein made up only 31 percent of the daily caloric intake of 2,310, which the reporter equated with malnutrition.[22] In 1997, meat (and for that matter, fruits and vegetables) were a very modest part of the Russian food basket (Table 13.4), while daily caloric intake had fallen to between 2000 and 2200.[23] A decline in production,[24] coupled with price increases, is to blame. In Saratov oblast in 1995, annual sales of meat, milk, and eggs per capita dropped precipitously from 1986–90 levels: meat, 110 to 31 kilograms; milk, 354 to 138 kilograms; and eggs, 213 to 83.[25] Strangely enough, in 1995, the price of vodka had risen less steeply than all other consumable

Table 13.1

Per Capita Consumption of Basic Food Products, Selected Years, 1960 to 1985 (kg)

Food Product	Blue- and White-Collar Workers			Kolkhozniki			USSR					Recommended Amount, 1974	Foodstuffs Program, 1990 (target)
	1960	1965	1968	1960	1965	1968	1970	1972	1973	1984	1985		
Meat and meat products	44	43	51	30	33	37	48	51	53	60.7	61	81.8	70
Dairy products	245	257	290	228	234	268	307	296	307	319	323	433.6	330–340
Eggs	117	124	143	122	123	146	159	185	195	258	260	292	260–266
Fish and fish products	12.0	14.4	15.9	5.4	7.1	9.0	15.4	15.1	16.1	17.5		18.2	
Sugar	32.4	36.7	38.8	18.2	26.5	32.9	38.8	38.8	40.8	44.0		36.5	
Vegetable oil	5.9	7.4	6.7	4.1	6.1	6.0	6.8	6.9	7.3	9.5	9.7		13.2
Potatoes	132	135	125	168	161	151	130	121	124	108		96.7	
Vegetables and melons	74	78	83	59	56	65	82	80	85	102	102	146.0	126–135
Fruits and berries	22						35			45	46	94.9	66–70
Grain products (bread, flour, grains, pasta, beans)	153	149	142	188	177	172	149	145	143	133		120.4	

Source: Stephen P. Dunn and Ethel Dunn, *The Peasants of Central Russia* (Prospect Heights, IL: Waveland Press, 1988), xx.

Table 13.2

Average Per Capita Annual Consumption of Selected Foodstuffs, 1965, 1970, and 1975 (kg)

Foodstuff	Recommended	1965	1970	1975
Grain products	110	156	149	141
Potatoes	97	142	130	120
Sugar	40	34.2	38.8	40.8
Fish	18.2	12.6	15.4	16.8
Milk products	405	251	307	316
Eggs	292	124	159	215
Meat products	82	41	48	57
Vegetables and melons	146	72	82	87

Source: Sel'skaia zhizn', 16 June 1998, 1.

products, to the point that a liter of milk cost almost 40 percent more than a liter of vodka.[26]

A report on the health of the Russian population in 1996 revealed that 45 percent of pregnant women and nursing mothers in Samara oblast were undernourished. Among the women surveyed, 53 percent to 66 percent were deficient in ascorbic acid, 77 percent to 93 percent were deficient in folic acid, and 27 percent to 36 percent were deficient in vitamins B1 and B2.[27]

In Tonshaevo raion, Nizhegorod oblast, a study of pregnant women was conducted at five-year intervals from 1981 to 1995. According to the study, in the town of Tonshaevo, with a population of 19,000, and basic areas for growth in agriculture and forestry, 53.2 percent of the population is female, of which 31.6 percent were of childbearing age. Unemployment of pregnant women increased from 4 percent in 1992 to 33.8 percent in 1994. Slightly more than one-fourth of these women were listed at the unemployment bureau but the rest were depending on husbands or relatives; 14.6 percent were single. In households where the woman did not work, the average income per family member was 304,000 rubles a month, compared to 422,000 rubles when the woman was employed. Even one child puts the family below the subsistence minimum, which on 6 January 1997 in Nizhegorod oblast was 325,000 rubles. Subsidiary economic activity (household plots and cattle) does not compensate for the deficit; only 26 percent of Tonshaevo households currently keep large livestock, and only 50.3 percent have other animals, mainly because fodder is difficult to obtain. The average person's diet consists mostly of flour, groats (consumed by 90 percent of the sample on a daily basis), and potatoes (daily fare for

Table 13.3

Average Per Capita Annual Food Consumption, Selected Years, 1989 to 1996 (kg)

Food Product	1989	1990	1991	1992	1993	1994	1996 Rural	1996 Urban
Meat and meat products	75	75	65	54	58	69	50	48
Beef	18.9		15.6	14.1	16.6			
Lamb	2.23		1.5	1.39	1.22			
Pork	10.35		9.5	10.29	10.98			
Poultry	13.55		12.6	10.31	8.7			
Sausage	14.4		13	10.37	10.54			
Milk and milk products	397	386	348	299	298	282	311	206
Whole milk	116.6		118	106.4	99.5			
Sour cream/cream	14.05		13.3	6.48	6.48			
Butter	7.14		5.51	5.57	5.87			
Eggs	237	297	229	243	255	225	183	168
Fish and fish products	16.1	20	14.1	11.6	12	11	6	10
Sugar and sweets	33	47	29	28	33	32	28	25
Sugar	20.8		17.5	17.32	21.56			
Vegetable oil, margarine	6.9	9.8	6.1	6.5	7.2	6		
Potatoes	93.83	106	98.1	106.65	117.58	140	151	92
Vegetables and melons	91.0	89	87.0	83.0	74	61	88	74
Fruits and berries	41.0	35	37.0	34.0	37	30	23	33
Grain products	98.0	119	98.0	104	109	128	117	89
Wheat bread	28.6		73.03	71.46	70.48			
Rye bread	23.62		24.7	26.69				

Notes: Figures for 1993 were calculated for the first six months of the year. According to *Izvestiia* (29 July 1994, 13), in 1989, 1991, 1992, and 1993, "not more than 50 percent of those surveyed used milk products," and "not more than 20 percent" ate fresh fruit.
Sources: 1990 and 1994 data from Stephen K. Wegren, "Rural Politics and Agrarian Reform in Russia," *Problems of Post-Communism* (January–February 1996): 27; 1989, 1991, 1992, and 1993 data from *Izvestiia*, 29 July 1994, 13; and 1996 data from L. V. Bondarenko, "Tendentsii v potreblenii sel'skogo naseleniia," *Ekonomika sel'skokhoziaistvennykh i pererabatyvayushchikh predpriyatii*, 3 March 1998, 39.

Table 13.4

Food Basket Chosen by the State Statistics Committee Based on
Recommendations by the Ministry of Labor, 1997 (kg/year)

Bread	121.6	Wheat flour	19.5	Cheese	2.3
Fresh cabbage	28.1	Sausage, cooked	0.45	Cottage cheese	9.9
Fish, frozen	11.7	Butter	2.5	Potatoes	124.2
Beef	8.4	Margarine	3.9	Sugar	20.7
Sour cream	1.6	Vermicelli	5.2	Poultry	17.5
Vegetable oil	6.4	Apples	19.4	Milk, liters	123.1
Millet	9.8	Rice	3.7	Eggs	151
Onion	28.4	Sausage, half-smoked	0.45	Carrots	37.6

Source: Sel'skaia zhizn' 16 June 1998, 3.

57 percent). In this survey, potatoes were classified as a vegetable. On a daily basis, 48 percent of the sample consumed milk products, 41 percent meat or fowl, 31 percent sweets, 20 percent fruits, and 10 percent fish. There are many complications of pregnancy, the leading one being anemia (37.9 percent), and among unemployed pregnant women, 81.3 percent suffered from anemia. The increase in anemia is seasonal, having to do with the slaughter of livestock; 44.4 percent of all cases of anemia occur between August and November, but in December through March, when most slaughtering occurs, cases of anemia fall to 26.4 percent. Morbidity among children over 10 years of age increased from 5.1 to 32.6 per 100, and birth anomalies from 1.2 to 4.8 per 100 newborns.[28]

Much has been made in the West of the introduction of private farming as a cure for the shortcomings of the Russian rural sector. Bridger compares the productivity of private farming and the private household plot, and notes that "by 1996 the new peasant farms were reported to be producing 3 percent of Russia's agricultural produce on 5 percent of the [arable] land. Figures from 1994 meanwhile, showed the plots producing 46 percent of gross agricultural product on 3.8 percent of the land."[29]

According to *Krest'ianskie vedomosti*, Russian farmers increased their share of the harvest in 1998 to 10.8 percent (up from 10.2 percent in 1997). However, grain output fell from 88.6 million tons in 1997 to 48.5 million in 1998. At the same time, farmers and people with household plots produced 95 percent of all potatoes, 76 percent of vegetables, and "thousands" of tons of meat and milk.[30] In early 1999, there were 270,000 private farms (down from 280,000 in 1998), and including rented land, private farms account for approximately 15 million hectares of arable land (up from 13 million in 1997).[31] Ioffe and Nefedova contend that "individual private farms . . . are so feeble that only some Western commentators continue to take them seriously. Besides, many private farms are no more than subsidiary plots."[32] The picture is further complicated by the fact that in Leningrad oblast, for example, 30 agricultural enterprises have declared their intention to turn themselves back into kolkhozy, i.e., to reverse privatization.[33] Some sovkhozy appear to have been dissolved to no good purpose.

According to the former chief engineer of a *sovkhoz* in Penza oblast, when the sovkhoz was shut down, it had 2,000 head of cattle, 400 students were attending the middle school, young children were in child-care facilities, the village boasted a bakery, good roads connected the village to the city, and the residents were proud of their House of Culture. Now there are less than 50 children in the school, and their parents have no work.[34]

Just as under the Soviet system, the success or failure of reforms is uneven; in fact, contemporary reforms are reasonably successful in some places. The Nizhniy Novgorod experiment, which reorganized 256 agricultural enterprises in the oblast in a five-year experiment, seems to have had some modest success. The experiment is being extended to 17 other regions of the country, aided by five agricultural funds (Nizhegorod, Moscow, Rostov, Orel, and Volgograd), now united in an Association of Funds for the Support of Agrarian Reform.[35] Certainly something needs to be done to improve the agricultural sector of the economy. Investment has sunk to 22 percent of the 1989 level and 90 percent of all farms are failing.[36]

According to Ioffe and Nefedova, "the peasant character of Russian agriculture is being de facto reproduced though without a numerous peasant class."[37] The Russian press is indeed having difficulty distinguishing between *fermery* (farmers) and *krest'ianstva* (peasants). Farmers were supposed to constitute a new stratum of the rural population, but in terms of their way of life, little separates them from peasants, except perhaps the size of their operations. Let us turn to some case studies, taken from recent Russian newspapers.

Vasil Bazhan is an example of Russians of peasant origin who are trying to reclaim their heritage. In 1993, Bazhan, the great-grandson of a *kulak* (wealthy peasant), returned to the village in which his great-grandfather had lived and prospered until he was dekulakized (politically and socially repressed) in 1932, and his mill, creamery, and brick factory were shut down. Bazhan had plans to restore all that and more, since flour had to be bought in Stavropol 130 versts away and butter and sausage from Ipatovo 90 versts away. Bazhan formed a partnership with his brother and other family members, using money and assets from his share of the sovkhoz in which he had worked as a link leader (head of a production unit). He was soon so successful that his enterprise had 100 million rubles invested, drawing the attention of Akkor-lezing (an agricultural equipment company), which promised even more investment. The envy of his neighbors expressed itself in the ruling that farmers' children would get school lunches at a higher price than other children, and their parents would not be able to buy bread at the bakery. Bazhan, however, did not retaliate, as others suggested he should, and instead made a mutually advantageous deal with the local sovkhoz director to open a shop. His partnership had 150 hectares of land, but Bazhan needed more land to keep the mill operating year round, and began looking for land to rent.[38] He therefore must be considered a success at adapting to new conditions.

Viktor Kuz'min, a farmer in Vologda oblast, was not so fortunate. He had all his assets seized to pay a court judgment against him for having willfully destroyed the private property of a citizen who brought suit against him. The matter went back to court when Kuz'min protested, but the fine was increased and Kuz'min was sentenced to three years in jail. To ensure that the order was carried out, armed soldiers appeared at his farmstead, leading to the cry in the village, "They're dekulakizing a farmer!" The matter ended with a lesser judgment against Kuz'min, and no time in jail, but the harassment continued. He was ordered to place himself on the list for the prison work detail.[39]

Vladimir Zolotov, described as the head of a peasant farm near Yaroslavl and a farmer from the beginning of the reform period, when credits and machinery were easier to get, was born in 1955 into a peasant family in a small village in Tugaevskii *okrug* of Yaroslavl oblast. After graduating from school, he entered the Poshekhon agricultural *tekhnikum*, where he earned a "red" diploma (entitling him to enter the Soviet system of professional and party placement) as a research agronomist. He worked in the Verzino sovkhoz as an agronomist, served in the army, and after demobilization worked in the Tunoshna sovkhoz as a brigadier and administrator, and then for seven years as the director of the Rodina sovkhoz. His wife works in rural administration, his daughter attends a teachers' college, and his twin sons are studying in the farmer division of an agricultural tekhnikum. In his spare time, Zolotov likes to fish for carp in a stream he dug out himself.

Now Zolotov has 62 hectares of his own and 25 rented hectares, from which he harvests 500 tons of potatoes and 500 tons of cabbage, carrots and beets, which he markets in nine shops and eateries in Yaroslavl, two military schools, and other cities. When he left the sovkhoz, he had no agricultural machinery, but after a year of building up his capital, he was able to acquire tractors, combines, automobiles, and tools. Then he acquired construction and road-building equipment, laid down a road to his work area, and recently built a modern, 1,000-ton vegetable storage facility costing a million new rubles. This facility allows him to get a better price for his vegetables, since he no longer has to sell his produce at any price immediately after the harvest. Credit for the construction was extended by SBS-Agro Bank.[40] The newspaper *Krest'ianskie vedomosti* did not mention whether Zolotov hires labor. However, if he uses the skills of his wife, daughter, and sons, he has achieved his success with a crew of four part-time workers in addition to his own labor. He also appears to be well connected both locally and regionally, but this can only be inferred from his biography. He is an undoubtedly also aided by his education and that of his family.

If farmers are not well connected, and perhaps not well liked, they have many problems. In 1994 in the center of Moscow, at the monument for Yuri Dolgoruki, Alevtin Chepenko, a Moscow area farmer, threatened to set himself on fire if nothing was done to help him. Here is his story:

In October 1991, when I decided to become a farmer, I had 22,000 rubles. At the time I could have bought a tractor and seed and plowed and sown the land. It's bad enough that relations with the local administration were irreparably spoiled, since I had to appeal repeatedly to the oblast administration and complain to the Minister of Agriculture, write to the Committee for Agricultural Reform, and to the administrative staff of the President, and even go to court. As a result I got the land, but after all this, the Kolomensk Bank refused me credit, although in 1993 the Kolomensk farmers were granted 90 million rubles in credit.

What am I to do? Now I have four hectares in private property, and I rent ten. Five years after receiving the land, I am obliged to build on it and create a farming operation; otherwise the raion administration can deprive me of the land. But a year has gone by, a second and then a third and the land is empty. I believe that this is not my fault but no one is interested in that. Not long ago the raion administration warned me that if I don't work the fields in the spring and don't build, they would take away the land. But where am I supposed to get the money?

And I need quite a bit. I need to build a large house, a building for the cattle, buy a tractor and a plow, and other agricultural implements, dig a well, plant a garden, plow, sow, grow and gather the harvest. Naturally, I tried to earn the money. Last summer I cut hay and proposed to the director of the Provodnik sovkhoz that he buy the hay. He answered that the sovkhoz had no problem with fodder. I called the outlying farms, but as soon as they learned that the hay was farmer's hay they refused to take it.

Everything is leading up to giving up the land. Last year four farmers in our raion were deprived of the land for the same reason, and this spring, according to my calculations about forty farmers will suffer the same fate.

That's why I've decided to appeal to people for help. I stand in the center of Moscow, a healthy man, and beg for alms. I am asking not for myself. Everyone like me wants that in the end we all live better. But those on whom the development of the farmers' movement depends, cannot understand this.

A Penza farmer, Viktor Chumak, when interviewed in Moscow about this story, was skeptical, saying that Chepenko could sow his 14 hectares by hand. Chumak had just finished working 700 hectares, and so had his neighbors. Chumak said reliance on the government for anything is a thing of the past for former *kolkhozniki*. He added, "There is always a risk to farming, and if you can't prove that you can handle it, no one will give you money." Chumak himself was looking for investors, because he'd like millions of rubles to expand his operation. If he doesn't get it, he said, he would consider it the breaks of the game and not blame anyone. It should be noted, however, that Chumak began his operation with a half-million-ruble line of credit from Agroprom Bank, extended without the usual guarantees from the kolkhoz.[41]

The president of AKKOR (Association of Peasant [Farmer] Operations and Agricultural Cooperatives of Russia), Vladimir Bashmachnikov, said the problem is that governmental decrees were not being implemented, and banks were not distributing the funds earmarked for farmers. He was planning an appeal to Yeltsin, asking that measures be taken, because in 1993 about 18,000 farmers stopped farming and the process is still continuing, although many farmers are still farming. In early 1994, farmers numbered 270,000 (about the same as in early 1999), and in May 1994, 280,000. The government should not simply abandon them, Bashmachnikov said.[42] One way around the credit crunch is credit cooperatives, such as the one in Voronezh oblast, which has been operating since 1998. The cooperative has 100 shareholders, and each shareholder contributed 5,000 rubles.[43]

In Lipetsk oblast, people have adapted to market conditions by increasing the size of private plots, or the amount of livestock held. Viktor Novikov, for instance, has six head of cattle, a pair of piglets, and a large number of geese, ducks, and chickens. A former sovkhoz that has been turned into a cooperative is doing well; in fact, the cooperative is owed 830,000 rubles by the oblast produce corporation. Cooperative employees earn approximately a thousand rubles a month, but these salaries are inadequate and the enterprise is not really making a profit. The sovkhoz sells a liter of milk for a ruble (about the price of a bottle of mineral water), and a kilogram goes for no more than 17 rubles, a third or fourth of the present market price.

The brigadier of the former Russia kolkhoz, which is now a cooperative called Chernava, was asked whether, given the fact that the cooperative had over a million rubles of debt, the kolkhoz ought to be dissolved. He said, "By no means. . . . [M]any [employees] would simply fall apart for lack of money, depression [*toska*], and drunkenness. Not everyone can work as an individual—where would you get the machinery? And there would not be enough land for everyone! No, something new is not always better. Best of all, before it is too late, to return to the former kolkhoz. Things were wonderful [*slavno*] in it." That last sentiment is heard frequently in these parts. At present, the government is not financing any social services in the village, because it doesn't have the money.

One of the most successful farmers in Lipetsk oblast, Alexander Suslov, from Volovskii raion, has more than 500 hectares, several tractors, combines, and trucks, purchased in Soviet times or in the early post-reform years. The machinery, however, has broken headlights and windshields, and is otherwise run down. Suslov started out at the beginning of the 1990s saying that he would show everyone that a Russian farmer could work as efficiently as a Dutchman or an American, and at first he did. Lately, things have begun to slip. Suslov told a *Sel'skaia zhizn'* reporter that he cannot do everything himself. He was a teacher by profession and is already a pensioner. He has to hire people, he said, who do not take the same care of the machinery that he would, or who do not show up because they are drunk. The reporter remarked, "You probably don't pay them much." Suslov answered,

> I'd be glad to pay them but with what? I myself sit without a kopek every month. Last year because the combine broke down, I didn't harvest 150 hectares of buckwheat. I had nothing to sell and that means nothing with which to buy gasoline and diesel fuel, and pay

wages. I didn't do the autumn plowing on time, and I had to do it in the spring, and we know that you don't get the same harvest with spring plowing. In general I'm in debt to everybody: my workers and the state.

The reporter thought to himself that if the boss lives in a house where the most valuable thing is an old TV set, he did not even want to know how the workers live. After visiting other nearby farms, the reporter learned that some live a little better and some live worse than Suslov. The exception was the farmer Vasilii Savenkov, from the village of Chernava, Iz-malkovskii raion. He does not hire workers, but all ten of the workers on his farm have shares in it of 7 or 14 hectares. They take better care of the machinery, and they earn 1,500 or 2,000 rubles a month, which before 17 August 1998, when the ruble was devalued, was the equivalent of 250 to 300 Soviet rubles—not bad wages for the area.

According to the *Sel'skaia zhizn'* reporter, in Moscow oblast, a person needs 700 to 800 rubles a month to make ends meet. He cited the case of a woman from a neighboring village who went to work at a milk process-ing plant equipped with Austrian machinery and built next to some former sovkhozy. She said that she was satisfied with the wages, but there is no better-paid work in the area. The plant provides no social benefits to its workers, such as housing, trips to sanatoriums, and the like. However, the plant has built a sports complex with an indoor swimming pool and bar, a recreation facility containing dance halls and banquet rooms, three apart-ments for plant managers, and a three-story house for the director.[44]

Nikolai Dobrinov combines farming and entrepreneurial activity. He is the founder and administrator of an enterprise called Spektr, serving collec-tives and farming operations over an area of more than 40,000 hectares in Tver oblast. He was born in Tver in 1954 and in 1964 he and his parents moved to the village of Kushalino. In 1970, he graduated from an agricul-tural tekhnikum, and in 1979 from the Kalinin Agricultural Institute, with a specialty of farm equipment operation. Beginning in 1971 (at age 17), he worked in the Kushalino interkolkhoz mechanics shop as a mechanic, rising to the post of chief engineer. In 1976, he became the deputy director of Kushalino, the largest kolkhoz in the oblast. Dobrinov has two sons, the oldest of whom is planning to enter the Tver Agricultural Academy in the Faculty of Farm Equipment Operation, following in his father's footsteps. In his spare time, Dobrinov likes to hike, but he has not had time to do it lately. When the kolkhoz was reorganizing in 1992, he spoke against the plan to divide the kolkhoz into two farmers' associations, which would have divided the machinery among the 600 members. He proposed putting the machinery in a single service center, but his proposal was turned down. He left the kolkhoz and returned to the interkolkhoz mechanics shop, and later created the Spektr enterprise. Spektr employs 27 workers and now includes a grain elevator, repair shops, a gasoline station, a drying facility, a motor pool, a factory for producing feed concentrates, and a center for processing wood. The enterprise collects fees for services in the form of agricultural produce at the end of the year, which is used to make feed concentrates, spirits, and other food products that the firm markets. In 1997, Spektr was building a fine grain milling facility and a bakery.[45]

Nikolai Ovchinnikov, who previously lived in the miners' settlement of Korkino in Chelyabinsk oblast, is another farmer with connections, some of which he probably acquired when he was working as a wildlife warden in the southern Urals. During his tenure, he blew the whistle on an important Communist Party boss who was poaching with forged documents, and Ovchinnikov stood his ground against threats of physical violence. The boss was later forced to leave the region. Ovchinnikov subsequently developed blood clots in his legs, and first one and then both legs were amputated (above the knees, to judge by a photograph showing him in his wheelchair), and he was given a disability pension.

Since Ovchinnikov had a diploma from the Tobol'sk tekhnikum for the fishing industry, and his son is an ichthyologist, he decided to become a fish farmer. He then rented Kamennoe Lake, which covers 18 hectares in the Etkul' raion of Chelyabinsk oblast. The lake had been serving as a reservoir for irrigating sovkhoz fields. A deputy to the rural soviet, the director of the middle school, and *ataman* (leader) of the Karatabanskaia Stanitsa supported Ovchinnikov in this activity. He was allowed to rent the lake for a 10-year period. He was also allowed to rent 5 hectares of land and a water tank for 25 years. When Ovchinnikov took over the lake, there were only a few carp in it, which were being forced out by small crabs, and weeds were everywhere. He cleared the lake of weeds and released 7,000 small carp to feed on the crabs. Now the carp are ready to be harvested for sale, and two other kinds of fish have been added, brought in from the Arakul' Fish Hatchery.

Ovchinnikov put a small mobile home with an awning on the land, cleaned the well, laid the foundation for a larger house with a bath, planted a hundred small pines on a hill and built a fence around the hill. He dug the holes for the fence posts himself, got a flock of 100 geese, and began to raise rabbits. All of this was accomplished without a kopek of credit. A teacher and her pupils from the Karatabanskii School helped plant the trees; two neighboring farmers helped with equipment, and the Korkino Power Department, through its chief engineer, helped put in electricity. In return, Ovchinnikov permits his helpers, as well as pensioners and disabled persons, to fish and swim in the lake. People who use the lake have stopped dumping chemicals into it, and have managed to prevent topsoil runoff. Ovchinnikov has an assistant, a former electrician, and his wife and son also help. He requires a specially equipped car in order to travel by himself, but the local Department of Social Protection does not respond to his requests.[46] To make matters worse, someone stole the boat he uses on his lake, and his pension of a little more than 200 rubles a month is wholly inadequate to cover the cost of a replacement.[47]

Even with his support network, Nikolai Ovchinnikov has to be considered unusually industrious. Anyone with his disability in Russia, at least in Russian cities, would usually be considered too disabled to work, although negative attitudes toward the disabled are changing. The presence in rural areas of a large number of pensioners, many of whom are disabled, places great strains on the social service network, and on any plans for rural development. In 1997, 630,000 of 1.8 million residents of Tula oblast were pensioners, and the average age of the 700,000 working-age people was 40. In an eight-month period in 1997, 21,826 persons died and 8,448 were born. About 70 percent of the oblast has been affected by pollution in the aftermath of the Chernobyl disaster.[48]

The huge numbers of elderly and disabled in rural areas are particularly at risk in Russia today, and some effort has been made by nonprofit organizations to attend to their needs. For example, the village of Trubegchino in Lipetsk oblast has 2,600 residents, and 320 of them have joined the All-Russia Society for the Disabled (ARSD), which has 2.5 million members. The Trubegchino chapter is supervised by the raion-level ARSD organization, and is visited by the head of the oblast-level organization. This chapter has five committees: daily life, legal questions, agriculture, education, and culture, each with its work plan, as well as a place for accepting contributions from citizens (apparently to redistribute).

Alexandra Sergeevna Breeva has served as chair of the Trubegchino chapter for several years. She has manifested unusual energy and initiative in making connections with the local administration and leaders of enterprises in the Dobrov raion, and as a result, the chapter gets holiday greetings, gifts, and trips to local tourist attractions and the health spa for its members. The village administration and workers in the Department of Social Protection help the ARSD in autumn and spring to plow the private plots of aged pensioners and people living alone, and also help them to get fuel and to repair their homes, among other types of assistance. The local social club director designated a special room in which members of a club for the disabled could meet. On the "Day for the Disabled," village entrepreneurs brought presents for disabled children. A gathering of elderly people designated as a "*posidel'ka*"[49] was organized to celebrate the old Rus' customs—mainly foods prepared from old recipes—and the effort was very well received.[50]

The best support for the rural elderly, many of whom live in villages where schools, hospitals, and stores have closed, would be an influx of new residents. Demobilized soldiers[51] and ethnic Russian migrants from non-Russian republics of the former Soviet Union might make such a revitalization possible. One example of the experience of migrants is the Novosel, an entire community comprised of ethnic Russians from Dushanbe (Tajikistan) who moved to a village in the Ferzikovskii raion, Kaluga oblast, called Sashkino. The move was coordinated by Galina Belgorodskaia, a senior research worker at the Institute of Seismology, and a deputy to the Dushanbe city soviet. With the help of the Federal Migration Service, the migrants laid 35 foundations and built ten homes, put roofs on the same number, laid down electric lines, and built an extension to an asphalt road. They received a loan from the Russian Compatriots Fund, and began to process lumber and to raise potatoes, geese, and pigs. The Novosel community has also set up a sewing shop, greenhouse, and bakery.

The Swedish Red Cross wanted to build a "Public Center for the Unprotected" in Novosel for use by the disabled and pensioners from hot spots of the former Soviet Union. However, the Kaluga oblast administration demanded that the money for construction be given to them in francs and dollars. The upshot was that the proposed building was forbidden, and, in fact, deemed useless for any purpose, so the Swedish Red Cross picked up and left. Belgorodskaia decided to build the center that the Swedish Red Cross had given up on. Her efforts were considered illegal, and she was actually arrested and questioned, and then released. This is only one of a number of conflicts, such as nonpayment of taxes, surrounding Belgorodskaia's efforts, during which accounts were closed, payments stopped, documents removed, and even land previously secured for the center withdrawn. The head of the Federal Migration Service in the oblast even threatened to bulldoze the village. These conflicts were caused in part by competition for scarce resources. Novosel had foreign backers, apart from the Swedish Red Cross. At the same time as all of this harassment was under way, the villagers had created a place for 150 people to work, as well as building roads and laying down water pipes. More than half of the teachers in the Sashkino school, the doctors in the Ferzikovskii raion, and even the investigator who was giving Belgorodskaia such a hard time are all from Dushanbe. However, in spite of their contributions to the region, the migrants from Dushanbe have not been given property rights to the land, which they were promised, as well as the *propiska* (residence permit), without which their children cannot get schooling or diplomas. Nor have they received compensation for the sale of their apartments in Dushanbe. During this time, the Federal Migration Service changed its mind about how to help the Russian-speaking population in the non-Russian former Soviet republics, mostly because of lack of money, saying that it was better to support them where they were.

In any case, ethnic Russians who have returned to Voronezh, Kaliningrad, Lipetsk, Yaroslavl, and Kaluga oblasts have found that their skills are not needed, but milkmaids and livestock tenders are.[52] As a result, 200,000 Russian-speaking people have returned to Uzbekistan.[53] No doubt one reason for the failure of recent migrants to rural areas of Russia to remain there is the appalling lack of physical infrastructure and social services—health care services, medicines, electricity, and even water are sometimes nonexistent. The training of new medical personnel is hampered by a lack of money to pay either teachers or students, or to buy microscopes, at least at the Altai State Medical University. Not only are doctors not paid on time, they say that they fear that the government intends to institute cost-cutting measures at the expense of public health. In the mid-1990s, 3,000 doctors and 18,000 paramedical workers left rural areas, with the result that the rural population has 13 times fewer doctors and 2 times fewer paramedical workers than Russia as a whole.[54]

Dukhobors (an ethno-religious group of Russian peasant origin), who had lived in the Georgian Republic for almost 200 years, have also been aided by the Federal Migration Service, although the aid has been less effective than in Soviet times, when entire families resettled in Tula oblast.[55] In February 1999, a group of 87 mostly elderly Dukhobors without warm clothing arrived in Briansk from Gorelovka, Georgia. After several years of harassment by their neighbors (Georgians and Armenians), the Dukhobors were forced to leave behind everything but their personal belongings, and to sell their houses and cattle for very little, with no compensation from the Georgian government. They were transported by bus to Vladikavkaz by the Georgians, and to Briansk by the Ministry for Extreme Situations. They were to settle in Mirnoe, 120 kilometers from Briansk, in an area contaminated by fallout from Chernobyl. Meanwhile, in the two years it has taken to complete the move, an advance party managed to build six cottages and a 12-unit apartment house.[56] One of my correspondents in Russia, a sophisticated scholar of the Dukhobor movement who was involved in the resettlement project, says that these recent events signal the death of the Dukhobor movement in Russia.

What conclusions can be drawn from all this? First of all, the question of whether the peasant wants private ownership of land is far from settled. If the answer is no, as it still is in some places, it is not because the peasant is unenlightened. There is a widely held belief that the land belongs to all and should not be the property of individuals. In addition, the peasant knows from experience that ownership brings responsibility, and he or she can see that under present conditions, ownership without the means of production means that the land can be taken away again without any consideration of how hard the owner had worked to keep it. There is also fear that wealthy foreigners will buy up the land. Some steps have been taken to see that this does not happen on a broad scale. In Tula oblast, for example, the Novo-moskovskbytkhim Stock Company bought 40 hectares of land from the Tula Property Fund, on which the company proposes to erect a number of buildings. The sale price of the land was 16 million rubles, an astonishing figure when we consider that one of the reasons for the sluggish pace of land reform is that establishing fair market prices for land has been enormously difficult. Procter and Gamble (a U.S. firm) holds 90 percent of the stock in Novomoskovskbytkhim. Vasilii Starodubtsev,[57] the governor of Tula oblast, does not like Procter and Gamble, but Americans have recently invested millions of dollars in the economy of the region, and in health care and other social programs, and they can be relied upon to pay their taxes.[58]

The Russian press frequently blames kolkhoz and sovkhoz administrators for the failure of the farmers' movement to thrive. For the most part, seed, fertilizer, and equipment has to come from the reorganized kolkhozy and sovkhozy. Many commentators feel that a variety of economic forms (*mnogoukladnost'*) are more appropriate for the Russian rural sector than private farming with individual ownership of land. Local administrators of rural agricultural enterprises have been shortchanged for a long time by agricultural policies that are still set by Moscow. That may change. Machine technology stations have been operating in Saratov, Rostov, and Lipetsk oblasts,[59] and the government announced that the 1999 budget had assigned 3.9 billion rubles to agriculture, though whether the government actually delivers this sum, or sets up effective equipment-leasing arrangements with SBS-Agro Bank or Rossagrosnab, remains to be seen.[60]

The Russian peasantry is not solely responsible for the "peasant character" of Russian agriculture noted by Ioffe and Nefedova. The Russian peasant can and does blame the government. The government believes that peasants are too politically passive to revolt. Peasant political parties, as Stephen Wegren has pointed out, are too fractured to defend their interests effectively against the urban majority.[61] The independent farmer faces enormous difficulties from local rural administrators[62] and tax collectors, and lacks government support.[63] People living in rural small towns and even large cities are currently feeding themselves from their own private plots or those of their relatives, and are thus in danger of reverting to the peasant class. I see no grounds for optimism about agricultural reform. If what is produced were to remain in the region, perhaps regional reformers would be able to craft a new federalism and a genuine democracy. The present difficult situation is not the fault of an allegedly inefficient peasantry but of continuous governmental neglect.

Notes

1. Ethel Dunn, "'They Don't Pay Attention to Us!': The Russian Peasant Today," in *Russia and Her Neighbors: Facts and Views on Daily Life* 6 (1992): 1–26.

2. Ethel Dunn, "Is There Feminization of Agriculture in the USSR?" *International Review of Sociology* n.s., no. 1 (1990): 166–83.

3. Sue Bridger, "Rural Women and the Impact of Economic Change," in *Post-Soviet Women: From the Baltic to Central Asia*, ed. Mary Buckley (Cambridge: Cambridge University Press, 1997), 40. Only 0.4 percent of women in 1991 had become owners of private farms or enterprises (Dunn, " 'They Don't Pay Attention to Us!,' " 26). *Sel'skaia zhizn'* (25 February 1999, 4) listed a woman economist, Galina Vladimirovna Kasym, the head of the Donets farm in the Kletskii *raion* of Volgograd oblast, who had just received a medal as Honored Economist of the Russian Federation. It should be noted that were she of retirement age, such a medal would entitle her to a number of pension benefits not extended to other pensioners.

4. I am not saying that women are totally prohibited from using machinery, but only that when rural people are trained to use equipment, it is usually men who get the training.

5. Sue Bridger, Rebecca Kay, and Kathryn Pinnick, *No More Heroines? Russia, Women and the Market* (London: Routledge, 1996), 149–53.

6. Such large families are a rarity, but Russian newspapers love to print stories of families that foster children, such as the Sorokins from the Rostov settlement, Rassvet. The Sorokins began their work in 1989, and a decade later, still foster 18 children, among whom there are 7 disabled children and 6 others who had their disability rating of developmentally retarded changed as a result of Mrs. Sorokin's efforts. *Sel'skaia zhizn'*, 4 March 1999, 1, 4.

7. *Izvestiia*, 11 November 1998, 5.

8. Bridger, "Rural Women and Economic Change," 45.

9. Ibid.

10. Bridger, Kay, and Pinnick, *No More Heroines*, 43–44.

11. *Sel'skaia nov'*, no. 11, 1997, 19.

12. *Sel'skaia zhizn'*, 2 March 1999, 1. This open letter was written by the editor, who was a teacher in the Nechaevka school.

13. *Sel'skaia nov'*, no. 1, 1999, 14.

14. *Sel'skaia nov'*, no. 9, 1997, 13.

15. *Sel'skaia nov'*, no. 7, 1997, 21.

16. Bridger, "Rural Women and Economic Change," 50.

17. Ibid., 46.

18. Ibid., 47.

19. Ibid., 46. The woman in Bridger's example lost her hands in an on-the-job accident. She and her four children were abandoned by her husband.

20. *Sel'skaia nov'*, no. 9, 1998, 11. See similar letters from a soldier's mother in Pskov oblast and a mother in Penza oblast with no wages and no child subsidy with which to feed her children and send them to school (*Sel'skaia nov'*, no. 4, 1998, 17). Another woman in Penza oblast received the money due her on the birth of her child only after she had gone from office to office, literally exhausting herself, her money, and her baby-sitters (*Sel'skaia nov'*, no. 3, 1998, 15). A woman in Kurgan oblast looking for "children's money" was satisfied with partial payment, probably because the agency itself did not receive its budget from the government (*Sel'skaia nov'*, no. 2, 1998, 13).

21. Stephen G. Wheatcroft, "The Great Leap Upwards: Anthropometric Data and Indicators of Crises and Secular Change in Soviet Welfare Levels, 1880–1960," *Slavic Review* 58, no. 1 (1999): 51.

22. *Sel'skaia zhizn'*, 24 October 1996, 7. He contrasts this to the 3,200/3,400-calorie diet in Western countries that allegedly was based on 60 percent to 65 percent animal protein.

23. *Sel'skaia zhizn'*, 16 June 1998, 1, 3.

24. In Orel oblast, for example, 28 percent of the land is not being planted for lack of equipment (*Sel'skaia zhizn'*, 16 March 1999, 1).

25. *Sel'skaia zhizn'*, 4 April 1995, 2.

26. *Izvestiia*, 5 April 1995, 11.

27. *Zdravookhranenie Rossissskoi Federatsii*, no. 5, 1998, 23.

28. I. V. Pokhoden'ko, M. G. Magomedov, A. V. Pokhoden'ko, and V. A. Strel'nikova, "Sotsial'no-gigienicheskaia kharakteristika bremennikh zhenshchin, prozhivaiushchikh v sel'skoi mestnosti," *Zdravookhranenie Rossissskoi Federatsii*, no. 2, 1999, 60–61.

29. Ibid., 52, citing an unpublished paper written by Vasilii Uzun in 1996, "Farm Reorganisation in Russia." Uzun worked on the Nizhniy Novgorod variant of agricultural reform; see *Krest'ianskie vedomosti*, 23–29 November 1998, 8.

30. In 1994, Saratov oblast farmers sold 2 percent of the grain, 4.3 percent of the sunflower seeds, 2 percent of the milk, and 20 percent of the cattle and fowl. P. P. Velikii, N. P. Kuznik, and L. G. Khaibulaeva, "Potentsial predpriimchivosti sel'skogo naseleniia," *Sotsiologicheskie issledovaniia*, no. 12, 1998, 41.

31. *Krest'ianskie vedomosti*, 4–17 January 1999, 2. See also *Sel'skaia zhizn'*, 25 February 1999, 4.

32. Grigory Ioffe and Tatyana Nefedova, *Continuity and Change in Rural Russia* (Boulder, CO: Westview Press, 1997), 305.

33. *Sel'skaia zhizn'*, 23 March 1999, 2.

34. *Sel'skaia zhizn'*, 9 February 1999, 1.

35. *Krest'ianskie vedomosti*, no. 47, 1998, 6.

36. *Sel'skaia zhizn'*, 14 January 1999, 3.

37. Ioffe and Nefedova, *Continuity and Change*, 305.

38. *Sel'skaia zhizn'*, 18 March 1994, 4.

39. *Sel'skaia zhizn'*, 31 May 1994, 5. Compare his story with that of the grandson of a kulak, equally gifted, who was on the edge of collapse both physically and financially because his family unit consisted of a wife and two small children. Dunn, " 'They Don't Pay Attention to Us!,' " 7–8.

40. *Krest'ianskie vedomosti*, 29 March–4 April 1999, 3.

41. Dunn, " 'They Don't Pay Attention to Us!,' " 9.

42. *Izvestiia*, 27 May 1994, 2.

43. *Krest'ianskie vedomosti*, 1–7 March 1999, 22.

44. *Sel'skaia zhizn'*, 11 February 1999, 4.

45. *Krest'ianskie vedomosti*, no. 15, 1997, 3.

46. The lack of response was probably because such automobiles are in very short supply. For further details, see Ethel Dunn, "Disabled Russian War Veterans: Surviving the Collapse of the Soviet Union," in *Disabled Veterans in History*, ed. David Gerber (Ann Arbor: University of Michigan Press, 2000), 251–71; and "The Disabled in Russia in the 1990s," in *Health and Social Welfare in Post-Communist Russia*, eds. Mark Field and Judyth L. Twigg (New York: St. Martin's Press, 2000), 153–71.

47. *Krest'ianskie vedomosti*, no. 40, 1997, 7.

48. *Sotsial'noe obespechenie*, no. 3, 1999, 23–24. Only Moscow oblast has the health care database from which an accurate figure could be obtained. *Sotsial'noe obespechenie*, no. 8, 1998, 22–24; *Sotsial'noe obespechenie*, no. 4, 1998, 23–27.

49. A traditional gathering dating back centuries, which originally had an important place in courtship and marriage rituals.

50. *Nadezhda*, no. 1, January 1999, 5.

51. As one officer put it: "Every officer should have land for private use, the way it was in the old days. If you served, you got your portion, and your family would have something to live on, and if you were wounded, you'd have something." *Sel'skaia zhizn'*, 16 July 1994, 3. However, young able-bodied veterans of the war in Afghanistan in one village in Moscow oblast were not finding the local administrator of the sovkhoz particularly supportive of their attempt to operate a construction brigade, since he failed to pay them for repairing a calf barn. *Sel'skaia zhizn'*, 19 February 1991, 2. On the other hand, the evidence is overwhelming that rural life in the 1990s proceeds without money.

52. Hilary Pilkington says that Novosel was the first compact resettlement of migrants in Russia. Pilkington, *Migration, Displacement, and Identity in Post-Soviet Russia* (London: Routledge, 1998), 77, 144–46. Pilkington believed that the program was promising, although what she calls "de-skilling," whereby the migrants are forced to take jobs unrelated to their specialties, was a really serious problem, especially for women, who are, in rural areas, more educated than men. However, the jobs available to women are mostly as manual laborers on the farms.

53. *Sel'skaia zhizn'*, 22 August 1998, 3.

54. *Sel'skaia zhizn'*, 20 June 1998, 3.

55. For details, see Ethel Dunn, "Spiritual and Economic Renewal Among Molokans and Doukhobors," *Canadian Ethnic Studies/Études Ethniques au Canada* 27, no. 3 (1995): 164–80.

56. *Izvestiia*, 4 February 1999, 6.

57. For a discussion of Starodubtsev before he became governor, see Dunn, " 'They Don't Pay Attention to Us!,' " 22–25.

58. *Izvestia*, 27 January 1999, 2.

59. *Sel'skaia zhizn'*, 15 September 1998, 2; 28 July 1998, 2; 8 September 1998, 2.

60. *Izvestiia*, 23 February 1999, 7.

61. Stephen K. Wegren, "Rural Politics and Agrarian Reform in Russia," *Problems of Post-Communism* (January–February 1996): 32–33.

62. A woman with agricultural experience who wanted land was told that the only land she would be given would be in the cemetery. Undeterred, she went on to establish a successful farming operation, but only through intense personal effort. *Sel'skaia zhizn'*, 29 June 1999, 2.

63. *Krest'ianskie vedomosti*, no. 26, 21–27 June 1999, 6.

14

Entrepreneurial Adaptations of Rural Households: Production, Sales, and Income

DAVID J. O'BRIEN

This chapter examines the growth of the informal economy of peasant household enterprises following the collapse of the Soviet command economy and the implementation of the Russian government's reform policies. While the persistence of small-scale peasant plot production is clearly linked to the Soviet model, and in that sense, is an example of *path* dependence,[1] certain actions by households reflect a new institutional environment that has been generated by government reforms in the 1990s (see the introduction to this book and chapter 5 by Patsiorkovski). Greater utilization of human and social capital in household enterprises, as well as the impact of rented land on household production, indicate that there have been some incremental changes in behavior in the Russian countryside that have supported increased household participation in a market economy. In this regard, the findings reported here are consistent with the analyses by Lerman in chapter 2 and Wegren and Belen'kiy in chapter 4.

The social organizational character of rural Russian household enterprises can be understood within the rubric of Scott's[2] and Netting's[3] descriptions of the *moral economy* of smallholder agriculture. This type of organization is based on rational principles, but these principles are fundamentally different than the principles by which large-scale, bureaucratic, wage-for-work enterprises are organized. Because the social organization of labor is based on highly dense networks of mutual trust and interdependence, rather than individualistic wage-labor contracts, these types of enterprises are able to substantially reduce transaction costs involving relationships between workers and "monitoring" of work performance.[4]

There is considerable evidence that small-scale enterprises based on principles of a moral economy can be an efficient way to adapt to certain types of economic exigencies in advanced industrial as well as in traditional societies. Examples include early twentieth-century, Japanese American, labor-intensive agriculture in the Central Valley of California[5] and small grocery stores, liquor stores, and restaurants owned by Cuban and Korean immigrants to the United States.[6] Coleman's oft-cited essay on social capital used several examples of highly dense social networks, such as those among the Hassidic Jews who control the diamond trade in New York City.[7]

Perhaps the most relevant example for our purposes is provided by Salamon's ethnographic comparison of German-Catholic and Yankee farm families in Illinois.[8] For Yankee farmers, the primary goal of farming was to maximize profits, and in the 1970s this meant specialization. Alternatively, the primary goal of German Catholic farm families, which operated culturally more along the lines of the moral economy model, was to preserve the family farm at all costs. This meant adopting a more conservative strategy of diversification that produced lower profits during boom periods in agriculture but also protected their farms against downturns, such as those that occurred in the American Midwest in the mid-1980s.

Because the vast majority of Russian peasant households have remained tied in some fashion to the large enterprise in their village, it may seem inappropriate to conceptually link them to the aforementioned examples of petit-bourgeois enterprises. Yet, the fundamental worldview of preserving the household and therefore adopting a conservative economic strategy is similar in both cases. Rural households in Russia, by and large, have opted for the more conservative strategy that preserves the household through the development of human and social capital. This strategy builds upon highly dense ties that were developed during the Soviet period but these relationships have become the basis for penetration into developing niche markets rather than merely household subsistence.[9]

The Russian Village Panel Survey

The economic and psychological adaptation of rural households to a changing economic environment has been the central focus of the Russian-

American panel study of households in three rural Russian villages, which is directed by Valeri Patsiorkovski and myself. Three waves of panel surveys, from 1995 to 1997, were funded by the National Science Foundation (NSF), in cooperation with the Russian Academy of Sciences.[10] An additional, fourth panel wave, sponsored by the Moskovski Obshestveni Nauchnii Fond (Moscow Public Science Foundation), was conducted in 1999 (see chapter 5 by Patsiorkovski). This chapter focuses on the findings from the 1995–97 NSF panel surveys, although the 1999 findings are noted where appropriate. Patsiorkovski's chapter provides an overview of the panel study's findings on overall institutional and social organizational changes that have occurred in the study villages from 1991 to 2001. In chapter 16, Dershem examines how the adaptation of different types of households to a market economy has affected their subjective quality of life. In this chapter, I report the panel study's findings on household production and sales and their impact on household income.

The panel study consisted of three waves of interviews in 1995, 1996, and 1997 of the same respondents in 463 households in three Russian villages. Respondents were asked to report the quantities of specific agricultural commodities produced and sold during each time period, as well as other sources of income from work in the large enterprises, other types of family business and trade, and government transfer payments.

The location of the three villages provided an opportunity to assess the impact of local and regional differences in the development of household enterprises. The village of Latonovo is located in Rostov oblast in the north Caucasus region. The village of Vengerovka is located in Belgorod oblast in the central black-earth region. The village of Bolshoe Sviattsovo (actually a collection of very small villages) is located in the central region. Locations of all three villages are shown in Map 14.1.

A proportional stratified random sample of households in each village permitted the researchers to examine the effects of differences in household human and social capital on household production, sales, and income.

Household Production and Sales

Table 14.1 provides a summary of the quantity of agricultural commodities produced and sold by households. Household respondents were asked to report specific amounts of commodities produced and sold during each of three years. These commodities were weighted to reflect their value in the marketplace and also to assess the nonmonetary[11] income value of the

Map 14.1

Locations of Study Villages

commodities consumed by the family. The market value of sales of these different commodities was obtained by a weighting procedure based on the ruble value (adjusted for inflation in each year of the panel study) of different products in the nearest regional marketplace. Potatoes and vegetables were sold for 4,500 rubles in 1995, which was approximately equal to one U.S. dollar at the time. Milk was sold for approximately 1.5 times the price of potatoes and vegetables, while meat was sold for approximately 6 times the price of potatoes and vegetables.

The increases in household production and sales in the panel sample are consistent with the national figures reported in earlier chapters (see chapter 2 by Lerman and chapter 5 by Patsiorkovski). What is most striking about the figures in Table 14.1, however, is that the rate of increase in household agricultural sales from 1995 to 1997 is almost double the increase in agricultural production. This indicates that in the new economic environment, especially weaker support for household income from the large enterprises, households have been selling a larger proportion of what they produce. The 1999 panel survey showed that the same trend was

Table 14.1

Weighted Household Production and Sales in Three
Russian Villages, 1995–97 (n = 463)

	1995	1996	1997
Production (kg)	6,679	7,080	8,236
Sales (kg)	2,326	2,325	3,630

Notes: Household production by year $F(2) = 7.46$, $p < .001$; household sales by year $F(2) = 20.50$, $p = < .001$.

continuing. Mean household production increased by 6.4 percent from 1997 to 1999, while mean household sales increased by 22.9 percent during the same time period.

One of the most impressive indicators of how even small institutional changes can produce a significant benefit for rural Russian households is the impact of land rental on household agricultural production. Although land rental has been legally permitted for only a relatively short period of time in Russia, and despite the fact that the portions of land that are rented are quite small,[12] the effect of this institutional change on household output has been quite dramatic. This is shown in Table 14.2. Households with rented land produced, on average, 80 percent more than other households did in 1995, and that advantage increased to 84 percent in 1996 and 93 percent in 1997.

These findings show the impact of formal institutional changes that were initiated by the Russian central government to promote land leasing. Ler-

Table 14.2

Land Rental and Household Agricultural Production, 1995–97
(n = 463)

Year	1995	1996	1997
Percentage of households that rent land	24.62	22.68	27.42
Mean amount of rented land	0.08	0.08	0.12
Mean weighted household production without rented land (kg)	5,583 ($n = 349$)	5,947 ($n = 358$)	6,565 ($n = 336$)
Mean weighted household production with rented land (kg)	10,037 ($n = 114$)	10,946 ($n = 105$)	12,657 ($n = 127$)

Note: Relationship between land rental and household agricultural production: 1995, $F(1) = 64.54$, $p < .001$; 1996, $F(1) = 52.95$, $p < .001$; 1997, $F(1) = 82.27$, $p < .001$.

man and Patsiorkovski described these changes in chapters 2 and 5, respectively. A 1991 presidential decree required that the large enterprises cede a portion of their land to the local governments of the villages in which they were located. This made it possible for local governments to distribute land to individual peasant households through formal-legal rental arrangements. The 1991 decree also allowed households, for the first time, to enter into informal land rental agreements with their neighbors or with other households. This permitted elderly or infirm persons, or individuals who had moved away from the village, to rent their household plots to younger families, thus increasing the size of the latter's holdings.

Oblast- and Village-Level Institutional Support for Household Enterprise Development

In chapter 3, Ioffe and Nefedova dealt at some length with spatial factors (e.g., distance from urban areas) and growing conditions that affect the prospects for agricultural development in different regions of Russia. The Russian village panel study examined how differences in governmental policies at the regional and village levels can create different amounts of institutional support for household enterprise development, over and above what can be accounted for by spatial, demographic, or other structural factors.

Two of the villages in the panel study, Latonovo in Rostov oblast and Vengerovka in Belgorod oblast, are located in the black-earth zone that contains good soil and climate, and both have approximately equal advantages with respect to distance to regional markets. The third village, Bolshoe Sviattsovo in Tver' oblast, is outside of the black-earth zone, but has some advantages over the other two villages because of its closer proximity to Moscow. The most interesting comparison with respect to the effects of subnational institutional changes is between Latonovo and Vengerovka. Despite the fact that these two villages have very similar climate, soil, and market conditions, they have responded quite differently to opportunities to make institutional changes at the local level. Following the Russian presidential decree on land reform in 1991 that required the large enterprises to cede a portion of their land to local governments, residents of Latonovo and Vengerovka took very different paths with respect to the use of this new land.[13]

Residents of Latonovo elected to use the land that was ceded to the local government by the large enterprise to create a communal land fund.

Households were allocated shares of communal land according to household composition criteria, and received the benefits of production on the land according to set criteria as well. Individual households, however, had no input into what was produced on this communal land. On the other hand, Vengerovka residents elected to make the ceded land available to individual households as rental shares. Once a household made an agreement, in the form of a contract, for renting a land share, household members had total discretion as to how the land was used. Although households in Latonovo have use of larger land holdings than their counterparts in Vengerovka, a much smaller proportion of the land in Latonovo is actually under the control of the household. Not only are the private plots almost twice as large in Vengerovka as in Latonovo, but households in Vengerovka are able to rent land directly from the village government, whereas this is not permitted in Latonovo.

In addition, Belgorod oblast, in which Vengerovka is located, created a special loan fund to support household improvements, such as building new homes and buildings for storing grain or silage or for keeping animals (*fond podderzhki individualnovo zhilishchnovo stroitel'stva na sele*).[14] This program allows households to borrow money for improvements that can be paid back in commodities, such as meat or dairy products. No such program exists in Rostov oblast. The governor of Belgorod oblast has maintained a high level of popularity by supporting other incremental mechanisms to improve the quality of life in rural villages. This has included, for example, a program to provide loans to local villages to purchase equipment to build their own bakeries. In June 1999, he soundly defeated the nationalist candidate Zhirinovsky in the gubernatorial election.

The effects of the different institutional developments in Latonovo and Vengerovka on household production and sales are quite dramatic. This is shown in Table 14.3.

Not only do households in Vengerovka produce more than 1.5 times as much on average as households in Latonovo, but household production in Vengerovka grew at a much faster rate over the three years (almost 29 percent) than the comparable rate of growth in Latonovo (approximately 18 percent). Most impressive is the fact that household sales increased by 61.2 percent in Vengerovka from 1995 to 1997, whereas the comparable figure for Latonovo during the same time period was only 16 percent. The 1999 panel survey showed a continuation of the same differences among the three villages. Average household sales in Vengerovka were 43.9 percent greater than in Latonovo and 48.3 percent greater than in Sviattsovo.

Table 14.3

Mean Weighted Household Production and Sales by Village, 1995–97
(n = 463)

	Production/Sales (kg)		
Village	1995	1996	1997
Latonovo, Rostov oblast			
(*n* = 157)	4,849/1,968	5,060/1,761	5,747/2,283
Vengerovka, Belgorod			
oblast (*n* = 156)	8,020/3,269	9,065/3,714	10,340/5,270
Sviattsovo, Tver' oblast			
(*n* = 150)	7,201/1,721	7,131/1,470	8,653/3,335
Total (*n* = 463)	6,679/2,326	7,080/2,325	8,236/3,630

Notes: Household production by village in 1995 F(2) = 14.95, *p* < .001; production by village in 1996 F(2) = 15.66, *p* < .001; household production by village in 1997 F(2) = 18.60, *p* < .001; household sales by village in 1995 F(2) = 10.98, *p* < .001; household sales by village in 1996 F(2) = 22.79, *p* < .001; household sales by village in 1997 F(2) = 22.77, *p* < .001.

Household Capital and Adaptation to a Market Economy

The Russian government's removal of restrictions on the ownership of animals and equipment and on certain land leasing arrangements, as well as provision of more opportunities for sales in the marketplace are critical institutional changes. While these changes at the national, regional, and local levels have had substantial effects on the development of rural household enterprises, households themselves have different capacities to take advantage of these changes. The most important of these differences pertain to levels of human and social capital and rental of land. In a labor-intensive peasant economy, human capital is defined largely in terms of the number of able-bodied hands to help to care for animals and to process meat and dairy products into value-added products. Drawing on the definition of peasant household labor by Chaianov,[15] the Russian village panel study developed a labor potential for each household by calculating the labor potential of each member within the household and then summing those figures. This weighted labor potential was based on the age of each household member: 0 (under 8 and 80 and older), 0.25 (8 to 11 years, and 75 to 79 years), 0.50 (12 to 14 years, and 71 to 74 years), 0.75 (15 to 16 years, and 66 to 70 years), and 1 (17 to 65 years).

Two types of social capital were also developed. The first was a measure of the extent to which a household possessed more *exclusive*, high-density helping networks that could provide assistance in six different areas. These areas included (1) borrowing money, (2) trading goods and services, (3) taking care of the household if someone is sick, (4) assisting with the cultivation of the household plot, (5) assisting with household tasks, and (6) discussing important matters. These helping networks were broken down further into redundant and nonredundant ties. Redundant helping network ties were calculated by adding up the number of helpers a household received in each of the six areas. Since the same individual could help in two or more areas, some of these ties were redundant. Nonredundant ties were the total number of persons that helped the household. A second measure of more *inclusive* ties was based on levels of village community involvement.[16] This was indicated by how much household members participated in village festivals and in the celebrations of other families in the village.

A complex structural equation model showing the indirect and direct relationships between the different human and social capital measures, household physical capital, and household production and sales is discussed elsewhere.[17] To simplify matters for this presentation, we present only the most important effects of differential levels of human and social capital and land rental on household enterprise development. These are shown via the standardized regression coefficients in Table 14.4. Only those variables that have a statistically significant relationship with the dependent variables are shown. The size of the regression coefficients indicates the *strength* of the relationship between a specific independent variable and a specific dependent variable.

The degree of economic success of a Russian rural household can be understood in a sequence of three overlapping tasks. The first is the household's ability to care for animals. Households with more household labor, indicated by higher values for the weighted number of adults, are clearly at an advantage in being able to care for more animals. At the same time, the size of a household's helping network, which includes persons who are not living in the household, is also critical in this area.

The relationship between size of household helping networks and ability to care for animals, however, is *curvilinear*. Increasing network size, *up to a certain point*, is associated with having more animals. The negative sign on the quadratic term for helping networks indicates that after a certain size additional members in the helping network do not bring additional benefits. Households with moderate-size networks are quite different than households with very large networks. Moderate-size helping networks, from seven to ten persons, are most likely to include a husband and a wife with children or a husband and a wife with children and other adults. Households with an extremely large number of persons in their

Table 14.4

Standardized Regression Coefficients Showing the Impact of Human and Social Capital on Household Production and Sales in Three Russian Villages, 1995–97[a]

	Number of Animals	Household Production	Household Sales
Weighted number of adults	.533	—	—
Number of people in helping networks	.284	.221	—
Quadratic of number of people in helping networks	−.261	−.173	—
Community involvement	.124	—	.104
Rented land	.214	.071	—
Number of animals	—	.756	.222
Household production	—	—	.494
Adjusted R^2	.421	.644	.522

[a] All coefficients are significant, at $p < .05$.

helping networks, 11 or more, typically consist of single persons or older retired couples. The networks of the former are more likely to be part of an ongoing household agricultural production and sales system, whereas the latter networks are more likely to consist of family members and neighbors who assist vulnerable persons in times of need.

Households with rented land have a greater ability to produce feed for animals. This is indicated by the strong positive relationship between rented land and number of animals in the household. The second task required in order for a rural household to be economically successful is to produce agricultural products, which include meat and dairy products, vegetables, fruits, and potatoes. As shown in column two of Table 14.4, the most important factor here is the number of animals possessed by the household, and thus, the amount of labor in the household has a strong indirect effect on household production. In this area, however, helping networks and rented land also have a direct effect, as well as an indirect effect through their association with care of animals.

Up to this point, the analysis of the panel data is entirely consistent with what one would expect on the basis of a classical peasant moral economy. The most successful households are those that are fortunate enough to have high levels of labor and high-density networks that can be depended upon for assistance in labor-intensive agriculture.

The picture changes in an important way, however, when we examine the third critical task faced by the rural Russian household: selling products in the marketplace to generate income for purchases that require cash, such as durable goods and clothing. While the strong effect of number of animals and household production on household sales is not surprising, it is important to note here that community involvement plays an important role. Community involvement, which is measured by the extent to which household members participate in village festivals and in the celebrations of other families in the village, contributes to success in selling products in the marketplace.

High labor-intensive production requires high-density personal ties, in the sense that persons who are feeding hogs or milking cows have to be very reliable day in and day out. This means that households with larger, but not too large, personal networks have an advantage in this regard. While personal networks obviously have a powerful indirect effect on household sales, through their positive association with agricultural production, it also appears that community involvement plays a uniquely direct role in agricultural sales. The presence of more *inclusive* village-level ties enhances opportunities to sell agricultural products, especially value-added products such as sour cream and processed meat, to restaurants and hotels. These ties may not approach the casual acquaintance character of American-style "weak ties,"[18] but it is clear that hearing about new opportunities for marketing in a regional center, for example, may require going outside a household's intimate helping network circle.

Opportunities for sales may be obtained from persons with whom one has good relations, but these relations need not be very strong. Moreover, the activities required to bring products to market, such as asking a neighbor for a ride to the city or having a neighbor watch one's livestock for a day, do not require the same level of intensity of relationship that would be required for sustained labor-intensive activities. Thus, in this area households that have more expansive, but less intense relationships with a larger number of households have a distinct advantage in the emerging market economy. It is also important to note in this regard that households with higher levels of community involvement are also more likely to rent land.

Overall levels of community involvement, as measured by participation in neighbors' and community-wide festivals and activities, declined in the villages from 1995 to 1997. In 1995, 35.9 percent of the sample reported that they never attended these events and this figure rose to 51.4 percent in 1997. In the 1999 survey, this percentage was even higher, at 58.3 percent.[19] Yet, households that had higher levels of community involvement had substantially higher levels of agricultural sales. In 1997, for example, households with a medium level of community involvement had double the sales of households with the lowest level of community involvement. The amount of sales increased 1.7 times again for households with the highest level of community involvement. Moreover, the relationship between community involvement and household sales remains even when controlling for other human, social, and physical capital variables that affect household economic performance.[20]

Income Differentation and Poverty

The increased importance of household production and sales for the overall income of peasant households in Russia is reflected in the proportion of household income that is generated from household enterprises. Household enterprises were an important part of overall household income in the Soviet period, generating a significant portion of food for the household to consume, as well as providing food for relatives living in urban areas. The inability of the large enterprises to maintain direct salary support for workers, coupled with the opportunity for households to find new sources of income in expanding niche markets, has resulted in a greater proportion of household income being generated by household enterprises.

Table 14.5 shows that income received from all types of household enterprises (nonagricultural businesses; benefits, usually from rental of land to other households; and agricultural sales), accounted for 36.5 percent of monetized and 61.4 percent of total (monetized plus nonmonetized) income in 1995. The comparable figures for 1997 were 41.7 percent and 60.2 percent.[21] Among retired couples and single-person households, income earned from some type of household enterprise rose from 19 percent in 1995 to 31 percent in 1997. For retired households, as a whole, the proportion of household income generated from nonagricultural businesses rose from 1.0 percent in 1995 to 5.7 percent in 1997.

The decline in the value of the ruble in 1998 created some significant advantages for small household producers that are reflected in findings from the 1999 survey. Because many Russian consumers could no longer afford imported meat, they began to purchase larger quantities of meat sold by domestic small-scale producers. This is reflected in a threefold increase in household income from 1997 to 1999. Monetary income from all types of household enterprises increased to 50.8 percent of all household income and the proportion of total (monetary plus nonmonetary) income from these sources increased to two-thirds (66.5 percent) of all household income.

Table 14.5

*Sources of Monthly Monetary (M) and Total Monetary and Nonmonetary
(TI) Household Income in Three Russian Villages, 1995–97 (n = 463)*

	1995 (%)		1996 (%)		1997 (%)	
	M	TI	M	TI	M	TI
Salary and wages						
Primary salary	30.6	19.0	35.1	21.9	30.5	21.0
Secondary salary	1.0	1.0	4.6	2.9	4.2	2.9
Transfer payments	33.2	20.2	34.9	21.7	27.6	18.9
Household enterprises						
Business	6.0	3.7	4.5	2.9	9.1	6.3
Benefits	3.2	1.9	6.5	4.1	4.1	2.8
Agricultural sales	27.3	16.6	19.0	11.8	28.5	19.5
Nonmonetized consumption	—	39.2	—	37.7	—	31.6
Subtotal monetary and nonmonetary income from household enterprises	36.5	61.4	30.0	56.5	41.7	60.2
Total household income	407.2	669.6	337.8	541.9	350.4	512.1

Note: Percentages are based on rubles adjusted for inflation.

Studies in urban areas have shown that the economic transition to a market economy has been accompanied by a steep rise in poverty and income differentiation.[22] Tables 14.6 and 14.7, however, show a different pattern of income differentiation and poverty for rural areas. Income differentiation in the three villages declined from 1995 to 1997. The coefficient of differentiation, which is created by dividing the mean income of the tenth decile income group by the mean income of the first decile income group, went from 9.4 in 1995 to 5.6 in 1997.

The 1999 survey showed a reversal of this trend, which was sparked by new opportunities for some small-scale producers that were brought on by the decline of the ruble in 1998. As a result, the coefficient of differentiation went from 5.6 to 10.2 from 1997 to 1999, but the latter figure is still considerably lower than the countrywide figures for income differentiation, which increased from 13.2 in 1997 to 14.7 in 1999.[23] What is most significant, however, is that *income for the bottom tenth of the rural sample also increased substantially during the same two-year period.* Adjusting for

Table 14.6

Differentiation of Monthly Income in Three Russian Villages, 1995–97 (rubles)

	1995	1996	1997
Mean income for bottom 10% income group	174.500	170.800	146.700
Mean income for the top 10% income group	1,636.300	1,100.600	825.100
Coefficient of differentiation[a]	9.4	6.4	5.6

[a] Coefficient of differentiation is calculated by dividing the mean income of the tenth decile income group by the mean income of the first decile income group.

inflation, the mean income of the bottom 10 percent of households increased more than two times from 1997 to 1999. During the same period, however, the mean income of the top 10 percent increased more than four times.

The 1995–97 panel data, and the subsequent 1999 survey, actually show a decrease in poverty in the villages over time. If we include nonmonetized sources of income (i.e., household production used for consumption) in our calculations of total household income, the percentage of households living below the official poverty line actually decreased from 62.4 percent to 28.9 percent from 1995 to 1997. This means that a substantially smaller proportion of rural households in the study were below the poverty line than the 36.9 percent reported for all of Russia in 1997.[24] Figures from the 1999 survey show a further drop in the percentage of households in poverty, to 17.1 percent.

Table 14.7

Households in Poverty in Three Russian Villages, 1995–97 (percent)

	1995	1996	1997
Per capita minimum consumption basket[a]	264,100	369,400	411,000
% households living in poverty by monetized income	91.1	83.8	69.8
% households living in poverty by monetized & nonmonetized income	62.4	42.3	28.9

[a] From N. M. Rimashevskaia, ed., *Rossiia, 1997* (Moscow: Institute for Socio-Economic Studies of Population, Russian Academy of Sciences, 1998), 119.

There are two causes of lower poverty rates in our rural sample than would be the case in urban samples in Russia. On the one hand, rural populations may have more effective ways than do urban households to compensate for income loss resulting from industry restructuring. As the large enterprises have become a less reliable source of income for rural households, these households are able either to grow their own food and sell it, or in the case of the elderly and infirm, rent their land to neighbors who compensate them with food. On the other hand, the lower levels of inequality in the rural sample may be due in part to the fact that the lack of more fundamental structural changes in the local economy has meant that no one has had an opportunity to gain extreme economic rewards. Hence the gap between the rich and the poor is not nearly as drastic as it is in urban areas. Finally, and perhaps most importantly, the strong "communal spirit" in the Russian village, described in chapter 6 by Paxson, chapter 9 by Gambold Miller, and chapter 12 by Allina-Pisano, undoubtedly serves as a brake on some of the excesses that have been shown by the "new Russians" in urban areas.

Conclusion

The preceding analysis is by no means an endorsement of small-scale household production over larger-scale, Western European or even American, farming operations. Rather, it should be viewed as an empirical analysis of *incremental* trends toward some type of *Russian* solution to the problems of agriculture and sustainable rural communities.

Significant numbers of rural Russian households have managed to adapt to the institutional constraints and opportunities of post-Soviet society by developing their household enterprises. By and large, these households have eschewed the "riskier" option of registering as private farmers. Instead they have remained connected, in some fashion, with the large farm enterprises and have focused on developing their household enterprises. They have used old social organizational forms that are based on the moral economy of peasant households. This has meant the development of household human and social capital, which is based on high-density social networks. This strategy is consistent with what other rational economic actors have employed in institutional environments where there is uncertainty about the long-term legitimacy of land tenure and land values.

It is certainly reasonable to criticize the policies of the Russian central government during the Yeltsin period for failing to understand the institutional and social organizational linkages between households and large farm enterprises (see chapter 12 by Allina-Pisano) and for not dealing with the problems of local services (see chapter 9 by Gambold Miller). But it is also important to recognize some successes of government policies. The very fact that the government removed legal constraints on household enterprises has been important in encouraging the development of household capital in a way that would never have been possible during the Soviet period. Most important, government institutionalization of leasing arrangements, especially ceding land from the large enterprises to local government, has had a positive effect on household production and sales.

At the same time, however, these adaptations have some serious downsides to them, which, if not dealt with, will limit further growth of economically viable independent farming in Russia. In order to develop a more efficient household-based agriculture, it will be necessary for *some* households to develop more expansive economic cooperatives with other households. The types of social relationships necessary to develop these kinds of cooperatives, however, are very difficult to establish in an environment where, up to now, there is no trusted third-party enforcement of contracts. By contrast, cooperatives in the United States and Western European nations have been developed within an institutional context of formal-legal contracts and trusted government enforcement. This is a theme we return to in detail in the concluding chapter.

Notes

1. Douglass C. North, *Institutions, Institutional Change and Economic Performance* (Cambridge: Cambridge University Press, 1990), 115–17.
2. James C. Scott, *The Moral Economy of the Peasant: Rebellion and Subsistence in Southeast Asia* (New Haven, CT: Yale University Press, 1976).
3. Robert McC. Netting, *Smallholders, Householders: Farm Families and the Ecology of Intensive, Sustainable Agriculture* (Stanford, CA: Stanford University Press, 1993).
4. Netting, *Smallholders, Householders,* 71–74.
5. Stephen S. Fugita and David J. O'Brien, *Japanese American Ethnicity: The Persistence of Community* (Seattle: University of Washington Press, 1991), 47–62.
6. Ivan Light, *Ethnic Enterprise in America* (Berkeley: University of California Press, 1972); Alejandro Portes and Julia Sensenbrenner, "Embeddedness and Immigration: Notes on the Social Determinants of Economic Action," in *The New Institutionalism in Sociology,* eds. Mary C. Brinton and Victor Nee (New York: Russell Sage Foundation, 1998), 127–49; Jimmy M. Sanders and Victor Nee, "Immigrant Self-Employment: The Family as Social Capital and the Value of Human Capital," *American Sociological Review* 63 (April 1998): 231–49.
7. James S. Coleman, "Social Capital in the Creation of Human Capital," *American Journal of Sociology* 94 (special supplement 1988): S95–S120.
8. Sonya Salamon, "Ethnic Communities and the Structure of Agriculture," *Rural Sociology* 50, no. 3 (1985): 323–40.
9. Larry D. Dershem, "Community and Collective: Interpersonal Ties in Three Russian Villages" (Ph.D. diss., University of Missouri, 1995); Larry D. Dershem, "Prevalence,

Sources and Types of Informal Support in Latonovo and Mayaki," in *Services and Quality of Life in Rural Villages in the Former Soviet Union*, eds. David J. O'Brien et al. (Lanham, MD: University Press of America, 1998), 163–98; Vladimir Shlapentokh, *Public and Private Life of the Soviet People: Changing Values in Post-Stalin Russia* (New York: Oxford University Press, 1989).

10. See David J. O'Brien, Valeri V. Patsiorkovski, and Larry D. Dershem, *Household Capital and the Agrarian Problem in Russia* (Aldershot, Hants, UK: Ashgate, 2000).

11. For a discussion of nonmonetary and monetary sources of income in Russia, see Richard Rose and Ian McAllister, "Is Money the Measure of Welfare in Russia?" *Review of Income and Wealth* 42 (March 1996): 1–16.

12. The average size of leased parcels of land was approximately 0.2 hectares in 1997 and increased to 0.4 hectares by 1999. See chapter 2 by Lerman for World Bank data on the impact of land leasing on agricultural production and sales.

13. An analysis of different types of institutional support for household enterprise development in Rostov, Belgorod, and Tver' oblasts is found in David J. O'Brien, Valeri V. Patsiorkovski, and Larry D. Dershem, "Rural Responses to Land Reform in Russia: An Analysis of Household Land Use in Belgorod, Rostov and Tver' *Oblasts* from 1991 to 1996," in *Land Reform in the Former Soviet Union and Eastern Europe*, ed. Stephen K. Wegren (London: Routledge, 1998), 35–61.

14. *Sel'skaia zhizn'*, 6 June 1996, 2.

15. A. V. Chaianov, *The Theory of Peasant Economy* (Homewood, IL: R. D. Irwin, 1966). See also C. D. Deere and A. de Janvry, "Demographic and Social Differentiation among Northern Peruvian Peasants," *Journal of Peasant Studies* 8 (1981): 335–66.

16. In the final chapter of this book we discuss the impact of different types of social capital on the future development of rural communities in Russia. For a general discussion of the different types of social capital and their impact on economic development, see Michael Woolcock, "Social Capital and Economic Development: Toward a Theoretical Synthesis and Policy Framework," *Theory and Society* 27 (1998): 151–208; and C. B. Flora and J. L. Flora, "Entrepreneurial Social Infrastructure: A Necessary Ingredient," *Annals AAPS* 529 (1993): 48–58.

17. See O'Brien, Patsiorkovski, and Dershem, *Household Capital*.

18. Mark Granovetter, "The Strength of Weak Ties," *American Journal of Sociology* 78 (1973): 1360–80.

19. The implications of the decline of bridging types of social capital for the development of civil society and more efficient household agriculture are discussed in the concluding chapter of this book.

20. See O'Brien, Patsiorkovski, and Dershem, *Household Capital*, 155–60.

21. The decrease in the proportion of income derived from agricultural sales in 1996 is due largely to a sharp drop in household sales of milk and eggs in Latonovo. In that year, the chairman of the large enterprise (*tovarishchestvo s ogranichennoi otvetstvennostiu*, or TOO) in Latonovo stopped the traditional practice of acting as a broker for household sales of milk and eggs. As a result, there was a great deal of dissatisfaction among households who provided the labor for the large enterprise. Eventually, someone more sympathetic to household needs replaced the chairman. Household sales increased markedly in 1997, resulting in an overall increase for the sample as a whole. This example illustrates the strong interdependent relationships between household enterprises and the large enterprises.

22. Jenni Klugman, *Poverty in Russia: Public Policy and Private Responses* (Washington, DC: World Bank, 1997).

23. N. M. Rimashevskaia, ed., *Rossiia, 1999* (Moscow: Institute for the Socio-Economic Studies of Population, Russian Academy of Sciences, 2000), 150.

24. N. M. Rimashevskaia, ed., *Rossiia, 1997* (Moscow: Institute for the Socio-Economic Studies of Population, Russian Academy of Sciences, 1998), 193.

15

Adaptation Strategies of Agricultural Enterprises During Transformation

ZEMFIRA KALUGINA

Introduction

The chapter is drawn from a survey of adaptation strategies of agricultural enterprises and families in an unstable environment conducted by the Department of Sociology, Institute of Economics and Industrial Engineering, Siberian Branch, Russian Academy of Sciences, under my direction and with my participation in two rural districts of the Novosibirsk oblast in summer 1998. It is a case study of four agricultural enterprises aimed at examining different patterns of adaptation. The data were collected through unstructured and focused interviews with enterprise managers and specialists ($n = 60$), a questionnaire survey of employees ($n = 404$), and analysis of statistics from 1992 to 1998 (the period of radical economic reforms), and related documents.[1]

The project's primary objective was to compare adaptation strategies used by economically strong and economically weak agricultural enterprises. The comparative analysis included measuring the effect of these strategies on the economic behavior of workers and their families in primary and secondary sectors of the economy, and assessment of economic results and social costs.

Adaptation strategies were analyzed along three dimensions: economic, social welfare, and labor. Economic strategies included choice of organizational-legal status, extent of output diversification, innovation policy, development of processing facilities and nonagricultural businesses, access to nonfarm employment, and policy regarding part-time commercial farming. Social welfare policy was assessed by two criteria: development of social infrastructure and maintenance of employees' living standards. Labor policy was evaluated by changes in the number of employees, the unemployment rate, financial and material support of young families (e.g., payment of educational fees), and opportunities for skill upgrading and education.

There were five specific goals of the approach just described: (1) examine special features in the enterprises' economic, social, and labor policies and assess objective and subjective factors in economic growth and social stability; (2) analyze how the different adaptation strategies affected the conditions and opportunities for employees to actualize their labor potential; (3) assess the social costs of a given strategy that were borne by the enterprise, its employees, and their families; (4) assess the degree of social tension among personnel as well as employees' involvement in or alienation from the enterprise; and (5) examine forms, means, and outcomes of employees' and their families' adaptive behavior geared to maintaining and improving their living conditions, offset social costs, and provide for the family's future.

Novosibirsk Oblast

Novosibirsk oblast is located in southwestern Siberia. The western Siberian region includes seven federal geopolitical units: Altai *krai*, the Republic of Altai, and Novosibirsk, Omsk, Kemerovo, Tiumen, and Tomsk oblasts. Novosibirsk oblast covers an area of 178.2 square kilometers and contains a population of 2,745,800. Population density, as of 1 January 1998, was 15.4 persons per square kilometer. The distance from Novosibirsk to Moscow is 3,191 kilometers. Map 15.1 shows the location of Novosibirsk oblast.

The entire western Siberian region, including Novosibirsk oblast, is in a zone of "risky" agriculture. Nonetheless, this region has a stable and rather high share—2.3 percent in 1997—in national agricultural output.[2] Principal products include grain, potatoes, and vegetables, as well as meat and dairy. Poultry products, honey, flax, and food processing also play important roles in the oblast's economy.

Monitoring the progress of the agrarian reform in Siberia (one of the test fields is Novosibirsk oblast) leads to the conclusion that the state of the

Map 15.1
Novosibirsk Oblast

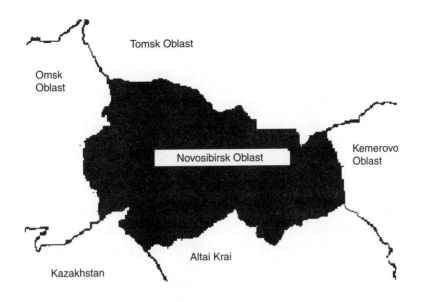

agrarian sector of the region is determined mainly by general national rather than local factors. A comparative analysis of survey findings in Siberia with other regions of the country shows basic similarities in the processes underway in the agrarian sector throughout the country.

Conditions in the Russian Agrarian Sector Before Reform

In the 1980s domestic agricultural production was not sufficient to provide a balanced diet to the Russian population. In many areas, food distribution was rationed. Attempts to improve the situation by the bureaucratic-administrative command system involved superficial adjustments that turned out to be futile in the long run. These incremental adjustments, such as intrafarm cost-benefit analyses, various types of contracts, and capital-intensive technologies, did not affect core problems. These efforts resulted in short-lived improvements and then only within specially chosen experimental farms that were artificially created and enjoyed more favorable conditions than elsewhere. After each "reform" campaign, everything returned to its previous condition. The socialist system repulsed the market elements that were alien to it. For the situation to be reversed radical reforms were needed.

Reorganization of Collective Agricultural Enterprises

The reorganization of collective and state farms was completed in 1994. Almost two-thirds (66 percent) of these large enterprises changed their organizational-legal status, while others retained the traditional collective organizational form. A total of 300 of the large enterprises registered as open joint stock companies, 11,500 as partnerships (of all types), 1,900 as agricultural cooperatives, 400 as farms affiliated with industrial enterprises or other organizations, 900 as associations of autonomous farms, and 2,300 as other forms of agricultural organization. Among *sovkhozy*, 3,600 retained their traditional form, as did 6,000 of the *kolkhozy*. By forms of ownership, agricultural enterprises were distributed as follows: state ownership, 26.6 percent; municipal ownership, 1.5 percent; private ownership, 66.8 percent; and mixed ownership, 5.1 percent.[3]

The reorganization of collective enterprises was supposed to be the first step toward the creation of a mixed agrarian economy based on equality of all forms of ownership and land management. Reorganization did not, however, result in higher efficiency and higher output for these large-scale collective enterprises. Agricultural output and the share of national agricultural production from these enterprises have been in steady decline. In 1990, the large-scale agricultural enterprises accounted for 74 percent of total output in Russian agriculture, but by 1998 they only accounted for 41 percent (see Figure 15.1). Livestock herds in the large enterprises continue to decline. Most of these enterprises are in a critical economic position. Average profitability of these enterprises at the end of 1991 was 43 percent, declining to –2 percent in 1995 and –20.5 percent in 1996.[4]

V. Khlystun, a former minister of agriculture of the Russian Federation, explains the unprofitable situation in Russian agriculture as the result of several factors, including the constantly increasing disparity between agricultural product prices and input prices; extremely low state subsidies; delays in the settlement of accounts receivable; and monopoly markets in agroindustry enterprises and organizations, such as processing, and diverse goods and services.[5]

The net result of reforms has been to replace an inefficient state sector of the economy with an inefficient private sector. The number of inefficient and unprofitable enterprises that have no working capital of their own and

Figure 15.1
Structure of Agricultural Production in Russia Based on Market Value of
Agricultural Commodities, 1990 and 1998

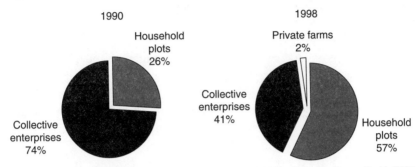

Sources: Rossiia v tsifrakh 1998 (Moscow: Goskomstat, 1998), 443; *Rossiia v tsifrakh 1999* (Moscow: Goskomstat, 1999), 203.

to whom bank loans proved inaccessible (due to high interest rates) was 96 in 1995, 137 in 1996, 138 in 1997, and 142 in 1998.[6]

In my view, the underlying cause of the failure of reform efforts was the formal character of the transformations. The organizational-legal status of collective and state farms was changed but in essence the social organization of economic relationships remained the same.

Because most workers have not observed any difference between their previous status as employed workers and the present one as co-owners, there has been no change in their work motivation or behavioral patterns. In the Russian Federation president's message to the Federal Assembly of 1997, it was noted that "the established mutual rights and responsibilities between owners (stockholders) and managers (directors) were not observed. Directors often merely pushed the stockholders, even major ones, aside when making important decisions in matters that were precisely within the owners' competence." The president's message asserted that stockholders' rights, a clear definition of the rights and responsibilities of stockholders and managers, and the perfection of a mechanism of corporate management were priority tasks for the government upon which the course of the reform in 1997 depended.

The formal-legal and market mechanisms by which peasants can exercise rights of ownership to their shares of land and other assets are not yet operational. In our surveys in Novosibirsk oblast, over 80 percent of the respondents had received no dividends for their shares of assets and land that they had handed over to the large-scale collective agricultural enterprises for use. Most enterprises are unable to pay dividends to their workers. This situation is typical of other regions of the country as well.[7]

The paradox of the reforms is that instead of developing in people a market mentality and behavior, they are in fact destroying work motivation in the large enterprises. The most vivid example of this is the gap between workers' expectations of higher earnings and the declining ability of agricultural enterprises to reward workers' contributions. Today agricultural workers' wages are less than 40 percent of the national average, the lowest among all categories of workers in Russia. Wages are below subsistence level and are typically paid several months late. Most important, the link between wage levels and work productivity and worker qualifications has been destroyed.

One-third of rural workers said that the amount of their remuneration was not contingent on the efficiency of the large enterprise in which they worked. Employment in the public sector has now ceased to be a primary source of income for rural workers. In our 1997 survey of the rural population (n = 553), only 38 percent of respondents said that their wages were the primary source of their livelihood. Part-time farming was listed as the primary source of income for 42 percent of the sample. See also see chapter 14 by O'Brien in this book.

In addition, opportunities for the large agricultural enterprises to use their own resources to solve the social problems of their workers have been drastically decreased. Before reform many social-welfare benefits in rural villages, such as free housing, preschool or child care for children, and health care, were contingent on having a job in the large enterprise. After reorganization, the collective and state farms were allowed to transfer the provision of social and cultural services to local governments. The latter, however, lacked sufficient financial resources and the appropriate infrastructure to provide these services. This has led to a substantial decline of social services provision in the countryside. See also chapter 9 by Gambold Miller in this book.

These processes are at the core of a sharply decreased motivation for professional, high-quality, and effective work in the large enterprises, as well as a drastic drop of the prestige of work in the public sector, especially among rural youth. In our 1997 survey, 31.9 percent of rural inhabitants said they would prefer not to work at all, if unemployment relief could provide for a fairly decent standard of living. Only three years earlier, only 10.6 percent of respondents would have preferred not to work in similar circumstances.

Other responses indicate attitudes toward work. Over half (65.8 percent) of the respondents indicated preference for a small but guaranteed income. Only 28.9 percent of those surveyed would accept higher risk in exchange for higher earnings. The current situation, in which work behavior is effectively disconnected with remuneration, encourages people to gradually lose their self-confidence and to become accustomed to state paternalism.

According to a survey ($n = 735$) in May 1998, however, managers of large enterprises believe that a different set of factors were responsible for their low productivity: buyers' insolvency (9 percent), shortage of finances (12 percent), high interest rates on loans (8 percent), increased share of imported foods in the domestic market (5 percent), high taxes (12 percent), instability of taxation and constant changes introduced into the "rules of the game" (9 percent), low product prices (14 percent), lack of working capital (7 percent), weak enterprise managers' powers and rights (3 percent), deterioration of the material technological base (13 percent), and impoverishment of natural resources (8 percent).[8]

Nevertheless, there are some large agricultural enterprises in each province that are successfully functioning under the current unfavorable conditions. These farms have managed to quickly adjust to the new economic conditions. They have studied the market situation; identified the most profitable channels to sell their products; restructured production according to market requirements; and successfully developed processing ventures and sell their products through their own network of shops, existing retail markets, or trusted wholesale agents. Some of these enterprises have become founders of large commercial structures and have set up modern agroindustrial companies.

Economic Strategies and Forms of Adaptation by Enterprises and Families

A distinctive feature of the present transition period for Russian enterprises and households is that concurrently with the appearance of new institutions, new processes, and new social phenomena, renovation of existing institutions is also under way. Such adaptation has included "response to innovations" as well as "response to transformation."[9] Adaptation can also be a response to change (novelty or alteration) occurring in the internal structure of the adapting person.[10] After the period of sweeping reorganization of agricultural enterprises from 1992 to 1994, it is very important to know how economic agents have adapted themselves to their new status, functions, and roles. In our study, the adapting persons are agricultural enterprises and rural households. The economic strategies of enterprises can be viewed as a way of adapting to the radically changing socioeconomic environment.

Our research has identified four different models of economic adaptation that have been used by agricultural enterprises and households in the current unstable environment.

Model 1. Active market strategy: productive and innovative adaptation of enterprises; orientation of most families is on improving or maintaining their present standard of living.

The characteristic feature of this economic strategy is an active innovative policy, which includes the introduction of advanced technologies, cooperation with domestic research and extension activities, cooperation with foreign firms, development of processing and storage facilities, effective schemes of work incentives, and a high level of organization of primary and auxiliary activities. The latter include repair of farm equipment and steady links with business partners to develop reliable markets for agricultural products.

The enterprise's adaptation is productive and innovative, based on the search and implementation of new ways of interacting with the environment. This type of adaptation is characterized by clearly defined objectives and the use of new and efficient methods. The accomplishments of these enterprises, found throughout Russia, were summarized above. Such enterprises, however, account for no more than 5 percent to 7 percent of all large agricultural enterprises in Russia.[11]

Under this adaptation strategy, the focus of social welfare policy is to maintain and develop rural social infrastructure, aid shareholders and employees with their part-time farming, organize summer vacation activities for children, and improve the landscape in the village community. Labor policy includes the retention of employees (in the 1992–98 period, worker numbers in the case-study farm increased by 11), the development of a labor contract system, regular cash payment of wages, incentives for high levels of work performance, economizing of input resources, and punitive dismissal for breaches of discipline. The latter has a special significance. The loss of a job is not only the loss of wages, but also loss of access to resources necessary for private farming. These resources are obtained by workers either in kind (grain, hay, young animals, and so on) or at discounted prices. In addition, machinery operators have at their disposal agricultural equipment and transport vehicles, which they use to render services for pay. In a recent study of adaptation models used in Siberia, Fadeyeva wrote: "The greater the difference between the total sum of goods and services obtained directly or indirectly by the job holder from his enterprise and his 'nominal' wage in the payroll sheet, the more 'valuable' is this job."[12]

Enterprises adopting this strategy have paid the tuition for villagers in institutions of higher education. In addition, these enterprises have organized business travel abroad for their employees. Young men returning home from military service are given a sum of money equal to five times the minimum wage. The chairperson of the case-study company regularly advised young people to purchase shares in their company. Retirees were given from 3,000 to 7,000 rubles (roughly between one and two years' wages).

The case study enterprise's economic performance was quite good overall. The higher efficiency of production (40 percent) in accounts receivables exceeding accounts payable was the result of the realization of the active market strategy and innovative adaptation of this enterprise. In the 1992–98 period following the introduction of reforms, arable land usage declined only slightly, and livestock herds declined by 20 percent (including a 10 percent reduction of the cattle herd). Livestock herd reduction at the oblast level was much higher.

Typical opinions of the managers and specialists in enterprises using this type of adaptation strategy are as follows:

Our company "prospers" only in comparison with other companies.

If the subsidy going away from the country for "Bush's legs" [refers to chicken legs imported from the United States] were given to our agriculture, it could really prosper.

Dividends—we don't speak of dividends! We would be satisfied at least to keep production and pay minimum wages. And pay taxes in due time not to destroy the enterprise.

When I was in France I paid 400 francs for shoes, while meat cost there 80 to 100 francs for one kilogram. So I had shoes for four kilograms of meat, when at home I would have to pay the price of a whole suckling pig for these shoes. You see the disparity; what use is it to talk about prospects for the countryside!

The dominant strategies of families working in this type of enterprise were to improve or maintain their present standard of living (26 percent and 49 percent of families, respectively) through small-scale commercial farming (76 percent of the workers had small-scale household enterprises) and secondary paid jobs (35.5 percent of respondents would like to have secondary employment). Over 60 percent of the persons interviewed in this type of enterprise preferred to work overtime on their primary job to increase their incomes. Regular payments, even if they were modest, plus cash income from household commercial enterprises provided people working in this type of large enterprise with an acceptable living. Over a fourth of respondents were quite satisfied with their standard of living.

Model 2: Conformity economic strategy: compensatory adaptation of enter-prise; most families' strategies are aimed at maintaining the present stan-dard of living.

Typically, large enterprises that have adopted this strategy are found in Soviet-era state farms specialized in meat and dairy and grain production that have been reorganized into closed joint stock companies. These farms' specializations have not changed, but they have built milk cooling and pas-teurizing facilities in partnership with processing enterprises. The reorga-nization of collective and state farms was aimed at changing the organi-zational-legal status of collective enterprises, giving workers a *right to free choice* of forms of entrepreneurship. There were plans to diversify dairy processing, including sour milk products (sour cream, yogurt, and cheese). In the case-study enterprise, the mill built next to the grain-collecting sta-tion was used on a sharing basis. Grain was stored for a fee in grain-collecting stations managed by the company. When an enterprise pays a certain amount of money or other resources (a share) for the building of some facility (in this case, a mill), then it becomes a co-owner and can ac-cordingly pay lower prices for the services of this facility (the mill).

These enterprises have steady partners in marketing and processing, but they believe that setting up their own retail trade enterprise would be more profitable. To this end, a retail store was being built in the district seat of the case-study enterprise. A construction shop was also available and in ad-dition to doing jobs for the large enterprise, it supplied services to village residents for a fee. The company also opened its own bakery.

The type of adaptation in this large enterprise is compensatory,[13] a com-bination of traditional primary agricultural production with partnership- or cooperative-based agricultural processing. The combination of primary and secondary activities allows these enterprises to more effectively market their commodities, obtain cash, and obtain higher profits. This mode of adaptation ensures steady growth under difficult economic conditions. We estimated that enterprises using this mode of adaptation account for 10 percent to 15 percent of large agricultural enterprises in Russia.

A large enterprise employing this adaptation strategy has a social-welfare policy that includes building a health-care rest home for the elderly and all workers in this enterprise; and providing infrastructure and services such as shops, schools, communications, and health care.

In the case-study enterprise, social-welfare sector workers have passed over their land shares to the company by contract. Working employee-shareholders and pensioners are assisted in part-time farming with hay, grain, other types of animal fodder, and young animals in return for their work (livestock growers are given calves as part of their work remuneration). Every quarter each employee-shareholder is given 15 to 20 metric centners (one centner equals one-tenth of a metric ton) of grain free of charge. Other employees buy grain at discounted prices. Shareholders are provided with 20 to 30 centners of hay, and an unlimited quantity of straw for their privately owned livestock. During the harvest, equipment operators are provided with food at discounted prices. Needy households are allowed to take foodstuffs from shops on credit against wages. The most acute problem is housing construction.

The labor policy of this company can be summarized as avoiding mass dismissals. The number of company employees has actually increased slightly, primarily via accepting forced migrants from former Soviet republics. Young shareholders starting households were given a one-time cash benefit, and they were assisted in starting their own part-time farm. Secondary school and higher education graduates were given jobs.

The profit margin of this company was 11 percent. Receivables were five times greater than payables. Payments to enterprise partners for supplied products were perpetually in arrears, which greatly undermined the company's ability to obtain loans. In the 1992–98 period, agricultural land area increased by 300 hectares, and the livestock herd declined by 30 percent (including a 35-percent reduction in the cattle herd, while the number of pigs increased). Livestock productivity has improved; for instance, between 1997 and 1998, the average milk yield per cow increased from 3,490 to 4,000 kilograms. The number of tractors decreased by seven. New equipment was not available. This problem was solved by purchasing second-hand equipment or repairing existing equipment by using parts from old equipment. These purchases were made primarily from private farmers who went out of business. In general, this type of enterprise has managed to maintain its position. The case-study company had plans to expand production, and to improve grain yields and cattle productivity.

Typical opinions of officials and specialists in this type of company are as follows:

> Our innovations? First, this involves general attempts, ranging from director to rank-and-file worker, to economize material inputs.

> We are fighting small thefts that still are practiced, but the scale of these thefts is quite moderate.

> Requirements for workers are very strict and discipline has improved.

> At our meetings we keep persuading people that they are owners, shareholders. But it is not easy to awaken this feeling.

> With support from the company, a man can gain maximum profit from his own part-time farm too.

> Before the reform we had 3,000 liters of milk per cow yield. The state farm was a millionaire. Many workers could purchase individual cars. It was prosperity then. And they could provide education for their children. . . . Now we work harder but live 10 times worse.

> At present, the work is very exciting, but it is very difficult too. Now it is self-reliance, how skillful you are, that determines what you will gain. It is beautiful!

The prevailing family strategy in this type of enterprise is to maintain the present standard of living. Half of the workers interviewed said they would like to have a paid secondary job or to work overtime for extra income. About half of the families earned additional cash from sales of products from household plots.

Model 3. Mimicry economic strategy: deprivation adaptation of enterprise; orientation of families to survival or maintenance of the present living level.

The mimicry economic strategy is characterized by low innovative activity. Its typical features are low diversification of production, low development of processing facilities, and no nonagricultural businesses. According to the enterprises' specialists, diversification opportunities have been missed. In their view, processing ventures and new production facilities should have been started six to seven years earlier. Lack of funds and difficulties in getting loans hindered planning for the development of new production and processing facilities. Commercial loans could not be repaid because agricultural product prices were lower than input costs. In the case-study enterprise, a dairy that had been under construction for four years was abandoned due to lack of funds. This company had opened a small bakery, and a small woodworking shop employed two persons.

In this model, economic strategy is directed more at survival than growth. This strategy is characteristic of more than half of the enterprises in our study.

The social welfare policy associated with this economic strategy has been to preserve the entire traditional social infrastructure, including the music school, the kindergarten, and the House of Culture, but housing construction was practically at a standstill. The situation in small villages was much worse. In some villages, the school, the club house, and shop were closed. In cases of urgent need, workers were given cash loans at a 10-percent interest rate. A loan of 1,000 to 3,000 rubles was usually taken for 12 months or 18 months. Typically, the money was spent on nondurable consumer goods instead of durable goods. If wages were delayed (often for 2 months), workers took goods from the village shop against future wage payments.

In the case-study enterprise using this adaptive strategy, the average number of workers on the payroll was reduced by 27 persons from 1992 to 1998. According to the specialists, one of the reasons for employee turnover is an expanding urban-rural gap. The average monthly wage in 1997 was 498 rubles, which is below the subsistence minimum. As a result, the majority of rural residents maintain small household plots, and thus take on a large amount of manual labor. Young people seek either to leave this environment or to find a nonagricultural job in the local labor market. The company could perhaps attract them by new housing, but home construction was not financially viable. Although workers' skills were generally satisfactory, constant skill upgrading is necessary. If workers do not leave home to upgrade skills or to meet with counterparts to exchange ideas and experiences, it is very difficult for them to maintain their skills at an adequate professional level. Specialists' skills were also becoming dated because most courses now must be paid for and the company could not afford to pay for employees' transportation to take courses.

The financial standing of companies employing this adaptation strategy is not good. According to their specialists, 80 percent to 100 percent of vehicles and equipment were worn out. In the case-study enterprise, the number of tractors decreased by five, and combines by three over the 1992–98 period. The last purchase of new equipment was five to seven years ago. Purchased equipment is second-hand and obtained with credit. The livestock herd, including cattle, declined by about a third, and productivity dropped by about a fourth. Cultivated area did not change. Profitability over the period of the study (1992–98) fell by one-third. In 1998, payables were 15 times higher than receivables. The company recorded a 3,000-ruble loss in 1997.

Typical opinions of officials and specialists in farms using this type of adaptation strategy included:

> No liberalization has occurred in the countryside. Everything has remained as it was in the past—one administrator, several specialists. All power is with the enterprise director, employees are under the director's authority and guidance. While nearby state farms are ruined, ours is still functioning. The director makes every effort not to let the enterprise be ruined and let people live in peace, be employed, be socially protected, and have high earnings.

The dominant strategies of those working in enterprises of this type were aimed at simple survival or maintaining the present standard of living (40 percent and 42 percent of families, respectively). Only 16 percent of the families seek to raise their living standard by farming household plots and a secondary paid job.

Model 4. Passive, biding-time economic strategy: destructive adaptation (disadaptation) of the enterprise and family survival strategy.

Typical features of this economic strategy include the reorganization of the enterprise into a closed joint stock company, passive biding of time and hoping for changes and aid from the top, total depreciation of fixed capital, absence of processing facilities or steady ties with retail or wholesale markets, and little diversification of production. Prior to the reforms, the case-study enterprise specialized in poultry production, and then switched to grain and meat and dairy production. The enterprise switched its specialization after reorganization; this production diversification was forced upon it.

This strategy indicates that the enterprise has been unable to find its niche in the new economic environment, which has led to disintegration of the workforce and financial ruin. In other words, this strategy is tantamount to "destructive adaptation." This situation characterizes, in our estimation, about 20 percent of all large agricultural enterprises.

The social welfare policy of this type of company is aimed mainly at giving help to employees and pensioners to farm their household plots, rendering services to residents at discount prices, and assisting with transportation problems and health-care facilities. The paucity of resources available to deal with social problems intensifies social tensions among workers.

In the case-study enterprise, labor policy from 1992 to 1998 included a reduction of employees by a factor of 2.3. Regular wages had not been paid for a long time. The financial standing of the enterprise was not good. The livestock herd had declined by 75 percent, including a 70-percent reduction of the cattle herd. Livestock productivity has declined; for instance, average milk yield per cow in 1998 was only 1,628 liters, which was below the oblast average. The number of tractors declined in the case-study enterprise during this period by 104, and combines by 38. Payables exceeded receivables by more than 200 percent.

Opinions of officials and specialists follow:

There's no help from anywhere, we are no one's concern.

No ideas, no innovations.

All has been ruined, equipment destroyed.

The only young people who come are odd persons, undisciplined, drinkers, those whom nobody needs.

Workers are stealing all things of whatever use, pilfer unused buildings, fodder, equipment—everything.

People live according to the old understanding—that it is not mine but everyone's.

It is a deadlock.

The result of this mode of adaptation was that employees barely subsist. Over 70 percent of them reported deterioration in their living standard over the past two years. The chief source of income was small household plots, which greatly increased employees' work load. Forty percent of the respondents reported that they work to exhaustion. Domestic strategies, including illegal actions, were oriented mostly to survival. The vast majority (89 percent) of the respondents excused this behavior, either in full or in part, by saying that they had no other choices. And about half of the workers attributed their disastrous situation to the poor financial standing of the company. Half of the employees could not recall any happy event in their life over the past year, and another 5 percent said that the past year had brought them only troubles. These families survived mainly on their small household plots, which account for up to 77 percent of their income. Most respondents expressed a willingness to take an additional paid job.

Conclusions

Notwithstanding the similarity of external conditions, the reorganized agricultural enterprises demonstrate drastically different models of economic strategies and adaptation to new socioeconomic conditions.

The choice of and results of a particular adaptation strategy were largely determined by the personality of the enterprise manager. This study has shown that the most successful enterprises did not change leadership during the period of reorganization. The most successful companies were those headed by so-called "red" directors who ideologically did not approve of the reforms but in practice demonstrated market models of economic behavior. In contrast, young directors, while embracing and supporting the ongoing transformations, did not possess adequate real-world experience and found themselves helpless in face of the difficulties in the present economic environment.

Rural people now understand the role of the leader. Forty percent of those surveyed believed that the lack of skills and erroneous actions of the leaders caused the deterioration in the economic situation of the enterprise. About the same share of rural respondents attributed their troubles to the erroneous course of reforms, ill-conceived state policies with regard to the agrarian sector, and a faulty tax system. Workers' hopes for their enterprise were associated with changes in the government's agrarian, tax, and financial-credit policies, and with the replacement of their enterprise manager. One of five employees believed that improving work motivations of rural people and improving work discipline are necessary. It is revealing that only 2 percent of the respondents hoped for a return to the former system and less than 1 percent thought that their enterprises could not be revived at all.

After reorganization, the economic situation of all agricultural enterprises deteriorated. But those enterprises specializing in production that was profitable under current market conditions were in better financial positions compared to others.

The economic situation of the enterprise at the beginning of the reforms had an impact on its process of reorganization and adaptation to new conditions, but was not always the decisive factor in causing its current financial situation.

The principal factors accounting for enterprise survival were diversification of production, a moderate innovation policy, and development of small processing facilities. The development of processing ventures was motivated by the desire of agricultural enterprises to achieve three goals. The first was to counter the pressure of large processing monopolies that dictate conditions to farm enterprises but do not always fulfill their obligations. The second was to ensure a small but secure source of cash. The third was to improve the profitability of processing ventures through the removal of middlemen.

Most large collective enterprises have no reliable channels for marketing their commodities. In the agricultural market, conditions are often dictated by wholesale dealers, racketeers, and criminals. Barter transactions make up a significant portion of transactions. In Novosibirsk oblast, barter accounted for 2 percent of all grain transactions in 1992 compared to 22 percent in 1998.

Lack of credit to replace and maintain agricultural equipment, and to purchase fertilizers, veterinary products, and other inputs led to falling productivity.

There were no mechanisms for regular skill upgrading of workers and specialists. Higher costs for education and a higher cost of living, in general, made it increasingly difficult for young people in rural areas to get secondary or post-secondary professional education in the city. The situation was exacerbated by the absence of opportunities for exchanging experiences and contacts among professionals and skilled workers.

The price disparity between agricultural and industrial products, as well as higher energy prices, increases the unprofitability of agriculture. In turn, this has led to a contraction of social welfare programs and housing construction. These conditions increase social tensions and conflicts in large farm enterprises. Nevertheless, enterprises still manage to provide many social services to workers and to assist them in small-scale private farming activities, thereby helping to maintain their standard of living.

The adaptation strategies used by large agricultural enterprises have had a major impact on dominant family strategies. The major means of survival of rural families were small-scale, part-time farming, secondary paid jobs, and illegal practices. In economically strong enterprises, most families were oriented to material affluence or maintenance of the present standard of living, while in economically weak enterprises, families were oriented only to subsistence.

Notes

1. The study was funded by the Russian Humanitarian Scientific Foundation, Project N 99N 99-03-00170.

2. *Regiony Rossii* (Moscow: Goskomstat, 1998), 432.

3. *Sel'skoe khoziaistvo Rossii* (Moscow: Goskomstat, 1995), 48–49.

4. Ye. Stroev, ed., *Konceptsiia agrarnoi politiki Rossii v 1997–2000 godax* (Moscow: Vershina Club, 1997), 343.

5. V. Khlystun, "Stabilizurovat rabotu agropromyshlennogo complekha Rossii," *APK: ekonomika, upravlenie,* no. 4 (April 1997): 7.

6. *Rossiia v tsifrakh 1998* (Moscow: Goskomstat, 1998), 319.

7. G. M. Orlov and V. I. Uvarov, "Sela i Rossiiskiye reformy," *Sotsiologicheskie issledovaniia* 5 (May 1997): 43–53.

8. *Rossiiskii statisticheskii ezhegodnik 1998* (Moscow: Goskomstat, 1998), 502.

9. G. Underwood, "Categories of Adaptation," *Evolution* 8 (fall 1954): 372.

10. L. Korel, *Sotsiologiia adaptatsii: etudy apologii* (Novosibirsk: IEIE SB RAS, 1997), 40–113.

11. B. Poshkus, "Vnutrennie rezervy APK Rossii," *APK: ekonomika, upravelenie* 3 (March 1997): 14.

12. O. P. Fadeyeva, "Sibirskoe selo: alternativnye model: adaptazii," in *Krestianovedenie, teoria, istoria, soveremennost,* eds. V. Danilov and T. Shanin (Moscow: MVShSEN, 1999), 227–40.

13. G. I. Tsaregorodsky, ed., *Philosophic Issues of Adaptation Theory* (Moscow: Mysl, 1975), 177.

16

How Much Does Informal Support Matter? The Effect of Personal Networks on Subjective Evaluation of Life

LARRY D. DERSHEM

Introduction

The collapse of the Soviet Union and the introduction of components of a market economy have led to decreasing standards of living and quality of life for the majority of Russians. To date, most research has focused on "objective" indicators, such as household income, wage arrears, and employment status. Although these are important indicators for understanding the economic transition in Russia, they may not correspond with "subjective" evaluations of these conditions. An individual's evaluation of his or her life obviously will be affected by material conditions and the extent to which he or she is experiencing adversity and hardship in trying to cope with those conditions. However, as Campbell, Converse, and Rodgers note:

> [T]he relationship between objective conditions and psychological states is very imperfect and . . . in order to know the quality of life experience it will be necessary to go directly to the individual himself for his description of how his life *feels* to him [my emphasis].[1]

The way rural Russians perceive the quality of their lives is critical in academic and policy assessments of how they are affected by social change. Much of public opinion research shows that individuals do not evaluate their lives in a simple unidimensional way. Rather, different domains of an individual's life are affected differently by social change. A change that may improve an evaluation of one area of life may reduce it in other areas of life. Most important, individuals differ in the resources they possess with which to deal with social change and this will have an important impact on how they evaluate different areas of their lives.

An important resource assisting individuals and households to deal with the socioeconomic transition of Russian society is personal exchange and support networks. Informal relationships pervaded the Soviet Union. Informal networks took care of needs that were not met by the command economy. Family and friends, rather than wages or salaries, were an institutionalized mechanism for dealing with everyday needs.[2] Informal ties were vital for obtaining scarce goods and services needed for a better life, a higher standard of living, and leisure. An environment of shortages, created by a command economy, encouraged and sustained interdependencies within and between families, friends, and neighbors.

The question being asked now is: What is the importance of informal ties and networks in the post-Soviet period? Some argue that the change from a command economy of shortages to some form of a market economy will undermine the basis of Russian informal relations of mutual help.[3] Others have shown that personal exchange and support networks remain meaningful resources for individuals and households in Russia today.[4]

Most research that measures informal exchange and support networks has focused on urban areas of Russia.[5] Moreover, studies typically focus on the impact of support networks on objective indicators of quality of life, such as access to financial capital, goods, and services. Few studies have examined personal exchange and support networks in rural Russia, or the impact of rural support networks on *subjective* evaluations of various life domains and overall quality of life. This chapter examines the effect of informal exchange and support networks on the way that rural Russians evaluate their subjective quality of life.

Data Collection

To study the effect of personal exchange and support networks on subjective quality of life in rural Russia, data were obtained from a three-wave panel study that was conducted each summer from 1995 to 1997 in three Russian villages. In this survey design, the same households, and the same informants within the households, were interviewed each summer during the three years. Chapter 5 by Patsiorkovski and chapter 14 by O'Brien in this book deal with other aspects of the panel study.

The locations of the three study villages are shown in Figure 14.1 on page 353. Two of the villages, Latonovo in Rostov oblast in the northern Caucasus region and Vengerovka in Belgorod oblast in the central black-earth region, are in the black-earth (chernozem) zone, and one village, Bolshoe Sviattsovo in Tver' oblast in the central region is outside of this zone.

The first village, Latonovo, is located 745 miles south of Moscow in the Matveev-Kurgen region on the southern edge of the Russian plains. In 1996, Latonovo had a population of 1,509 people (532 households). The second village, Vengerovka, is located 500 miles south of Moscow, approximately 31 miles north of the Ukrainian border in south central Russia. In 1996, Vengerovka had a population of 1,010 people (267 households). The third village, Bolshoe Sviattsovo ("greater Sviattsovo"), which is a collection of eight very small villages in Tver' oblast, is located 150 miles northwest of Moscow and 300 miles south of St. Petersburg. In 1996, the population of Bolshoe Sviattsovo was 920 (241 households).

The household sample was constructed from the official list of permanent residents in each village, which is called the *kniga ucheta domashnikh khoziaistva* (book of household accounts).[6] The village council updates this list at the beginning of each calendar year.

The following is an overview of the demographic characteristics of the 463 panel respondents at the start of the panel study in 1995.[7] Almost three-quarters of household respondents were women (74.5 percent). Respondents were, on average, 52 years of age—50 for men and 52 for women. Two-thirds (65.8 percent) of all respondents were married, 27.5 percent were widowed, 4.1 percent were divorced, and 2.6 percent were single (never married). The average number of years of education was 8, and almost one-third had 11 or more years of education. Slightly more than two-thirds (68.3 percent) of the respondents were employed in the local TOO (*tovarishchestvo s ogranichennoi otvetstvennostiu*, closed joint stock company) or *kolkhoz*, 25.8 percent worked in the social sphere, 2.3 percent were newly registered private farmers, 1.4 percent were involved in other agriculture-related businesses, and 2.3 percent were engaged in nonagricultural businesses.

Personal Networks and Subjective Evaluation of Life

Personal exchange and support networks were measured with items that were similar to the social network items used in Fischer.[8] These items were adapted to meet the specific social organization, needs, and cultural characteristics of the Russian village. Respondents were asked to identify up to five individuals who assisted members of their household in 6 areas. These included: (1) borrowing money, (2) trading goods and services, (3) taking care of the household if someone is sick, (4) assisting with the cultivation of the household plot, (5) assisting with household tasks, and (6) discussing important matters. The total number of unique individuals across the six exchange areas was used to gauge the size of a respondent's exchange network.[9]

The subjective evaluation of life consists of five domains that had different degrees of immediacy in a person's life, and one overall measure. The first three domains pertain to an individual's household relations: current marital status, family life, and income. The next two domains pertain to an individual's external household relations—satisfaction with the village and with the overall situation in the country.[10] Finally, individuals assessed their level of satisfaction with life in general.

Measurement of different levels of satisfaction with each of the five domains and life in general was obtained from responses to three pairs of semantic differential seven-point scales. In each of the domains and life in general, respondents were asked to identify the extent to which they were "dissatisfied (1) to satisfied (7)," and the extent to which they found each to be "unpleasant (1) to pleasant (7)," and "disappointing (1) to rewarding (7)." An index for each of the five domains and life in general was created from the three pairs of semantic differential scales. The alpha reliabilities of the indexes ranged from 0.91 to 0.98.

Domain and Overall Satisfaction from 1995 to 1997

The size of personal exchange and support networks over the three-year period ranged from 0 to 17 people, with respondents mentioning, on average, slightly more than 5 people (see Table 16.1). During this time, the average size of exchange and support networks was 5. The average size of personal networks increased slightly during this time period, but the change was not statistically significant.

Table 16.1

Size of Personal Exchange and Support Networks in Three Russian Villages, 1995–97 (n = 463)

Network Characteristics	1995	1996	1997
0	0.2%	0.2%	0.6%
1–2	8.0%	7.7%	5.4%
3–5	47.5%	43.0%	41.2%
6–12	44.4%	48.5%	51.5%
13+	0.2%	0.6%	0.3%
Mean	5.5	5.6	5.8
Maximum	17.0	14.0	15.0
Standard deviation	2.4	2.4	2.4

The average size of exchange and support networks in Russian villages is not much different than those found in other national studies. The average size of networks, for example, in Jacksonville, Florida, was 6.88 persons, 2.95 in Mexico City, 5.8 in a random sample of college students in the United States, 5.18 for Dutch volunteers, and 5.00 in one study and 4.7 in another study in Toronto, Canada.[11] A precise comparison cannot be made among these studies and the findings reported in this chapter because the question to solicit a respondent's network members was slightly different in each study. Nonetheless, it is reasonable to conclude that the size of personal exchange and support networks in Russia has not changed dramatically as a result of the transition from the Soviet to the post-Soviet period.

The mean levels of satisfaction of the total sample for the five life domains and life in general from 1995 to 1997 are shown in Table 16.2. On average, the respondents evaluated their overall quality of life as less than fair, that is, slightly lower than the midpoint of four on the seven-point scale. This seems to be contrary to popular press reports, which suggest that rural Russians would overwhelmingly rate their quality of life as extremely low. There was a slight increase in the mean level of satisfaction with overall quality of life, from 3.51 in 1995 to 3.58 in 1997, but this increase is not statistically significant. These mean evaluations of overall quality of life in rural Russia, however, are much lower than mean evaluations of overall quality of life of Americans in earlier studies: 5.5 in May 1972, 5.3 in November 1972, and 5.4 in April 1973.[12]

Three of the five life domains had mean levels of satisfaction above the midpoint: family, marital status, and village life. Of these three life domains,

Table 16.2

Mean Level of Satisfaction with Five Life Domains and Life in General in Three Russian Villages, 1995–97 (n = 419)[a]

Domain Satisfaction[b]	1995	1996	1997
Life in general	3.51	3.54	3.58
Marital status	4.33	4.45	4.42
Family	4.71	4.79	4.80
Income	2.85	3.07	3.07
Village	4.39	4.04	3.92
Country	1.97	1.93	2.05

[a] Forty-four respondents had one or more missing values in the quality-of-life questions.
[b] Scale: 1 = dissatisfied to 7 = satisfied.
Notes: Marital status by year $F(2) = 0.82$, p = not significant; family by year $F(2) = 0.62$; income by year $F(2) = 6.12$, $p < .01$, Scheffe 1995 by 1996 $p < .01$, 1995 by 1997 $p < .01$; village by year $F(2) = 24.86$, $p < .000$, Scheffe 1995 by 1996 $p < .000$, 1995 by 1997 $p < .000$; country by year $F(2) = 3.38$, $p < .05$, Scheffe 1996 by 1997 $p < .05$, life in general by year $F(2) = 0.69$, p = not significant.

only satisfaction with village life decreased significantly over the three years, even though its mean level remained near the scale average. Evaluations of the most personal domains of interaction within the household remained unchanged, while the next level of personal interaction outside the household, with village institutions and services, began to decline during this period.

The mean level of satisfaction with two life domains, income and country, were substantially below the scale midpoint in 1995. The lowest mean level of satisfaction for income was 2.85 in that year. Although still low, the mean satisfaction level of 3.07 in 1996 and 1997 was a significant increase from the 1995 level. Satisfaction with the situation in the country was evaluated the lowest of all life domains, reaching a mean low of 1.93 in 1996. Despite some worsening conditions in Russia as a whole during this time, the mean level of satisfaction with the situation in the country actually increased to 2.05 in 1997, which was a statistically significant change. The increases in satisfaction with income and the situation in the country are explained in large measure by the successful adaptation strategies developed by households, especially the growth of household enterprises.[13] The impact of these strategies on household income is discussed by Lerman in chapter 2 and O'Brien in chapter 14. These strategies have produced some visible material and economic gains for a substantial number of households in the three villages.

A comparison of the mean levels of satisfaction with different life domains shows that important changes occurred in a relatively brief period of three years. There was increased optimism about material and economic conditions represented by an increase in satisfaction with income and the situation in the country, but this was offset by a substantial decrease in level of satisfaction with the village. One of the most important reasons for the lower assessment of village life is that the villages in the study have not adapted their social, economic, and political institutions to the realities of a market economy as fast as have households. While households have managed to develop and expand interpersonal helping networks to increase informal exchange of goods, services, and labor, which improves the effectiveness of their enterprises, the institutional structures in villages have not adapted to assist the new household enterprises in purchasing inputs, processing raw agricultural commodities, or marketing these products. In general, villages have not developed many important institutions of civil society, such as government-private partnerships and for-profit and not-for-profit organizations, and have not found ways to replace the social service infrastructure support once obtained from the *kolkhozy* and *sovkhozy*. In chapter 5, Patsiorkovski discusses this point at length.

Despite fluctuations, the large difference between the mean levels of satisfaction with interpersonal relations (family, marital status, and village) and economic and political structures (income and situation in the country) remained constant. For each of the three years of the study, respondents were twice as satisfied with their family, marital status, and village as they were with the situation in the country. Satisfaction with the most intimate types of interpersonal relations reflects a normative commitment and capacity to support kith and kin during a crisis.

Domain and Life Satisfaction by Size of Personal Exchange and Support Networks

Table 16.3 shows evaluations of five life domains and overall subjective quality of life by size of personal exchange and support networks. There are positive bivariate relationships between the size of exchange and support networks and satisfaction with marital status, family, and income. However, the relationships between size of networks and satisfaction with marital status and family are not linear. In 1996 and 1997, respondents with middle-size networks had higher levels of satisfaction with their marital status and family life than did respondents with smaller or larger networks. The association between small and large networks and lower levels of satisfaction with marital status and family life is due to a disproportionate number of

Table 16.3

Mean Level of Satisfaction with Five Life Domains and Life in General by Size of Helping Network, 1995–97[a]

Size of Helping Network	Marital Status	Family	Village	Income	Country	Life in General
			1995			
0–3 (n = 79)	3.51	4.00	4.03	2.53	2.17	3.33
4–5 (n = 146)	4.35	4.73	4.39	2.74	1.98	3.51
6 (n = 64)	4.30	4.70	4.46	3.18	2.07	3.57
7–10 (n = 116)	4.81	5.10	4.58	2.96	1.78	3.60
11–17 (n = 14)	4.98	5.45	4.67	3.33	1.88	3.48
Total (n = 419)	4.33	4.71	4.39	2.85	1.97	3.51
			1996			
0–3 (n = 70)	3.85	4.26	3.91	2.75	2.22	3.45
4–5 (n = 129)	4.35	4.75	4.00	2.88	1.84	3.55
6 (n = 74)	4.52	4.83	4.00	3.19	1.99	3.52
7–10 (n = 133)	4.89	5.13	4.20	3.35	1.86	3.62
11–17 (n = 13)	3.87	4.31	3.85	3.28	1.64	3.26
Total (n = 419)	4.45	4.79	4.04	3.07	1.93	3.54
			1997			
0–3 (n = 69)	3.83	4.31	3.82	2.73	2.28	3.37
4–5 (n = 117)	4.25	4.75	3.94	2.99	2.09	3.54
6 (n = 78)	4.68	4.89	3.97	3.17	2.17	3.77
7–10 (n = 139)	4.68	5.01	3.94	3.26	1.93	3.64
11–17 (n = 16)	4.75	4.94	3.71	3.02	1.31	3.23
Total (n = 419)	4.42	4.80	3.92	3.07	2.05	3.58

[a] Scale: 1 = dissatisfied to 7 = satisfied.

Notes: 1995—marital status by helping network F(4) = 10.69, $p < .000$, Scheffe 1 × 2 $p < .001$, 1 × 3 $p < .05$, 1 × 4 $p < .000$, 1 × 5 $p < .01$; family by helping network F(4) = 10.78, $p < .000$, Scheffe 1 × 2 $p < .001$, 1 × 3 $p < .05$, 1 × 4 $p < .000$, 1 × 5 $p < .01$; income by helping network F(4) = 4.59, $p < .001$, Scheffe 1 × 3 $p < .01$; village by helping network F(4) = 3.70, $p < .000$, Scheffe 1 × 4 $p < .01$; country by helping network F(4) = 3.72, $p < .01$, Scheffe 1 × 4 $p < .01$; life in general by helping network F(4) = 0.97, p = not significant.

1996—marital status by helping network F(4) = 8.76, $p < .000$, Scheffe 1 × 4 $p < .000$, 2 × 4 $p < .05$; family by helping network F(4) = 7.56, $p < .000$, Scheffe 1 × 3 $p < .000$; income by helping network F(4) = 4.89, $p < .001$, Scheffe 1 × 4 $p < .01$, 2 × 4 $p < .05$; village by helping network F(4) = 1.78, p = not significant; country by helping network F(4) = 5.11, $p < .001$, Scheffe 1 × 2 $p < .01$, 1 × 4 $p < .01$; life in general by helping network F(4) = 0.97, p = not significant.

1997—marital status by helping network F(4) = 6.67, $p < .000$, Scheffe 1 × 3 $p < .01$, 1 × 4 $p < .001$; family by helping network F(4) = 4.44, $p < .01$, Scheffe 1 × 4 $p < .01$; income by helping network F(4) = 4.03, $p < .01$, Scheffe 1 × 4 $p < .01$; village by helping network F(4) = 0.47, p = not significant; country by helping network F(4) = 9.21, $p < .000$, Scheffe 1 × 4 $p < .01$, 1 × 5 $p < .000$, 2 × 5 $p < .001$, 3 × 5 $p < .000$, 4 × 5 $p < .01$; life in general by helping network F(4) = 3.58, $p < .01$, Scheffe 1 × 3 $p < .05$.

smaller networks being reported by single parents and larger networks being reported by a larger households and elderly persons.[14]

The size of helping networks was positively associated with satisfaction with village only in 1995 and the strength of the association is minimal. The size of personal networks, however, is positively associated with income satisfaction in each of the three years; respondents with smaller size networks are least satisfied whereas respondents with larger size networks are the most satisfied with their household income. Larger networks assist households in producing, processing, and marketing agricultural commodities, which translates into higher overall household income.

There is a consistently negative relationship between size of helping networks and satisfaction with the country. Respondents with smaller networks reported higher levels of satisfaction with the situation in the country than did respondents reporting larger networks. As noted earlier, size of helping networks is positively associated with satisfaction with income. These same households, however, are also the most likely to be frustrated with the lack of local and national institutional change that hinders expansion of their nascent enterprises. More often than not, these more successful enterprises have reached the limit of what they can produce with the land, technology, and credit available to them. Central and regional government inaction in land reform and opportunities for household credit are basic causes of these limitations. See chapter 5 by Patsiorkovski for a discussion of these points.

The size of personal networks is associated with satisfaction with life in general only in 1997. In that year, respondents with moderate-size networks had higher mean levels of satisfaction with life in general than did respondents with small and large networks.

In the structural equation model that is described below (see Figure 16.1 and Appendix), all bivariate relationships between personal networks and life domains remain except for satisfaction with village life and the situation in the country. Personal exchange and support networks, however, have *indirect* effects on overall life satisfaction that operate through four of the five life domains.

Modeling the Effects of Household Capital on Subjective Quality of Life

The relationships between the various respondent and household characteristics, size of exchange networks, domain satisfactions, and satisfaction

Figure 16.1
Effects of Household Labor and Social Capital on Five Quality-of-Life Domains and Life in General

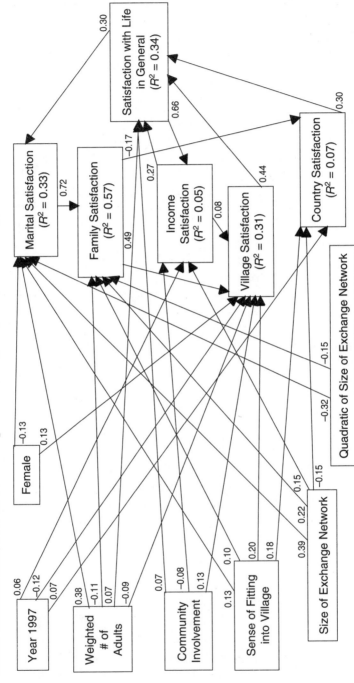

Notes: $X^2 = 41.00$, $df = 30$, $p < .09$, GFI = 0.99, AGFI = 0.99. For the standardized regression coefficients for observed exogenous variables and explained variance (R^2) for the structural model, see Table 16A.1 in the Appendix.

with life in general are shown in Figure 16.1. The model of these relationships includes the effects of a number of individual and household characteristics: gender, the weighted number of adults in the household,[15] two measures of community attachment,[16] year, and size of exchange network. The data were analyzed in a structural equation model using the computer program Amos, rev. 3.62.[17] The database of 463 cases for each of the three years of the study is inverted to represent 1,389 separate cases (463 cases × 3 years), which allows for the testing of the "pure" effect of a variable on another variable over the three-year period of time.

The arrows show the statistically significant relationships ($p < .01$) between personal and household characteristics and satisfaction with the five life domains and life in general. The number next to each arrow is a standardized beta coefficient. The multiple squared correlation (R^2) is the amount of explained variance for each of the quality-of-life issues accounted for by the respondent, household characteristics, and size of exchange networks. The quadratic of size of personal exchange network is added to measure the curvilinear relationship between size of exchange network and satisfaction with marital status and family life.

When controlling for personal and household characteristics, personal exchange networks directly impact on satisfaction with marital status, family life, income, and the situation in the country. The statistical significance between the quadratic of size of exchange network and satisfaction with marital status and family life shows that the curvilinear relationship presented in Table 16.3 is maintained. The standardized beta coefficients in Figure 16.1 indicate, in rank order, that the effect of personal networks is greater on satisfaction with marital status (0.39) and family life (0.22), which is almost twice as much as the effect on satisfaction with income or the situation in the country.

Figure 16.2 presents the curvilinear relationships between the size of personal exchange and support networks and marital and family satisfaction as shown by the positive coefficient from size of network and negative coefficients for the quadratic of network size. The level of marital satisfaction increases up to approximately nine network members, and then decreases. Respondents with the smallest and the largest personal networks evaluated their level of marital satisfaction quite low. These two groups represent different demographic types of families. Respondents with low marital satisfaction and small personal networks are primarily single parents. At the other extreme, low marital satisfaction and large personal networks are found primarily among respondents who are married with children and have one or more other adults living in the household. Low levels

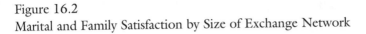

Figure 16.2

Marital and Family Satisfaction by Size of Exchange Network

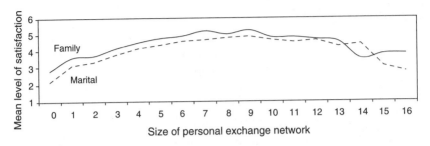

of available household labor without large personal exchange and support networks to substitute for its absence increase dissatisfaction with marital status. A large number of persons in the household will supply more labor and increases the size of personal support networks but it also appears to increase stress between husband and wife.

Figure 16.2 shows that the greatest level of family satisfaction occurs for respondents with personal networks of nine to ten members. Like marital satisfaction, respondents with the smallest (3 or fewer) and largest personal networks (12 or more) have low levels of family satisfaction. Once more, respondents with small personal networks and low family satisfaction are primarily from households comprised of single parents and retired couples. Respondents with low levels of family satisfaction and large personal networks are primarily individuals who are married with children and other adults living in the household.

Personal networks have an equally strong, but opposite, effect on satisfaction with income and the situation in the country (0.15 and –0.15, respectively). This is shown in Figure 16.3. Respondents with larger-size personal networks are more satisfied with their household income, but, conversely, less satisfied with the situation in the country.

The increase in satisfaction with income is explained in large measure by the successful adaptation strategies developed by households, especially the growth of household-based enterprises. Because household production and sales have such an important bearing on household income, they also have a critical bearing on the quality of life of the Russian peasant household. Household income resulting from sales of a household's production will directly affect the ability of the household to purchase more expensive, often imported, goods that have begun to appear in shops in regional centers and large cities. The ability of a household to pay for these goods with

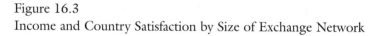

Figure 16.3

Income and Country Satisfaction by Size of Exchange Network

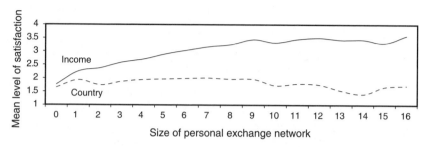

money gained from sales of pork, poultry, or sour cream will determine to a significant degree whether the household is able to experience any of the material benefits of a new market economy. However, peasant household production is extremely labor intensive. Although peasant households have obtained some types of mechanical equipment, their ability to maintain plots, produce crops, care for animals, and process their harvest depends on the size and availability of household labor and personal exchange networks. Households reporting larger personal networks produce more agricultural commodities and higher household incomes than households reporting smaller personal networks.[18] See chapter 14 by O'Brien for elaboration on this point. Thus, large personal exchange networks increase the opportunities for households to gain access to information, equipment, land, and animals, thereby increasing production and sales.

The declining satisfaction with the situation in the country by those with large personal networks is the result of their improved economic situation, which has been brought about in part through these same helping networks. Persons in these households are more likely to be dissatisfied with the slow pace of institutional change at the village, regional, and national levels. There has been very limited development of a market infrastructure, including land and credit markets, that would meet the needs of these households with growing enterprises, as well as a failure to develop formal-legal, member-owned, and managed cooperatives for them to purchase inputs or to market their products.

Moreover, there has been a failure at different levels of government, and in the private sector, to deal with the social service needs that have emerged in the post-Soviet era. Among those households that have made more successful economic adaptations to the market economy, there is a very real concern that they will not be able to meet their health, education, and other social-welfare needs. See chapter 14 by O'Brien, chapter 9 by Gambold Miller, and chapter 5 by Patsiorkovski for more details on these points.

Summary

Personal exchange and support networks in rural Russia have not disappeared, nor are they withering in the post-Soviet transition. Rather, the size of personal exchange and support networks of rural Russians increased slightly from 1995 to 1997. Respondents reported, on average, five people from whom they receive material goods, labor, and emotional support.

Personal exchange and support networks did not significantly affect a respondent's evaluation of his or her overall subjective quality of life but they operated *indirectly* through their association with specific life domain satisfaction. Moderate-size personal exchange and support networks were associated with higher levels of marital and family satisfaction. However, the larger the personal and exchange network the greater the satisfaction with household income and the greater the dissatisfaction with the situation in the country.

In summary, personal exchange and support networks are important contributors to how satisfied rural Russians are with various aspects of their lives. In the more intimate and exclusive parts of life, however, bigger is not always better. Large networks are used to compensate for elderly persons, usually widows, who have lost a spouse, but large networks cannot overcome personal dissatisfaction with intrahousehold conditions.

When dealing with issues outside the household, especially income, larger personal exchange networks are better. Large exchange and support networks provide better access to multiple sources of income. In addition, the weakened capacity of the state to provide social services and the emergence of market-based service alternatives provide an advantage to households with larger networks. At the same time, however, the findings show that those households that are better off are also more likely to be frustrated with the slow pace of structural change and thus perhaps to be a source of pressure for more fundamental reforms of rural institutions and social organization in the future.

Appendix

Table 16A.1

Standardized Regression Coefficients for Observed Exogenous Variables and Explained Variance (R^2) for Structural Model of Peasant Household Quality of Life

Observed Endogenous Variable	R^2	Standardized Regression Weights	Observed Exogenous Variable
Life in general	0.34		
		0.44	Village satisfaction
		0.30	Country satisfaction
		0.27	Income satisfaction
		0.07	Community involvement
		0.07	Weighted number of adults
Life Domains			
Family satisfaction	0.57		
		0.72	Marital status satisfaction
		0.22	Size of exchange and support network
		−0.14	Quadratic of size of network
		−0.11	Weighted number of adults
		0.10	Sense of "fit" into village
Marital satisfaction	0.33		
		0.39	Size of exchange and support network
		−0.32	Quadratic of size of network
		0.38	Weighted number of adults
		0.20	Overall satisfaction with life
		−0.13	Female
		0.13	Sense of "fit" into village
Village satisfaction	0.31		
		0.49	Family satisfaction
		0.20	Sense of "fit" into village
		0.13	Community involvement
		0.13	Female
		−0.12	Year 1997
		−0.09	Weighted number of adults
		−0.08	Income satisfaction
Country satisfaction	0.07		
		0.18	Sense of "fit" into village
		−0.17	Family satisfaction
		−0.15	Size of exchange and support network
		0.07	Year 1997
Income satisfaction	0.05		
		0.66	Overall life satisfaction
		0.15	Size of exchange and support network
		−0.08	Community involvement
		0.06	Year 1997

Notes

1. Angus Campbell, Philip E. Converse, and Willard L. Rodgers, *The Quality of American Life: Perceptions, Evaluations and Satisfaction* (New York: Russell Sage Foundation, 1976), 4.

2. Vladimir Shlapentokh, *Public and Private Life of the Soviet People* (New York: Oxford University Press, 1989); Alena V. Ledeneva, *Russia's Economy of Favours: Blat, Networking and Informal Exchange* (Cambridge: Cambridge University Press, 1998).

3. Ibid.

4. Larry D. Dershem, Valeri V. Patsiorkovski, and David J. O'Brien, "The Use of the CES-D for Measuring Symptoms of Depression in Three Rural Russian Villages," *Social Indicators Research* 38 (1996): 1–20; David J. O'Brien, Valeri V. Patsiorkovski, and Larry D. Dershem, "Rural Responses to Land Reform in Russia: An Analysis of Household Land Use in Belgorod, Rostov and Tver' Oblasts from 1991–1996," in *Land Reform in the Former Soviet Union and Eastern Europe*, ed. Stephen K. Wegren (London: Routledge, 1998), 35–61; Ledeneva, *Russia's Economy of Favours*.

5. Vladimir Yakubovich, "Economic Constraints and Social Opportunities: Participation in Informal Support Networks of Russian Urban Households" (Warwick, UK: Centre for Comparative Labour Studies, University of Warwick, 1999), available at *www.warwick.ac.uk/fac/soc/complabstuds/russia/network.doc*; Ledeneva, *Russia's Economy of Favours*.

6. A stratified sample was obtained based on the proportion of seven different household types in each village. These seven types and their specific proportions in the villages in 1995 follow: *single adult household* (23.2 percent) includes people of various age groups who live separately and keep an independent household; *retired couples* (9.3 percent) contains a married couple in which the male is 60 years of age or older; *employed couples without children* (8.7 percent) typically includes parents who are of employment age who are helping their children who have migrated to urban areas; *employed couples with children* (28.9 percent), nuclear families; *employed couples with children and other adults* (10.0 percent), nuclear families with relatives, such as parents of one of the spouses, or a grandfather/mother, brother or sister; *single parents with children* (2.6 percent), usually a mother with a child under age 16; *other extended family* (17.3 percent), primarily parents living with adult but unmarried children or grandmothers living with their grandchildren, but also includes households comprised of a brother and a sister, or an aunt/uncle with a niece/nephew, or some other combination of adults living together.

7. A total of 524 individuals were interviewed in the first wave of the panel study in 1995. Over the next two years (1996 and 1997), 61 of the original respondents had moved, died, or were unwilling to participate, resulting in a panel of 463 of the same respondents who were interviewed three times over the three-year time period. The attrition rate was 11.6 percent.

8. Claude S. Fischer, *To Dwell Among Friends: Personal Networks in Town and City* (Chicago: University of Chicago Press, 1982).

9. Redundant exchange networks can be calculated using the total number of persons identified in each helping area, regardless of whether a person was identified in another area, referred to as multistranded ties. Fischer, *To Dwell Among Friends*, 139.

10. Two life domains, health and employment satisfactions, are not presented in this analysis. Health is not included because it is highly correlated with age. Employment is not included due to a large proportion (approximately one-third) of respondents who are not employed, which would greatly reduce the sample size.

11. Robert M. Milardo, "Comparative Methods for Delineating Social Networks," *Journal of Social and Personal Relationships* 9 (1992): 447–61.

12. Frank M. Andrews and Stephen B. Withey, *Social Indicators of Well-Being: Americans' Perceptions of Life Quality* (New York: Plenum, 1976), 311.

13. David J. O'Brien, Valeri V. Patsiorkovski, and Larry D. Dershem, *Household Capital and the Agrarian Problem in Russia* (Aldershot, Hants, UK: Ashgate, 2000).

14. Larry D. Dershem, David J. O'Brien, and Valeri V. Patsiorkovski, "Social Capital: Community Attachment and Social Networks," in O'Brien, Patsiorkovski, and Dershem, *Household Capital.*

15. Weighted number of adults is the labor potential given for each household based on age. The weights follow: 0 (under 8, and 80 or older), 0.25 (8 to 11, and 75 to 79), 0.50 (12 to 14, and 71 to 74), 0.75 (15 to 16, and 66 to 70), and 1.00 (17 to 65).

16. The first measure of community attachment asked respondents the extent to which they attended both family and village events and ceremonies: never (0), sometimes (1), and often (2). These responses were summed for a total community involvement score. The alpha reliability of community involvement was 0.72 in 1995, 0.69 in 1996, and 0.70 in 1997.

The second measure was based on an index of two items (using a seven-point scale) to ascertain a respondent's subjective evaluation of whether he or she "fit" into the local community. The first item asked respondents, "How well do people in the village relate to you?" The second item asked respondents, "How much do you have in common with most of the people in your village?" These responses were summed for the total sense-of-fit score. The alpha reliability of sense of fit was 0.68 in 1995, and 0.67 in 1996 and 1997.

17. James L. Arbuckle, *Amos User's Guide Version 4.0* (Chicago, IL: SmallWaters Corporation, 1999).

18. O'Brien, Patsiorkovski, and Dershem, *Household Capital.*

Conclusion

Where Do We Go From Here?
Building Sustainable Rural Communities

DAVID J. O'BRIEN AND STEPHEN K. WEGREN

The term "sustainable rural community" has become increasingly popular in scholarly and public policy discussions. Local places no longer can continue to exist simply because they have always been there or because they have some cultural significance. Sustainability means the capacity of a local community to provide individuals and households with a way to make a living, as well as supplying them with services such as health care and education, and a sense of personal attachment.[1] The question for us is whether it is possible to create sustainable rural communities in Russia.

The problem of building and maintaining sustainable rural communities is by no means a uniquely Russian problem. Geographically isolated and low-population-density places throughout the world face increasing challenges to their sustainability, especially with respect to attracting talented people and being economically competitive. Indeed, much more is written about this subject in North America and the European Union, where persons in rural areas have a much higher material quality of life than Russian or Eastern European residents, but they still lag behind metropolitan areas with respect to economic and social development.

In recent years, researchers have devoted a good deal of attention to identifying universal characteristics of sustainable rural communities. One result of these efforts has been empirical documentation that even within the same country and region, rural communities differ in the strategies they use to deal with the same macroeconomic, demographic, and other structural constraints, and that the outcomes of these strategies differ markedly as well. Studies have shown that the social networks and social capital of more sustainable communities are quite similar, irrespective of differences in cultural legacies and economic conditions. Sustainable places are more likely than less sustainable communities to contain *horizontal* networks within which community members relate to one another in such a way that they are able to engage in cooperative collective action. Sustainable communities also contain *vertical* bridging types of social networks that link them to outside sources of information, ideas, and resources. The first type of social network is based on similarities in some combination of culture, identity, or interests that forms a basis for identifying a common good. The second type of social network creates bridges that allow the community to become integrated into larger national and international economic, social, political, and informational systems.[2] The precise way in which individual communities create these networks may vary considerably but their structural properties have some fundamental similarities.[3]

Also important, but perhaps least understood, is that many times the development of both horizontal and vertical social networks in sustainable rural communities has involved the active support of national governments. Despite de Tocqueville's observations on the propensity of small-town Americans to join voluntary associations,[4] for example, the development of horizontal and vertical ties in these areas oftentimes has been difficult and has required government programs to facilitate collective action. One of the most noteworthy examples in this regard was government support for the development of the Farm Bureau Cooperative. This involved the creation of county agents and what later became the Cooperative Extension Service of U.S. Department of Agriculture.[5] Similar government assistance for the development of horizontal and vertical social networks to facilitate economic development in rural communities is now taking place on a massive scale in the European Union.[6]

The challenge in developing social networks for sustainable communities in post-communist societies is much greater than it is in Western nations for two reasons. First, totalitarian societies, by definition, view competing loyalties and associations as a threat. Thus, the historical institutional climate in such societies has suppressed competing social organizational forms.[7] Given this legacy, it is not surprising that we frequently find a lack of motivation, let alone organizational capacity, to facilitate the development of indigenous forms of social organization. We are more likely to encounter situations where government either takes a laissez-faire attitude toward local institution building or sees indigenous social organization as a threat.

Second, while the post-communist survival strategies of ordinary citizens have produced benefits, they have also produced costs for long-term institutional change. On the benefit side, these survival strategies strengthen indigenous sources of social capital and provide households with positive experiences in building social networks to accomplish collective goals.[8] In this regard, the building of helping networks that draw upon and strengthen local social capital are similar to what has occurred in the development of ethnic small-business enterprises in Western nations.[9] Persons who do not have access to "normal" channels to accomplish economic goals find alternative means through informal networks, often outside of the tax code. The kinds of social relationships that hold these types of economic systems together are highly embedded and take on a quasi-kin quality. This ensures that the individuals interacting within such a system are dealing with highly trusted persons in a very insecure environment.

These survival strategies have produced some important incremental institutional changes that move in the direction of a more sustainable adaptation to a market economy. A problem with these strategies, however, is that they also reinforce aspects of social organization and institutional arrangements that may retard the development of broader bridging social networks that are necessary for economic development and the growth of civil society. Survival strategies that rely on highly dense personal networks of trusted persons[10] reduce the risks involved in business transactions when there are no trusted third-party enforcement mechanisms to regulate more formalized contractual agreements. The networks and the institutional values and norms that underlie them, however, reduce competitive bidding for the small entrepreneur's products and services and reduce opportunities for community-wide economic growth.[11]

Exclusive reliance on highly dense personalized networks prevents the development of more *inclusive* kinds of social relationships that are necessary to support the institutions of civil society, such as agricultural or nonagricultural cooperatives, and nongovernmental voluntary organizations. Too much dependence on strong ties prevents the development of what Woolcock terms *bridging* social capital,[12] and Granovetter refers to as "weak ties."[13] Communities and societies that lack bridging network ties are unable to create the kinds of concerted collective action that are necessary for both political and economic action.[14]

A frequent mistake of outside observers is to assume that a high dependence on highly dense networks is the result of a basic cultural conservatism or rejection of the marketplace. A more accurate explanation is simply that individuals and households depend on these types of relationships when they have very little faith in the ability of governments or other economic actors to follow a set of rules that they see as dependable and fair. In short, individuals who are utilizing these highly dense networks are indeed behaving as *rational economic actors*, but they are operating in an environment in which it would be foolish to risk transactions with persons outside of their known circle of associates.[15]

Assessing Behavioral and Institutional Change in Rural Russia

A significant portion of the problems in creating institutions to support viable rural communities in Russia can be traced to the same unique Soviet history that has created general problems in the agrarian sector of Russian society, which have been described in earlier chapters. Foremost among these limitations has been the absence of institutionalized property rights and a class of independent farmers. These problems are more perplexing than those faced by the former communist bloc nations in Eastern Europe in which the central task of post-communist agrarian policy was to reinstitute property relations and resurrect a dormant farmer class.[16] This has meant that rural Russian communities have been struggling to create the kinds of bridging capital linkages for economic development and civil society that in Western nations would be supported by a middle class of independent farmers who had significant resources because of the land they owned.

Moreover, as Macey described earlier, in comparison with the broad-based agrarian reforms of the Stolypin period, the reforms proposed by the Yeltsin government were in some ways quite limited. In particular, the latter-day reforms did not include any significant effort to restructure social relationships in the countryside. Nonetheless, even though the Yeltsin government was not especially supportive of rural citizens, the formal changes that have occurred in rural Russia since 1991 have been significant.

As Wegren and Belen'kiy point out from their survey data, a land market is developing in Russia. Land ownership is certainly in no way as transferable and secure as it is in Western nations and there are restrictions on who may purchase land. In addition, the amounts of land purchased remain, on average, quite small. To put the matters in perspective, however, it is important to keep in mind DeSoto's observation that even in the West, "reliance on integrated property systems is a phenomenon of at most the last two hundred years. In most Western countries, integrated property systems appeared only about a hundred years ago; Japan's integration happened little more than fifty years ago."[17]

The beginning of a property rights system in Russia, no matter how limited at present, is significant not only for agricultural development per se but also for the long-term development of nonagricultural business enterprises in rural areas as well. The lack of secure titles to land or other forms of property is a major obstacle to more efficient use of existing household physical capital.[18] Thus, the institutionalization of secure titles to land is a major step in the development of the capacity of smaller-scale entrepreneurs and ordinary citizens to obtain collateral for loans. The Belgorod oblast credit program that allows rural households to borrow money to build improved facilities for household enterprises is an important step in this direction, since it is based on the assumption that rural households have secure rights to the use of their plots.[19]

Land leasing, which is a less radical departure from Soviet institutions regarding land use, has become fully institutionalized in the countryside. Again, the amounts of land involved in these new institutional arrangements are quite small, but their effect on the ability of some ordinary Russians to increase their household production has been substantial. As Lerman points out, this institutional development has expanded the horizons of a certain portion of the rural population. The panel study survey findings reported by O'Brien, Patsiorkovski, and Dershem show that these small incremental institutional changes have encouraged households to develop their own human and social capital. These informal adjustments by households have produced a growth of entrepreneurial activity in the countryside that is much greater than many experts had expected in the early days following the collapse of the Soviet Union. In turn, these changes set the stage for future grassroots pressures for additional institutional changes that will include the development of both horizontal and bridging ties to support expanded economic and social development.

Other important institutional changes have occurred in rural Russia. Drawing on ten years of longitudinal and panel survey research, Patsiorkovski observes that institutional and social organizational arrangements at the local level have changed considerably since the end of the Soviet period. The large enterprises still exist in reorganized forms in most rural areas, but there has been some growth of formal legal institutions and most certainly growth in informal, social helping networks. The local government no longer merely provides clerical functions for the large enterprise—during the Soviet period its responsibilities were largely restricted to keeping records of the demographic, economic, and health status of the *kolkhoz* workforce—but actually has some additional social welfare functions and formal legal control over some land. In turn, this land, which can then be leased to village residents, provides some resources for the local administration. This administrative structure does not in any way compare to local administrative organizations in Western countries. Local formal institutional development is by no means complete, but the monolithic, vertically integrated bureaucratic organization of Soviet times is no longer the sole formal social organization in the Russian countryside.

The most dramatic evidence of incremental institutional change in the Russian countryside is found by looking at the experiences of ordinary rural families. In this regard, it is useful to recall the modest expectations of many Western observers about the capacity of these households to deal with the demands and choices presented by a market economy and the loss of social service support from the large enterprises. Research by Dunn and Dershem shows, however, that households were able to survive primarily by utilizing informal networks and community attachments that pre-date the Soviet experience. The fact that they were able to quickly adapt their personal networks to cope with dramatic and unexpected exigencies in spite of the collapse of institutions and organizations they had depended on for economic and social support is a significant feat. It clearly belies the argument that these individuals lack the initiative to cope with the competitive challenges of capitalism. Most important, it reinforces the argument that the problem of generating more efficient economic activity in post-communist nations is not a lack of motivation or resources among the poor, but rather the macroeconomic and legal environment in which they must operate.[20]

Opportunities for
Further Development of Sustainable Communities

This volume has presented evidence from a variety of sources to show that more change has occurred in rural Russia than is often recognized by scholars and certainly more than is generally reported in the popular press, either in Russia or in the West. As we have taken pains to point out repeatedly, however, the development of economically and socially sustainable rural communities in Russia is barely beginning. Moreover, some aspects of the adaptation of rural Russian households to the immediate post-Soviet period create some serious challenges for the further development of the kinds of bridging networks that are essential for the long-term economic and social sustainability of rural communities. We now turn our attention to these issues and the way in which the findings presented in this volume may be helpful in understanding them.

The growth and decline of different types of social capital in rural Russian households and villages during the 1990s provide insights into the opportunities and limitations of efforts to make incremental changes in institutional paths that have created obstacles to the growth of social capital to support community economic development. There are several features of the recent rural Russian situation that are especially relevant in this regard. Compared to rural residents in other nations with developing economies, rural Russians are fairly well educated—the average number of years of schooling of adults is more than ten—and thus the problems encountered in trying to develop social capital cannot be attributed to illiteracy or lack of education. In addition, the demographic structure of rural Russian villages and rural communities in the American Midwest are remarkably similar in terms of age, family structure, and number of children per household.[21] Thus, the Russian case provides us with a natural experiment in which *some* of the formal institutional structures that restricted the development of social capital were altered by actions of the central government. The mixed results of these efforts demonstrate the opportunities as well as the difficulties involved in attempting to improve the quality of social capital.

Three main findings are most important in terms of our general understanding of social capital formation. First, household social capital, especially highly dense helping networks, has grown considerably and has contributed to the development of nonagricultural as well as agricultural household enterprises. This illustrates how the growth of household social capital can be stimulated relatively easily by macro-level, formal institutional changes.

The second main finding, however, is that it is much more difficult to alter social relationships to build the kind of bridging social capital that will facilitate community-wide economic development. In fact, for many households, increasing their own social capital through the extension of highly dense personal helping networks has resulted in less involvement in village-wide community activities.

Third, as noted earlier, this negative association between the growth of highly dense personal networks and involvement in community-wide bridging networks is not due to cultural resistance to bridging-type relationships. Rather, it arises from the lack of more complete formal institutional changes that would provide protections to households when they enter into less dense, weaker-tie relationships.

In order to develop a more efficient economy, it is necessary to let go of *exclusive* dependence on traditional economic relationships, at least to the extent of allowing some broader network connections within and outside of the community.[22] Yet, as North points out, all institutional systems create mechanisms to reinforce and perpetuate their own existence. This reinforcement, which produces path dependence,[23] emerges from the social organizational forms that reinforce the cultural values and norms upon which they were spawned in the first place. In places where the institutional environment does not contain a set of formal and informal norms that encourage trust among persons, individuals and households will invest most of their energy in maintaining highly dense networks of persons with whom they do business.[24]

Despite the resilience of institutional forms, which is empirically observed in the "elastic budget constraints" described in Amelina's study, however, it is important to remember that institutions can change. She notes that regional governmental actors have considerable discretion in the manner in which they interpret, implement, and create strategies to adapt to formal institutional changes decreed by the central government. Kalugina's case studies show that even within the same economic and ecological environment, managers of large enterprises have shown considerable diversity in the kinds of strategies they have used to deal with pressures from central and oblast governments, workers, and market constraints.

Marsh and Warhola's study reminds us that support or opposition to reform measures enacted or debated during the Yeltsin administration varied considerably from one ethnic region of Russia to another. Ioffe and Nefedova point out that there are vast differences in the ecological and economic advantages among Russia's rural regions, and these differences are associated with greater or lesser adjustment of institutions and social organizational arrangements to become more or less competitive in a market economy. Rural areas that are adjacent to large metropolitan areas have distinct advantages in forming new vertically integrated, production-processing relationships with foreign investors.[25]

A major obstacle to recognizing the possibilities of how institutions may change is a failure to appreciate that unique "hybrid" institutional and social organizational forms can emerge. The new institutions may contain certain strengths of the traditional historical paths, along with the acquisition of new elements that permit a certain degree of economic and social adaptation that was not possible with the old institutions in their original "stand-alone" form. This is seen, for example, in the "flexible rigidities" that linked Japanese traditional culture and Western technology[26] and the actions of the U.S. federal government in the nineteenth century that institutionalized extant informal property rights institutions, including "squatters' rights," into formal laws.[27] Thus, sustainable communities are not built with a "one-size-fits-all" cultural template, and traditional cultures are not necessarily an obstacle to social and economic development.

Major adjustments in the institutions supporting economic activity, in the direction of supporting the development of capitalist enterprise, were shown in Volgine's study of the adaptation of the Russian commune to an international market-based venture. His study also shows that such an adjustment was by no means easy and involved not only social and economic but also ecological factors, as evidenced by the changes in the commune that occurred as Russian peasants moved from European Russia to Siberia.

The critical question that remains is what are the *precise mechanisms* by which communities develop the more sustainable institutions and social organizations that incorporate the principles of more inclusive bridging networks and social capital?

There is a growing body of research that shows that what we may perceive as the evolutionary development of new institutional arrangement in fact is the result of conflict between different actors over which set of alternative institutional arrangements will prevail. Changes in the "rules of the game," especially in economic matters, are not merely cultural struggles but rather are conflicts over how a given set of rules will enhance or weaken the power of one group vis-à-vis another.[28]

The struggle between interest groups over institutional change or preservation is no more evident than in the case of the transitional economies of Central and Eastern Europe. Different outcomes in the struggles over the rules of the game have resulted in different directions of government policies regarding land use and tenure, transfer of property, and use of property for collateral or availability of other sources of credit or taxation. These policies have had profound effects on the ability of different households to participate in the development of a market economy and, in turn, have resulted in the emergence of different systems of stratification.[29]

A central empirical research task is to measure how individuals and families at the micro-level respond and *initiate their own unique adaptation strategies* while macro-level institutional rules of the game are changing. A crucial assumption here is that actors at the local level do more than simply respond or react to institutional changes that are initiated at the macro-level governmental or economic spheres. These actors also may initiate the process of social change themselves by developing their own informal institutional changes that eventually force macro-level actors to respond with changes in macro-level institutional arrangements.

It is at the household level that decisions are made with respect to investments of time, energy, and various forms of human, social, and physical capital.[30] It is also at the household level that decisions are made with respect to engagement, noninvolvement, or outright opposition to emerging institutional changes. None of these decisions, of course, minimizes the importance of macro-level changes in the rules of the game. Changing government policies regarding land use and tenure, transfer of property, and use of property for collateral or availability of other sources of credit or taxation, for example, will have profound effects on the choices available to households.[31] Yet, even within the limitations offered by macro-level economic or political processes, individual households and local communities do respond differently to these constraints and opportunities.[32] The Russian village panel study, for example, has shown overall a substantial drop in community-wide bridging social networks among residents in the study villages, which is measured by a decline in household involvement in community social events. At the same time, there has been an overall increase in the amount of tasks that are carried out by highly dense personal helping networks. This would seem to indicate that a majority of households are investing more in their personal helping networks and becoming less involved in the life of their villages. Nonetheless, those households with the highest levels of sales have maintained their high levels of community involvement, indicating that these households are much more engaged in bridging networks than their less productive neighbors.[33]

Long-term ethnographic, longitudinal, and panel studies of household strategies in a transitional economy are especially useful in identifying the relationship between macro- and micro-level institutional change. Such studies can identify how informal institutions and social organizational arrangements at the local level support or thwart the development of new institutional arrangements that would support the development of a market economy and civil society.

One of the most striking relationships to emerge from the Russian village panel surveys is that over time respondents have become more satisfied with their incomes but less satisfied with village life. These findings are due to the increased effectiveness of personal helping networks in expanding household productivity, but the transfer of energy from village-wide bridging-type associations has been produced at a serious cost to more inclusive types of community-wide networks.[34]

A deeper understanding of why village residents are upset about the costs they have experienced with respect to community solidarity is found in the ethnographic data reported by Paxson. The frustration with the Yeltsin government reforms expressed by ordinary people was not simply an indictment of the marketplace. After all, even in the Soviet period rural households in Russia had considerable experience in dealing with the marketplace, typically more so than their urban counterparts. The frustration of rural residents, so clearly expressed in this study, was due in significant measure to the government's lack of sensitivity to their situation, as well as to the situation itself.

As Gambold Miller points out, local residents were angry that the reformers in Moscow seemed to have very little understanding of or empathy with the breakdown of traditional service-delivery providers. The government seemed to be without any realistic plan to create new institutional arrangements to compensate for the collapse of the traditional Soviet-style, social service delivery system, in which the large enterprise was the central player. In addition, Donahue's findings show that certain human capital disadvantages in rural areas that were present in the Soviet period have been exacerbated by lack of government attention during the early post-Soviet period.

Allina-Pisano's study shows the central government reformers seemed to be quite naive about the intricate relationships between ownership and control of the means of production, which is an ironic failure of understanding, given the official Marxian ideology of the Soviet period. They simply did not anticipate how changes in one element in a complex social and economic system could affect ordinary people's lives so adversely. Obsessions with creating a new class of private farmers (the reformers' goal) or the preservation of the large enterprises (the conservatives' goal) left ordinary Russian households without any real base of support. In that environment it is not surprising that households devoted most of their energy to their helping networks and that broader-based bridging networks suffered.

One way to overcome these limitations of earlier reform efforts is to examine which government strategies in other nations have been most successful in developing sustainable rural communities, in both an economic and a social sense. Historically, some of the most successful transitions to institutional arrangements that have supported the development of more secure property rights have occurred when national governments have not attempted to try to force centralized solutions on grassroots populations. Institutional development has been enhanced when governments have made the effort to become knowledgeable about the informal institutions with which ordinary people do business on a day-to-day basis. This does not mean endorsing inefficient economic institutions or rejecting the eventual development of formal-legal property-rights structures or other institutions of sustainable communities, such as formal voluntary associations. Nonetheless, the transition from informal to formal property rights is smoother when government officials ask the question of how they can find ways to extend or improve extant informal relationships, rather than assume that existing institutions can be replaced whole cloth with new ones. This improvement may involve the development of formal institutional arrangements, but in such a process the formal institutions will have been connected to a foundation of informal, broad-based, institutional history.[35]

Similarly, it would seem that the process of transforming rural Russian villages into sustainable communities will require a greater understanding of the nature of rural institutions and social organization. It is our hope that this book has contributed in some small way to this effort.

Notes

1. The relationship between community attachment and mental health in American rural communities is shown in David J. O'Brien, Edward W. Hassinger, and Larry D. Dershem, "Community Attachment and Depression Among Residents in Two Rural Midwestern Communities," *Rural Sociology* 59 (1994): 255–65. The relationship between community attachment and mental health in rural Russian communities is found in David J. O'Brien, Valeri V. Patsiorkovski, Larry Dershem, and Oksana Lylova, "Household Production and Symptoms of Stress in Post-Soviet Russian Villages," *Rural Sociology* 61 (1996): 674–98.

2. For a discussion of the importance of bridging social capital in community development, see Cornelia B. Flora and Jan L. Flora, "Entrepreneurial Social Infrastructure: A Necessary Ingredient," *Annals AAPS* 529 (1993): 48–58.

3. A comparative study of the economic success of similar-size rural Midwestern communities during the difficult times of the American "farm crisis" in the mid-1980s found that places that fared better than others had leaders with more *inclusive* horizontal and vertical networks. It was striking, however, that the way in which horizontal ties between leaders developed varied considerably from one viable place to another. In one highly successful place, horizontal ties were based on kin relations, whereas in another similarly effective place the equivalent network structures were produced by high levels of involvement in voluntary associations. See David J. O'Brien, Edward W. Hassinger, Ralph B. Brown, and James R. Pinkerton, "The Social Networks of Leaders in More and Less Viable Rural Communities," *Rural Sociology* 56 (1991): 699–716; and David J. O'Brien, Andrew Raedeke, and Edward W. Hassinger, "The Social Networks of Leaders in More and Less Viable Communities Six Years Later: A Research Note," *Rural Sociology* 62 (1998): 109–27.

4. Alexis de Tocqueville, *Democracy in America* (New York: Vintage Books, 1960), 2: 102–20.

5. See, for example, the discussion of the U.S. federal government's assistance in the development of political pressure groups in Mancur Olson, Jr., *The Logic of Collective Action: Public Goods and the Theory of Groups* (Cambridge, MA: Harvard University Press, 1971), 148–59.

6. The Leaders community development program in the European Union has developed extensive databases and offers practical programming to assist local communities to market their agricultural and nonagricultural (often tourism) resources, as well as develop linkages to international markets. See their Web site at *www.rural-europe.aeidl.be/rural-en/index.html*.

7. See William Kornhauser, *The Politics of Mass Society* (New York: Free Press, 1959); and Hannah Arendt, *The Origins of Totalitarianism* (New York: Harcourt Brace, 1951).

8. See, for example, David J. O'Brien, Valeri V. Patsiorkovski, and Larry D. Dershem, *Household Capital and the Agrarian Problem in Russia* (Aldershot, Hants, UK: Ashgate, 2000).

9. See, for example, Ivan Light, *Ethnic Enterprise in America: Business and Welfare Among Chinese, Japanese and Blacks* (Berkeley: University of California Press, 1972); and Stephen S. Fugita and David J. O'Brien, *Japanese American Ethnicity: The Persistence of Community* (Seattle: University of Washington Press, 1991).

10. See V. Shlapentokh, *Public and Private Life of the Soviet People: Changing Values in Post-Stalin Russia* (New York: Oxford University Press, 1989); and Larry D. Dershem, "Prevalence, Sources and Types of Informal Support in Latonovo and Mayaki," in *Services and Quality of Life in Rural Villages in the Former Soviet Union: Data from 1991 and 1993 Surveys*, eds. David J. O'Brien et al. (Lanham, MD: University Press of America, 1998), 163–98.

11. See Douglass C. North, *Institutions, Institutional Change and Economic Performance* (Cambridge: Cambridge University Press, 1990), 98–100.

12. Michael Woolcock, "Social Capital and Economic Development: Toward a Theoretical Synthesis and Policy Framework," *Theory and Society* 27 (1998): 151–208.

13. Mark S. Granovetter, "The Strength of Weak Ties," *American Journal of Sociology* 78 (1973): 1360–80.

14. See Robert D. Putnam, "The Prosperous Community: Social Capital and Public Life," *The American Prospect* 13 (1993): 35–42; Francis Fukuyama, "Social Capital and the Global Economy," *Foreign Affairs* 74 (September/October 1995): 89–102; Flora and Flora, "Entrepreneurial Social Infrastructure."

15. This explains, for example, why most rural Russian households were not eager to become officially registered private farmers in the early 1990s. Ordinary people viewed the efficacy of the new Russian economic institutions with the same skepticism as many Western economists at that time. A new institutional economist's explanation of the rationality involved in utilizing highly dense social networks for economic transactions in risky environments is found in North, *Institutions*, 38–39. Moreover, even if such individuals were able to trust persons outside of their dense networks, the absence of secure property rights that prevents them from obtaining collateral for loans would not make them very attractive parties with whom to do business. See Hernando DeSoto, *The Mystery of Capital: Why Capitalism Triumphs in the West and Fails Everywhere Else* (New York: Basic Books), 56.

16. See Johan F.M. Swinnen, ed., *Political Economy of Agrarian Reform in Central and Eastern Europe* (Aldershot, Hants, UK: Ashgate, 1997).

17. DeSoto, *Mystery of Capital*, 56.

18. Ibid., 62–66.

19. *Sel'skaia zhizn'*, 6 June 1996, 2.

20. DeSoto, *Mystery of Capital*, 189–91.

21. Valeri V. Patsiorkovski and David J. O'Brien, *Research Methodology and Quality of Rural Life in Russia and the USA* (Moscow: Institute for the Socio-Economic Studies of Population, Russian Academy of Sciences, 1996), 135–40.

22. The reference here is to "adaptive efficiency" rather than "allocative efficiency." North explains that, "Adaptive efficiency . . . is concerned with the kinds of rules that shape the way an economy evolves through time. It is also concerned with the willingness of a society to acquire knowledge and learning, to induce innovation, to undertake risk and creative activity of all sorts, as well as to resolve problems and bottlenecks of the society through time." North, *Institutions*, 80. This adaptive capacity is, in the long run, dependent on the development of secure but flexible bridging network ties.

23. Ibid., 93–98.

24. Ibid., 67.

25. See also L. Alexander Norsworthy, ed., *Russian Views of the Transition in the Rural Sector: Structure, Policy Outcomes and Adaptive Responses* (Washington, DC: World Bank, 2000).

26. Ronald Dore, *Flexible Rigidities: Industrial Policy and Structural Adjustment in the Japanese Economy 1970–80* (London: Athlone, 1986).

27. DeSoto, *Mystery of Capital*, 105–52.

28. Paul Ingram, "Changing the Rules: Interests, Organizations and Institutional Change in the U.S. Hospitality Industry," in *The New Institutionalism in Sociology*, eds. Mary Brinton and Victor Nee (New York: Russell Sage Foundation, 1998), 258–76; Jack Knight, *Institutions and Social Conflict* (Cambridge: Cambridge University Press, 1992).

29. See Swinnen, ed., *Political Economy of Agrarian Reform*; Ivan Szelenyi, *Privatizing the Land: Rural Political Economy in Post-Communist Societies* (London: Routledge, 1998); Szelenyi and Kostello, "Outline of an Institutionalist Theory of Inequality"; Stephen K. Wegren, *Agriculture and the State in Soviet and Post-Soviet Russia* (Pittsburgh, PA: University of Pittsburgh Press, 1998), 227–40.

30. Gary S. Becker, *A Treatise on the Family* (Cambridge, MA: Harvard University Press, 1981); James S. Coleman, "Social Capital in the Creation of Human Capital," *American Journal of Sociology* 94 (special supplement 1988): S95–S120; Jimmy M. Sanders and Victor Nee, "Immigrant Self-Employment: The Family as Social Capital and the Value of Human Capital," *American Sociological Review* 16 (April 1998): 231–49.

31. DeSoto, *Mystery of Capital*, 39–68.

32. Becker, *A Treatise on the Family*, 135–71; O'Brien, Patsiorkovski, and Dershem, *Household Capital and the Agrarian Problem in Russia*, 131–90.

33. O'Brien, Patsiorkovski, and Dershem, *Household Capital and the Agrarian Problem in Russia*, 93–108.

34. Ibid., 213–36.

35. DeSoto pointed out, for example, that a significant portion of property rights in the United States evolved from institutionalizing the informal, but previously illegal, "squatters rights." See DeSoto, *Mystery of Capital*, 122–36. A classic social science study of the give-and-take in a major development project between government and the grassroots, along with subsequent institutional adjustments, is Phillip Selznik, *The TVA and the Grassroots* (1949; reprint, New York: Harper and Row Torchbooks, 1966).

Contributors

Jessica Allina-Pisano, Ph.D. Candidate, Department of Political Science, Yale University, New Haven, Connecticut

Maria Amelina, Economist, The World Bank, Washington, DC

Vladimir R. Belen'kiy, Director, Research Institute on Land Relations and Land Tenure, Moscow

Larry D. Dershem, Rural Sociologist, Save the Children Federation Inc., Tbilisi

Dennis J. Donahue, Ph.D. Candidate, Department of Sociology and the Population Research Center, University of Texas, Austin, Texas

Ethel Dunn, Executive Secretary, Highgate Road Social Science Research Station, Berkeley, California

Grigory Ioffe, Professor of Geography, Radford University, Radford, Virginia

Zemfira Kalugina, Department of Sociology, Institute of Economics and Industrial Engineering, Siberian Branch, Russian Academy of Sciences, Novosibirsk

Zvi Lerman, Economist, the World Bank, Washington, DC

David A.J. Macey, Professor of History, C.V. Starr Professor of Russian Studies, and Director of the Russian and East European Area Studies Program at Middlebury College, Middlebury, Vermont

Christopher Marsh, Assistant Professor of Political Science, Baylor University, Waco, Texas

Liesl L. Gambold Miller, Ph.D. candidate, Department of Anthropology, University of California, Los Angeles, California

Tatyana Nefedova, Geographer, Institute of Geography, Russian Academy of Sciences, Moscow

David J. O'Brien, Professor of Rural Sociology, University of Missouri, Columbia, Missouri

Valeri V. Patsiorkovski, Laboratory Chief, Institute for Socio-Economic Studies of Population, Russian Academy of Sciences, Moscow

Margaret L. Paxson, Anthropologist, Kennan Institute Scholar, Washington, DC

Igor V. Volgine, Ph.D. Candidate, Department of History, Novosibirsk State University, Novosibirsk, Russia

James W. Warhola, Professor of Political Science, University of Maine, Orono, Maine

Stephen K. Wegren, Associate Professor of Political Science, Southern Methodist University, Dallas, Texas

Index

419